TEXTBOOK

Land:
THE LAW OF REAL PROPERTY

Fifth Edition

PROFESSOR CEDRIC D BELL

LLB, LLM, PhD, Barrister
Chief Executive, Holborn College
Visiting Professor of Legal Practice, University of Hertfordshire
Guest Professor of Law, Northern University, Bangladesh

OLD BAILEY PRESS

OLD BAILEY PRESS
at Holborn College, Woolwich Road,
Charlton, London, SE7 8LN

First published 1997
Fifth edition 2005

ISBN 1 85836 602 X

British Library Cataloguing-in-Publication.
A CIP Catalogue record for this book is
available from the British Library.

Acknowledgement
The publishers and author would
like to thank the Incorporated
Council of Law Reporting for
England and Wales for kind
permission to reproduce extracts
from the Weekly Law Reports, and
Butterworths for their kind
permission to reproduce extracts
from the All England Law Reports.

Printed and bound in Great Britain

Contents

Preface   *vii*

Table of Cases   *ix*

Table of Statutes   *xix*

Glossary   *xxv*

1 The Study of Land Law   *1*

The problem of land law – The 1925 property legislation – Methods of study of land law

2 Historical Introduction   *3*

Origins of the feudal system – The feudal system in England – The decline of the feudal system – The intervention of statute

3 Tenures   *10*

Introduction – Free tenures – Unfree tenures – Copyhold – Conclusion: tenures today

4 Estates   *18*

Introduction – Classification of estates – Possession, remainder, reversion and seisin – The fee simple – The fee tail – The life estate – Waste – Fixtures – Reverter of Sites Act 1987

5 Law and Equity   *35*

Two legal systems – Contributions by equity to land law – The difference between legal and equitable rights – The doctrine of notice – Powers

6 The 1925 Legislation – Including Registration of Incumbrances   *40*

Introduction – The purpose of the 1925 legislation – Reduction of legal estates and interests – Protection of equitable interests – Local Land Charges Act 1975 – Entries on the land charges register – Searching in the land charges register – Priority notices – Vacation of the registration of a land charge – Worked example

7 Registration of Title   *57*

Introduction – Registration of title and the doctrine of notice – Relationship between the Land Charges Act 1972 and the Land Registration Act 2002 – Key principles of registration – Registrable estates and interests – Overriding interests under the Land Registration Act 1925 – Other aspects of registration under the Land Registration Act 1925 – Land Registration Act 2002

8 Settlements of Land   *89*

Introduction – Settlements under the Settled Land Act 1925 – How is a settlement created? – Who is the tenant for life? – When there is no tenant for life – Who are the trustees of the settlement? – Powers of the tenant for life – Personal nature of the statutory powers: s108 – Protection of the statutory powers: s106 – Powers remain with the tenant for life: s104 – Death of the tenant for life – Acquisition by the tenant for life of the settled land: s68 – Dispositions by the tenant for life and protection of purchasers – Capital money – Functions of Settled Land Act trustees – Trusts for sale under Law of Property Act 1925 – Position of trustees for sale – Position of the beneficiaries – Ad hoc settlements and trusts for sale – Strict settlements and registered land – Comparison of the strict settlement and the trust for sale – Trusts of Land and Appointment of Trustees Act 1996

9 Co-ownership *124*

Introduction – Creation of a joint tenancy – Creation of a tenancy in common – Resulting trusts and co-ownership – Aspects of co-ownership under the 1925 legislation – Co-ownership under the Trusts of Land and Appointment of Trustees Act 1996 – House deposit and co-ownership – Ending of co-ownership – Rights between co-owners – Other forms of co-ownership – Worked example

10 Leases and Tenancies *149*

Introduction – Definitions – Assignments and subtenancies – The essentials of a lease – Distinction between a lease and a licence – Types of tenancy – Terms implied into leases – Express covenants in leases – Determination of tenancies – Forfeiture – Enforceability of covenants in leases – Statutory protection of tenants – Residential tenancies – Agricultural tenancies – Business tenancies

11 Enforcement of Covenants between Freeholders *211*

Introduction – Definitions – The creation of covenants – Enforcement of covenants at common law between original parties – Enforcement of covenants at common law by assignees – Example of the running of covenants at common law – Enforceability of covenants in equity – Enforceability in equity: original parties – Enforceability in equity by successors in title – Example of the running of covenants in equity – Effect of Contracts (Rights of Third Parties) Act 1999 – Discharge of restrictive covenants – Reform – Worked example

12 Easements and Profits *245*

Introduction: examples of easements – Essentials of an easement – Legal and equitable easements – Acquisition of easements – Prescription – Extent of the easement – Remedies for infringement of easements – Extinguishment of easements – Access to Neighbouring Land Act 1992 – Profits à prendre – Acquisition of profits à prendre – Remedies for infringement of profits – Extinguishment of profits – Worked example

13 Licences *271*

Introduction – Bare licences – Licences coupled with an interest – Contractual licences – Licences protected by estoppel or in equity

14 Mortgages *287*

Introduction – Creation of a mortgage – Legal and equitable mortgages – The right to redeem and the equity of redemption – The rights of the mortgagor – Redemption – The rights of the mortgagee to enforce his security: remedies of the mortgagee – The remedies of the legal mortgagee – The remedies of the equitable mortgagee – Other rights of the mortgagee – The right to tack further advances – The right to consolidate – The rights common to both parties – Priority of mortgages – Priority of mortgages of an equitable interest

15 Adverse Possession   *330*

General principles – Limitation periods – Running of time – Effect of lapse of time – Proof of squatter's title

16 Future Interests: The Rules against Perpetuities and Accumulations   *342*

Introduction – Vested and contingent interests – The rule against perpetuities – The common law rule against perpetuities – Modifications to the common law rule before 1964 – Determinable and conditional interests – Perpetuities and Accumulations Act 1964 – Powers – Exceptions to the perpetuity rule – The rule against accumulations – Revision summary – Proposals for reform

17 Statutory Restrictions on the Use of Land   *363*

Introduction – Planning control – Protection of tenants – Public health and housing provisions – Taxation – Environmental issues – Conclusion

Index   *367*

Preface

The new edition, like its predecessors, is written specifically for students of Real Property law. Its primary aim is to better help students understand the tenets and principles of Real Property law so that they can more confidently approach their examinations and assessments. At first sight many students find land law daunting and difficult to comprehend, not least because most have no practical experience of the transactions/concepts comprising the subject. Accordingly, the text endeavours to present material clearly and concisely and in an easy-to-read, user-friendly format. The coverage is comprehensive but not verbose. The style and structure of the text is particularly suited to the semesterised teaching now prevalent in most UK university law degree courses.

The text is designed for use by any undergraduate who has Real Property/Land Law within its syllabus. It is equally useful for CPE/LLDip students who must study Land Law as one of the 'core subjects'. In addition, students of certain professional examinations, including those of the Royal Institution of Chartered Surveyors, the Institute of Legal Executives and the Council for Licensed Conveyancers, should find that the text gives them ample information for their land law examinations.

A companion 150 Leading Cases, Revision WorkBook and Statutes Book (all of which are published by Old Bailey Press) can be advantageously read in conjunction with this textbook. Indeed these four titles comprise a complete and integrated package of materials ideal for students wishing to maximise their examination performance in the subject.

The new edition features a substantially revised chapter on Registration which aims to provide a succinct summary of the significant changes made to registered land by the Land Registration Act 2002, but at the same time provide the reader with an understanding of the 'old regime' under the now repealed Land Registration Act 1925. New cases dealt with include *Crest Nicholson Residential (South) Ltd* v *McAllister* [2004] 2 All ER 991 (on statutory annexation of restrictive covenants), *Sweet* v *Sommer* (2004) The Times 25 August (on the doctrine of implied reservation of an easement of necessity) and *Yorkshire Bank plc* v *Tinsley* (2004) The Times 12 August (on undue influence in respect of mortgages). Some relevant aspects of the Civil Partnership Act 2004 and Housing Act 2004 are also included.

I would like to thank my colleague John Cassidy of Royds Solicitors for making some helpful comments as to the practical effect of the Land Registration Act 2002.

This textbook endeavours to state the law as at 1 May 2005.

Professor Cedric D Bell

Table of Cases

Abbey National Building Society v Cann [1990] 2 WLR 832   *73, 74, 76*

Abbey National Building Society v Maybeech Ltd [1984] 3 All ER 262   *188*

Abbey National plc v Moss [1993] 1 FLR 307   *107, 119*

Abbeyfield (Harpenden) Society Ltd v Woods [1968] 1 WLR 374; [1968] 1 All ER 352   *160*

Aberconway's Settlement Trusts, Re, McLaren v Baron Aberconway [1953] Ch 647; [1953] 2 All ER 350   *101*

Acklom, Re [1929] 1 Ch 195   *101*

Adamson v Halifax plc [2003] 1 WLR 60   *302*

Addiscombe Garden Estates Ltd v Crabbe [1958] 1 QB 513; [1957] 3 All ER 563   *160*

Adler v Upper Grosvenor Street Investments Ltd [1957] 1 WLR 227; [1957] 1 All ER 229   *173*

AG Securities v Vaughan [1988] 3 WLR 1205; [1988] 2 All ER 173   *162, 164, 204, 272*

Aldred's Case (1610) 9 Co Rep 57b, 58b   *246, 249*

Alefounders' Will Trusts, Re, Adnams v Alefounder [1927] 1 Ch 360; (1927) 96 LJ Ch 264   *93, 104*

Allen v Greenwood [1979] 2 WLR 187   *260*

Allied Irish Bank v Byrne (1 February 1994 – unreported)   *318*

Amsprop Trading v Harris Distribution [1997] 1 WLR 1025   *200*

Andrews v Partington (1791) 3 Bro CC 401   *350, 351, 356, 361*

Anstruther-Gough-Calthorpe v McOscar [1924] 1 KB 716   *178*

Antoniades v Villiers [1988] 3 WLR 1205; (1988) EG 30 April 122   *162, 163, 204, 272*

Argyle Building Society v Hammond (1984) 49 P & CR 148   *87*

Ashburn Anstalt v Arnold [1989] Ch 1; [1988] 2 All ER 147   *159, 161, 270, 276*

Aslan v Murphy [1989] 3 All ER 130   *164*

Atkin's Will Trusts, Re, National Westminster Bank Ltd v Atkins [1974] 1 WLR 761; [1974] 2 All ER 1   *350*

Attorney-General v Shadwell [1910] 1 Ch 92   *33*

Attorney-General of Southern Nigeria v John Holt & Co (Liverpool) Ltd [1915] AC 599   *246, 270*

Austerberry v Oldham Corporation (1885) 29 Ch D 750; (1885) 55 LJ Ch 633   *217, 219, 241*

B & Q plc v Liverpool and Lancashire Properties Ltd (2000) The Times 6 September   *264*

Ballard's Conveyance, Re [1937] Ch 473; [1937] 2 All ER 691   *225, 226*

Bank of Baroda v Dhillon & Another (1997) The Times 4 November   *118, 119*

Bank of Scotland v Bennett [1999] 1 FLR 1115   *313, 314*

Bank of Scotland v Grimes [1985] 2 All ER 254   *307*

Bannister v Bannister [1948] 2 All ER 133; (1948) 92 SJ 377   *278, 283*

Barclays Bank plc v Boulter and Another [1999] 1 WLR 1919   *314*

Barclays Bank plc v Caplan (1997) The Times 12 December   *318*

Barclays Bank plc v Coleman [2000] 1 All ER 385   *317*

Barclays Bank plc v O'Brien and Another [1993] 3 WLR 786   *61, 62, 311, 312, 313, 314, 315, 316, 317, 318, 319, 320*

Barnett v Hassett [1981] 1 WLR 1385; [1982] 1 All ER 80   *48, 55*

Barrett v Lounova (1982) Ltd [1989] 1 All ER 351   *177*

Barton v Morris [1985] 2 All ER 1032   *132*

Basham (Deceased), Re [1986] 1 WLR 1498   *281, 282*

Bass Holdings Ltd v Lewis (1986) 280 EG 771   *167*

Batchelor v Marlow (2001) 82 P & CR 36   *247, 261*

Bates v Donaldson [1896] 2 QB 241; [1895–9] All ER Rep 170   *174*

Bathurst (Earl) v Fine [1974] 1 WLR 905; [1974] 2 All ER 1160   *185*

Baxter v Four Oaks Properties Ltd [1965] Ch 816; [1965] 1 All ER 906   *229*

Beacon Carpets Ltd v Kirby [1984] 2 All ER 726
    173
Bedson v Bedson [1965] 2 QB 666; [1965] 3 All
    ER 307   *106*
Benn v Hardinge (1992) The Times 13 October
    265
Berkeley Road (No 88), London NW9, Re [1971]
    Ch 648; [1971] 1 All ER 254   *143*
Berkley v Poulett (1976) The Times 3 November
    31
Bernard v Josephs [1982] Ch 391; [1982] 3 All
    ER 162   *106*
Bernstein of Leigh (Lord) v Skyviews & General
    Ltd [1978] QB 479; [1977] 3 WLR 136;
    [1977] 2 All ER 902   *24, 246*
Beswick v Beswick [1968] AC 58; [1967] 2 All
    ER 1197   *215*
BHP Petroleum GB Ltd v Chesterfield Properties
    Ltd [2001] All ER (D) 451   *194*
Bickel v Duke of Westminster [1977] QB 517;
    [1976] 3 WLR 805; [1976] 3 All ER 801
    174
Biggs v Hoddinott [1898] 2 Ch 307   *295*
Binions v Evans [1972] Ch 359; [1972] 2 All ER
    70   *49, 56, 157, 167, 276, 278, 283*
Birmingham Midshires Mortgage Services Ltd v
    Sabherwal (2000) 80 P & CR 256   *45, 114,
    281, 319*
Bland v Ingram's Estate Ltd (2001) The Times
    18 January   *186, 188*
Bocardo SA v S & M Hotels Ltd [1980] 1 WLR
    17; [1979] 3 All ER 737   *173*
Bookman (Thos) v Nathan [1955] 1 WLR 815
    174
Borman v Griffith [1930] 1 Ch 493; (1930) 99 LJ
    Ch 295   *253, 254, 269*
Bradford Corporation v Pickles [1895] AC 587
    26
Bretherton v Paton (1986) 278 EG 615   *161*
Brew Bros v Snax [1970] 1 QB 612   *178*
Bridges v Mees [1957] Ch 475; [1957] 2 All ER
    577   *70, 71*
Bridgett and Hayes' Contract, Re [1928] Ch 163;
    [1927] All ER Rep 191   *104*
Brikom Investments Ltd v Seaford [1981] 2 All
    ER 783   *170*
Brinnand v Ewens (1987) 19 HLR 415; (1987)
    The Times 4 June   *178, 282*
Bristol & West plc v Bartlett [2003] 1 WLR 284
    331
Bristol & West Building Society v Ellis and
    Another (1996) 73 P & CR 158   *308*
British Railways Board v Glass [1965] Ch 538;
    [1964] 3 All ER 418   *262*

Brockbank, Re [1948] Ch 206   *122*
Bromley Park Garden Estates Ltd v Moss [1982]
    1 WLR 1019; [1982] 2 All ER 890   *174*
Browne v Flower [1911] 1 Ch 219; (1911) 80 LJ
    Ch 181   *168, 169*
Brunner v Greenslade [1971] Ch 993; [1970] 3
    All ER 833   *229*
Bruton v Quadrant Housing Trust [1999] 3 WLR
    150   *204*
Buchanan-Wollaston's Conveyance, Re [1939] Ch
    738   *106, 147*
Buchmann v May [1978] 2 All ER 993   *160*
Buckinghamshire County Council v Moran [1989]
    2 All ER 225   *332*
Bull v Bull [1955] 1 QB 234; [1955] 1 All ER 253
    124, 131, 134, 145
Burden, Re, Mitchell v St Luke's Hostel
    Trustees [1948] Ch 160; [1948] 1 All ER 31
    101
Burgess v Rawnsley [1975] Ch 429; [1975] 3 All
    ER 142   *144*
Burns v Burns [1984] Ch 317; [1984] 1 All ER
    244   *106, 136*

Calgary and Edmonton Land Co Ltd v Dobinson
    [1974] Ch 102   *55*
Carr-Saunders v Dick McNeil Associates Ltd
    [1986] 1 WLR 922   *260*
Caunce v Caunce [1969] 1 WLR 286; [1969] 1
    All ER 722   *49*
Celsteel Ltd v Alton House Holdings Ltd [1985]
    1 WLR 204   *70, 85, 250, 263*
Celsteel Ltd v Alton House Holdings Ltd (No 2)
    [1987] 1 WLR 291   *169*
Centaploy Ltd v Matlodge Ltd [1974] Ch 1;
    [1973] 2 All ER 720   *166*
Central Estates (Belgravia) Ltd v Woolgar (No 2)
    [1972] 1 WLR 1048; [1972] 3 All ER 610
    182
Central London Property Trust v High Trees
    House Ltd [1947] KB 130   *277*
Central Midlands Estates v Leicester Dyers
    [2003] 2 P & CR D2   *247*
Centrax Trustees Ltd v Ross [1979] 2 All ER 952
    307
Chandler v Kerley [1978] 1 WLR 693   *275*
Chastey v Ackland (1895) 11 TLR 460   *246*
Chatsworth Estates Co v Fewell [1931] 1 Ch 224
    233
Chelsea Yacht & Boat Club Ltd v Pope [2001] 2
    All ER 409   *31*
Cheltenham & Gloucester Building Society v
    Grattidge (1993) The Times 9 April   *306*

Cheltenham & Gloucester Building Society *v* Norgan [1996] 1 WLR 343; [1996] 1 All ER 449 *307, 308, 309*

Chester *v* Buckingham Travel Ltd [1981] 1 WLR 96; [1981] 1 All ER 386 *171*

Chowood *v* Lyall [1930] 2 Ch 156 *70, 79*

Chowood's Registered Land, Re [1933] Ch 574; [1933] All ER Rep 946 *80*

Church of England Building Society *v* Piskor [1954] Ch 553 *73, 73–74*

CIBC Mortgages plc *v* Pitt and Another [1993] 3 WLR 802 *312*

Citro, Domenico (A Bankrupt), Re [1991] Ch 142; [1990] 2 WLR 880 *107, 119, 120*

City and Metropolitan Properties Ltd *v* Greycroft Ltd (1987) 283 EG 199 *192*

City of London Building Society *v* Flegg [1987] 2 WLR 1266 *75, 114*

Cityland and Property (Holdings) Ltd *v* Dabrah [1968] Ch 166; [1967] 2 All ER 639 *294–295*

Clark and Another *v* Chief Land Registrar and Another [1994] 4 All ER 96 *78*

Clayton's Deed Poll, Re [1980] Ch 99; [1979] 2 All ER 1133 *34*

Clore *v* Theatrical Properties Ltd [1936] 3 All ER 483 *276*

Colls *v* Home & Colonial Stores Ltd [1904] AC 179; (1904) 73 LJ Ch 484 *260*

Commission for the New Towns *v* Cooper (GB) Ltd [1995] 2 All ER 929 *156*

Copeland *v* Greenhalf [1952] Ch 488; [1952] 1 All ER 809 *247, 248, 249, 270*

Cornish *v* Brook Green Laundry Ltd [1959] 1 QB 394 *157*

Corpus Christi College *v* Gloucestershire County Council [1982] 3 WLR 849; [1982] 3 All ER 995 *5, 16*

Countrywide Banking Corporation *v* Robinson [1991] 1 NZLR 75 *303*

Crabb *v* Arun District Council [1976] Ch 179; [1975] 3 All ER 865 *279*

Crago *v* Julian [1992] 1 All ER 744 *157*

Credit Lyonnais Bank Nederland NV *v* Burch [1997] 1 All ER 144 *317, 318*

Crest Nicholson Residential (South) Ltd *v* McAllister [2004] 2 All ER 991 *vii, 227, 233*

Cricklewood Property and Investment Trust Ltd *v* Leightons Investment Trust Ltd [1945] AC 211 *172*

Crow *v* Wood [1970] 3 WLR 516; [1970] 3 All ER 425 *220, 246, 249*

Cuckmere Brick Co Ltd *v* Mutual Finance Ltd [1971] Ch 949; [1971] 2 All ER 633 *302, 303*

Curryer's Will Trusts, Re [1938] Ch 952 *352*

Dalton *v* Angus & Co (1881) 6 App Cas 740 *246*

Dance *v* Triplow [1992] 1 EGLR 190 *259*

Dances Way, West Town, Hayling Island, Re [1962] Ch 490 *87*

Dano Ltd *v* Earl Cadogan and Others [2004] 1 P & CR 169 *236*

Dashwood *v* Magniac [1891] 3 Ch 306; (1891) 60 LJ Ch 809 *29*

Davies *v* Du Paver [1953] 1 QB 184; [1952] 2 All ER 991 *258*

Davis *v* Whitby [1974] Ch 186; [1974] 1 All ER 806 *256*

Dean *v* Andrews (1985) The Times 25 May *30, 33*

Dearle *v* Hall (1828) 3 Russ 1 *41, 58, 62, 110, 290, 329*

Dennis (A Bankrupt), Re [1995] 3 All ER 171 *143*

Dennis *v* McDonald [1982] Fam 63 *106, 145*

Deptford High Street (No 139), Re, ex parte British Transport Commission [1951] Ch 884; [1951] 1 All ER 950 *80*

D'Eyncourt *v* Gregory (1866) LR 3 Eq 382; (1866) 36 LJ Ch 107 *31*

Di Palma *v* Victoria Square Property Co Ltd [1985] 3 WLR 207 *187*

Diligent Finance Co Ltd *v* Alleyne (1972) 23 P & CR 346 *53*

Dillwyn *v* Llewellyn (1862) 4 De GF & J 517; (1862) 31 LJ Ch 658 *278*

Dodds *v* Walker [1981] 2 All ER 609 *179, 210*

Doherty *v* Allman (1878) 3 App Cas 709; (1878) 39 LT 129 HL *29*

Dolphin's Conveyance, Re, Birmingham Corporation *v* Boden [1970] 1 Ch 654; [1970] 2 All ER 664 *229*

Downsview Nominees Ltd *v* First City Corporation Ltd [1993] AC 295 *304*

Drake *v* Whipp [1996] 1 FLR 826; (1995) The Times 19 December *135, 284*

Draper's Conveyance, Re, Nihan *v* Porter [1969] 1 Ch 486; [1967] 3 All ER 853 *143*

Dudley & District Benefit Building Society *v* Emerson [1949] Ch 707 *327*

Dyce *v* Lady James Hay (1852) 1 Macq 305 HL *249, 261*

E & G C Ltd *v* Bate (1935) 79 LJ News 203 *217*

Earnshaw and Others *v* Hartley [2000] Ch 155
337
Elite Investments Ltd *v* T I Bainbridge Silencers
Ltd (1986) 280 EG 1001   *177*
Elitestone Ltd *v* Morris & Another [1997] 2 All
ER 513   *33*
Ellenborough Park, Re, Re Davies, Powell *v*
Maddison [1956] Ch 131; [1955] 3 All ER
667   *248, 249, 267*
Elliston *v* Reacher [1908] 2 Ch 374; (1908) 77 LJ
CH 617; affirmed [1908] 2 Ch 665; [1908–10]
All ER Rep 612 CA   *229*
Elmcroft Developments Ltd *v* Tankersley Sawyer
(1984) 270 EG 140   *177*
Emile Elias & Co *v* Pine Groves [1993] NPC 30
229
Epps *v* Esso Petroleum Co [1973] 1 WLR 1071;
[1973] 2 All ER 465   *72, 80, 81*
Errington *v* Errington and Woods [1952] 1 KB
290; [1952] 1 All ER 149   *160, 276*
Esso Petroleum Co Ltd *v* Harper's Garage
(Stourport) Ltd [1968] AC 269; [1967] 1 All
ER 699   *295*
Eves *v* Eves [1975] 1 WLR 1338   *135*
Evers' Trust, Re, Papps *v* Evers [1980] 1 WLR
1327; [1980] 3 All ER 399   *106, 107*

Fairclough *v* Swan Brewery Co Ltd [1912] AC
565; [1911–13] All ER 397   *293, 294*
Fairweather *v* St Marylebone Property Co Ltd
[1963] AC 510; [1962] 2 All ER 288   *336, 340*
Family Housing Association *v* Jones [1990] 1
WLR 779   *164*
Federated Homes Ltd *v* Mill Lodge Properties
Ltd [1980] 1 WLR 594; [1980] 1 All ER 371
225, 226, 227, 228, 233, 243, 244
Fitzpatrick *v* Sterling Housing Association Ltd
[1999] 3 WLR 1113   *203*
Formby *v* Barker [1903] 2 Ch 539; (1903) 72 LJ
Ch 716   *224*
Four Maids Ltd *v* Dudley Marshall (Properties)
Ltd [1957] Ch 317; [1957] 2 All ER 35   *306*
Freeguard *v* Royal Bank of Scotland plc [2002]
EWHC 2509   *303*
Frewen, Re [1926] Ch 580; (1926) 95 LJ Ch 297
94
Fuller *v* Judy Properties Ltd [1992] 1 EGLR 75
187

Gaite's Will Trusts, Re, Banks *v* Gaite [1949] 1
All ER 459; (1949) 65 TLR 194   *349*
Gardner *v* Hodgson's Kingston Brewery Co Ltd
[1903] AC 229; (1903) 72 LJ Ch 558 HL
255, 258

Gilbert *v* Spoor [1983] Ch 27   *235, 246, 249*
Gill *v* Lewis [1956] 2 QB 1   *187*
Gillett *v* Holt and Another [2000] 2 All ER 289
(CA); [1998] 3 All ER 917   *282*
Glass *v* Kencakes [1966] 1 QB 611; [1964] 3 All
ER 807   *183*
GMS Syndicate Ltd *v* Gary Elliott Ltd [1982]
Ch 1; [1981] 1 All ER 619   *186*
Go West Ltd *v* Spigarolo and Another [2003] 2
All ER 141   *175*
Goldberg *v* Edwards [1950] Ch 247; (1950) 94
Sol Jo 128   *254*
Gore and Snell *v* Carpenter (1990) 61 P & CR
456   *144*
Gough *v* Wood & Co [1894] 1 QB 713   *322*
Graham *v* Philcox [1984] 3 WLR 150   *263*
Grant *v* Edwards [1986] Ch 638; [1986] 3 WLR
114   *106, 137, 284*
Greasley *v* Cooke [1980] 3 All ER 710; [1980] 1
WLR 1306   *279*
Grigsby *v* Melville [1974] 1 WLR 80; [1973] 3
All ER 455   *248, 249, 270*
Groves and Another *v* Minor (1997) The Times
20 November   *262*

Hadjiloucas *v* Crean [1987] 3 All ER 1008   *161*
Hall *v* Howard (1989) 57 P & CR 226   *170*
Halsall *v* Brizell [1957] Ch 169; [1957] 1 All ER
371   *218, 219, 286*
Hambro *v* Duke of Marlborough [1994] 3 All ER
332   *99*
Hamilton *v* Martell Securities Ltd [1984] 1 All
ER 665   *185*
Hammersmith and Fulham London Borough
Council *v* Monk [1991] 3 WLR 1144   *145*
Hammond *v* Mitchell [1991] 1 WLR 1127   *137*
Hamp *v* Bygrave (1982) 266 EG 722   *32, 33*
Hardwick *v* Johnson [1978] 1 WLR 683; [1978] 2
All ER 935   *275*
Harris *v* De Pinna (1886) 33 Ch D 238   *249*
Harris *v* Goddard [1983] 3 All ER 242   *143*
Harrop, Re (1883) 24 Ch D 617   *95*
Haslemere Estates Ltd *v* Baker [1982] 1 WLR
1109; [1982] 3 All ER 525   *47*
Haywood *v* Brunswick Permanent Benefit
Building Society (1881) 8 QBD 403; (1881)
51 LJ QB 73   *224, 230, 242*
Hazell *v* Hazell [1972] 1 WLR 301   *136*
Healey *v* Hawkins [1968] 1 WLR 1967; [1968] 3
All ER 836   *255*
Heath *v* Drown [1973] AC 498   *160*
Hill *v* Harris [1965] 2 QB 601   *169*
Hill *v* Tupper (1863) 2 H & C 121; (1863) 2
New Rep 201   *248, 270*

Hobson *v* Gorringe [1897] 1 Ch 182   *32*

Hodgson *v* Marks [1971] Ch 892; [1971] 2 All
   ER 684   *72, 75*

Holland *v* Hodgson (1872) LR 7 CP 328   *30*

Hollington Brothers Ltd *v* Rhodes [1951] 2 All
   ER 578; [1951] 2 TLR 691   *47, 56, 157*

Hollins *v* Verney (1884) 13 QBD 304; (1884) 53
   LJ QB 430   *256*

Honywood *v* Honywood (1874) LR 18 Eq 306;
   (1874) 43 LJ Ch 652   *29*

Hooper *v* Sherman [1994] NPC 153   *156*

Hopgood *v* Brown [1955] 1 WLR 213; [1955] 1
   All ER 550   *278*

Hopkin's Lease, Re, Caerphilly Concrete
   Products Ltd *v* Owen [1972] 1 WLR 372;
   [1972] 1 All ER 248   *167*

Horrocks *v* Forray [1976] 1 WLR 230; [1976] 1
   All ER 737   *160*

Hughes' Application, Re [1983] JPL 318   *234*

Hulme *v* Brigham [1943] KB 152; [1943] 1 All
   ER 204   *322*

Hunt *v* Luck [1902] 1 Ch 428; [1900–3] All ER
   295   *37*

Hussey *v* Palmer [1972] 1 WLR 1286; [1972] 3
   All ER 744   *135, 136*

Hyde *v* Pearce [1982] 1 WLR 560   *341*

Inns, Re [1947] Ch 576   *108*

International Drilling Fluids Ltd *v* Louisville
   Investments (Uxbridge) Ltd [1986] 2 WLR
   581   *174, 175*

Inwards *v* Baker [1965] 2 QB 29; [1965] 1 All ER
   446   *278, 285*

Ives (E R) Investments Ltd *v* High [1967] 2 QB
   379; [1967] 2 WLR 789; [1967] 1 All ER 504
   49, 281, 286

J A Pye (Oxford) Ltd *v* Graham [2002] 3 WLR
   221; [2000] 3 WLR 242   *334, 339*

J T Developments *v* Quinn (1991) 62 P & CR 33
   283

Jee *v* Audley (1787) 1 Cox Eq Cas 324   *349*

Jennings *v* Ward (1705) 2 Vern 520   *294*

Jeune *v* Queens Cross Properties Ltd [1974] Ch
   97   *178*

Jones *v* Barnett [1984] Ch 500   *187*

Jones *v* Challenger [1961] 1 QB 176; [1960] 1 All
   ER 785   *106, 147*

Jones *v* Jones [1977] 1 WLR 438; [1977] 2 All
   ER 231   *145*

Jones *v* Lavington [1903] 1 KB 253   *168*

Jones *v* Price (1992) The Independent 16 January
   255

Jupp, Re (1888) 39 Ch D 148   *145*

Kataria *v* Safeland plc [1998] 1 EGLR 39   *182*

Kelly, Re, Clearly *v* Dillon [1932] IR 255   *347*

Kelsen *v* Imperial Tobacco Co [1957] 2 QB 334
   24

Kilgour *v* Gaddes [1904] 1 KB 457; (1904) 73 LJ
   KB 233   *256*

Kinch *v* Bullard (1998) The Times 16 September
   143

King *v* David Allen & Sons Billposting Ltd
   [1916] 2 AC 54; [1916–17] All ER 268   *276*

Kingsnorth Finance Co Ltd *v* Tizard [1986] 1
   WLR 783; [1986] 2 All ER 54   *37*

Kingsnorth Trust Ltd *v* Bell [1986] 1 WLR 119
   310

Knightsbridge Estates Trusts Ltd *v* Byrne [1939]
   Ch 441; [1938] 4 All ER 618 (CA); affirmed
   [1940] AC 613; [1940] 2 All ER 401 (HL)
   293, 297

Kreglinger *v* New Patagonia Meat and Cold
   Storage Co Ltd [1914] AC 25; (1914) 83 LJ
   Ch 79   *293, 295*

Lace *v* Chantler [1944] KB 368; [1944] 1 All ER
   305   *158*

Lake *v* Craddock (1732) 3 P Wms 158   *131*

Land Securities plc *v* Receiver for the
   Metropolitan Police District [1983] 1 WLR
   439   *184*

Layton *v* Martin [1986] 2 FLR 227   *285*

Lee-Parker *v* Izzet [1971] 1 WLR 1688; [1971] 3
   All ER 1099   *71, 179*

Leigh *v* Taylor [1902] AC 157   *31*

Lever Finance Ltd *v* Needleman's Trustee and
   Kreutzer [1956] Ch 375   *320*

Leverhulme, Re, Cooper *v* Leverhulme (No 2)
   [1943] 2 All ER 274; (1943) 169 LT 294
   347

Lewis *v* Frank Love Ltd [1961] 1 WLR 261;
   [1961] 1 All ER 446   *293*

Lister *v* Lane and Nesham [1893] 2 QB 212   *178*

Liverpool City Council *v* Irwin [1977] AC 239;
   [1976] 2 All ER 39   *169*

Liverpool Corporation *v* H Coghill & Son Ltd
   [1918] 1 Ch 307   *255*

Lloyds Bank plc *v* Byrne [1993] 1 FLR 369
   120, 121

Lloyds Bank plc *v* Carrick & Another [1996] 4
   All ER 630   *51*

Lloyds Bank plc *v* Rosset [1991] 1 AC 107;
   [1990] 2 WLR 867; [1988] 3 WLR 1301
   74, 134–135, 137, 284

London and Blenheim Estates Ltd v Ladbroke
Retail Parks Ltd [1992] 1 WLR 1278 *246,
247*

London and Cheshire Insurance Co Ltd v
Laplagrene Property Co Ltd [1971] Ch 499;
[1971] 1 All ER 766 *75*

London and County (A & D) Ltd v Wilfred
Sportsman Ltd [1971] Ch 764 *192*

London and Suburban Land and Building Co
v Carey (1991) 62 P & CR 480 *262*

London Borough of Hounslow v Twickenham
Garden Developments Ltd [1971] Ch 233;
[1970] 3 All ER 326 *274*

London Corporation v Riggs (1880) 13 Ch D
798; (1880) 49 LJ Ch 297 *251*

London County Council v Allen [1914] 3 KB 642
230, 242

Long v Gowlett [1923] 2 Ch 177; (1923) 92 LJ
Ch 530 *254*

Lurcott v Wakeley [1911] 1 KB 505 *178*

Lyme Valley Squash Club Ltd v Newcastle
under Lyme Borough Council [1985] 2 All
ER 405 *255*

Lyus v Prowsa Developments Ltd [1982] 1 WLR
1044; [1982] 2 All ER 953 *61*

McGreal v Wake [1984] 1 EGLR 42 *170*

McHardy and Sons v Warren (1994) The Times
8 April *140*

McMorris v Brown & Another [1999] 1 AC 142
234

Malayan Credit Ltd v Jack Chia MPH Ltd
[1986] 1 All ER 711 *132*

Malzy v Eichholz [1916] 2 KB 308 *168*

Manfield & Sons v Botchin [1970] 2 QB 612
210

Marchant v Charters [1977] 1 WLR 1181; [1977]
3 All ER 918 *160*

Marjorie Burnett Ltd v Barclay (1980) 258 EG
642 *167*

Marsden v Miller (1992) The Times 23 January
334

Martin's Application, Re (1989) 57 P & CR 119
235

Maryon-Wilson's Instruments, Re, Blofeld v
Maryon-Wilson [1971] Ch 789; [1969] 3 All
ER 558 *101*

Matharu v Matharu (1994) 68 P & CR 93 *281*

Mayo, Re, Mayo v Mayo [1943] Ch 302; [1943] 2
All ER 440 *106, 147*

Medforth v Blake [2000] Ch 86 *304*

Michael & Others v Miller (2004) The Times 30
March *302*

Midland Bank Ltd v Farmpride Hatcheries Ltd
(1981) 260 EG 493 *37, 276*

Midland Bank plc v Cooke & Another [1995] 4
All ER 562 *134, 137, 141*

Midland Bank Trust Co Ltd v Green [1981] AC
513; [1981] 2 WLR 28; [1981] 1 All ER 153
36, 46, 52, 56

Midland Railway Co's Agreement, Re, Charles
Clay & Sons Ltd v British Railways Board
[1971] Ch 725; [1971] 1 All ER 1007 *159,
165*

Mikeover v Brady [1989] 3 All ER 618 *164*

Mills v Silver [1991] 2 WLR 324; (1990) The
Times 13 July *257*

Ministry of Housing and Local Government v
Sharp [1970] 2 QB 223 *54*

Mogridge v Clapp [1892] 3 Ch 382; (1892) 61 LJ
Ch 534 *103*

Moody v Steggles (1879) 12 Ch D 261; (1879) 48
LJ Ch 639 *246*

Moore v Rawson (1824) 3 B & C 332 *265*

Moore, Re [1901] 1 Ch 936 *347*

Morgan's Lease, Re, Jones v Norsesowicz [1972]
Ch 1; [1971] 2 All ER 235 *103*

Morris v Liverpool City Council (1988) 14 EG
59 *170*

Mortgage Corporation v Shaire & Others [2001]
Ch 743 *108, 120, 148*

Moule v Garrett (1872) LR 7 Ex 101 *191*

Mount Carmel Investments Ltd v Peter Thurlow
Ltd [1988] 3 All ER 129 *335*

Multiservice Bookbinding Ltd v Marden [1978] 2
WLR 535; [1978] 2 All ER 489 *296*

Mulvaney v Jackson [2002] EWCA Civ 1078
246

Mundy and Roper's Contract, Re [1899] 1 Ch
275 *95*

National and Provincial Building Society v Lloyd
[1996] 1 All ER 630 *309*

National Carriers Ltd v Panalpina Northern Ltd
[1981] AC 675 *172, 180*

National Provincial Bank Ltd v Ainsworth [1965]
AC 1175; [1965] 2 All ER 472 HL; reversing
sub nom National Provincial Bank Ltd v
Hastings Car Mart [1964] Ch 665 *71, 72*

National Westminster Bank plc v Amin [2002] 1
FLR 735 *315*

National Westminster Bank plc v Kosto Poulos
(2000) The Times 2 March *320*

National Westminster Bank plc v Morgan [1985]
2 WLR 588 *310*

Nationwide Building Society v Registry of
Friendly Societies [1983] 3 All ER 296 *296*

New Zealand Government Property Corporation
v H M & S Ltd [1982] 2 WLR 837; [1982] 1
All ER 624   *32*

Newbould, Re (1913) 110 LT 6   *105*

Newman *v* Jones (22 March 1982 – unreported)
246, 247

Newman *v* Real Estate Debenture Corporation
[1940] 1 All ER 131   *169*

Newport Farms Ltd *v* Damesh Holdings Ltd
(2003) 147 SJLB 1117   *302, 304*

Newton Abbot Co-operative Society Ltd *v*
Williamson & Treadgold Ltd [1952] Ch 286;
[1952] 1 All ER 279   *228*

Nickerson *v* Barraclough [1980] Ch 325; [1979] 3
All ER 312; reversed [1981] Ch 426; [1981] 2
All ER 369 (CA)   *251*

Nisbet and Pott's Contract, Re [1906] 1 Ch 386;
(1906) 75 LJ Ch 238   *341*

Norfolk Capital Group Ltd *v* Kitway [1977] QB
506; [1976] 3 All ER 787   *174*

Norris *v* Shecksfield [1991] 1 WLR 1241   *164*

Norwich and Peterborough Building Society *v*
Steed [1993] Ch 116   *79*

Oak Co-operative Building Society *v* Blackburn
[1968] Ch 730; [1968] 2 All ER 117   *53, 54*

Official Custodian for Charities *v* Parway Estates
Developments Ltd [1984] 3 All ER 679
188

Oliver *v* Hinton [1899] 2 Ch 264; (1899) 68 LJ
Ch 583   *56*

O'May *v* City of London Real Property Co Ltd
[1982] 1 All ER 660   *210*

P & A Swift Investments *v* Combined English
Stores Group plc [1988] 2 All ER 885   *172*

Paddington Building Society *v* Mendelsohn
(1985) 50 P & CR 244   *73*

Palk *v* Mortgage Services Funding [1993] 2 All
ER 481   *305*

Palmer (Deceased) (A Debtor), Re [1994] 3 All
ER 835   *144*

Palmer and Another *v* Bowman and Another
[2000] 1 WLR 842   *247, 257*

Paragon Finance plc *v* Nash and Another;
Paragon Finance plc *v* Staunton and Another
[2002] 1 WLR 685   *296*

Parker *v* British Airways Board [1982] 1 All ER
834   *26*

Parker-Tweedale *v* Dunbar Bank plc (No 1)
[1990] 3 WLR 767   *303*

Parkin *v* Boggon [1947] KB 346   *174*

Parkus *v* Greenwood [1950] Ch 644; [1950] 1 All
ER 436   *167*

Pascoe *v* Turner [1979] 1 WLR 431; [1979] 2 All
ER 945   *277, 279*

Passee *v* Passee [1983] 1 FLR 263   *136*

Payne *v* Adnams [1971] CLY 6486   *69*

Payne *v* Cardiff RDC [1932] 1 KB 241   *301*

Peffer *v* Rigg [1978] 3 All ER 745   *61*

Perera *v* Vandiyar [1953] 1 WLR 672   *168*

Perrin *v* Lyon (1807) 9 East 170   *22*

Pettitt *v* Pettitt [1970] AC 777; [1969] 2 WLR
996; [1969] 2 All ER 385   *136, 275*

Pettkus *v* Becker (1980) 117 DLR (3d) 257   *135*

Phipps *v* Pears [1965] 1 QB 76; [1964] 2 All ER
34   *246, 249*

Pimms Ltd *v* Tallow Chandlers Co [1964] 2 QB
547   *174*

Port *v* Griffith [1938] 1 All ER 295   *169*

Post Office *v* Aquarius Properties Ltd [1987] 1
All ER 1055   *177*

Powell *v* McFarlane (1977) 38 P & CR 452
332

Powys *v* Blagrave (1854) 4 De GM & G 448;
(1854) 2 Eq Rep 1204   *29*

Premier Confectionary (London) Ltd *v* London
Commercial Sale Rooms Ltd [1993] Ch 904
174

Prior's Case, The (1368) YB 42 Ed 3 Hil, pl 14
216

Pritchard *v* Briggs [1980] Ch 338; [1980] 1 All
ER 294   *47*

Proctor *v* Bishop of Bath and Wells (1794) 2 Hy
BL 358   *353*

Proudfoot *v* Hart (1890) 25 QBD 42   *178*

Prudential Assurance Co Ltd *v* London
Residuary Body [1992] 3 WLR 279   *158,
161, 165*

Pwllbach Colliery Co Ltd *v* Woodman [1915] AC
634; [1914–15] All ER Rep 124   *252*

Pyx Granite Co Ltd *v* Minister of Housing and
Local Government [1958] 1 QB 554   *364*

Quennel *v* Maltby [1979] 1 WLR 318   *306, 327*

Quick *v* Taff-Ely Borough Council [1985] 3 All
ER 321   *177*

R *v* Oxfordshire County Council, ex parte
Sunningwell Parish Council [1999] 3 WLR
160   *255*

R *v* Suffolk County Council, ex parte Steed
(1996) 75 P & CR 102   *255*

Raja *v* Lloyds TSB (2001) 82 P & CR 19   *337*

Ramsden *v* Dyson (1866) LR 1 HL 129   *277*

Rance *v* Elvin (1985) The Times 27 February
246

Ravenseft Properties Ltd *v* Davstone (Holdings) Ltd [1980] QB 12; [1979] 1 All ER 929   *177*

Reeve *v* Lisle [1902] AC 461; (1902) 71 LJ Ch 768   *293*

Regan & Blackburn Ltd *v* Rogers [1985] 1 WLR 870   *47*

Regent Oil Co Ltd *v* J A Gregory (Hatch End) Ltd [1966] Ch 402; [1965] 3 All ER 673 *224*

Regis Property Co Ltd *v* Dudley [1959] AC 370 *178*

Regis Property Co Ltd *v* Redman [1956] 2 QB 612; [1956] 2 All ER 335   *249*

Reilly *v* Orange [1955] 2 QB 112; [1955] 2 All ER 369   *259*

Renals *v* Cowlishaw (1879) 11 Ch D 866   *225, 243*

Reynolds *v* Ashby & Son [1904] AC 466   *32*

Rhodes *v* Dalby [1971] 1 WLR 1325   *327*

Rhone *v* Stephens [1994] 2 All ER 65; (1993) The Times 21 January   *218, 219, 241*

Roake *v* Chadha [1983] 3 All ER 503   *226, 228*

Rogers *v* Hosegood [1900] 2 Ch 388; [1900–3] All ER Rep 915   *216, 224, 225, 243*

Ropaigelach *v* Barclays Bank plc [2000] QB 263 *309*

Rowhook Mission Hall, Horsham, Re [1985] Ch 62; [1984] 3 All ER 179   *34*

Royal Bank of Scotland *v* Etridge (No 2) [2001] 4 All ER 449 (HL); [1998] 4 All ER 705 (CA) *314, 315, 316*

Royal Philanthropic Society *v* County (1985) 276 EG 1068   *161*

Rugby Joint Water Board *v* Walters [1967] Ch 397   *26*

Rugby School Governors *v* Tannahill [1935] 1 KB 87; [1934] All ER Rep 187   *183*

Saeed *v* Plustrade Ltd [2001] EWCA Civ 2011 *246, 247*

Sainsbury (J) plc *v* Enfield London Borough Council [1989] 2 All ER 817   *228*

Sampson *v* Hodson-Pressinger [1981] 3 All ER 710   *169, 189*

Samuel *v* Jarrah Timber and Wood Paving Corporation Ltd [1904] AC 323; (1904) LJ Ch 526   *293*

Santley *v* Wilde [1899] 2 Ch 474; (1899) 68 LJ Ch 681   *287*

Saunders *v* Vautier (1841) 4 Beav 115; (1841) Cr & Ph 240   *122, 360*

Savva & Savva *v* Hussein (1997) 73 P & CR 150 *183*

Scala House and District Property Co Ltd *v* Forbes [1974] QB 575; [1973] 3 All ER 308 *173, 183*

Sea View Gardens, Re, Claridge *v* Tingey [1967] 1 WLR 134; [1966] 3 All ER 935   *80*

SEDAC Investments Ltd *v* Tanner [1982] 1 WLR 1342; [1982] 3 All ER 646   *184*

Seddon *v* Smith (1877) 36 LT 168   *333*

Sekhon *v* Alissa [1989] 2 FLR 94   *134, 136*

Selim Ltd *v* Bickenhall Engineering Ltd [1981] 1 WLR 1318; [1981] 3 All ER 210   *47*

Seton *v* Slade (1802) 7 Ves 265   *292*

Shanly *v* Ward (1913) 29 TLR 714   *173*

Sharpe *v* Rickards [1909] 1 Ch 109   *325*

Sharpe (A Bankrupt), Re [1980] 1 WLR 219; [1980] 1 All ER 198   *72, 137, 284*

Shell-Mex and BP *v* Manchester Garages [1971] 1 WLR 612; [1971] 1 All ER 841   *160*

Shiloh Spinners Ltd *v* Harding [1973] AC 691; [1973] 1 All ER 90   *48, 49, 250, 281*

Silverman *v* Afco (UK) Ltd [1988] 1 EGLR 51 *187*

Simmons *v* Dobson [1991] 1 WLR 720   *256*

Skipton Building Society *v* Bratley (2000) The Times 12 January   *302*

Smith *v* Marrable (1843) 11 M & W 5   *169*

Smith and Snipes Hall Farm *v* River Douglas Catchment Board [1949] 2 KB 500; [1949] 2 All ER 179 CA   *198, 216*

Snaith *v* Dolding's Application, Re (1996) 71 P & CR 104   *234*

Somma *v* Hazelhurst [1978] 1 WLR 1014; [1978] 2 All ER 1011   *160, 203*

Southern Centre of Theosophy *v* State of South Australia [1982] AC 706; [1982] 1 All ER 283 *26*

Sovmots Investments Ltd *v* Secretary of State for the Environment [1977] 2 WLR 951; [1977] 2 All ER 385   *254*

Spectrum Investment Co *v* Holmes [1981] 1 WLR 221; [1981] 1 All ER 6   *340*

Stafford *v* Lee (1992) 65 P & CR 172   *252*

Standard Chartered Bank *v* Walker [1982] 3 All ER 938   *302*

Standard Pattern Co Ltd *v* Ivey [1962] Ch 432 *186*

Stent *v* Monmouth Borough Council (1987) 282 EG 705   *177*

Strand Securities *v* Caswell [1965] Ch 958; [1965] 1 All ER 820   *72*

Street *v* Mountford [1985] 2 WLR 877   *159, 160, 161, 163, 164, 204, 287*

Stribling *v* Wickham (1989) 27 EG 81   *164*

Swansborough *v* Coventry (1832) 2 M & S 362
   254
Sweet *v* Sommer (2004) The Times 25 August
   vii, 251
Swindon Waterworks Co Ltd *v* Wilts & Berks
   Canal Navigation Co (1875) LR 7 HL 697   *26*

Tandon *v* Trustees of Spurgeon's Homes [1982]
   AC 755; [1982] 1 All ER 1086   *207*
Tanner *v* Tanner [1975] 1 WLR 1346; [1975] 3
   All ER 776   *160, 275*
Target Home Loans *v* Clothier and Clothier
   [1994] 1 All ER 439   *308, 309*
Taylor Fashions Ltd *v* Liverpool Victoria
   Trustees Co Ltd [1982] QB 133; [1981] 1 All
   ER 897   *48*
Terunnanse *v* Terunnanse [1968] AC 1086   *272*
Texaco Antilles Ltd *v* Kernochan [1973] AC 609
   236
Thames Guaranty Ltd *v* Campbell [1984] 2 All
   ER 585   *130*
Thellusson *v* Woodford (1799) 11 Ves 112   *359,*
   361
Tiltwood, Sussex, Re, Barrett *v* Bond [1978] Ch
   269; [1978] 2 All ER 10   *236*
Titchmarsh *v* Royston Water Co Ltd (1899) 81
   LT 673   *251*
Tito *v* Waddell (No 2) [1977] Ch 106   *218*
Tomlin *v* Luce (1889) 43 Ch D 191   *302*
Treloar *v* Nute [1976] 1 WLR 1295; [1977] 1 All
   ER 230   *332*
Trenchard, Re [1902] 1 Ch 378   *101*
Truman, Hanbury, Buxton & Co Ltd's
   Application, Re [1956] 1 QB 261   *235*
TSB Bank plc *v* Camfield [1995] 1 All ER 951
   317
TSB Bank plc *v* Marshall [1998] 39 EG 208
   108, 120, 148
Tse Kwong Lam *v* Wong Chit Sen [1983] 1
   WLR 1349; [1983] 3 All ER 54   *304, 305*
Tulk *v* Moxhay (1848) 2 Ph 774; (1848) 1 H &
   Tw 105   *197, 222, 223, 224*
Turner *v* Wright (1860) 2 De GF & J 234   *29*
Twentieth Century Banking Corporation Ltd *v*
   Wilkinson [1977] Ch 99; [1976] 3 All ER 361
   301, 305

Union Lighterage Co *v* London Graving Dock Co
   [1902] Ch 557; (1902) 71 LJ Ch 791   *251*
United Bank of Kuwait plc *v* Sahib and Others
   [1996] 3 All ER 215   *289*
University of Westminster, Re [1998] 3 All ER
   1014   *234*

Vane *v* Lord Barnard (1716) 2 Vern 738; (1716) 1
   Eq Cas Abr 399   *30*
Verrall *v* Great Yarmouth Borough Council
   [1981] QB 202; [1980] 1 All ER 839   *274*
Villar, Re, Public Trustee *v* Villar [1929] 1 Ch
   243; [1928] All ER Rep 535   *347*

Wakeham *v* Wood (1981) 43 P & CR 40   *230*
Wallis's Cayton Bay Holiday Camp Ltd *v* Shell-
   Mex & BP Ltd [1975] QB 94; [1974] 3 WLR
   387 CA; [1974] 3 All ER 575   *332*
Walsh *v* Lonsdale (1882) 21 Ch D 9   *157*
Warner *v* Jacob (1882) 20 Ch D 220   *302*
Warren *v* Keen [1954] 1 QB 15; [1953] 2 All ER
   1118   *171*
Webb *v* Pollmount Ltd [1966] Ch 584; [1966] 1
   All ER 48   *71*
Westhoughton UDC *v* Wigan Coal and Iron Co
   Ltd [1919] 1 Ch 159   *217*
Westminster City Council *v* Clarke [1992] 2
   WLR 229   *164*
Weston *v* Henshaw [1950] Ch 510   *103*
Wheeldon *v* Burrows (1879) 12 Ch D 31; (1879)
   48 LJ Ch 853   *70, 250, 252, 253, 254, 255,*
   267, 269, 270
Wheeler and Another *v* J J Saunders Ltd and
   Others [1995] 2 All ER 697   *253*
Wheelwright *v* Walker (1883) 23 Ch D 752;
   (1883) 52 LJ Ch 274   *97*
White *v* City of London Brewery Co (1889) 42
   Ch D 237; (1889) 58 LJ Ch 855   *310*
White *v* Grand Hotel, Eastbourne [1913] 1 Ch
   113   *262*
White *v* Richards [1993] RTR 318   *262*
Williams *v* Hensman (1861) 1 J & H 546; (1861)
   30 LJ Ch 878   *127*
Williams *v* Staite [1978] 2 WLR 825; [1978] 2 All
   ER 928   *280*
Williams *v* Wellingborough Borough Council
   [1975] 1 WLR 1327; [1975] 3 All ER 462
   304
Williams & Glyn's Bank *v* Boland [1981] AC 487;
   [1980] 3 WLR 138; [1980] 2 All ER 408
   49, 61, 62, 71, 72, 75, 133, 310, 320
Winter Garden Theatre (London) Ltd *v*
   Millennium Productions Ltd [1948] AC 173;
   [1947] 2 All ER 331   *274*
Wong *v* Beaumont Property Trust [1965] 1 QB
   173; [1964] 2 All ER 119   *246, 252*
Wood *v* Leadbitter (1845) 13 M & W 838   *273*
Woodhouse & Co Ltd *v* Kirkland (Derby) Ltd
   [1970] 1 WLR 1185; [1970] 2 All ER 587;
   (1970) 114 SJ 589; (1970) 21 P & CR 534
   262

Woolwich plc *v* Gomm & Another (2000) 79 P &
    CR 61   *37*
Wright *v* Macadam [1949] 2 KB 744; [1949] 2
    All ER 565   *246, 247, 248, 254, 270*
Wroth *v* Tyler [1974] Ch 30   *48*

Yaxley *v* Gotts & Gotts [1999] 3 WLR 1217
    155, 156

Yellowly *v* Gower (1855) 11 Exch 274   *171*
Yorkshire Bank plc *v* Tinsley (2004) The Times
    12 August   *vii, 319*

Zetland *v* Driver [1939] Ch 1   *226*

Table of Statutes

Access to Neighbouring Land Act 1992   72,
    245, 264, 266
    s1   266
    s3   266
    s5   72, 266
    s7   266
Accumulations Act 1800   359, 361
Administration of Estates Act 1925   11, 17, 40
    s33   105, 106
    s34   41
    s45   41, 145
    s46   41
    Schedule 1   41
Administration of Justice Act 1970
    s36   307, 308, 309, 310
Administration of Justice Act 1973
    s8   300, 307
Administration of Justice Act 1982   79
Administration of Justice Act 1985
    s55   187
Agricultural Holdings Act 1948   32, 179
    s13   32
Agricultural Holdings Act 1984   179
Agricultural Holdings Act 1986   208, 209, 365
Agricultural Tenancies Act 1995   208, 209, 365

Bankruptcy Act 1914   144
Bodies Corporate (Joint Tenancy) Act 1899   125
Building Societies Act 1986
    s13   302
    Schedule 4   302

Charging Orders Act 1979   49
Civil Aviation Act 1982
    s76   25
Civil Partnership Act 2004   133
    s65   133
    s66   133
Coal Act 1938   25
Coal Industry Act 1987
    s1   25
Common Law Procedure Act 1852   186
    ss210–212   186
    s212   186

Commonhold and Leasehold Reform Act 2002
    237–240, 242
Commons Registration Act 1965   85, 268
    s16   267
Consumer Credit Act 1974   292, 296, 297
    s94   297
    s137   296
    s138   296, 297
    s139   296
    s140   296
Contracts (Rights of Third Parties) Act 1999
    198–201, 211, 233
    s1   199, 200, 233
    s2   199
    s3   199
Conveyancing Act 1881   27
    s58   228
County Courts Act 1984
    s71   306
    s138   187
    s148   174
Criminal Law Act 1977
    s6   182

Deeds of Arrangement Act 1914   47
Defective Premises Act 1972   170
    s4   170

Environment Act 1995   366
Environmental Protection Act 1990   366

Family Law Act 1996   48
Financial Services Act 1986   155
Fines and Recoveries Act 1833
    s1   xxv, 21, 28
Fires Prevention (Metropolis) Act 1774   322

Housing Act 1957
    s6   170
Housing Act 1961
    s32   169
Housing Act 1980   203, 206, 365
Housing Act 1985   193, 203, 205, 365
    s609   230
    s610   236

Housing Act 1987   *203, 365*
Housing Act 1988   *176, 202, 203, 204, 205,*
    272, 365
        s1   *31*
        s15   *176*
        s21   *206*
        s27   *208*
Housing Act 1996   *202, 203, 204, 207, 365*
        s105   *207*
        Schedule 7   *202*
        Schedule 9   *208*
Housing Act 2004   *201, 205, 206*
        s212   *206*
        ss254–259   *206*
        Part 1   *205*
        Part 2   *205*
        Part 6   *206*
Human Right Act 1998   *88*

Judicature Act 1873   *35*
Judicature Act 1875   *35*

Land Charges Act 1925   *40, 46, 62*
        s13   *46*
Land Charges Act 1972   *xxvii, 38, 41, 46, 47,*
    48, 49, 50, 52, 57, 62, 63, 66, 77, 285
        s1   *46, 55*
        s2   *47, 48, 49*
        s3   *53*
        s4   *46, 50, 51, 55, 223*
        s6   *266*
        s10   *53*
        s17   *36, 46, 56*
Land Clauses Act   *24*
Land Registration Act 1925   *40, 51, 57, 58, 60,*
    61, 62, 63, 64, 65, 67, 68, 71, 74, 76, 77, 78,
    81, 82, 86, 88, 223, 250, 328, 340
        s3   *68, 77*
        s20   *60, 61*
        s49   *72*
        s59   *60, 61*
        s70   *52, 60, 61, 69, 70, 71, 72, 73, 74,*
            75, 76, 77, 81, 82, 85, 119, 133, 250,
            283, 340
        s74   *61*
        s75   *70, 340*
        s82   *79*
        s83   *80*
        s86   *72*
        s102   *58, 110, 329*
Land Registration Act 1986   *41, 58, 110*
        s4   *70*
        s5   *58, 62, 329*

Land Registration Act 1988   *41, 59*
Land Registration Act 1997   *41, 58, 59, 83*
        s1   *59*
        s2   *80*
        s3   *60*
Land Registration Act 2002   *vii, 27, 41, 57, 58,*
    60, 61, 62, 63, 64, 66, 68, 70, 76, 77, 81–88,
    110, 223, 243, 250, 283, 287, 288, 289, 290,
    322, 328, 329, 340
        s4   *63*
        s6   *64*
        s7   *64*
        s9   *64, 65*
        s10   *65*
        s23   *288*
        s65   *87*
        s116   *283, 285*
        Part 2   *83*
        Part 7   *87*
        Part 8   *82*
        Part 9   *85*
        Part 11   *88*
        Schedule 1   *84, 85*
        Schedule 3   *84, 85, 283*
        Schedule 4   *87*
        Schedule 6   *86*
Landlord and Tenant Act 1927   *195*
        s1A   *195*
        s18   *178*
        s19   *173, 174, 176, 195, 196*
Landlord and Tenant Act 1954   *203, 210, 272,*
    365
        s23   *210*
        s25   *210*
        s30   *210*
        s51   *184*
        s53   *174*
        Part II   *179, 210*
Landlord and Tenant Act 1985   *365*
        ss8–10   *170, 365*
        s10   *170*
        ss11–16   *169*
        s11   *168, 170*
Landlord and Tenant Act 1988   *175, 176*
        s1   *175, 176*
Landlord and Tenant (Covenants) Act 1995
    41, 190, 193, 194, 196
        s3   *194*
        s5   *194*
        s7   *194*
        s8   *194*
        s11   *194*
        s16   *195*

Landlord and Tenant (Covenants) Act 1995
(*contd.*)
    s17   *195*
    s19   *195*
    s22   *195*
    s24   *194*
    s25   *196*
    s28   *194*
Law of Property Act 1922   *11, 16, 17, 40*
    s128   *16*
    s145   *167*
    Schedule 12   *16*
    Schedule 15   *167, 190*
Law of Property Act 1925   *8, 23, 40, 49, 77,*
  89, 90, 105, 111, 117, 126, 140, 156, 288,
  301, 345, 361
    s1   *xxviii, 23, 42, 43, 44, 45, 76, 126,*
    138, 149, 150, 249–250, 288
    s2   *44, 114*
    s3   *34*
    s7   *23, 24, 33, 34, 43*
    s25   *105, 106, 108, 111, 114*
    s26   *108, 109, 111, 116, 117*
    s28   *108, 111, 115, 116, 141*
    s29   *109, 116*
    s30   *106, 107, 108, 109, 118, 119, 120,*
    121, 147, 148
    ss34–36   *138*
    s34   *138, 139, 140*
    s35   *118, 139*
    s36   *127, 139, 140, 143*
    s37   *145*
    s40   *144, 155, 156, 289*
    s52   *154*
    s53   *134, 284, 289*
    s54   *154, 155*
    s55   *250*
    s56   *190, 200, 215*
    s60   *xxvii, 7, 27, 42*
    s62   *70, 157, 247, 250, 253, 254, 255,*
    267, 269, 270
    s77   *191*
    s78   *198, 216, 217, 225, 226, 227, 228,*
    232, 233, 244
    s79   *197, 230, 243*
    s84   *234, 235, 236*
    ss85–87   *42*
    ss85–120   *288*
    s85   *288*
    s87   *44, 288, 290*
    s91   *300, 301, 305, 306, 321*
    s93   *325*
    s94   *50, 322, 323*

Law of Property Act 1925 (*contd.*)
    s95   *306*
    s96   *50, 298*
    s98   *299*
    s99   *327*
    s100   *328*
    s101   *301, 305, 320, 322*
    ss101–107   *300*
    s103   *301*
    s104   *301*
    s109   *320*
    s115   *298*
    s130   *27, 41*
    s135   *30*
    s137   *41, 329*
    s138   *290, 329*
    s139   *290*
    s141   *192, 193, 196*
    s142   *192, 193, 196*
    s146   *173, 181, 183, 184, 185, 186, 187,*
    197, 340
    s149   *150, 157, 166, 167, 168*
    s152   *98*
    s153   *180, 181, 218*
    s155   *39*
    s156   *39*
    s157   *39*
    s160   *360*
    s163   *350, 352, 355, 356, 361*
    ss164–166   *359, 361*
    s164   *360*
    s176   *28*
    s196   *143*
    s198   *38, 46, 50, 51, 55*
    s199   *37, 38*
    s205   *xxvi, xxvii, xxviii, 20, 43, 44, 105,*
    111, 149, 150, 157, 161, 254
Law of Property Act 1969   *41, 51*
    s23   *53*
    s24   *51, 53*
    s25   *53*
    s28   *234, 236*
Law of Property (Amendment) Act 1926   *41,*
  43, 142
    s1   *93*
    Schedule   *23*
Law of Property (Joint Tenants) Act 1964   *41,*
  141
    s1   *142*
    s3   *142*
Law of Property (Miscellaneous Provisions) Act
  1989   *41*
    s1   *157*
    s2   *144, 155, 156, 289*

Law of Property (Miscellaneous Provisions) Act
  1994   *123*
    s14   *106, 338*
    s15   *46*
Leasehold Property (Repairs) Act 1938   *179,*
  184, 185
    s1   *184*
Leasehold Reform Act 1967   *72, 174, 203, 206,*
  207
    s5   *72*
Leasehold Reform Act 1979   *206*
Leasehold Reform, Housing and Urban
  Development Act 1993   *203, 207*
    s63   *207*
    s65   *207*
    s66   *207*
Limitation Act 1980   *xxvii, 299, 300, 330, 333,*
  335, 336, 337, 340
    s5   *330, 331*
    s15   *330, 335, 339*
    s16   *330*
    s17   *339*
    s18   *338*
    s20   *330, 331*
    s21   *337*
    s28   *338*
    s29   *337, 339*
    s32   *339*
    s38   *336*
    Schedule 1   *331, 333, 336, 337*
Limitation (Enemies and War Prisoners) Act
  1945   *339*
Local Land Charges Act 1975   *40, 41, 52*
    s1   *52*
    s10   *52, 54*

Magna Carta 1215   *12, 14*
Married Women's Property Act 1882   *145*
Matrimonial Causes Act 1973   *133*
    s23   *133*
    s24   *133, 143*
    s25   *133*
Matrimonial Homes Act 1967   *48, 71, 72*
Matrimonial Homes Act 1983   *48, 71, 72, 285*
    s2   *71, 72*

Perpetuities and Accumulations Act 1964   *22,*
  41, 342, 345, 352, 354–357, 358, 359, 360,
  361, 362
    s1   *354, 361*
    s2   *354, 361*
    s3   *354, 355, 361*
    s4   *352, 354, 355, 356, 361*

Perpetuities and Accumulations Act 1964 (*contd.*)
    s5   *354, 356*
    s9   *357, 358*
    s10   *357*
    s11   *359*
    s12   *22, 357*
    s13   *359, 361*
Prescription Act 1832   *xxvii, 250, 255, 257,*
  258, 259, 267
    s1   *267*
    s2   *258, 259, 269*
    s3   *259, 260, 261*
    s4   *258, 259, 261*
Protection from Eviction Act 1977
    s1   *168, 208*
    s3   *182, 208*
    s5   *165, 179, 208*

Quia Emptores 1290   *6, 7, 267*

Race Relations Act 1976
    s24   *174*
Rent Act 1977   *160, 202, 203, 204, 205, 272,*
  307, 328, 365
    s70   *203*
Rentcharges Act 1977   *24, 41, 44, 91, 219*
    s2   *44, 219*
Reverter of Sites Act 1987   *18, 24, 33–34, 34*
    s1   *34*
Rights of Light Act 1959   *53, 261*

School Sites Act 1841   *33*
Settled Land Act 1882   *103, 111, 112, 345*
Settled Land Act 1925   *xxvii, 23, 33, 40, 44,*
  49, 72, 77, 85, 89, 90, 92, 93, 94, 95, 98, 99,
  100, 102, 103, 104, 105, 108, 110, 111, 112,
  113, 114, 116, 122, 278, 283, 285, 288
    s1   *33, 90, 93, 105*
    s4   *91, 92, 111*
    s5   *91*
    s9   *92*
    s13   *92, 102*
    s16   *93, 111*
    s17   *104*
    s18   *103*
    s19   *93, 111*
    s20   *93, 167, 278, 283*
    s23   *94*
    s24   *102, 104*
    s30   *94, 95*
    s34   *95*
    s38   *96, 97, 111*
    s39   *96, 97, 111*

Settled Land Act 1925 (*contd.*)
    s40   *96, 97*
    ss41–48   *96, 97*
    s42   *96*
    s46   *96*
    s51   *96, 98*
    s52   *96*
    s53   *96*
    s58   *96, 99*
    s64   *96, 99*
    s65   *96, 99*
    s66   *96, 99*
    s67   *96, 99*
    s68   *89, 95, 102*
    s71   *96, 98*
    s73   *104, 111*
    s75   *104, 111*
    ss83–89   *96, 100*
    s90   *98*
    s95   *103*
    s101   *97*
    s104   *89, 101*
    s105   *101*
    s106   *89, 95, 101, 108, 111, 116*
    s107   *96*
    s108   *89, 93, 100*
    s110   *103, 104*
    s117   *94, 105*
    Schedule 3   *100*
Sex Discrimination Act 1975   *174*
Statute De Donis Conditionalibus 1285   *27*
Statute for the Abolition of Military Tenures *see*
    Tenures Abolition Act 1660
Statutes of Mortmain 1279 and 1290   *14*
Statute of Uses 1535   *7, 8*
Statute of Wills 1540   *14*
Supreme Court Act 1981
    s37   *321*

Tenures Abolition Act 1660   *8, 9, 10, 11, 13, 17*
Town and Country Planning Act 1962
    s37   *235*
Town and Country Planning Act 1971
    s52   *235*
Town and Country Planning Act 1990   *363*
    s55   *363, 364*

Town and Country Planning Act 1990 (*contd.*)
    s70   *364*
    s106   *235*
    s237   *236*
Treasure Act 1996   *25, 26*
Trustee Act 1925   *40, 122*
Trustee Act 2000   *41*
    s8   *115*
    Schedule 2   *115*
Trusts of Land and Appointment of Trustees Act
    1996   *23, 33, 41, 49, 50, 56, 89, 90, 91, 93,*
    106, 108, 109, 111–123, 124, 139, 140, 145,
    146, 147, 148, 167, 278, 339, 365
    s1   *113, 139*
    s2   *91, 113*
    s3   *109, 114*
    s4   *114, 139, 147*
    s6   *115, 117*
    s7   *115, 121, 141*
    s8   *115*
    s9   *116*
    s10   *116, 117*
    s11   *117, 121*
    s12   *117, 118, 145*
    s13   *118, 145*
    s14   *106, 108, 118, 119, 120, 147, 148*
    s15   *106, 108, 119, 120, 147, 148*
    s16   *121*
    s19   *122*
    s20   *122*
    s21   *122*
    s22   *118, 122*
    Part I   *113*
    Part II   *113, 121, 122*
    Part III   *113*
    Schedule 1   *28, 41, 91, 93, 145, 335,*
    359
    Schedule 2   *34, 106, 140*

Universities and College Estates Act 1925   *49,*
    90, 114

Variation of Trusts Act 1958   *365*

Water Resources Act 1991   *366*
Wills Act 1837   *27*

Glossary

Some terms used in land law

Use of the glossary

Some terms used in land law

Absolute:	not conditional or determinable (used in relation to estates)
Alienation:	the act of disposing of or transferring to another
Ante-nuptial:	before marriage
Appendant:	attached to land by operation of law
Appurtenant:	attached to land by act of parties
Base fee:	a fee simple produced by partially barring an entail, not absolute: see s1 Fines and Recoveries Act 1833
Beneficial owner:	a person entitled for his own benefit
Caution:	a form of entry protecting an interest in registered land
Cestui que trust:	a beneficiary under a trust
Cestui que use:	a person to whose use property was conveyed
Cestui que vie:	a person for whose life an estate pur autre vie (during the life of another) lasts
Charge:	an encumbrance securing the payment of money – compare legal charge with equitable charge
Commorientes:	persons dying at the same time
Constructive:	inferred or implied
Contingent:	operative only upon an uncertain event
Conversion:	a change in the nature of the property, from real to personal or vice versa
Corporeal:	able to be physically possessed
Coverture:	the continuance of a marriage
Cy-près:	as nearly as possible
Deed:	a document signed, sealed and delivered
Deed poll:	a deed with only one party
Defeasance:	the determination of an interest on a specified event
Demise:	a transfer, usually the grant of a lease

Determine:	come to an end
Devise:	a gift of real property by will
Distrain, distress:	the lawful seizure of chattels without a court action by a landlord to enforce a right against his tenant; usually for non-payment of rent
Dominant tenement:	land to which the benefit of a right is attached
Easement:	a right over land, eg a right of way
Emblements:	growing crops which an outgoing tenant of agricultural land may take
En ventre sa mère:	conceived but not born
Entail:	an estate or interest descending only to the issue of the grantee (fee tail)
Equity of redemption:	the sum of a mortgagor's rights in mortgaged property
Escrow:	a deed which will be completed by delivery
Estoppel:	prohibition of a party from denying facts which he had led another to believe to be true
Execute:	1. to perform or complete, eg a deed
	2. to convert, eg transform the equitable interest under a use into a legal estate
Executory:	not yet completed
Feme covert:	married woman
Feme sole:	single woman
Feoffment:	conveyance by livery of seisin, ie formal ceremony of handing over title to the land
Foreclosure:	proceedings by a mortgagee which free mortgaged property from the equity of redemption
Heirlooms:	1. inheritable chattels
	2. settled chattels
Hereditaments:	inheritable rights in property
Heritable issue:	descendants capable of inheriting
In esse:	in existence
In gross:	existing independently of a dominant tenement
Incorporeal:	not able to be physically possessed
Incumbrance:	a liability burdening property
Indenture:	a deed between two or more parties, cf deed poll
Instrument:	a legal document
Interesse termini:	the rights of a lessee before entry
Issue:	descendants of any generation
Jus accrescendi:	right of survivorship in joint tenancy
Jus tertii:	a third party's title
Land:	see s205(1)(ix) Law of Property Act 1925
Licence:	a permission, eg to occupy land
Lien:	a form of security for unpaid money

Limitation of actions:	statutory barring of rights of action after a specified period: see Limitation Act 1980
Limitation, words of:	words delimiting the estate granted: see s60 Law of Property Act 1925
Limited owner:	an owner with an estate less than a fee simple
Merger:	the fusion of two or more estates or interests, cf surrender
Mesne:	intermediate
Minority:	the state of being an infant
Mortmain:	holding of land by a corporation
Notice:	actual constructive or imputed knowledge, cf Land Charges Act 1972
Occupancy:	occupation of land
Overreach:	to transfer rights from land to its purchase money
Override:	to render rights void
Partibility:	divisibility of inheritance among children
Per capita:	one share for each person
Per stirpes:	one share for each line of descendants
Portions:	provisions for children, especially lump sums for younger children under a settlement
Possession:	defined to include the receipt of rent and profits: s205(1)(xix) LPA 1925
Prescription:	the acquisition of easements by long user: see Prescription Act 1832
Privity of contract:	the relation of the original landlord and tenant
Privity of estate:	the relationship between the present landlord and tenant
Puisne mortgage:	a legal mortgage not protected by deposit of title deeds, see land charge Class C(i)
Pur autre vie:	for the life of another
Purchase, words of:	words conferring an interest
Purchaser:	one who takes by act of parties, not by operation of law
Release:	waiver of some right or interest
Quicquid plantatur solo, solo cedit:	whatever is affixed to the soil, belongs to the soil
Remainder:	the interest of a grantee subject to a prior grant to another
Restrictive covenant:	a covenant restricting the use of land
Resulting:	returning to the grantor by implication of law or equity
Reversion:	the interest remaining in a grantor
Riparian owner:	the owner of land adjoining a watercourse or road
Seisin:	possession of land by a freeholder
Servient tenement:	land burdened by a right, eg an easement
Settlement:	provision for persons in succession (or the instrument creating it: see Settled Land Act 1925)

Severance:	the conversion of a joint tenancy into a tenancy in common in equity only: see s1(6) Law of Property Act 1925
Severance, words of:	words showing a tenancy in common – must be in the deed itself
Specialty:	contract by deed
Spes successionis:	a possibility of succeeding to property
Squatter:	a person wrongfully occupying land
Statutory trusts:	trusts imposed by statute
Subinfeudation:	alienation by creating a new tenure
Sui juris:	not subject to any legal disability
Surrender:	the transfer of an interest to the person next entitled, cf merger
Tacking:	extension of a mortgagee's security to cover a later loan
Tenement:	property held by a tenant
Term of years absolute:	a defined period for which a tenant holds the land: see s205(1)(xxvii) Law of Property Act 1925
Time immemorial:	from 1189, the first year of the reign of Richard I
Title:	the evidence of a person's right to property
Undivided share:	the interest of a tenant in common which only arises in equity after 1925
User:	use enjoyment (*Note*: not the person who uses)
Vested:	unconditionally owned
Voluntary conveyance:	a conveyance not for valuable consideration
Waiver:	abandonment of a legal right
Waste:	an act altering the nature of the land

Use of the glossary

Other words and phrases will appear in the study of land law and the reader should make his or her own supplement to this glossary when such words appear in his or her reading material. Always do this immediately the word is discovered. In this way the context of the word will be appreciated and recalled for future reference.

1

The Study of Land Law

1.1 The problem of land law

1.2 The 1925 property legislation

1.3 Methods of study of land law

1.1 The problem of land law

Most students have difficulty when they start to study English land law. This is partly because of the strange technical terms used, and a list of some of the most common of them can be found in the glossary. The main reason, however, is that land law is a logical system, but one that is strange to most people because they rarely encounter it in their daily lives. Almost everyone has made at least one contract, and most people can understand torts such as negligence and know about crime at least from television and newspapers, but they only encounter land law when they buy a house.

English land law is firmly based in English history, and can only be understood in the light of its feudal origins. That is why this textbook starts with a historical introduction, which is intended to give those students who have never studied English history the basic information they need. Others may find it a useful revision of a period of history they probably studied several years ago.

1.2 The 1925 property legislation

Arguably the most important year for land law was 1925, when a scheme of legislation was passed, coming into force on 1 January 1926, which reformed and largely codified land law and related subjects, trusteeship and administration of estates. The 1925 legislation was a reform of the old system, not a totally new one, and some knowledge of the pre-1925 law may still be required for examination purposes.

1.3 Methods of study of land law

In view of the fact that land law is a complete system, it is not possible to study it in small, self-contained sections, and it is necessary in the early parts of the textbook to refer briefly to topics which will not be studied until later, and which may not be understood when first encountered. However, do not despair! Many students find that during the first few months of land law study they are in a 'fog', but that suddenly all the pieces of the puzzle fall into place, and the subject becomes much easier.

In the case of certain topics in the land law syllabus, there are techniques which can help the student to answer the type of questions often set on that topic. These techniques are embodied in worked examples which are included at the end of some of the chapters.

There are a number of references in the text to 'Cheshire' and 'Megarry and Wade'. The works referred to are *Cheshire and Burn's Modern Law of Real Property* by E H Burn (16th edn, 2000), Butterworths, and *The Law of Real Property* by Megarry and Wade (6th edn, 1999), Sweet and Maxwell. Students wishing to build upon their understanding of the subject derived from this text should peruse the aforementioned works.

2

Historical Introduction

2.1 Origins of the feudal system

2.2 The feudal system in England

2.3 The decline of the feudal system

2.4 The intervention of statute

2.1 Origins of the feudal system

Around about the fourth century AD the Roman Empire, which had ruled the greater part of Europe for about four to five hundred years, began to collapse. The Roman armies, which had provided law and order, were gradually withdrawn to Rome, and when they left there was no strong local government to replace them. The border areas were attacked by 'barbarians', peoples who had not been under Roman rule who came from the north of Europe. The attacks on England came first from the Picts and Scots, who lived north of the Roman (Hadrian's) Wall, which ran from Carlisle to Newcastle, and then from the Saxons, a Germanic people. The Saxons settled in many parts of the country, being known as the Anglo-Saxons. Later, the eastern part of the country was raided by the Vikings, who came from Scandinavia, and they settled in many parts of eastern England.

The same pattern of withdrawal of troops, attacks by barbarian tribes and breakdown of law and order was repeated in most of Europe. The result was not only murder and pillage; people were unable to farm their land, which resulted in famine. The only way of getting any protection to enable him to farm his land was for the farmer to give his land to the strongest person in the area who had the biggest army, who would then allow the farmer to work it and pay him in kind. In return, the lord was bound to protect his tenant. This became known as the *feudal system*, where land was held from a lord in return for services, the lord being bound to protect his tenant from those who might seek to dispossess him. Feudalism was the original 'protection racket'.

3

2.2 The feudal system in England

Not a great deal is known about English land-holding before the Norman Conquest, but there is evidence that there was a form of feudalism in places. However, as in Europe, there was no universal feudal system covering the whole country, because the system had grown from the bottom upwards. The importance of the Norman Conquest of 1066, and the reason why it is the start of English land law, is that a feudal system was imposed from the top, which produced an unusually complete and logical system. This is because the king, William the Conqueror, declared that all the land belonged to him by reason of his victory, and this is why it is still in legal theory correct to say that ultimately all land in the country belongs to the Crown, and that all 'owners' are merely tenants of one sort or another. This will be examined in more detail in Chapter 4.

William then rewarded his chief followers by making them tenants of large areas of land, and they in turn granted smaller areas to their followers, who might in turn grant land. This meant that a pyramid of land-holding was created, with the king at the top, under him a few chief lords, known as barons, and so on, with a large number of tenants, who each farmed a small area, at the bottom (see diagram).

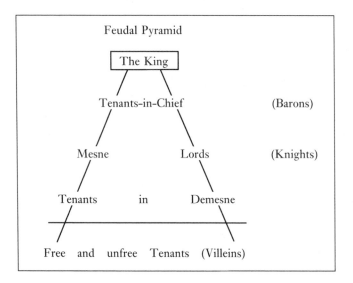

The basis of the feudal system

The basis of the feudal system is that land was given in return for services. At the time of the Norman Conquest, and for some time thereafter, the economy was purely agricultural and everyone produced their own food. There was very little money, which was not much used, and bartering was the method of obtaining things the people could not produce themselves. This meant that land was the only real source of wealth, and the 'richest' man was the one with the most land. Today we have a money economy, and if we want a pair of shoes, or we want our car repaired, we pay for the goods or services with money. In feudal times, goods and services were bought with land. If a 'wealthy' man, a man with ample land, wanted a cook, he would grant enough land to support a man and his family to someone in return for that man's services as a cook. When that man died, the lord would grant the land to someone else, often the man's son, in return for the same services.

The type of service for which the land was granted was known as the 'tenure', various forms of which are examined in more detail in Chapter 3. Most of the king's tenants, who were known as tenants-in-chief, held land in return for providing the king with a specified number of soldiers. They would seek to fulfil this obligation by in turn granting part of the lands granted to them to tenants ('tenants in desmesne' or 'mesne lords') who had to supply some of these soldiers. This would continue down the pyramid until at the bottom there was the soldier who was granted enough land to keep himself and his family in return for doing the required military service.

The manor

The basic unit of the feudal system was the manor. Each manor had a lord (the lord of the manor) and usually consisted of the lord's own land (known as the lord's desmesne), consisting of the manor house and the lord's agricultural land, land held by tenants and waste land on which the tenants grazed their cattle. The lord's land was cultivated by the tenants in return for the land he had granted them. Some of the tenants would be freemen, others would be serfs or villeins. Villeinage was a personal status which was akin to slavery, but was not exactly slavery. The villein had no rights against his lord, except that of physical protection. Further, he might belong either to the lord or to the manor, but against third parties he had all the rights of a freeman. In *Corpus Christi College v Gloucestershire County Council* [1982] 3 All ER 995 Lord Denning MR concluded that:

'In medieval times the manor was the nucleus of English rural life. It was an administrative unit of an extensive area of land. The whole of it was owned originally by the lord of the manor.'

2.3 The decline of the feudal system

The feudal system in its original form was probably in operation for less than 200 years, and thereafter it began to decline for a number of reasons, the most important of which are identified below.

The impracticability of maintaining an army by feudal means

As we have seen, many of the tenants-in-chief held their land in return for the supply of troops. Such troops, however, were only obliged to serve in the king's army for a fixed number of days per year. It was very difficult to wage an effective military campaign when an army was entitled in the middle of a battle to pack up and go home, and so the king very soon preferred to hire full-time soldiers, especially as money was becoming more important in the economy. He would therefore commute the requirement of actual soldiers to a requirement of a fixed sum of money, which facilitated the raising of a mercenary army.

The rise of a monetary economy and ensuing inflation

As money became more important, many mesne lords preferred to receive from their tenants an easily enforced payment of money rather than actual services, which were harder to enforce. Such payments were fixed, and as the value of money declined, so many lords did not find it worth the trouble of enforcing the payments.

2.4 The intervention of statute

The Statute of Quia Emptores 1290

Originally, as previously noted, a tenant would usually provide the services he was bound to render by himself granting land in return for services. This creation of 'subtenants' was known as *subinfeudation*. Lords were entitled to various valuable incidents to their grant as well as the services (see Chapter 3 for details of incidents), but subinfeudation could effectively deprive a lord of these. For example, if A granted to B in knight's service and B then granted to C for a rose each midsummer's day, then if B died leaving an infant heir, A was entitled to wardship of the heir, but instead of being entitled to the land by reason of the wardship all he got was an annual rose. In order to protect their incomes arising from incidents, the barons ensured the passing of the Quia Emptores Statute which included the following provisions:

1. Alienation by subinfeudation was forbidden.
2. All free tenants were authorised to alienate all or part of their land by *substitution*, without the lord's consent, the new tenant standing in the old tenant's place and holding directly from the lord by the same services.
3. On alienation of part the services were to be apportioned.
4. The statute only applied to grants in fee simple.

The effect of this statute was to make land-holding a piece of property which could be freely alienated (the modern concept) rather than a personal relationship between a lord and his tenant (the feudal concept) It also prevented the creation of new tenures, and so thereafter the feudal pyramid could no longer grow – it could only contract. It is useful to see the extent of the statute from its opening words:

'Forasmuch as purchasers of lands and tenements of the fees of great men and other lords have many times heretofore entered into their fees, to the prejudice of the lords, to whom the freeholders of such great men have sold their lands and tenements to be holden in fee of their feoffers, and not of the chief lord of the fees, whereby the same chief lords have many times lost their escheats, marriages, and wardships of land and tenements belonging to their fees which thing seemed very hard and extream unto those lords and other great men and moreover in this case manifest disheritance: Our lord the King (Edward I) in his Parliament at Westminster after Easter, the eighteenth year of his reign … at the instance of the great men of the realm, granted, provided and ordained, that from henceforth it shall be lawful to every freeman to sell at his own pleasure his lands and tenements, or part of them; so that the feoffee shall hold the same lands or tenements of the chief lord of the same fee by such service and customs as his feoffor held before.'

It should be noted that the Statute of Quia Emptores is still in force today. Its effect is demonstrated by any conveyance of land whereby the purchaser takes over completely the role of the vendor. This is further recognised by s60(1) Law of Property Act (LPA) 1925 which provides as follows:

'A conveyance of freehold land to any person without words of limitation … shall pass to the grantee the fee simple or other the whole interest which the grantor had power to convey in such land unless a contrary intention appears in the conveyance.'

The use and the Statute of Uses 1535

Quia Emptores 1290 preserved the lord's rights to feudal incidents and thus prevented 'tax avoidance' by means of subinfeudation. This did not, however, prevent tenants from trying to avoid the incidents, which could sometimes amount to a crippling financial burden. There were other defects of the feudal system from the tenant's point of view which he might wish to avoid, the most important of these being:

1. Freehold land could not be devised by will but passed automatically to the heir.
2. Land could only be conveyed by a public ceremony called 'feoffment with livery of seisin' at which both parties had to be present. This made conveyancing difficult or inconvenient.
3. Seisin had to pass immediately, and so it was not in general possible to create future interests in land.
4 If the tenant was convicted of a felony his land was escheat (ie forfeit) to the lord. This was particularly serious in times of political uncertainty, such as the Wars of the Roses, when being on the losing side would usually be followed by escheat.

These disadvantages could all be avoided by the *use*, whereby land was conveyed to a sufficient number of trusted persons (feoffees) who held the land on behalf of the person whom the tenant really intended to benefit, the *cestui que use*. By selecting a sufficient number of feoffees (sometimes as many as ten, and as they died off new feoffees could be put in their place) the land rarely, if ever, vested in one feoffee whose death would give rise to the same feudal incidents as would fall due when the tenant died. By having a wall of feoffees it was possible to greatly reduce the lord's chances of reliefs since there was likely to be *no* wardship, inheritance, marriage, etc. For example, if Blackacre was conveyed by A to B, C, D and E and their heirs to the use of F and his heirs, the effect was as follows:

A	–	Feoffer
B, C, D and E	–	Feoffees
F	–	Cestui que use

Under the contemporary trust, B, C, D and E would have equated to trustees and F to the beneficiary.

The common law looked on the feoffee to uses as the absolute owner and refused to enforce what it regarded as only a moral obligation, but once the Court of Chancery became established the Chancellor would enforce the use, and thus protect the cestui que use. The use became very popular in the fifteenth century. In 1535 Henry VIII, realising that his feudal income from incidents had been seriously eroded by the use of the use forced Parliament to pass the Statute of Uses in order to improve his finances. The effect of the statute was to execute all uses and take the legal estate away from the feoffees to use and transfer it to the cestui que use. So, applying the statute to the previous example where B, C, D and E were seised of Blackacre to the use or trust of F (beneficiary), F was deemed to be the legal owner of the property the use being executed. Accordingly, if F married or when he died feudal incidents would become payable since he was seised of Blackacre. In reality the Statute of Uses 1535 was an early example of anti tax-avoidance legislation. In due course after the Crown had obtained a substantial amount of income from this reimposition of the feudal system a device – a use upon a use – was allowed by the courts to get round the 1535 statute. For example, if Whiteacre was granted to X and his heirs to the use of Y and his heirs to the use of Z and his heirs, the statute executed the *first* use so that Y became the legal owner but the Chancellor and Court of Chancery did not execute the *second* one so that Z was the beneficiary (ie Y was left holding the legal estate 'on trust for Z'). The Statute of Uses was repealed by the Law of Property Act 1925. Thereafter the modern law of trusts developed, with important effects on land law as will be seen in Chapter 5.

The Tenures Abolition Act 1660 (also known as the Statute for the Abolition of Military Tenures)

The payment of services had ceased to be of any importance by the fifteenth century, but feudal incidents remained important. In particular the Crown, which was always lord and never tenant, derived a great deal of revenue from these incidents. After the triumph of Parliament over the king in the Civil War,

Parliament sought to ensure its supremacy by abolishing any independent source of income of the Crown. The Long Parliament in 1646 abolished all forms of tenure, except freehold and copyhold, and most of the feudal incidents, and this was confirmed by Charles II in 1660 by the Tenures Abolition Act. The Crown was instead granted a tax on beer!

3

Tenures

3.1 Introduction

3.2 Free tenures

3.3 Unfree tenures

3.4 Copyhold

3.5 Conclusion: tenures today

3.1 Introduction

Tenure is the method of holding land, the services to be rendered by the tenant in return for the grant of the land. While these could be of any kind, depending on the lord's needs, in practice they became in general standardised and could be classified. The main division was between free and unfree, and there were various types of free tenure. These are demonstrated in the diagram overleaf.

3.2 Free tenures

Tenures in chivalry

These were also called military tenures and were of two sorts: grand serjeanty and knight's service.

Grand serjeanty
These were tenures granted by the king in return for personal services of an honourable nature, such as carrying his banner or being his marshal. There were many such services connected with court ceremonial and with coronations. This type of tenure eventually became confined to tenants-in-chief and was abolished by the Tenures Abolition Act 1660 which, however, preserved some of the honorary services.

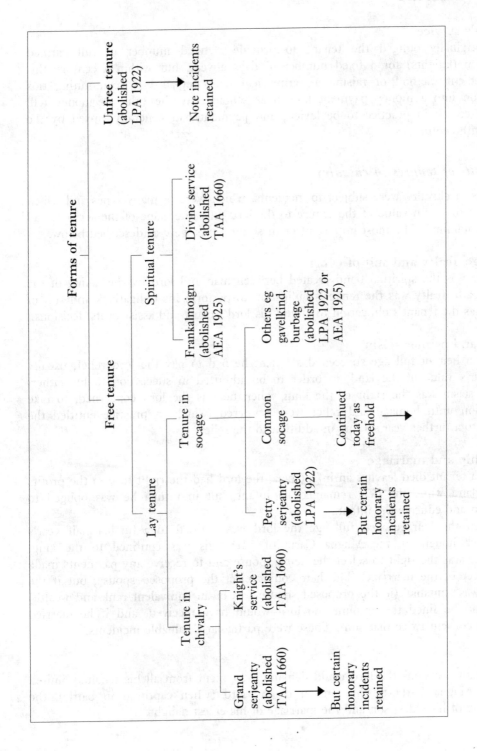

Knight's service
This originally obliged the tenant to provide a fixed number of fully armed horsemen (knights) for a fixed number of days a year, but within a century this inconvenient method of raising an army had been replaced by commuting this obligation into a money payment known as scutage. As the value of money fell, scutage ceased in practice to be levied, and payment had generally lapsed by the fourteenth century.

Incidents of tenures in chivalry

Tenures in chivalry were subject to incidents, which were of many types and which provided the main value of the tenure to the lord once the value of the services had become nominal. The most important of these incidents were as described below.

Homage, fealty and suit of court
Homage was the spiritual bond created between man and lord by the taking of the feudal oath, fealty was the tenant's obligation to perform his obligations and suit of court was the tenant's obligation to attend his lord's court and assist in its decisions.

Relief and primer seisin
When an heir of full age succeeded a tenant he had to pay the lord relief, usually one year's value of the land, in order to be admitted in succession to his father. Primer seisin was the right of the king, when he was the lord concerned, to take possession until homage and relief were rendered, which in practice entitled the Crown to a further year's value in addition to the relief.

Wardship and marriage
Where a tenant died leaving an infant heir, the lord had the right to take the profits of the land while the heir remained an infant, but in return he was obliged to maintain and educate the infant.

   When the heir reached full age the lord was entitled to a further half year's profits, although by the Magna Carta of 1215 this was confined to the king. Marriage was the right to select the heir's spouse and to receive any payments made in respect of the marriage. The heir could reject the proposed spouse, but if the match was 'suitable' (ie the proposed spouse was of an equivalent rank and wealth) he would be fined the amount the lord would have received, and if he married without consent twice that sum. These were particularly valuable incidents.

Aids
On certain occasions the lord could demand a payment from all his tenants, limited by the Magna Carta to the ransom of the lord (when captured in battle), the knighting of his eldest son and the marriage of his eldest daughter.

Escheat and forfeiture

Escheat was the right of the lord to the land when the tenancy came to an end for any reason. The most common causes were the failure of heirs, *escheat propter defectum sanguinis*, and when the tenant was convicted of a felony and sentenced to death, *escheat propter delictum tenentis*. Before the land returned to the lord, the Crown had the right to hold it for a year and a day and commit acts of waste.

Forfeiture was the right of the Crown to keep the lands of any person attainted of high treason.

However, almost all of these incidents were abolished by the Tenures Abolition Act 1660, the only ones of importance which were retained being escheat and forfeiture. Grand serjeanty and knight's service were converted into tenures of free and common socage.

Tenures in socage

These were less exalted than military tenures and were found in the bottom part of the feudal pyramid, see Chapter 2, section 2.2. They were of two types:

Petty serjeanty

The tenant was obliged to perform some services for the king of a non-honourable, non-personal nature, such as supplying arrows or firewood. It quickly ceased to be of importance as money became more important, and the king found it easier to receive payment instead. After the fifteenth century it could only exist as a tenure-in-chief.

Socage

This was by far the commonest form of tenure, and after 1660 became the only kind of free tenure. While any kind of services could be reserved, the most usual services were of an agricultural nature. They would be fixed both as to nature and extent, and by the end of the fifteenth century had generally been commuted to money payments.

The socage tenures were only subject to aids, relief and escheat, and the relief was fixed at one year's rent, rather than the one year's profit to which military tenures were subject.

Inheritance of free tenures

Primogeniture

In general the system of primogeniture applied, ie the land went automatically to the eldest son. However, socage tenure could vary depending on local customs. When the tenure was 'common socage' the rule of primogeniture applied, but there were some important variations as set out below.

Exceptions to the rule of primogeniture

Gavelkind. This applied automatically to all land in Kent and could apply elsewhere. The main feature of such land was partibility, ie on intestacy it descended to all males of the same degree equally and not to the eldest son alone. Other peculiar features of gavelkind were:

DEVISABILITY. This land, unlike all other types, could be freely disposed of by will. Free devisability did not apply to other land until the Statute of Wills 1540, and even then restrictions remained, some as late as 1925.

NO ESCHEAT. No escheat on felony, although forfeiture for high treason applied.

DOWER. A widow was entitled to dower until remarriage in one-half of her deceased husband's estate (in common socage it was only in one-third).

CURTESY. A husband was entitled to a life estate ('curtesy') in all his deceased wife's realty, whether or not issue capable of inheriting the land had been born. In common socage he only received curtesy if there was such an issue.

Borough English. This custom applied in various parts of the country, and was not confined to towns as the name might suggest. When this custom applied, socage land descended to the youngest rather than the eldest son.

Spiritual tenures

These were of two types, *frankalmoign* by which land was granted to an ecclesiastical corporation in return for no specific services, but under an obligation to pray for the tenant's soul, and *divine service* in which the tenure was subject to defined services such as saying Mass weekly or giving a specified sum to the poor. This service could be enforced by the normal methods of distraint and forfeiture, unlike the obligations of frankalmoign which could only be enforced by the ecclesiastical courts.

The conveyance of land to ecclesiastical corporations, known as mortmain, was very unpopular with lords because, as a corporation never dies and leaves heirs, there would be a loss of feudal dues from incidents. The Magna Carta and the Statutes of Mortmain 1279 and 1290 forbade the conveyance of land to religious bodies, but pious tenants who were concerned for their spiritual health found a way to avoid this prohibition by the *use*.

3.3 Unfree tenures

Villeinage

Unfree tenure was called villeinage, and later became known as copyhold – see section 3.4. The main differences between free and unfree tenures were as described below.

No seisin
The tenant of a free tenure had seisin, which meant that the king's courts would protect him if his lord unlawfully sought to eject him from the land. In unfree tenure, the tenant was deemed to hold on behalf of the lord who had the seisin, so the king's courts would not at first protect the tenant whose only remedy was in the lord's court.

Services not fixed
The services attached to free tenure were always fixed in quantity and quality, while those of unfree tenure were not fixed and were usually more onerous. The villein had to work for his lord for a fixed number of days a week, doing whatever was required in the manner in which the lord required him to do it.

Status
Only a free man could hold land in free tenure. The converse was not true, because although a man of villein status could only hold in unfree tenure, some land of villein tenure was held by free men. It was the quality of the services, not the status of the tenant, that distinguished the two forms of tenure.

At first the villein's position was precarious, but it became established that the lord should not forfeit his land unless the tenant had done some act which by the custom of the manor merited forfeiture. The principal incidents were:

1. Agricultural services. They later became commuted to money payments.
2. Fealty and suit of court.
3. Escheat and forfeiture.
4. Heriots. This was a custom that the lord was entitled to take the tenant's best beast or other chattel on the tenant's death.
5. Fines payable on alienation of the land.

Later history of villeinage

During the fourteenth and fifteenth centuries most villein services were commuted to money payments, so the villein became a rent-paying tenant and the lord hired the necessary labour, and at the same time villein status was dying out. By 1550 the king's courts were prepared to protect any tenant whether he held by free or villein tenure.

3.4 Copyhold

Origin of title

The change in status of the villein tenant from an agricultural labourer, often of servile status, to a rent-paying farmer was marked by a change of name, and villein tenure became known as copyhold. The particulars of each holding were entered in the manorial rolls, and copyhold land was conveyed by surrender to the lord who then admitted the new tenant, the transaction being recorded in the court rolls. The transferee was given a copy of the entry, hence 'copyhold'. The transfer was governed by the custom of the manor. Certain incidents, notably fines, heriots and reliefs, continued to apply.

Enfranchisement

Various Acts of Parliament throughout the nineteenth century made possible the enfranchisement (ie conversion to freehold) of copyhold, but much remained until the Law of Property Act 1922 which by s128 and Schedule 12 compulsorily enfranchised all remaining copyhold. The Act divided manorial incidents attached to copyhold into three categories:

1. Those which were obsolete (eg forfeiture for alienation without the lord's consent): these were abolished immediately.
2. Those which had some existing monetary value (eg quit rents): these continued until 1935 to give the parties an opportunity to arrange voluntarily for the incident to be extinguished on the payment of compensation. Failing agreement, application was to be made to the then Minister of Agriculture and Fisheries. These incidents were subsequently extended to 1 November 1950 before they were finally extinguished.
3. Those which were not extinguished and which still attach to the land unless extinguished by mutual agreement and compensation. These are:

   a) tenant's right of common;
   b) rights to minerals;
   c) rights of the lord in respect to markets, fairs and sporting rights;
   d) liability for dykes, ditches, sea or river walls and bridges.

Copyhold today

It should be noted that the third category remains in existence today. For a consideration of these rights in relation to the 'manor' see: *Corpus Christi College* v *Gloucestershire County Council* [1982] 3 All ER 995.

3.5 Conclusion: tenures today

The Tenures Abolition Act 1660 (also known as the Statute for the Abolition of Military Tenures) effectively marked the end of the tenurial system by converting all tenures into socage. A number of forms and incidents were preserved – see diagram in section 3.2 – but these, in turn, were brought to an end by the 1925 property legislation. This means that the only form of tenure which remains today is the former socage tenure now known as freehold. In addition a number of honorary incidents relating to grand and petty serjeanty remain together with the four incidents preserved by the LPA 1922 from the enfranchisement of copyholds (ie rights of common rights to minerals, rights in respect of markets and fairs etc and liability for dykes, ditches etc).

While it is still technically correct to state that no one owns land in England and Wales, except the Crown, and that all freeholders are in reality 'tenants' of the Crown (this is because tenure continues as a legal fact), for most practical purposes the doctrine is now obsolete. The one circumstance when it is submitted that the doctrine of tenures still has an impact is when a freehold tenant dies *intestate* leaving no heirs able to take under the Administration of Estates Act 1925. In that particular circumstance the property would revert to the Crown.

4

Estates

4.1 Introduction

4.2 Classification of estates

4.3 Possession, remainder, reversion and seisin

4.4 The fee simple

4.5 The fee tail

4.6 The life estate

4.7 Waste

4.8 Fixtures

4.9 Reverter of Sites Act 1987

4.1 Introduction

Tenure involves the quality of land-holding, that is, the types of services for which land is granted. Estate is the quantity of land-holding, the period for which the land is granted. The importance of estates, and the reason why the law relating to land is much more complicated than the law relating to ownership of other property, is that several people can have different estates in the same piece of land. So, for example, A might have a life interest, B a life interest in remainder and C the fee simple reversion, while D had a 99-year lease and had granted a seven-year sublease to E. At the same time A may have mortgaged the land to F, while G had a right of way over the land.

The system of estates was amended by the 1925 legislation, but it is necessary to know the old classification to understand the new law.

4.2 Classification of estates

The two main classes are *freehold* and *leasehold*. Each class may then be subdivided – but note how some of these subdivisions did not continue, in that form, after 1925.

The position in 1925 (ie before the 1925 property legislation came into force on 1 January 1926) can be represented in the diagram below:

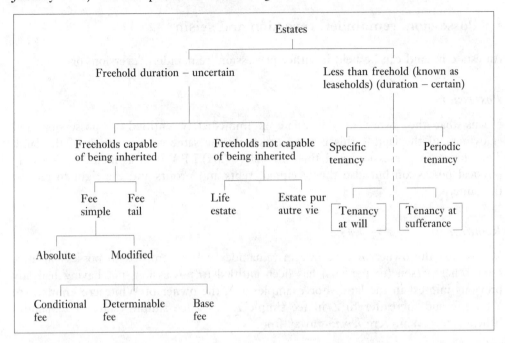

Freehold estates

There were prior to 1925 three freehold estates: fee simple, fee tail, and life estate. These will be dealt with in detail in sections 4.4 to 4.6 below.

Leasehold estates (sometimes referred to as estates less than freehold)

At first the common law refused to recognise the lease as an interest in land, treating it as a mere personal contract. The leaseholder only became fully protected by the law at the end of the fifteenth century following the introduction of the Action of Ejectment, and in theory a leasehold is still inferior to a freehold. Another result of this historical situation is that leaseholds are treated as personal property, while freeholds and other legal rights in land are real property.

The main categories of leasehold are:

1. Fixed term of certain duration – specific tenancy.
2. Fixed term with duration capable of being rendered certain – renewable periodic tenancies.
3. Tenancies at will and at sufferance may also be classified under leaseholds, although they do not fit easily into the above two major divisions of specific and periodic tenancies – hence the parentheses.

The various types of lease are dealt with in detail in Chapter 10.

4.3 Possession, remainder, reversion and seisin

An estate in land can be held in either possession, remainder, reversion, or seisin.

Possession

Means that the owner of the estate is immediately entitled to possession and enjoyment of the land – this is not necessarily the same as occupation of the land. The phrase 'in possession' is defined in s205(1)(xix) LPA 1925 as including not only physical possession but also the receipt of rents and profits and the right to receive the same.

Remainder

Means that the owner of an estate in remainder will be entitled to possession after some other person (or persons) has been entitled to possession, not having had any previous interest in the land. For example, if X the owner of Whiteacre grants it to Y for life and thereafter to Z in fee simple Z has a fee simple estate in remainder (when Y dies Whiteacre *remains* away from X).

Reversion

Means the residue of the interest possessed by a person who has granted away a lesser estate in possession than he owns. For example, if A the fee simple owner of Blackacre grants the land to B for life then during B's lifetime A has an estate in reversion and upon B's death the land will *revert* to A or if by then A is dead to his personal representatives.

Seisin

The concept of seisin was extremely important in early land law, and denoted quiet possession of the land. It was a status, not a right, and so a lawful owner put out of possession was 'disseised' and the interloper gained seisin until himself dispossessed by force or law. The important fact was that only freeholders could have seisin, and so if a leaseholder or a copyholder was in possession the seisin remained in the freeholder or lord. For a person to be seised he must hold the freehold estate; the land must be of freehold tenure; and either he must have physical possession of the land or a tenant/leaseholder holds the land for him.

4.4 The fee simple

Definition

While in theory the fee simple owner holds his land in tenure, in practice he is the absolute owner, save that the land will revert to the lord (usually the Crown) if the fee simple owner dies *intestate* leaving no heirs capable of taking it under the Administration of Estates Act 1925.

It is important to appreciate the distinction between a fee simple which is absolute and a modified fee simple.

Fee simple absolute

This type of fee is an estate which continues indefinitely, and is the most common.

Modified fee simple

There are three types of modified fee simple:

1. Determinable fee: this is a fee simple which automatically comes to an end on the happening of some specified event which is not certain to occur. If the specified event does occur the land reverts to the grantor. A grant of Blackacre to John until he becomes a barrister would give rise to a determinable fee.
2. Fee simple upon condition (conditional fee): this is the grant of a full fee simple to which is attached a condition that may operate upon the happening of some specified uncertain event, a condition subsequent. A grant of Blackacre to John provided he does not become a barrister would create a conditional fee.
3. Base fee: this is a special type of fee which arises after the barring of an entail (see below) and is determinable upon the failure of heirs of the body of the original grantor. See s1 Fines and Recoveries Act 1833.

Distinction between the determinable fee and the conditional fee

It is often difficult to determine whether a particular grant creates a determinable fee or a conditional fee. A determinable fee has an in-built limitation, often indicated by 'while', 'until', 'so long as', while a conditional fee is a full fee simple with an extra condition tacked on, often shown by words such as 'provided that', 'but if', 'on condition that'. The main differences between the two types of modified fee are set out below.

Determination

The grantor of a determinable fee simple retains a 'possibility of reverter' which means that a determinable fee terminates automatically on the happening of the specified event. The effect is that the legal estate reverts automatically to the original grantor or his heirs. If, however, the happening of the determining event becomes impossible the 'possibility of reverter' is destroyed. Thereafter the fee simple becomes absolute.

A conditional fee gives the grantor a *right of entry* on the happening of the specified event, and until that right is *exercised* the fee continues.

Validity of the condition

If the condition attached to a determinable fee is void for any reason other than perpetuity the whole grant fails. If the condition attached to a conditional fee is void the grantee takes a fee simple absolute.

Effect of a void condition

The courts are therefore readier to find that the condition of a conditional fee is void than to make the same finding in respect of a determinable fee. If the condition in a conditional fee simple is held to be void it is the condition alone that is void, and the grantee takes an absolute interest in the property free from the condition. If the determining event in a determinable fee simple is void then the whole grant is also void. The grounds on which a condition may be held to be void are:

1. Uncertainty: the condition will be void unless it can be precisely determined what will cause its operation; for example, a clause requiring 'residence' may be too vague and imprecise.
2. Alienation: the condition must not take away the power of alienation, because this is totally against the idea of ownership. A partial restraint, not to sell to a particular person, may be valid.
3. Course of law: the condition must not attempt to alter a course of devolution prescribed by law, for example on intestacy, or making it a condition that the grantee does not become bankrupt.
4. Restraint of marriage: the condition must not impose a total or wide restraint on marriage, although a partial restraint may be valid. In *Perrin* v *Lyon* (1807) 9 East 170 a prohibition on marrying a Scotsman was held to be valid.
5. Public policy: the condition must not be illegal, immoral or otherwise against public policy. Any condition which encouraged separation and divorce would come within this category.

Remoteness and effect of rule against perpetuities

The rule against perpetuities does apply to any such right of re-entry, and the condition must not offend against the rule against perpetuities (see Chapter 16). The perpetuity rules do not apply to determinable fees granted before 1964, but s12 of the Perpetuities and Accumulations Act 1964 provides that the possibility of reverter arising on a grant of a determinable fee simple is subject to the rule against perpetuities.

Existence at law

A determinable fee cannot exist as a legal estate after 1925. Prior to the coming into force of the Trusts of Land and Appointment of Trustees Act 1996 it was a settlement under the Settled Land Act 1925 (see Chapter 8). While originally legislation also made a conditional fee a settlement under that Act, it is arguable that the effect of the Schedule to the Law of Property (Amendment) Act 1926 is that a conditional fee can now exist as a legal estate, because the Schedule adds the following words to s7(1) LPA 1925:

> '... a fee simple subject to a legal or equitable right of entry or re-entry is for the purposes of this Act [the Law of Property Act 1925] a fee simple absolute.'

The reason for this amending legislation was to address an oversight in the LPA 1925 as to 'rentcharge conveyancing'. Prior to mortgage finance becoming the dominant way in which people who cannot buy a property for cash aquire a freehold estate, there had been a second method – 'rentcharge conveyancing' – for such acquisitions. This method was common in two parts of England: the north-west (around Manchester) and the south-west (around Bristol). Under 'rentcharge conveyancing' the purchaser paid a lower capital sum for the property but had to pay an annual sum charged on the land in perpetuity (a perpetual rentcharge). The right to sue and the liability to be sued ran respectively with the rentcharge and the land. For example, if a rentcharge was imposed on Blackacre by A in favour of B and subsequently Blackacre was bought by C and the rentcharge was assigned to D, D would be able to sue C on the rentcharge.

The attraction of 'rentcharge conveyancing' to a purchaser was that he had to find a lower capital sum, while the attraction for a vendor was that he and his successors obtained an annual income from the land which, over a period of time, would amount to more than the difference between the lesser capital sum originally taken and the larger capital sum which the property would have been sold for if sold by way of a mortgage. If the 'rentpayer' did not pay the rentcharge, the rentcharge owner could temporarily re-enter the land and collect rent and profits. The effect of s1 LPA 1925 was to render freehold estates acquired by rentcharge conveyancing prior to 1926 no longer legal ones because since they were subject to a right of entry for non-payment of the rentcharge the estate was less than absolute. To preserve the legal status of rentcharge estates the Law of Property (Amendment) Act 1926 provides that a fee simple subject to a right of entry or re-entry is for the purposes of the LPA 1925 a fee simple absolute. However, in swiftly amending s7(1) LPA 1925 the draftsmen overlooked conditional fee simples. The amending legislation was widely drawn. In consequence of the 1926 Act it can be argued that a conditional fee simple is a legal estate. However, given the rationale for the amendment to s7(1) LPA 1925 – to safeguard the legal status of freeholds acquired by rentcharge conveyancing – it is submitted that it is a moot point whether it is realistic to so regard conditional fee simples.

Finally, 'rentcharge conveyancing' is no longer used to acquire properties in

England and Wales. The effect of the passing of time and inflation was to reduce the real value of the annual rentcharge payment and thus the attraction of this method of property disposal to vendors. Further, under the Rentcharges Act 1977, every rentcharge other than those created to enforce positive covenants or to secure a family annuity is to be extinguished 60 years after 22 July 1977 or the date on which the relevant rentcharge became payable, whichever is the later.

Section 7(1) LPA 1925 provides that a fee simple which, by virtue of the Land Clauses Act or any similar statute, is liable to be divested is for the purposes of the Act a fee simple absolute. This subsection covers statutes which enable public bodies to acquire land compulsorily for a public purpose (eg for a highway or a school) and they usually provide that if the land is not used for that public purpose or ceases to be so used in the future, the land shall re-vest in the original owner or his successors. The effect of s7(1) is to ensure that the possibility of such re-vesting does not render the land less than absolute while vested in the relevant public body. As a result of the Reverter of Sites Act 1987, when the special purpose for the use of the land comes to an end the legal estate remains vested in the current owners, although they now hold it on a trust of land for those entitled under the reverter: see section 4.9.

In similar vein is s7(2) LPA 1925, which provides that a fee simple vested in a corporation is a fee simple absolute (it could be argued that a company's fee simple is determinable on its dissolution).

Rights of the fee simple owner

The right of alienation
The fee simple owner may dispose of his land as he wishes, either by will or inter vivos (in lifetime).

The right to everything in, on or over the land
This was expressed by the medieval lawyers as 'cujus est solum, ejus est usque ad coelum et ad inferos' – all is his, up to the sky and down to the centre of the earth – but this is much wider than reality today. These rights have several limitations:

Rights of others over the land. The owner is subject to rights such as easements, tenancies and mortgages.

Airspace. While the owner of the land can sue in trespass or nuisance for intrusion of his airspace *(Kelsen* v *Imperial Tobacco Co* [1957] 2 QB 334), his rights are restricted to such height as is necessary for the ordinary use of the land and the structures on it *(Bernstein* v *Skyviews Ltd* [1977] 3 WLR 136). In *Bernstein's* case Griffiths J expressed the modern rule as to rights in airspace as follows:

'The problem is to balance the rights of an owner to enjoy the use of his land against the rights of the general public to take advantage of all that science now offers in the use of airspace. This balance is in my judgment best struck in our present society by restricting the rights of an owner in the airspace above his land to such a height as is necessary for the ordinary use and enjoyment of his land and the structures upon it: and declaring that above that height he has no greater rights in the airspace than any other member of the public.'

Section 76(1) of the Civil Aviation Act 1982 provides that no action shall lie in respect of trespass or nuisance by a flight of an aircraft over property at a reasonable height.

Minerals. The right of the fee simple owner to all minerals under his land has been considerably eroded by statute. At common law the Crown is entitled to all gold and silver, by the Coal Act 1938 all coal was vested in the Coal Commission and then subsequently in the National Coal Board. However, following a government privatisation initiative coal is now vested in the British Coal Corporation (s1(2) Coal Industry Act 1987).

Treasure trove. By common law the Crown was entitled to treasure trove, which was anything discovered that was made of 'substantial' proportions of gold or silver. Such discoveries had to be reported to the local coroner who would hold an inquest with a jury. If the property appeared to have been concealed by the original owner with a view to later recovery and now had no known owner it was treasure trove and belonged to the Crown by prerogative. The common law of treasure trove was not without problems. For example, some valuable finds were not of precious metal. Further, it did not protect items (even precious metal ones) found to have been *lost* rather than hidden.

The Treasure Act 1996 replaced the common law of treasure trove with a new regime. The following key features of the 1996 Act should be noted:

1. There is a new statutory definition of treasure the effect of which is to extend the protection formerly afforded to gold and silver objects to a wider range of archeological finds;
2. It removes the need to establish that objects were hidden with the intention of being recovered (ie an object has the status of treasure even if it was lost, abandoned or buried in a grave);
3. The Treasure Valuation Committee is to give advice on ex gratia payments to be made to finders;
4. The jurisdiction of coroners over treasure is the same as over treasure trove. However, treasure inquests shall usually be held without a jury;
5. It creates a new offence of non-declaration of treasure to a coroner within 14 days of the find; and
6. Treasure when found vests in the Crown or, if there is one, the franchisee, subject to prior interests and rights existing over the treasure.

The Treasure Act 1996 Code of Practice contains an account of the legislation, the actual code of practice as to how treasure proceeds will be disposed of, details of the various bodies that deal with treasure and a short appendix on how to look after finds.

Other chattels found on land. The general question of other chattels found on land has been considered by the Court of Appeal in *Parker* v *British Airways Board* [1982] 1 All ER 834. The owner of the land upon which the chattels are found must clearly show he is in control of the land before he can claim title to the chattels.

Wild animals. Wild animals belong to no one, although the land owner has the right to hunt them. As soon as the animal is killed it belongs to the owner of the land on which it was killed.

Water. A landowner has no property in water which flows or percolates through his land, and his rights to draw it off for his own purposes are now severely limited by statute. However he has the sole right to fish in the water, provided that it is not tidal. See *Swindon Waterworks Co Ltd* v *Wilts and Berks Canal Navigation Co* (1875) LR 7 HL 697 and *Rugby Joint Water Board* v *Walters* [1967] Ch 397.

The landowner does have the right to abstract subterranean water flowing in undefined channels beneath his land without regard to the consequences to his neighbours. This was established by the House of Lords in *Bradford Corporation* v *Pickles* [1895] AC 587.

Liability in tort. A landowner may be liable in tort for acts done on his land. In particular note the duties of a landowner to his neighbours not to commit acts of trespass, nuisance or negligence.

Statute. Besides the statutes mentioned above there are many other statutes which limit an owner's right to do what he likes with his land including, for example, the Town and Country Planning Acts, the Rent Act and the Housing Acts – see Chapters 10 and 17.

Accretions to land. The owner is entitled to land added by gradual accretion from the sea. See *Southern Centre of Theosophy* v *State of South Australia* [1982] 1 All ER 283.

Creation of a fee simple
The words needed to create a particular estate are known as the words of limitation.

The rules relating to the words required to create a fee simple are as follows:

	Inter vivos	*By will*
At common law	'to A and his heirs'	No formal words needed but intent must be shown
By the Wills Act 1837	–	The fee simple passes unless the contrary is shown
By Conveyancing Act 1881 By LPA 1925 s60(1)	'to A in fee simple' the fee simple passes unless the contrary is shown	– –

Note: By the Land Registration Act 2002 the legal estate in registered land does not pass to the transferee until the transfer is completed by registration.

4.5 The fee tail

(see the Statute De Donis Conditionalibus 1285)

Definitions

Students interested in the history of the entail should consult Megarry and Wade at pp72–78. There are three types of entail:

1. Tail general, in which the fee is limited to a person and heirs of his body, ie lineal descendants, of either sex.
2. Tail male, in which the fee is limited to a person and the male heirs of his body.
3. Tail female, limited to a person and the female heirs of his body (very rare).
4. Each of these can be either general, ie not limited to children by a particular spouse, or special, ie limited to children by a particular spouse.

Creation of an entail – words of limitation

The necessary words of limitation were as follows:

	Inter vivos	*By will*
At common law	'heirs' + words of procreation	Informal words showing intent
By Conveyancing Act 1881 By LPA 1925 s60(4)	'in tail' 'in tail'	– 'in tail'

See also s130 LPA 1925.

Ending the entail

This is known as barring the entail. A tenant in tail after possibility, that is, when he cannot possibly have heirs of the requisite type, cannot bar the entail. Otherwise the right to bar cannot be excluded or restricted. The methods available are:

By a disentailing assurance
This can be executed by a tenant in tail in possession of full age, and the effect is to enlarge the fee tail into a fee simple. This defeats the interests of his issue and all subsequent interests but not prior interests.

By a disentailing deed
A tenant in tail in remainder, ie who has not yet succeeded to the entail, can bar the entail by deed with the concurrence of the protector of the settlement who is the owner of the prior life interest under the settlement; and, if there is more than one prior life interest, the first in time or any person who would have a prior interest if he had not disposed of it.

A tenant in tail in remainder can execute a disentailing deed without this consent, but he will only create a base fee (see sl Fines and Recoveries Act 1833). However, a base fee may be enlarged into a fee simple by the following:

1. Execution of a fresh disentailing deed with the consent of the protector or after the former tenant in tail in remainder becomes entitled to possession.
2. By union of the base fee with the reversion or remainder in fee simple.
3. By will, if the testator is in possession.
4. By expiry of 12 years after the date on which the tenant in tail in remainder became entitled to possession.

By will
Section 176 LPA 1925 made it possible for entails to be barred by wills executed after 1925. This only applies to entails in possession and the tenant in tail must be of full age. The will must refer specifically to the entailed property, or the instrument creating the entail, or entailed property generally. Entails cannot be barred by infants, lunatics and bankrupts. No new entailed interests can be created after 31 December 1996 (Schedule 1 para 5 of the Trusts of Land and Appointment of Trustees Act 1996).

4.6 The life estate

Definition

There are two types of life estate, which since 1925 can only exist as *equitable interests*:

1. For the life of the tenant – this can arise expressly or by operation of law, eg a tenant in tail after possibility.
2. Estate for life of another – estate pur autre vie – this may be granted expressly or may arise when a tenant for life assigns his interest.

Rights of a tenant for life

The rights of a tenant for life over the land are considerably restricted by the common law rules relating to waste and to fixtures.

4.7 Waste

Waste is any act which alters the nature of the land. This change in the land is not necessarily detrimental to the land. The idea behind the rules is that a tenant for life is only entitled to the income from the land, and must not act so as to affect its capital value.

Types of waste

There are four types of waste: ameliorating, voluntary, permissive and equitable.

Ameliorating waste

This is an act which improves the land. A court would not in general look favourably upon an action to restrain such acts unless the whole character of the property is changed. See *Doherty* v *Allman* (1878) 3 App Cas 709.

Voluntary waste

This is a positive act which damages the land, such as opening a mine or cutting timber. A tenant for life is liable for voluntary waste unless the grant expressly exempts him from such liability, when he is said to be 'unimpeachable of waste'. See *Honywood* v *Honywood* (1874) LR 18 Eq 306 and *Dashwood* v *Magniac* [1891] 3 Ch 306.

Permissive waste

This is a failure to do something which ought to be done. A tenant for life is not liable for permissive waste unless the grant imposes upon him an obligation to repair. See *Powys* v *Blagrave* (1854) 4 De GM & G 448.

Equitable waste

This was defined by Lord Campbell in *Turner* v *Wright* (1860) 2 De GF & J 234 as '... that which a prudent man would not do in the management of his own property'.

Even when a tenant for life is unimpeachable for waste, equity will not allow him to ruin the property by acts of destruction (*Vane* v *Lord Barnard* (1716) 2 Vern 738), unless he can show that the document giving his life interest also shows a clear intention to allow him to commit such acts of equitable waste. See s135 LPA 1925 which provides as follows:

> 'An equitable interest for life without impeachment of waste does not confer upon the tenant for life any right to commit waste of the description known as equitable waste, unless an intention to confer such right expressly appears by the instrument creating such equitable interest.'

4.8 Fixtures

The law of fixtures is important in relation to leaseholds as well as freeholds. In respect of leaseholds some special rules apply in addition to the general principles.

Definition

A fixture is a chattel which has become part of the land by being attached to it, often stated as the Latin maxim 'quicquid plantatur solo, solo cedit' (whatever is affixed to the soil, belongs to the soil). Fixtures are real property, and belong to the owner of the land unless a contrary intention can be shown. For example, a brass front door knocker when purchased is a chattel. However, when in place on the front door it becomes part of the house and thus part of the land.

The distinction between fixtures and chattels

In order to decide whether a particular object is a fixture or a chattel, the courts apply two tests known as the degree of annexation and the purpose of annexation:

The degree of annexation
This is the first test to be applied and means that, prima facie, an object is a fixture if it is firmly attached to the land, but not a fixture if it is only resting on the ground by its own weight. In *Dean* v *Andrews* (1985) The Times 25 May, a large prefabricated greenhouse bolted to a concrete plinth which was not affixed to the ground but merely rested on the ground under its own weight (and that of the greenhouse) was held *not* to be a fixture. See also *Holland* v *Hodgson* (1872) LR 7 CP 328. When considering fixtures in relation to leases the test is often said to be whether the object can be removed without doing serious damage to the premises. Originally the degree of annexation was the only test applied by law, but it operated harshly, and so the courts began to use a second test.

The purpose of annexation

If the object was attached to the land with the intention that it should be part of the land, it is a fixture; if it was attached to the land merely for its better enjoyment as a chattel, it remains a chattel. The test was at first applied only to limited owners, eg life tenants. In *Leigh* v *Taylor* [1902] AC 157 a tenant for life had securely fastened valuable tapestries to the walls, but the House of Lords held that she had done this merely for their better enjoyment and they passed to her estate.

The same test was applied in *D'Eyncourt* v *Gregory* (1866) LR 3 Eq 382 to objects (garden statues) not attached to the land but merely resting on it. They were held to be an integral part of the landscaping and therefore fixtures.

In *Berkley* v *Poulett* (1976) The Times 3 November the same test was applied as between vendor and purchaser by the majority of the Court of Appeal. It is not possible to reconcile the many cases on fixtures, and even the above two tests may not always be conclusive.

Moored houseboat

The question whether a boat, if sufficiently attached to the shore, could become part of the land has been considered. In *Chelsea Yacht & Boat Club Ltd* v *Pope* [2001] 2 All ER 409, P (the defendant) lived on a moored houseboat, which was attached to land at several points by various ropes and cables (including to rings in the embankment wall and to a pontoon), and a line also went from the bow of the boat to an anchor on the river bed. The boat received supplies of gas, water and electricity from connections on the pontoon. It had been let to P by an agreement which described the relevant parties as landlord and tenant. When CYBC (the current owners of the boat) sought possession, P successfully argued at first instance that he had an assured tenancy by virtue of s1(1) of the Housing Act 1988. CYBC appealed, arguing that despite its attachment the houseboat had not become part of the land (the 1988 Act only applies to lettings of *land*) and that therefore the agreement did not come within the terms of that Act.

After considering the *degree* and *purpose* of annexation of the houseboat, the Court of Appeal allowed CYBC's appeal. It concluded that the houseboat could 'without due effort' be removed from its position by undoing the various attachments and detaching it from its service connections. As such, the boat's degree of annexation did not require it to be regarded as part of the land. Rather, it remained a chattel. As to the purpose of the annexation, the Court rejected P's contention that the purpose was to enable the boat to be used as a home. Rather, it concluded that the houseboat could be used as a home without the various attachments and that the purpose of those attachments was to prevent the boat being carried up or downstream by the tide and to provide it with services.

It is submitted that the decision reached by the Court was clearly correct. Here all the various attachments of the houseboat to the land could be undone and the boat could be moved to another mooring. In essence, a boat on a river is not on land or anything like land (ie it is not of the same genus as real property).

The right to remove fixtures

Prima facie a fixture cannot be removed from the land. There are, however, certain limited exceptions to this rule.

Landlord and tenant

Certain fixtures, known as 'tenant's fixtures', may be removed by the tenant during his tenancy or a reasonable time thereafter. There are three classes of tenant's fixtures.

1. Trade fixtures, those attached by the tenant for the purpose of his trade or profession. See *New Zealand Government Property Corporation* v *H M & S Ltd* [1982] 1 All ER 624.
2. Ornamental and domestic fixtures which can be removed without substantial damage to the building.
3. Agricultural fixtures. By s13 Agricultural Holdings Act 1948 an agricultural tenant may remove fixtures which he installed for agricultural purposes before the end of the term or within two months thereafter if he gives one month's written notice; and all rent is paid and obligations performed, no avoidable damage is done in the removal and any damage done made good; and the landlord has not served a written counter-notice and paid a fair value for the fixtures.

Tenant for life and remainderman

The position is the same as between landlord and the tenant, except that the 1948 Act provisions do not apply.

Mortgagor and mortgagee

All fixtures on mortgaged land are included in the mortgage, and the mortgagor may not remove them during the currency of the mortgage, even those affixed after the mortgage commenced. This becomes important where the mortgagee contemplates the remedy of taking possession of the mortgaged property. See *Hobson* v *Gorringe* [1897] 1 Ch 182 and *Reynolds* v *Ashby & Son* [1904] AC 466.

Vendor and purchaser

The importance of the distinction between a fixture and a chattel is that if an article is a chattel it can be removed by the seller of land, whereas if it is a fixture it comprises part and parcel of the land (ie it passes to the purchaser on conveyance unless otherwise agreed: see *Hamp* v *Bygrave* (1982) 266 EG 722). Disputes frequently arise as to whether an article is a fixture or a chattel between the vendor/seller (claiming that the article is not a fixture with the consequence that he may remove it) and a purchaser (claiming that it is a fixture with the consequence that it has become his property along with the land).

In the vast majority of situations, houses/bungalows on land will be fixtures. However, *Elitestone Ltd* v *Morris & Another* [1997] 2 All ER 513 demonstrates that in those rare cases where the status of such a structure on land falls to be determined the question whether it is a fixture or a chattel will all depend (as it does in cases of tapestries or garden statues) on the degree and purpose of annexation of the structure in question. There a chalet resting on concrete pillars with no physical attachment to land was held to be a fixture because it could only be removed by being demolished. In *Hamp* v *Bygrave* where certain garden ornaments could have been either fixtures or chattels in their own right, it was held that the ornaments were part of the property on which they were situated because they had been expressly referred to as such in both the particulars of sale and the inquiries before contract. In addition they had been regarded as part of the freehold by the vendors during their negotiations with the purchasers and, as such, were held to pass with the land on the conveyance to the purchasers. (See also *Dean* v *Andrews* (1985) The Times 25 May.)

4.9 Reverter of Sites Act 1987

Background

Prior to the introduction of compulsory state education in England schools were usually endowed by private benefactors. To encourage private landowners to convey parcels of land to trustees to provide schools for the poor the School Sites Act 1841 was passed. It provided for a simple and cheap form of conveyance to facilitate such conveyances. Further, it provided that when land ceased to be used as a school it would automatically revert back to the grantor (ie the Act gave rise to a determinable fee simple).

Under the 1925 legislation, as previously noted, a determinable fee ranks as an equitable interest and prior to the coming into force of the Trusts of Land and Appointment of Trustees Act (TOLATA) 1996 the creation of such a fee gave rise to a strict settlement under the Settled Land Act 1925 (see s1(ii)(c) of the 1925 Act). However, by virtue of s7(1) of the Law of Property Act 1925 a determinable fee simple arising under the School Sites Act 1841 is stated to be a *fee simple absolute in possession for the purpose of the 1925 Act.*

There were certain problems associated with the reverter provision when a piece of land ceased to be used as a school under the 1841 Act – in particular, what happened to the legal estate? Under the pre-1926 law where a site ceased to be used as a school the legal estate and the beneficial interest automatically passed to the person entitled on reverter (*Attorney-General* v *Shadwell* [1910] 1 Ch 92). However, after the 1925 property legislation came into force the position was less certain. This was because ss7(1) and 3(3) of the Law of Property Act 1925 seemed to be at variance with each other. Section 7(1) of the 1925 Act provides that a fee simple which is liable to be divested under the School Sites Act 1841 'remains liable to be divested as if this Act had not been passed'. In contrast s3(3) of the 1925 Act provides that where by reason of a statutory right of reverter a person becomes entitled to require a legal estate to be vested in him 'the estate owner whose estate is affected shall be bound to convey or create such legal estate as the case may require'.

In *Re Clayton's Deed Poll* [1980] Ch 99 it was held that when land ceased to be used as a school only the beneficial interest passed to the person entitled in reverter with the trustees continuing to hold the legal estate on a bare trust for him. However, in *Re Rowhook Mission Hall, Horsham* [1985] Ch 62 the court declined to follow the aforementioned view and held that s7(1) LPA 1925 had the effect of preserving the pre-1926 position and therefore when land ceased to be used as a school the legal estate automatically vested in the revertee.

Scheme of the Act

The Act preserves the right of the reverter. It provides that when land ceases to be used as a school there is no automatic shifting of the legal estate to the revertee. Rather, the trustees continue to hold the legal estate on trust for the revertee with a power to sell the land (originally it was held on a trust for sale but since 1 January 1997 on a trust of land: see s1 of the 1987 Act as amended by Schedule 2 para 6 of TOLATA 1996). Further, the trustees may if they cannot ascertain the identity of the revertee entitled to the land apply to the Charity Commissioners to have his interest extinguished and a scheme drawn up so that the land can be used for other charitable purposes.

Finally, the Act departs from the traditional approach of ss3(3) and 7(1) of the Law of Property Act 1925 by stipulating that when land ceases to be used as a school the trustees are to continue to hold the legal estate.

5

Law and Equity

5.1 Two legal systems

5.2 Contributions by equity to land law

5.3 The difference between legal and equitable rights

5.4 The doctrine of notice

5.5 Powers

5.1 Two legal systems

The common law rules concerning land were almost fully developed when the Chancellor started to exercise a separate jurisdiction in the fifteenth century, because matters concerning land were the first to come to the king's courts.

The Chancery jurisdiction over land developed because the Chancery would enforce the *use*, or trust as it was later called. Land was put into uses for several purposes, often to evade the effects of the common law. From this jurisdiction developed a whole range of equitable estates, ie enforceable only in the Court of Chancery, brought into being by the *use* or the *use upon a use*, which exactly mirrored the range of legal estates, and so in one piece of land one person could have a fee simple protected by the common law courts (the legal fee) and a different person a fee simple protected by the Court of Chancery (the equitable fee). Until the Judicature Acts of 1873 and 1875 these were two separate court systems, with their own rules and procedure. Now, although law and equity are 'fused' in that they are administered by the same courts by the same process, they are still to some extent different systems of law. Land law, more than any other subject, uses and exploits these parallel legal and equitable interests in land to produce often elegant, sometimes bewildering, solutions to complex problems of land ownership.

Definition

Equity may be defined as a system of doctrines and procedures which developed side by side with the common law and statute law.

5.2 Contributions by equity to land law

1. The trust.
2. Remedies such as specific performance of contracts for the sale or leasing of land. This also gave rise to the rules relating to the agreement for a lease. See Chapter 10.
3. Mortgagor's equity of redemption. This will be explained in Chapter 14.
4. Restrictive covenants. These are dealt with in Chapter 11.

5.3 The difference between legal and equitable rights

The difference arose because of the fact that the common law only recognised legal ownership and gave no effect to trusts, which were enforceable only in equity. Legal interests in land are therefore rights *in rem*, enforceable against anyone; equitable interests were at first rights only *in personam*, enforceable against the trustee personally. This was clearly a very limited protection, and so the Court of Chancery gradually extended it, enforcing equitable interests against persons who took under the trustee on various grounds. Equity, however, would not enforce a trust against an innocent purchaser of the land who knew nothing about the trust, as that enforcement would itself be inequitable, and so an equitable right was still not as strong as a legal right.

5.4 The doctrine of notice

These equitable rules became embodied in what is known as the doctrine of notice. This doctrine can be expressed as follows:

> 'Legal rights are good against the whole world; equitable rights are good against all persons except a bona fide purchaser of the legal estate for value without notice of the equitable interests in that land, and those claiming under him.'

This bona fide purchaser is often known as *'equity's darling'*. The essential features of this privileged person are that he is:

1. *Bona fide* – any dishonesty, sharp practice or other inequitable practice will forfeit equity's protection.
2. *Purchaser for value* – 'purchaser ' excludes those who inherit the land or acquire it by operation of law. 'For value', while it does not necessarily mean 'full value', means money or money's worth or marriage. The decision of the House of Lords in *Midland Bank Trust Co Ltd* v *Green* [1981] AC 513 shows that the consideration need not be adequate. (See also s17(1) Land Charges Act 1972 for the definition of 'purchaser'.)

3. *Of a legal estate* – this is essential; the purchaser of an equitable interest is in general bound by prior equitable interests whether he had notice of them or not.

4. *Without notice* – the purchaser must have no knowledge of the equitable interest at the time he purchased his interest. There are three types of notice:

   a) *Actual notice* – this must be within his own knowledge and must not be merely a vague reference, except that such vague knowledge might lead to constructive notice (below).

   b) *Constructive notice* – a purchaser cannot attempt to avoid equitable interests by shutting his eyes and ears and thus not having actual notice. He is deemed to have notice of all matters about which a reasonably diligent purchaser would have inquired and which would have come to his notice on such an inquiry. This would be derived either from not following up some information or by deliberately abstaining from making any inquiries. As to the need to inspect the land, see *Hunt* v *Luck* [1902] 1 Ch 428.

   If a person in occupation deliberately withholds information about his interest he may be estopped from relying on the defence that the inquirer had constructive notice arising from the occupation. See *Midland Bank Ltd* v *Farmpride Hatcheries Ltd* (1981) 260 EG 493.

   c) *Imputed notice* – if a purchaser employs an agent, eg a solicitor, in the purchase, any actual or constructive notice which that agent receives in the course of *the same* transaction is imputed to the purchaser.

   Section 199(1)(ii) of the Law of Property Act 1925 provides that a purchaser will not be prejudicially affected by notice of any fact unless '(b)... it has come to the knowledge of his solicitor or other agent ... or would have come to the knowledge of his solicitor or other agent, as such, if such inquiries and inspections had been made as ought reasonably to have been made by the solicitor or other agent'.

   The application of s199(1)(ii)(b) LPA 1925 in the context of a surveyor acting on behalf of a mortgagee was seen in *Kingsnorth Finance Co Ltd* v *Tizard* [1986] 2 All ER 54. There the surveyor was held to have imputed notice, on behalf of the mortgagee, of a wife's occupation where the potential mortgagor had described himself as being 'single'. This gave the court the opportunity to consider the meaning of 'occupation' in the context of unregistered land. The wife had made contributions to the purchase price and her occupation was such as to give the mortgagee imputed notice of her equitable rights in the property.

   In *Woolwich plc* v *Gomm & Another* (2000) 79 P & CR 61 the Court of Appeal concluded that the test to be applied in deciding whether a bank providing a mortgage had been fixed with notice under s199(1)(ii)(b) LPA 1925 was objective and did not depend on the particular instructions given by the bank to its solicitor.

5. *Successors in title* – the protection, once acquired, extends to all persons claiming through the original purchaser, even though they are not purchasers for value.

While the doctrine of notice has become less important since the passing of the 1925 legislation, for reasons set out in the next chapter, it still has a part to play in several aspects of land law. See the Land Charges Act 1972, and note ss198 and 199 Law of Property Act 1925. It is essential to know the above rules and when they may still apply today, eg restrictive covenants created before 1926, equitable rights of entry and equitable easements.

5.5 Powers

A power enables a person who is not the owner of property to dispose of it or exercise certain administrative powers over it. Since 1925 most powers are equitable.

The most important types of power are powers of trustees and powers of appointment. Powers of appointment can be classified as:

1. *General powers* – the appointor may appoint to any person including himself. For example, a will or trust may contain a devise 'to A for life with remainder to whomsoever he should appoint'. A may appoint to anyone including himself. Accordingly, a general power may be regarded as tantamount to absolute ownership.
2. *Special powers* – here the donee of the power has to exercise it among a specified class of persons (the objects of the power). For example, '£20,000 to such of B's children as he (B) shall appoint'. The essence of this type of power is that the donee's choice is restricted. It is possible for the donee himself to be a member of the class in whose favour the power may be exercised.
3. *Hybrid powers* – here the donee may appoint to anyone except a certain class of person. For example, '£20,000 to C to whomsoever he shall appoint except my brothers and sisters and their descendants'.

Exercise of powers of appointment

When the donor specifies that the power is to be exercised in a certain way or subject to certain formalities, the direction must be followed or the exercise is void. An appointor of a special power must observe the limits imposed on the exercise. If he makes an appointment which partly comes within the scope of the power but is otherwise too wide, the part within the scope is valid and the rest void. If he makes an appointment which does not come within the scope at all, the whole appointment is void.

Fraud on a power

A fraud on a power is where the power has been used for a purpose beyond that intended by the instrument creating the power, and the effect is that the appointment is void in so far as it is fraudulent. By s157 LPA 1925 a purchaser in good faith of property fraudulently appointed is protected provided that he bought for money or money's worth without notice of the fraud from an appointee aged more than 25 who was entitled in default of appointment.

Release and disclaimer of powers

A power is discharged by exercise. A donee of a power may release it or contract not to exercise it by s155 LPA 1925 unless it is a trust power when he is under a duty to exercise it. He may disclaim it by deed: s156 LPA 1925. He may also impliedly extinguish it by any dealing inconsistent with the further exercise of the power.

6

The 1925 Legislation – Including Registration of Incumbrances

6.1   Introduction

6.2   The purpose of the 1925 legislation

6.3   Reduction of legal estates and interests

6.4   Protection of equitable interests

6.5   Local Land Charges Act 1975

6.6   Entries on the land charges register

6.7   Searching in the land charges register

6.8   Priority notices

6.9   Vacation of the registration of a land charge

6.10   Worked example

6.1 Introduction

There had been considerable statutory reform of land law during the nineteenth century, but a need for a comprehensive code of property legislation was felt, which resulted in the magnificent achievements of the draftsmen and legislature known as the 1925 legislation. This was a series of Acts, most of which were passed in 1925 and came into effect on 1 January 1926, which are the:

Law of Property Act 1922	(LPA 1922)
Settled Land Act 1925	(SLA 1925)
Law of Property Act 1925	(LPA 1925)
Land Charges Act 1925	(LCA 1925)
Land Registration Act 1925	(LRA 1925)
Trustee Act 1925	(TA 1925)
Administration of Estates Act 1925	(AEA 1925)

Since 1925 there has been further, piecemeal, legislation. The most important Acts are the:

Law of Property (Amendment) Act 1926	(LP(A)A 1926)
Perpetuities and Accumulations Act 1964	(PAA 1964)
Law of Property (Joint Tenants) Act 1964	(LP(JT)A 1964)
Law of Property Act 1969	(LPA 1969)
Land Charges Act 1972	(LCA 1972)
Local Land Charges Act 1975	(LLCA 1975)

(The LCA 1972 and LLCA 1975 consolidate the law of land charges, replacing the LCA 1925)

Rentcharges Act 1977	
Land Registration Act 1986	(LRA 1986)
Land Registration Act 1988	(LRA 1988)
Law of Property (Miscellaneous Provisions) Act 1989	
Landlord and Tenant (Covenants) Act 1995	
Trusts of Land and Appointment of Trustees Act 1996	(TOLATA 1996)
Land Registration Act 1997	(LRA 1997)
Trustee Act 2000	(TA 2000)
Land Registration Act 2002	(LRA 2002)

6.2 The purpose of the 1925 legislation

There are two main purposes of the legislation:

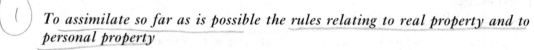

To assimilate so far as is possible the rules relating to real property and to personal property

This is of lesser importance in the study of land law. The main reforms were:

1. By s130 LPA 1925 an entailed interest could be created in personalty as well as realty. However, no new entailed interests can be created after 31 December 1996 (Schedule 1 para 5 of the Trusts of Land and Appointment of Trustees Act 1996).
2. On intestacy by ss45 and 46 AEA 1925 (as amended) both real and personal property pass in the same way (apart from entails).
3. Realty and personalty are now both available to pay the deceased's debts, which formerly had to be satisfied from personalty alone, s34(3) and Schedule 1 AEA 1925.
4. The rule in *Dearle* v *Hall* (1828) 3 Russ 1 governing the priority of assignment of equitable interests applies equally to interests in realty and personalty by s137 LPA 1925.

5. By s60(1) LPA 1925 a conveyance of freehold land passes the whole interest of the vendor without the need for words of limitation.
6. Substantial changes were made in the method of creating legal mortgages. See ss85–87 LPA 1925 (Chapter 14).

The simplification of conveyancing

When a purchaser buys land he wants to know, first, whether the vendor in fact owns the title he is purporting to sell and, second, whether the land is incumbered by any interests belonging to third parties. We have already seen that a purchaser is in a much better position in respect of equitable interests owned by others than legal interests, and so the fewer legal interests there are the easier the purchaser's task is. On the other hand, owners of equitable interests also need protection. The 1925 legislation sought to satisfy as far as possible these conflicting claims of the purchaser and the owner of the equitable interest by:

1. Reducing the number of legal estates and interests that can exist in land (see s1 LPA 1925 below).
2. Protecting certain equitable interests by registration or transferring them to money in the hands of trustees (overreaching).
3. Expanding the system of title registration.

6.3 Reduction of legal estates and interests

Section 1 LPA 1925

Legal estates
Section 1(1) LPA 1925 states that:

'The only estates in land which are capable of subsisting or of being conveyed or created at law are –
1. an estate in fee simple absolute in possession;
2. a term of years absolute.'

This means that all other interests, eg entails, life estates, which could previously be legal estates can now only exist as equitable interests behind a trust.

Legal interests
Section 1(2) deals with legal interests, that is rights over another's land, as follows:

'The only interests or charges in or over land which are capable of subsisting or of being conveyed or created at law are:
1. an easement, right or privilege in or over land for an interest equivalent to an estate in fee simple absolute in possession or a term of years absolute;
2. a rentcharge in possession issuing out of or charged on land being either perpetual or for a term of years absolute;

3. a charge by way of a legal mortgage;

4. a charge on land not created by an instrument;

5. rights of entry exercisable over or in respect of a legal term of years absolute, or annexed, for any purpose, to a legal rentcharge.'

Equitable interests

Section 1(3) concludes the reorganisation by stating that:

'All other estates interests and charges in or over land take effect as equitable interests.'

Estates and interests under s1 LPA 1925

Fee simple absolute in possession

'Fee simple' – the meaning of fee simple has been dealt with in Chapter 4 (see section 4.4). 'Absolute' in the definition is used to distinguish the fee simple absolute in possession from a modified fee such as a determinable fee simple or a conditional fee. The effect of the Law of Property (Amendment) Act 1926 has already been noted, and the full effect of s7(1) in relation to fee simples which may be divested together with the 1926 amendment should be considered when any right of re-entry has been reserved (see Chapter 4, section 4.4).

'In possession' means that the estate is immediate, not in remainder or reversion, and is defined to include the receipt of rents and profits as well as physical possession. (See s205(1)(xix) LPA 1925.) Thus a landlord who owns the fee simple absolute in possession has a legal estate even though he has parted with possession to the tenant (who may also have a legal estate). In addition s1(5) provides that: 'A legal estate may subsist concurrently with or subject to any other legal estate in the same land.' This may be demonstrated by the following diagram:

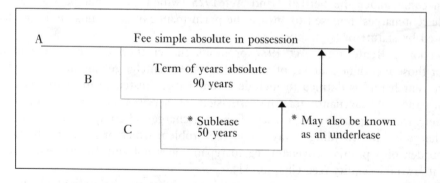

In this case A owns the fee simple absolute in possession. He grants a lease to B for 90 years. A continues to be in 'possession' because of s205(1)(xix) LPA 1925 which defines possession to include the receipt of rents and profits. B has a term of years absolute which will remain 'absolute' even if A has reserved a right of re-entry in the event that B breaks any covenants in the lease.

In turn B has granted a sublease to C. This is also a legal estate, being a term of years absolute. There is no requirement that B must be 'in possession'.

The whole example illustrates the fact that any number of legal estates may subsist concurrently within the terms of s1(5) LPA 1925.

Term of years absolute

A 'term of years absolute' is defined by s205(1)(xxvii) LPA 1925 as including a term of less than one year, or for a year or years, or from year to year, which appears to include all periodic tenancies. 'Absolute' does not appear to have any meaning, because a term of years is absolute even though it is subject to determination by notice, re-entry or operation of law. Megarry and Wade refer (at p114) to an interesting example of a term of years absolute that is neither a term of years nor absolute. This would arise in the case of a monthly tenancy, 'less than a year', subject to a right of re-entry for failure to pay rent or breach of any other covenant in the lease.

Legal easements: s1(2)(a) LPA 1925

This covers both easements and profits à prendre (see Chapter 12), but note that they can only be *legal* if held for equivalents of the two legal estates. An example of a non-legal easement would be an easement for life which only exists as an equitable easement today. See s2(3) LPA 1925.

Rentcharges: s1(2)(b) LPA 1925

A rentcharge is a right to be paid a periodical sum of money charged on land. This section has been considerably modified by the effect of the Rentcharges Act 1977, which forbids the creation after 22 August 1977 of any new rentcharges except those which come under the Settled Land Act 1925 (which could not be legal anyway), 'estate rentcharges' imposed to ensure the performance of covenants, and rentcharges imposed by statute or by a court.

Section 2 Rentcharges Act 1977 prohibits the creation of any new rentcharge except those mentioned above, of which the 'estate rentcharge' should be noted. The 'estate rentcharge' is defined to include a rentcharge created to meet the cost of the performance of covenants for the provision of services or the carrying out of maintenance or repairs by the owner of the rentcharge. The importance of the estate rentcharge lies in providing a way round the problem which arises from the fact that the burden of a positive covenant, eg to repair, does not run directly with freehold land at law or in equity (see Chapter 11).

The effect is to preserve certain rentcharges paid by the individual owners of some freehold properties on estates which have been deliberately laid out for landscape or amenity purposes, the upkeep of which is financed by such payments. All other existing rentcharges are to be phased out within 60 years.

Legal charge: s1(2)(c) LPA 1925
This is one of the two methods of creating a legal mortgage after 1925. It was introduced by s87 of the Law of Property Act 1925 (see Chapter 14).

A charge on land not created by an instrument: s1(2)(d) LPA 1925
Unimportant today due to the repeal of the significant parts of the subsection.

Rights of entry: s1(2)(e) LPA 1925
These are rights of entry reserved in a lease enabling the landlord to recover the land if the tenant does not pay the rent or breaks his covenants, or those which allow a rentcharge owner to secure payment by taking possession of the land.

Any other former estate or interest which does not come within the above list must be equitable: s1(3) LPA 1925.

6.4 Protection of equitable interests

The 1925 legislation makes a broad distinction between what can be called 'commercial' and 'family' interests in land. Those estates and interests which are legal estates and interests under s1 LPA 1925 are those which are commonly bought and sold; those which are equitable only, such as life interests, generally arise as a result of a will or a family settlement. The same broad distinction is made between those equitable interests which arise from, or may be the subject of, a commercial transaction, which are generally protected by registration, and those arising from settlements which are protected by the mechanism of overreaching. In *Birmingham Midshires Mortgage Services Ltd* v *Sabherwal* (2000) 80 P & CR 256 the Court of Appeal confirmed the well established view that commercial equitable interests, but not family equitable interests, are exempt from the overreaching regime. The former equitable rules of notice have been greatly affected by the 1925 legislation. Since 1925 they continue to have a role to play in the protection of equitable interests in respect of *unregistered* land but it is much less significant than hitherto.

The land charges register

The word 'registration' relates to two distinct concepts. The first is the registration of incumbrances (in *unregistered land*) as a replacement for the equitable doctrine of notice. This must not be confused with the *registration of title* at the Land Registry which is dealt with later (Chapter 7). The land charges register was intended to provide a means of protecting owners of equitable interests coming within the registrable classes, while at the same time making it easy for a purchaser to discover what equitable incumbrances he will be bound by. The problems which arise are due to the exceptions which make the land charges register an incomplete record of incumbrances which may affect unregistered land.

Prior to 1 July 1995, a land charge could only be registered against an estate owner and nobody could be an estate owner after he had died. Since that date it has been easier to register a land charge where an owner has died because s15 of the Law of Property (Miscellaneous Provisions) Act 1994 enables the charge to be registered against the owner's name after his death.

Principles of registration

The registration of a registrable interest replaces the doctrine of notice, so far as that interest is concerned. The principles relating to a registered land charge represent the combined effect of:

Section 4 Land Charges Act 1972: failure to register makes the interest void against a 'purchaser' – as defined in s17 LCA 1972. See *Midland Bank Trust Co Ltd v Green* [1981] AC 513 (below).

Section 198 Law of Property Act 1925: registration is deemed to constitute actual notice to all persons for all purposes connected with the land. This means that a registered charge is binding on a purchaser whether he knew about it or not, and an unregistered charge is not binding on a purchaser even if he had notice of it.

The meaning of the word 'purchaser' was considered in *Midland Bank Trust Co Ltd* v *Green*, where a wife purchased a farm from her husband for a considerable undervalue, the purpose of the sale being to defeat the exercise of an option by the son. The option was not registered. The House of Lords held that the unregistered option, under s13(2) Land Charges Act 1925 (now s4(6) Land Charges Act 1972), was void against 'a purchaser of a legal estate for money or money's worth'. These words contained no requirement that the purchaser must take in good faith or that the 'money or money's worth' must be more than nominal. See also s17 LCA 1972.

Registrable interests

The 1925 Act – now replaced by the LCA 1972 – imposed a duty to keep five separate registers; these are set out in s1(1) LCA 1972 as a:

1. Register of land charges.
2. Register of pending actions.
3. Register of writs and orders affecting land.
4. Register of deeds of arrangement affecting land.
5. Register of annuities.

The register of land charges is undoubtedly the most important for land law purposes and this will be dealt with later. The following points should be noted in relation to the other registers:

The register of pending actions. This relates to 'any action information or proceeding pending in court relating to land or any interest in or charge on land' (s17(1) LCA 1972). The meaning of 'pending land action' is further considered in

Selim Ltd v *Bickenhall Engineering Ltd* [1981] 1 WLR 1318 and *Haslemere Estates Ltd* v *Baker* [1982] 1 WLR 1109.

An action for breach of a landlord's repairing covenant is not a pending land action because it does not amount to a claim to an interest in the particular land. See *Regan & Blackburn Ltd* v *Rogers* [1985] 1 WLR 870.

The register of writs and orders affecting land. These include writs and orders enforcing judgments and orders of the court and would include any receiving order in bankruptcy made after 1925.

The register of deeds of arrangement affecting land. A deed of arrangement is defined in the Deeds of Arrangement Act 1914 as any document whereby control over a debtor's property is given for the benefit of his creditors.

The register of annuities. This register was closed in 1925 and dealt with annuities created after 25 April 1855 and before 1 January 1926.

The register of land charges. As indicated above this is the most important of the registers for land law purposes, and is dealt with in more detail below.

The register of land charges
Registrable land charges are divided into five classes by s2 LCA 1972.

Class A – charges imposed by statute which only arise on application by some interested person (unimportant): s2(2) LCA 1972.

Class B – charges imposed automatically by statute: s2(3)LCA 1972.

Class C – this class is divided into four categories: s2(4) LCA 1972.

C(i) – a puisne mortgage, ie a legal mortgage of the legal estate not protected by deposit of title deeds. *Note*: this is a legal interest and is an example of a non-equitable matter covered by the LCA 1972.

C(ii) – a limited owner's charge. This charge is given to a tenant for life who himself pays any inheritance tax and entitles him to the same rights as a mortgagee against the settled land.

C(iii) – a general equitable charge. This is a residuary class, and covers things such as equitable mortgages of a legal estate unprotected by deposit of title deeds and an unpaid vendor's lien.

C(iv) – an estate contract, in other words a contract by the owner of a legal estate to convey or create a legal estate which is binding and enforceable. This covers contracts for the sale, lease or mortgage of land, and equitable leases arising from a purported lease lacking in the necessary formalities. See *Hollington Brothers Ltd* v *Rhodes* [1951] 2 All ER 578. The class also includes options to purchase and a right of pre-emption: see *Pritchard* v *Briggs* [1980] Ch 338, in which a conflict arose between persons holding a right of pre-emption and an option to purchase respectively on the same property where both were correctly registered as estate contracts under s2(4)(iv) LCA 1972. Although the right of pre-emption was registered first, it was held by the Court of Appeal that the option to purchase had priority because a right of pre-emption is not an interest in land, even though it is registrable under the LCA 1972. A person who has a right to have land offered to him first if the owner of the land decides to sell can take no initiative. He cannot call for a conveyance to himself, he has only the hope that the owner will decide to sell the land. The grant of a right of pre-emption confers no present or contingent interest in land. See also *Taylor Fashions Ltd* v *Liverpool Victoria Trustees Co Ltd* [1981] 1 All ER 897.

An estate contract does include a lessee's option to renew an estate contract even though the option runs with the reversion.

Class D – this class is divided into three categories: s2(5) LCA 1972.

D(i) – a charge for unpaid inheritance tax in favour of the Inland Revenue.

D(ii) – restrictive covenants made after 1925, not being covenants in a lease (covenants created before 1926 continue to depend on the rules of notice).

D(iii) – equitable easements arising or created after 1925. This section is very vaguely worded but has been interpreted by the House of Lords in *Shiloh Spinners Ltd* v *Harding* [1973] AC 691 as having a narrow meaning, confined to rights equivalent to easements and profits. Lord Wilberforce considered whether an equitable right of entry was included and said: '... Class D(iii) should be given its plain prima facie meaning and that so read it does not comprise equitable rights of entry'.

Class E – annuities created before 1926 but registered after 1925: s2(6) LCA 1972.

Class F – charge arising from the Family Law Act 1996 (formerly the Matrimonial Homes Act 1983): s2(7) LCA 1972. This is the right of a spouse who does not own a legal estate in the matrimonial home to occupy the home; see *Wroth* v *Tyler* [1974] Ch 30 in which Megarry J described the effect of the original Act of 1967 as follows:

> '... the essentials of the right given by the Act [1967] to an occupying spouse [are] as follows. The right is in essence a personal and non-assignable statutory right not to be evicted from the matrimonial home in question during marriage or until the court otherwise orders: and this right constitutes a charge on the estate or interest of the owning spouse which requires protection against third parties by registration.'

The use of Class F land charges was considered in *Barnett* v *Hassett* [1981] 1 WLR 1385, in which it was held that a spouse who has no intention to occupy the matrimonial home is not permitted to register a Class F charge merely in an attempt to freeze the proceeds of an intended sale.

Unregistrable interests

There are certain interests which do not come within the provisions of the Land Charges Act 1972, but do *not* arise under a trust of land (post 1996), trust for sale (pre 1997) or a strict settlement, and so are not overreachable. Some of these are clearly unregistrable because of the wording of s2 LCA 1972, eg restrictive covenants and equitable easements created before 1926. Others have been declared by the courts to be unregistrable, for example:

1. Beneficial interests under bare trusts. A bare trust is where the entire beneficial interest is vested in one person and the legal estate in another. Such trusts came within neither the trust for sale nor the strict settlement and therefore the overreaching machinery provided by the 1925 legislation did not apply to bare trusts with the result that there could have been situations where a purchaser failed to obtain a good title. However, since the Trusts of Land and Appointment of Trustees Act 1996 came into force on 1 January 1997 bare trusts are now within the new trusts of land regime (ie from that date equitable interests under such trusts are subject to the overreaching machinery).
2. Equitable rights of entry: *Shiloh Spinners* v *Harding* (see Lord Wilberforce, above).
3. Beneficial interests under resulting trusts: see *Caunce* v *Caunce* [1969] 1 WLR 286, and cf *Williams & Glyn's Bank* v *Boland* [1981] AC 487.
4. Contractual licences: see *Binions* v *Evans* [1972] Ch 359.
5. Equitable easements: see *E R Ives Investments Ltd* v *High* [1967] 2 QB 379.
6. Equitable rights based on estoppel: this is probably the most significant application of the doctrine of notice today as the courts continue to develop the rules relating to proprietary estoppel.
7. A charging order on an undivided share of land is now possible under the Charging Orders Act 1979, but the Act did not make such an order registrable under the Land Charges Act 1972.

The doctrine of notice applies to unregistrable interests. However, given that most equitable interests in respect of unregistered land are now protected by registration as land charges or by overreaching, the doctrine is much less significant today than it was prior to 1926.

Overreaching

A settlement of land, in the broadest meaning of the word, is an arrangement creating a succession of interests in property. The 1925 legislation allowed two methods of doing this, a strict settlement under the Settled Land Act and a trust for sale under the Law of Property Act 1925. This dual system was replaced by a new unitary system of holding land on trust when the Trusts of Land and Appointment of Trustees Act 1996 came into force on 1 January 1997. Since that date all trusts of land (except pre-Act strict settlements and land to which the Universities and College Estates Act 1925 applies) are now subject to the new trust of land regime. Because limited interests in land are now necessarily equitable, in both trusts of land or a pre-1996 Act strict settlement there are one or more persons holding the legal estate on trust for the beneficiaries.

In order to enable easy dealing with land subject to a trust of land or pre-1996 Act strict settlement, a method of selling it free from the equitable interests of the beneficiaries, while protecting them, is necessary. This is done by providing that if the purchase money for the land is paid to at least *two trustees* of the settlement (unless a trust corporation is a trustee, when the money may be paid to it) the purchaser takes free of equitable interests under the settlement, which are said to be 'overreached'. The beneficiaries' interests are transferred to the purchase money. This concept was also invoked in respect of pre-1997 trusts for sale (all trusts for sale became trusts of land under the 1996 Act whether created before or after 1 January 1997).

Effects of a sale of unregistered land on legal and equitable rights

Unregistered land means land of which the title is not registered as explained in Chapter 7.

1. The purchaser takes subject to all *legal rights* except:

   a) those legal rights which are registrable and are unregistered, eg puisne mortgage (land charge Class C(i));
   b) those few legal rights which are overreachable.

2. The purchaser takes subject to all equitable rights except:

   a) registrable equitable rights which are unregistered: s4 LCA 1972;
   b) overreachable equitable rights, provided that the overreaching mechanism is gone through;
   c) unregistrable and non-overreachable rights in respect of which he is a bona fide purchaser of a legal estate for value *without notice*.

The general effect of the registration of land charges

Section 198 LPA 1925 provides that registration under the Land Charges Act is deemed to constitute notice of the matter registered 'to all persons and for all purposes'. There are, however, a few exceptions to s198 LPA 1925 where *actual knowledge* is required. These are:

Tacking: s94(2) LPA 1925
Where a prior mortgage expressly states that it is to be a security for any further advances, then registration of such a later mortgage is not deemed to be actual notice and will not prevent tacking (see Chapter 14).

Discharge of a mortgage: s96(2) LPA 1925
When a mortgagor has discharged his first mortgage, the first mortgagee is not deemed to have notice of any subsequent mortgages simply because the later

mortgages were registered. Thus subsequent mortgagees, who will not have the title deeds, must both register their mortgage as land charges Class C(i) or Class C(iii) and give actual notice to the prior incumbrancers.

Actual knowledge at the date of the contract: s24 LPA 1969

Whether a purchaser knew of a registered land charge when he entered into the contract is to be decided by reference to his actual knowledge. Section 24 LPA 1969 provides:

> 'Where under a contract for the sale or other disposition of any estate or interest in land the title to which is not registered under the Land Registration Act 1925 ... any question arises whether the purchaser had knowledge at the time of entering into the contract, of a registered land charge, that question shall be determined by reference to his actual knowledge and without regard to the provisions of s198 of the Law of Property Act 1925.'

The effect of s24 LPA 1969 is to make a land charge search before the exchange of contracts unnecessary because the only knowledge which counts at the time of exchange of contracts is the actual knowledge of the prospective purchaser. It should be noted that the Act refers to 'actual knowledge', which appears to exclude the rules of constructive notice in this particular area.

The two major exceptions to the application of s24 are that the section does not relate to contracts for the sale of registered land, and nor does it dispense with the need for a search in the local land charges register (see section 6.5 below).

Conclusion

A clear weakness of the unregistered land system is that it does not protect people in *occupation* of land. This was demonstrated in *Lloyds Bank plc* v *Carrick & Another* [1996] 4 All ER 630. There the first defendant (RC) held a legal leasehold of a maisonette title to which was *unregistered*. When his brother died, he suggested to the second defendant (MC) his brother's widow that she should sell her house, pay the sale proceeds to him and move to the maisonette (RC did not live there) which would become hers (ie the sale proceeds would be the payment for the maisonette). MC accepted this offer, sold her house, paid the sale proceeds of £19,000 to RC and moved into the maisonette. However, the lease remained in the name of RC alone. The agreement between RC and MC was an oral one. Subsequently, unbeknown to MC, RC mortgaged the maisonette to the plaintiff bank as security for a loan. He did not inform the bank that MC was living there nor of the basis under which she did so. Further, the bank made no inquiries as to who was in possession. In due course, RC defaulted on the mortgage and the bank sought an order for possession of the property. MC claimed she had an interest which bound the bank.

The Court of Appeal concluded that no equitable interest had been established either by way of bare trust, constructive trust or proprietary estoppel. Rather the court held that MC's only interest arose under the *estate contract* with RC (ie she had a valid contract with RC for the grant of a legal estate). This estate contract should have been registered as a Class C(iv) land charge under the Land Charges Act 1972 in order to be binding on a purchaser for valuable consideration (ie the bank). Since MC's interest had not been registered it was void against the bank under s4(6) of the 1972 Act and the bank was accordingly awarded possession.

The outcome of the case – once the court decided that MC's interest arose under an estate contract – was in line with established case law (see *Midland Bank Trust Co Ltd v Green* [1981] AC 513). However, it is submitted that the outcome for MC would have been entirely different if the title to the maisonette had been *registered*. In such a situation, the interest of MC who was in possession at the time RC took out the mortgage and of whom no enquiry was made by the bank would have been an overriding interest under s70(1)(g) of the Land Registration Act 1925 (for a person to successfully claim an overriding interest under s70(1)(g) he must have a proprietary interest in the land and an estate contract would rank as such an interest, but note the effect on overriding interests of LRA 2002). As such it would have bound the bank thus demonstrating the greater protection afforded to persons in actual occupation (who are not legal owners) by the registered land system over the unregistered land one.

6.5 Local Land Charges Act 1975

Definition of a local land charge

A local land charge is broadly defined in s1 Local Land Charges Act 1975 to include charges under the Public Health and Highways Acts, restrictions and positive obligations imposed by a local authority or Minister of the Crown if they bind successive owners of the land, and matters expressly declared to be local land charges. Entries in the land charges register are made against the relevant land.

Effect of failure to register a local land charge

Section 10 LLCA 1975 should be noted; it provides that from 1 August 1977 failure to register a charge in the local land charges register shall not affect the enforcement of the charge, but that a purchaser shall be entitled to compensation for any loss suffered by reason that the charge was not registered or was not shown as registered by an official search certificate. Previously a local land charge had been void against a purchaser for money or money's worth of a legal estate in the land affected unless registered before completion of the purchase. The result is that while a local land charge certificate will no longer be conclusive, a certificate from the central land charges register still remains conclusive under s10(4) Land Charges Act 1972.

Examples of local land charges

Local land charges include various public matters relating to financial charges, some planning charges and lists of buildings of special architectural or historical interest.

The one private matter which will be found in the local land charges register is a light obstruction notice registered under the provisions of the Rights of Light Act 1959 (see Chapter 12).

6.6 Entries on the land charges register

The land charges register is a 'names' register and a person wishing to protect a registrable interest must register it against the name of the landowner for the time being: s3(1) LCA 1972. This gives rise to several problems which are summarised below.

Registration against the wrong name

This does not invalidate the registration if it is made in a name which could reasonably be regarded as a usual variation of the correct name (*Oak Co-operative Building Society* v *Blackburn* [1968] Ch 730), although it will not bind a purchaser who searches against the correct name because a clear search is conclusive by virtue of s10(4) LCA 1972 (*Diligent Finance Co Ltd* v *Alleyne* (1972) 23 P & CR 346).

Search against the wrong name

A purchaser who searches against the wrong name will be bound by the interests registered against the correct name, or even against a usual variant of the correct name (*Oak Co-operative* v *Blackburn* (above)).

Names behind the root of title

Before a purchaser buys land the vendor must prove that he has title, ie he owns the interest he is selling. This is done by producing the documents that trace the title to the land in question. It would be an impossible task for a vendor to produce every document, and instead he need not produce a document older than a specified date before the transaction which shows the ownership of the land unless the contract provides otherwise. This is known as the 'root of title'. Until 1969 the specified period was 30 years; it is now *15 years* (s23 LPA 1969). As registration of incumbrances goes back to 1925, it is often the case that there are previous owners whose names are not revealed by examination of the title documents against whom incumbrances may have been registered. A scheme of compensation for purchasers affected by undiscoverable land charges was introduced by s25 LPA 1969. See also section 6.4 as to the effect of s24 LPA 1969.

6.7 Searching in the land charges register

A prospective purchaser can only discover registered incumbrances by searching the register against the correct names of all the persons he knows to have owned the land in question. In view of the decision in the *Oak Co-operative* case (see above) he would also be well advised to search against all the usual variants of the correct names.

The search may be made in person, but it is much safer to have an official search made by the Land Registry and obtain an official certificate. Nowadays an official search is done by computer. The advantages of an official search certificate are:

1. It is conclusive in favour of the person requesting the search, provided that his application correctly specifies the persons and the land concerned. This means that he takes free of any rights it fails to disclose, even if properly registered.
2. It protects any solicitor or trustee making a search from liability for any error in the certificate.
3. It provides protection from incumbrances registered in a period of 15 working days from the date of the certificate, so that if the purchase is completed within that period the purchaser takes free from such incumbrances.

If the official search certificate fails to reveal a properly registered charge the purchaser takes free of the charge and so the owner of the interest loses it. No provision was made by Parliament to compensate the owner of the interest in such a case, but an action for damages for negligence lies against the public authority responsible. This should be compared with the local land charges position since 1 August 1977: see *Ministry of Housing and Local Government* v *Sharp* [1970] 2 QB 223. Compare s10 Local Land Charges Act 1975 (section 6.5 above).

6.8 Priority notices

Very often on the sale of land a series of operations all take place at the time of completion; for example, the conveyance which, inter alia, creates a restrictive covenant will be completed a few moments before a mortgage on the property. If the normal rules of registration applied, the restrictive covenant would be void as against the mortgagee. The vendor can, however, protect his restrictive covenant by giving a priority notice to the registrar at least 15 days before the transaction. Then, if he registers his covenant within 30 days of the entry of the priority notice the registration dates back to the moment of the creation of the restrictive covenant and hence is binding on the mortgagee. This priority notice provision applies to all registrable charges.

6.9 Vacation of the registration of a land charge

The court has a wide jurisdiction, both inherent, *Calgary and Edmonton Land Co Ltd* v *Dobinson* [1974] Ch 102, and statutory under s1(6) LCA 1972, to order the removal of any registration from the register when the registration was improper or has ceased to apply. See *Barnett* v *Hassett* [1981] 1 WLR 1385.

6.10 Worked example

The following is an example of a typical LLB examination question set on the contents of this chapter.

The answer is only intended to set out the points which should be covered by the student when answering, and it is for each student to develop his or her own style of writing.

Q In 1970 Peter bought the fee simple absolute of Windmill Farm. The farm is subject to a covenant prohibiting any further building, entered into by Peter's predecessor in title in 1920, and in 1975 Peter covenanted with his neighbour not to use the Long Meadow for other than agricultural purposes. In 1980 Peter mortgaged the farm to the Temple Building Society by way of legal charge.

The Society took the title deeds, but later allowed Peter to borrow them and never asked for their return. In 1988 Peter let Tithe Cottage, one of the farm buildings, to Mrs Stanley for 15 years at £500 pa in writing but not under seal. In 1990 Peter executed a deed declaring himself to be trustee of the farm for his wife. Peter recently sold and conveyed the legal fee simple in the whole farm to William without disclosing any of the above matters. Advise William as to whether he is bound by them.

A Assuming this to be *unregistered land*, the effect of the various transactions is as follows:

The 1920 restrictive covenant
Covenants made before 1926 are not registrable as land charges and the doctrine of notice applies. William does not have actual notice, and provided that he does not have constructive or implied notice he will not be bound by this covenant. This is one of the occasions when the examiner will require a knowledge of pre-1926 land law.

The 1975 restrictive covenant
This is registrable as a Class D(ii) land charge. If it is registered, registration constitutes actual notice (s198 LPA 1925), and so William is bound; if it is not registered it is void against a subsequent purchaser for money or money's worth of a legal estate (s4 LCA 1972), and so William will not be bound. As to the

meaning of 'purchaser', see *Midland Bank Trust Co Ltd* v *Green* [1981] 2 WLR 28 and s17 LCA 1972.

The 1980 mortgage

This was originally protected by deposit of title deeds and so was a legal interest not requiring registration. William would be bound irrespective of notice. It is possible, however, that the return of the title deeds to Peter made the mortgage registrable as a puisne mortgage, Class C(i), and, if so, it would be binding if registered and void if unregistered. Even if it does not become registrable it is possible that the Society has lost its priority against William if its failure to regain the title deeds was gross negligence (see Chapter 14). See *Oliver* v *Hinton* [1899] 2 Ch 264.

The 1988 lease

This is an equitable lease as it is for more than three years but not made by deed (see Chapter 10) and is registrable as an estate contract, Class C(iv). If registered it is binding on William, if unregistered it is void. See *Hollington Brothers Ltd* v *Rhodes* [1951] 2 All ER 578.

The 1990 trust

This appears to be a bare trust rather than a settlement. Prior to 1 January 1997, bare trusts were not overreachable nor were they registrable and so the doctrine of notice applied. This was assumed to be the position by the Court of Appeal in *Binions* v *Evans* [1972] Ch 359.

However, since the coming into force of the Trusts of Land and Appointment of Trustees Act 1996 on 1 January 1997 bare trusts are now within the new trusts of land regime (ie from that date equitable interests under such trusts are subject to the overreaching machinery).

In recent years LLB examiners have gone on to ask if the answer would differ if the title to the land was *registered*. After Chapter 7 has been studied the reader is advised to return to this example to check if his answer would differ if the title to Windmill Farm was registered.

7

registered & unregistered land.

Registration of Title

7.1 Introduction

7.2 Registration of title and the doctrine of notice

7.3 Relationship between the Land Charges Act 1972 and the Land Registration Act 2002

7.4 Key principles of registration

7.5 Registrable estates and interests

7.6 Overriding interests under the Land Registration Act 1925

7.7 Other aspects of registration under the Land Registration Act 1925

7.8 Land Registration Act 2002

7.1 Introduction

Registration of title was introduced in the nineteenth century and extended by the Land Registration Act 1925. The idea lying behind registration is that there should be a register containing all the relevant details about all land in England and Wales. Compulsory registration of title has been extended to the whole of England and Wales since 1 December 1990.

There were two reasons for the establishment of such a system:

1. To provide a simpler and faster method of proving title when the land is conveyed.
2. To provide better protection for purchasers and for the owners of equitable interests in the land conveyed.

At the outset of the chapter it is important to emphasise that the system of registration was substantially reformed on 13 October 2003 with the coming into force of the Land Registration Act 2002 and the repeal of the Land Registration Act 1925.

Proof of title

A vendor must be able to prove that he is entitled to the land before he can pass good title to a purchaser. Under the pre-1926 system such proof was provided by the production of the title documents to the land, ie the conveyances or leases. The vendor had to be able to show the chain of ownership for the last 30 (now 15) years. This meant that each time the land was sold, all these documents had to be examined which was time consuming and thus added to the cost of conveyancing. Under the LRA 2002 (and previously under the LRA 1925) a single register entry is substituted for the series of title deeds as proof of title, and a prospective purchaser need only examine this register entry.

Protection of interests in the land

A purchaser learnt of the existence of some of the interests, both legal and equitable, affecting the land from the title deeds, but many were not disclosed. All purchasers were bound by any legal interests and all purchasers, except a bona fide purchaser for value of the legal estate without notice, were bound by any equitable interests. On the other hand the owner of an equitable interest in the land would lose that interest to a purchaser of the legal estate without notice. In order to protect both purchasers and the owners of equitable interests, the register entry under the LRA 2002 is intended to provide an accurate record of most interests in or over all land (this was also the position under the LRA 1925).

Over the years the range of transactions requiring registration has widened. Initially every conveyance on the sale of freehold land and every lease for more than 40 years or the assignment of a lease with more than 40 years to run had to be submitted for registration within two months of the date of the deed. The Land Registration Act 1986 which came into force on 1 January 1987 reduced the required period relevant for leases from 40 to 21 years. The range of transactions requiring registration was further extended by the Land Registration Act 1997 (see below) and the Land Registration Act 2002 extended the compulsory first registration to leases with more than seven years to run and to assignments of leases with more than seven years to run.

Minor interests index

Section 5 of the Land Registration Act 1986 repealed s102(2) LRA 1925. With consequent changes to the Land Registration Rules 1925 the effect was to abolish the Minor Interests Index and provide that priority between dealings with equitable interests in registered land was to be determined by the rule in *Dearle* v *Hall* (1828) 3 Russ 1, under which priority would be the order in which notice was received by the trustees.

Land Registration Act 1988

This Act came into force on 3 December 1990 and opens the Land Registry to inspection by anyone, removing the restrictions on access to the register without the authorisation of the registered proprietor. This new right of access extends to inspecting and making copies of entries on the register and any consequent documents held by the Land Registry, but does not include leases and charges on the land.

The consequences of having an 'open register' are many and varied. For example, a developer trying to assemble a site for development can now discover who owns the plot he needs to acquire and can then approach the owner directly with an offer to buy it. Further, the tenant of a long lease can now discover the identity of his landlord without having to correspond with, for example, a managing agent. It also greatly facilitates the enforcement of judgments and could be of use to private investigators and investigative journalists. Finally, the open register now records the price paid on the last sale, which is of interest to those 'reading' the market.

Registration of Title Order 1989

The Registration of Title Order 1989 (SI 1989/1347) completed the extension of registration of title to the whole of England and Wales. Since 1 December 1990 the whole of England and Wales has been subject to compulsory registration of title at the next appropriate transaction.

Land Registration Act 1997

The Act received the Royal Assent on 27 February 1997. Section 1 (which came into force on 1 April 1998) made first registration compulsory in a number of new situations (ie over and above registration on sale etc). The new triggers for registration were:

1. conveyances by way of gift;
2. conveyances pursuant to a court order;
3. conveyances by way of assents, vesting assents and vesting deeds;
4. first legal *mortgages* of freehold or leaseholds having more than 21 years to run.

The aim of s1 LRA 1997 was to accelerate the completion of a comprehensive register of title covering the whole of England and Wales (at present there are well over 16 million separate registered titles out of an estimated potential total of about 21 million). Of the new LRA 1997 triggers for registration, the 'assent one' is proving to be the most significant in terms of the number of additional registrations.

Many commentators expected the mortgage trigger to be the most significant, the fact that it is not is probably due to the fact that since compulsory registration on sale has been going in much of the country for many years, and for at least ten years in any event (compulsory registration of title has applied to the whole of England and Wales since 1 December 1990), most property has changed hands since the area in question became one of compulsory registration of title.

Section 3 enabled orders to be made providing for reduced fees to be charged for voluntary first registration. The Lord Chancellor has exercised the power to reduce fees by 25 per cent in order to encourage voluntary registration of title in situations where compulsory first registration has not yet been triggered (see Land Registration (Fees) Order 1999 (SI 1998/2254), art 2(5)).

Land Registration Act 2002

As previously mentioned the new Act repeals LRA 1925 and substantially reforms the system of registered title. One of the key catalysts for the new Act is the anticipation that during the first decade of the twenty-first century conveyancing will switch to electronic form and the Act establishes the requisite framework to facilitate electronic (ie paperless) conveyancing.

The Act came into force on 13 October 2003. However, not all of its provisions took effect immediately. Further, it is submitted that students of land law will better understand the new regime if they have an understanding of the system of registered title operated under the 1925 legislation and which the new Act substantially reforms. Accordingly, in this chapter, the 'old system' of registered title (ie that operated under LRA 1925) is outlined in advance of a consideration of the main changes effected by the new Act.

7.2 Registration of title and the doctrine of notice

The equitable doctrine of notice so far as it relates to land with registered title was abolished by the LRA 1925. Its place was taken by registration. Failure to register rendered an equitable interest void against a purchaser, whether or not he had notice. This simple principle was however modified by s70(1) LRA 1925, in particular s70(1)(g) (see section 7.6 below), so that unregistered equitable interests might still bind a purchaser of registered land who had constructive or imputed notice of their existence. The effect of the saving provision in s70(1)(g) LRA 1925 was important to understand.

Minor interests and the doctrine of notice

The general rule was that only minor interests protected on the register would bind a purchaser: s20(1) LRA 1925.

Actual knowledge or notice of an unprotected minor interest would not affect a purchaser who took free from that interest. This was the effect of s59(6) LRA 1925, which provided that notice would not make an unprotected minor interest bind a purchaser.

This was part of the general policy of the LRA 1925 (maintained under LRA 2002): that *the state of the register was the paramount feature*. This rule should have created the distinction between estates and interests on the register which were binding against everyone and those not on the register which were not binding unless they came within s70(1) as overriding interests. This was the intention of the LRA 1925 and should have been the only distinction which could be made. Attempts have been made, however, to reintroduce the concept of 'notice' into registered land, in spite of s20(1) LRA 1925 (see *Barclays Bank plc* v *O'Brien and Another* [1993] 3 WLR 786).

Section 20(1) LRA 1925 provided that a transferee for value under a registered disposition of an absolute freehold title took free of 'all estates and interests whatsoever' unless they were protected on the register *or* took effect as overriding interests.

Problem areas

Under the system of registered title the state of the register, not the state of the purchaser's mind, is what is paramount. A purchaser is bound by what is on the register and by overriding interests. In essence the aim of the 1925 legislation was to do away with the doctrine of notice in respect of registered land.

In the years after 1925 some incursions by the doctrine of notice into registered land have taken place. First, two cases sought to introduce the concept of 'notice': *Peffer* v *Rigg* [1978] 3 All ER 745 and *Lyus* v *Prowsa Developments Ltd* [1982] 1 WLR 1044. The effect of these two cases was that if a purchaser had express knowledge of an unprotected minor interest he might still be bound by it if circumstances arose where a constructive trust ought to be imposed. This appeared to be the introduction of the doctrine of notice into registered land without regard to s59(6) LRA 1925.

The aforementioned view of these two cases could be countered in two ways.

1. By refering to s74 LRA 1925 which provided that no person dealing with a registered estate was to be affected by notice of a constructive trust, or
2. By relying upon the words of Lord Wilberforce in *Williams & Glyn's Bank* v *Boland* [1980] 2 All ER 408 who, when considering the effect of the doctrine of notice in relation to s70(1)(g) LRA 1925, concluded that:

> '... to have regard to ... the doctrine of notice ... would run counter to the whole purpose of the Act. The purpose, in each system, is the same, namely, to safeguard the rights of persons in occupation, but the method used differs. In the case of unregistered land, the purchaser's obligation depends on what he has notice of, notice actual or constructive. In the case of registered land, it is the fact of occupation that matters. If there is actual occupation, and the occupier has rights, the purchaser takes subject to them. If not he does not. No further element is material.'

To some extent the issue was clouded by Parliament itself by virtue of s5 Land Registration Act 1986, which abolished the Minor Interests Index and provided that priority between dealings with equitable interests in registered land was to be determined by the rule in *Dearle* v *Hall* (1828) 3 Russ 1. This meant that priority was established by the order in which notice was received by the trustees. This must undermine the clear distinction Lord Wilberforce was seeking to establish in *Williams & Glyn's Bank* v *Boland* [1980] 2 All ER 408 referred to above.

Conclusion

It is a danger if the clear principles of registered land are allowed to became clouded by the introduction of the rules of notice, and it may be that the words of Lord Wilberforce will become the basis for future decisions on this matter. This, at least, would uphold the main ethos of the 1925 property legislation to simplify conveyancing.

However, more recently the doctrine of notice has been reintroduced in cases of mortgages where a wife is seeking to have a legal charge of a lender attaching to the matrimonial home set aside on the ground that her consent to the charge (usually to help finance her husband's business) was obtained by undue influence or misrepresentation on the part of the husband of which the lender has constructive notice (see *Barclays Bank* v *O'Brien and Another* [1993] 3 WLR 786 and Chapter 14, section 14.8 below). As a result of this development a registered interest may now be defeated by notice.

7.3 Relationship between the Land Charges Act 1972 and the Land Registration Act 2002

Land Registration Act 2002

The system of registration established under the LRA 1925 now extends to cover the whole of England and Wales. However, this system was introduced gradually, starting in the larger towns. Once land is registered under the LRA 2002 (or LRA 1925 previously) it is called 'registered land'. Until the land is so registered, it remains 'unregistered land'. This will continue for some time in the future.

Land Charges Act 1925 (now 1972)

The LCA 1925 (now the LCA 1972) was introduced as a stop-gap measure, to provide protection for equitable interests and some legal interests (eg puisne mortgages) in land not yet registered under the now repealed the LRA 1925. The LCA 1972 applies to all land until that land is registered under the LRA 2002.

The relationship

The two systems of registration are independent and should not be confused. If land is *registered* the LRA 2002 applies. If land is *unregistered* the LCA 1972 applies. It is impossible for both systems of registration to apply to the same land at the same time. Either one or the other applies, not both. In relation to examination questions the candidate must be able to distinguish the respective effects of the two systems within any one problem area. The invitation is often to consider whether the answer would differ if the title to the land were not registered, or vice versa. However, the system of registered land is defined partly in terms of the LCA 1972, and so there is some link between the two systems.

7.4 Key principles of registration

In this section consideration is afforded to the following:

* Compulsory registration
* Time limit for registration
* Effects of non-compliance with registration
* Titles to freehold estates
* Titles to leasehold estates
* Contents of the title register
* The three principles

At the outset it is important to emphasise that the LRA 2002 is in many respects a restatement of the law under the LRA 1925. So, for example, the register of title is kept in the same way under the 2002 Act as under the LRA 1925. Likewise the classes of title and the broad effect of the registration of each is the same under thr LRA 2002 as under the LRA 1925. However, there are nevertheless a good number of changes in the law, some of which are very significant.

Compulsory registration

There are a number of situations which trigger compulsory registration, including the following three. First, where there is the transfer of a qualifying estate for valuable or other consideration, by way of a gift or in pursuance of a court order or by way of an assent. A qualifying estate is an unregistered legal estate which is either a freehold estate or a leasehold estate for a term which at the time of the transfer, grant or creation has more than seven years to run. Under the LRA 2002 the meaning of 'valuable or other consideration' (s4(1)) has been extended to include an estate transferred or granted for a negative value (s4(6)). Second, registration is also required upon the grant of a right to buy lease out of an unregistered legal estate in land. Third, registration is compulsory upon the creation of a first legal mortgage of a qualifying estate.

There are certain transfers which are not subject to compulsory registration, including the assignment of a mortgage term and the assignment or surrender of a lease to the owner of the immediate reversion with the result that the term merges with that reversion.

Time limit for registration

The period for registration is two months beginning with the date on which the relevant event occurs or such longer period as the Land Registrar may provide (s6(4) LRA 2002). The same arrangements applied under the LRA 1925. Given that the aim of the LRA 2002 is to maximise registration of land, it will almost always be the case that late registration will be allowed. The duty to register rests with the responsible estate owner (or his successor in title). This is the person to whom the relevant grant is made unless the trigger event is the first legal mortgage of a qualifying estate when the mortgagor has to apply for registration. In the event of a mortgagor not so applying rules can be made to enable a mortgagee to apply for registration.

Effect of non-compliance with registration

If a requirement to register is not complied with the relevant transaction becomes void so far as the transfer, grant or creation of the legal estate is concerned, ie the legal estate remains vested in the transferor. Where the transfer is of a qualifying estate for valuable or other consideration, by way of gift or in pursuance of a court order or by way of an assent, then the transferor holds the property on a bare trust for the transferee.

However, where the trigger for registration is the creation of a first legal mortgage of a qualifying estate the transferor holds the land subject to a contract 'made for valuable consideration to grant or create the legal estate concerned' (s7(2) LRA 2002). In either situation the transferee can apply for registration at any time subject to complying with the land registration rules.

Titles to freehold estates

There are three classes of title with which an applicant may be registered as proprietor in respect of a freehold estate – absolute title, qualified title and possessory title (they are the same as under the LRA 1925).

A person may be registered with an absolute title if the Registrar is of the view that the person's title to the estate is such that a willing buyer could properly be advised by a competent professional adviser to accept. This is a test which can be objectively applied by the court in assessing the decision of the Land Registry. Further, under s9(3) LRA 2002 the Registrar may disregard the fact that a person's title appears to him to be open to some objection 'if he is of the opinion' that the defect will not cause the holding under the title to be disturbed. Accordingly, the Registrar has a discretion to register a person with an absolute title even though the title is defective in some very minor way. Absolute title is the highest category.

A person may be registered with a qualified title if the Registrar is of the view that the person's title to the estate has been established for only a limited period or is subject to certain reservations which cannot be disregarded under s9(3) LRA 2002. However, in reality registration with a qualified title is in the words of the Land Registry 'extremely rare'.

A person may be registered with a possessory title if the Registrar is of the view that the person applying is in actual possession of the land and there is no other class of title with which he could be registered. There are in essence two main situations when a possessory title will be granted. First, where the person applying is in adverse possession of the land in question. Second, where the title deeds to the property cannot be found.

Titles to leasehold estates

There are four classes of title with which an applicant may be registered as proprietor in respect of a leasehold estate – absolute title, good leasehold title, qualified title and possessory title (they are the same as under the LRA 1925).

A person may be registered with an absolute title if the Registrar is of the view that the person's title to the estate is such that a willing buyer could properly be advised by a competent professional adviser to accept and the Registrar approves the lessor's title to grant the lease (ie the Registrar has to examine the freehold title and satisfy himself that the lease was properly granted out of it).

A person may be registered with a good leasehold title if the Registrar is of the view that the person's title to the estate is such that a willing buyer could properly be advised by a competent professional adviser to accept. However, the reality in practice is that many competent professional advisers would not favour the acceptance of a good leasehold title. They would much prefer securing absolute title.

In considering an absolute or good leasehold title the Registrar may, by virtue of s10(4), disregard the fact that a person's title appears to be open to some objection 'if he is of the opinion that the defect will not cause the holding under the title to be disturbed'. Accordingly, as with freehold titles the Registrar has a discretion to register a person with an absolute title (and additionally in the case of leaseholds with a good leasehold title), even though the title is defective in some very minor way.

A person may be registered with a qualified title if the Registrar is of the view that the person's title to the estate or the lessor's title to the reversion has been established for only a limited period or is subject to certain reservations which cannot be disregarded under s10(4) LRA 2002. As with freehold estates, registration with a qualified title is 'extremely rare'.

Finally, a person may be registered with a possessory title if the Registrar is of the opinion that the person applying is in actual possession of the land and there is no other class of title with which he could be registered. The situations in which such a title will most frequently arise have already been noted.

Contents of the title register

Where land is registered under the LRA 2002 all legal estates in land, both freehold and leasehold (except where the lease is for seven years or less), have a title register. This takes the place of title deeds and is kept in the Land Registry. Each register is divided into three sections – the property register, the proprietorship register and the charges register.

The *property register* gives the county or other administrative area and the parish where the land is situated. It describes the land, giving the address and a map reference, and shows where it is on a map. It also includes details of rights over other land of which the registered land has the benefit, ie where the registered land is the dominant tenement in respect of a legal easement.

The *proprietorship register* contains the name and address of the estate owner (freeholder or leaseholder) and gives details of any limitation on his powers of dealing with the land. It also specifies what title applies to the land (see above). This register tells you who owns the land.

The *charges register* contains details of encumbrances or charges owned by others over the registered land – interests which *burden* it, eg restrictive covenant. However, not included are local land charges which are registered separately in the registers kept in the local land charges registries.

Under the LRA 2002 the land is registered under the description of the land (most properties have a street number but fields, for example, are described by their location), not under the name of the estate owner as is the case with charges under the LCA 1972.

The three principles

It is often suggested that registered land is made up of three principles – the mirror principle, the curtain principle and the insurance principle. The register is designed to operate as a mirror, accurately reflecting the totality of estates and interests affecting the registered land. Set against this principle are overriding interests (which are not shown on the register but nevertheless bind the registered proprietor) and as such they are often referred to as a 'crack in the mirror'. As to the curtain principle, only the legal title is shown on the register – not equitable interests (they are behind the curtain!). The insurance principle involves the state guaranteeing the accuracy of the registered title. An indemnity is paid from public funds if a registered proprietor is deprived of his title or is otherwise prejudiced by the operation of the registered land scheme.

7.5 Registrable estates and interests

Estates and interests that are registrable comprise the following:

1. Fee simple absolute in possession.
2. Legal leases exceeding seven years.
3. Legal easements.
4. Legal rentcharges.
5. Legal mortgages.

The conveyance or creation of these estates or interests can only be accomplished by registration. Until and unless the grant is registered in the appropriate way it is ineffective. The legal estate or interest remains vested in the grantor but an equitable interest will pass to the transferee, mortgagee, etc (the effect of which is to render void an attempt to use unregistered conveyances to effect a disposition of a registered estate).

The proper method of registration depends on the estate or interest:

Fee simple

The grantee's (transferee's) name is entered in the proprietorship register in substitution of the previous proprietor's name (now done electronically). The transferee thereupon becomes the registered proprietor of the freehold estate.

Legal lease

A lease cannot be a registered disposition if the term is for seven years or less, or if it has a mortgage term subject to a right of redemption.

All other leases are registered dispositions. On their creation or assignment, the lessee's name is entered in the proprietorship register of the *leasehold estate*. A notice is also entered in the charges register of the superior estate affected.

The exclusion of short leases (ie leases for seven years or less under the LRA 2002 or leases for 21 years or less under the LRA 1925) from the list of registrable interests merits explanation. It would have been impracticable to require all short leases to be noted on the register. This could only have been done if there had been a significant increase in the Land Registry's resources (ie taxpayers money) which successive Governments did not find an attractive proposition. Further, many leases not required to be created by deed (ie those for three years or less) are often entered into informally and it was felt that it would have been unrealistic to expect a tenant of such a lease to protect his interest on the register.

Legal easement

A notice is entered in the charges register of the servient tenement; the details may also be entered in the property register of the dominant tenement.

Legal rentcharge

A notice is entered in the charges register of the land subject to the rentcharge. A rentcharge title is also created.

Legal mortgage

The charge (mortgage) is entered in the charges register of the mortgaged land and the chargee is also entered as proprietor of the charge. During the charge the chargee will have a charge certificate.

7.6 Overriding interests under the Land Registration Act 1925

Overriding interests loomed large in the scheme of the LRA 1925 – 'the crack in the mirror' – and they regularly featurered in examination questions on land registration. To better understand the scheme of overriding interests under the Land Registration Act 2002 an appreciation of the law prior to 13 October 2003 is recommended. A summary of that law is set out below.

Definition

Overriding interests were defined in s3(xvi) LRA 1925 as:

> '... all the incumbrances, interests, rights and powers not entered on the register, but subject to which registered dispositions are to take effect'.

Effect

The register was designed to act as a mirror accurately reflecting the totality of estates and interests affecting the registered land in question. However, overriding interests constitute a major qualification to this principle (sometimes referred to as a 'crack in the mirror'). They were rights which bound a purchaser without appearing on the register, even though he had no knowledge of them. They provided the most common pitfall for a purchaser of registered land. Hayton (*Registered Land*) put the matter thus:

> '... [overriding interests] provide a cavernous crack in the fundamental mirror principle under which the register is supposed to reflect accurately and irrefutably the current facts material to a particular title.'

Types of overriding interest

There were two classes of overriding interest:

1. Those specifically listed in s70(1) LRA 1925, although often in broad and uncertain terms.
2. Minor interests which were not protected by registration but were protected under s70(1)(g) LRA 1925 and converted into overriding interests.

Section 70(1) LRA 1925

The interests listed under s70(1) LRA 1925 were:

'(a) Rights of common, drainage rights, customary rights (until extinguished), public rights, profits à prendre, rights of sheepwalk, rights of way, watercourses, rights of water and other easements not being equitable easements required to be protected by notice on the register.

(b) Liability to repair highways by reason of tenure and other tenurial obligations.

(c) Liability to repair the chancel of a church.

(d) Liability in respect of embankments and sea and river walls.

(e) Tithe redemption annuities.

(f) Rights acquired or being acquired under the Limitation Act 1980.

(g) The rights of every person in actual occupation of the land or in receipt of the rents and profits thereof save where inquiry is made of such person and the rights are not disclosed.

(h) In the case of a possessory, qualified, or good leasehold title, all estates, rights, interests and powers excepted from the effects of registration.

(i) Rights under local land charges unless and until registered on the register at the Land Registry on the particular title concerned. [Such registration at the Land Registry was rare and the normal practice was to rely upon registration in the local land charges register.]

(j) Fishing, sporting, seignorial and manorial rights and franchises.

(k) Leases granted for a term not exceeding 21 years (s70(1)(k) LRA 1925 as amended by s4(1) LRA 1986).

(l) Mineral rights in respect of land registered before 1926.'

The most important of these were s70(1)(a), (f), (g) and (k), which will now be considered in more detail.

Section 70(1)(a). Most problems with this section arose from the strange jumble of interests listed, this jumble being due to the legislative history of this provision. The section was obviously intended to protect legal easements and profits, which was the position in unregistered land, but the meaning of the words 'equitable easements required to be protected by notice' was unclear, because there was no such requirement elsewhere in the Act. Equitable interests might be protected by notice, but they might also be protected by a caution. It was held in a county court case, *Payne* v *Adnams* [1971] CLY 6486, that this meant no equitable easements were excluded from s70(1)(a), but the general opinion of textbook writers and the Land Registry was that equitable easements could not be overriding interests. However, this opinion had to be read in the light of the decision of Scott J in *Celsteel Ltd* v *Alton House Holdings Ltd* [1985] 1 WLR 204. There the judge decided that under r258 of the Land Registration Rules 1925 an equitable easement was 'a right enjoyed with the land' for the purpose of that rule. As it affected the registered title it was an 'overriding interest' which did not need to be protected by notice on the register. However, under the Land Registration Act 2002, equitable easements and profits do not have overriding status (see section 7.8 below). Equitable profits à prendre can, on the other hand, be interests that overrode.

In addition the interests covered by s70(1)(a) included:

1. Legal easements or profits à prendre created before the servient tenement was registered.
2. Legal easements or profits à prendre created *other* than by express grant or reservation, ie by implied grant, under s62 LPA 1925 or the rule in *Wheeldon* v *Burrows* (1879) 48 LJ Ch 853, or by prescription.

Section 70(1)(f). This provided for rights arising by adverse possession. Once the owner's title had been extinguished the squatter could apply to be registered in the owner's place, and until this was done the owner held the property on trust for the squatter. See s75 LRA 1925. If he sold before this was done the squatter's title was binding on the purchaser. See *Bridges* v *Mees* [1957] Ch 475; *Chowood* v *Lyall* [1930] 2 Ch 156.

Section 70(1)(k). Section 70(1)(k) was intended to protect those leases which could not be registered dispositions because they were for 21 years or less.

Section 4 LRA 1986 amended s70(1)(k) LRA 1925. Any lease granted for a term of 21 years or less was henceforward an overriding interest. This removed the previous exemptions relating to leases without a rent or granted with a premium. Thus, the provisos for such a lease were that the term did not exceed 21 years, and that the lease was *granted*.

Section 70(1)(g). All the interests specifically listed in s70(1) were legal interests. The intention of the Act was to preserve legal interests as good against all the world, while making equitable interests registrable as minor interests. However, the wording of s70(1)(g) allowed the courts to interpret this subsection as including equitable interests, which were thereby made overriding interests. This distorted the basic structure of the Act and could result in bona fide purchasers of the legal estate of registered land being bound by unregistered equitable interests of which they had no notice, actual or constructive.

Section 70(1)(g) provided:

'The rights of every person in actual occupation of the land or in receipt of the rents or profits therefrom save where inquiry is made of such person and the rights are not disclosed.'

Before s70(1)(g) could apply *three conditions had to be satisfied*:

1. There had to be a right 'subsisting in relation to the land' which was capable of being protected by s70(1)(g). In *Webb* v *Pollmount Ltd* [1966] Ch 584 such a right was defined as being:

    > 'an interest in the land capable of enduring through different ownerships of the land according to normal conceptions of title to real property'.

    Neither occupation nor notice of occupation could by itself create the overriding interest. There had to be an existing 'right', protected by occupation, before s70(1)(g) could apply.

    Interests in land which were held to qualify as such 'rights' included:

    a) The equitable interests of co-owners holding under a pre-1997 statutory trust for sale: *Williams & Glyn's Bank* v *Boland* [1981] AC 487. The implications of this decision were considered by the Law Commission which concluded that as the law stood little could be done to alleviate the problems caused to purchasers or mortgagees by the protection afforded to the rights of persons in actual occupation. (Law Commission Report on the Implications of *Williams & Glyn's Bank* v *Boland*: Law Com No 115).

        In early 1985 the government introduced, in the House of Lords, a Land Registration and Law of Property Bill to take account of some of the problems posed by the decision in *Williams & Glyn's Bank* v *Boland*. However, there was failure to agree on the limits of any necessary amendments to s70(1)(g) LRA 1925 and the Bill was withdrawn.

    b) The right to specific performance of an estate contract: *Bridges* v *Mees* [1957] Ch 475.

    c) The right to specific performance of an option: *Webb* v *Pollmount* (above).

    d) The right of a tenant to make deductions from his rent in respect of the cost of repairs when the landlord was in breach of a repairing covenant: *Lee-Parker* v *Izzet* [1971] 1 WLR 1688.

    e) The rights of the deserted wife in occupation of the matrimonial home were considered by the Court of Appeal in *National Provincial Bank Ltd* v *Hastings Car Mart* [1964] Ch 665 but reversed by the House of Lords on appeal in *National Provincial Bank Ltd* v *Ainsworth* [1965] AC 1175, which led to the passing of the Matrimonial Homes Act 1967 – now the Matrimonial Homes Act 1983. Section 2(8)(b) of the 1983 Act provides that:

        > '... a spouse's right of occupation shall not be an overriding interest within the meaning of that Act [LRA 1925] affecting the dwelling house notwithstanding that the spouse is in actual occupation of the dwelling house.'

        However, see (c) below.

    Rights which could only be minor interests, and hence could not be protected by s70(1)(g), were:

a) The rights of a beneficiary under a Settled Land Act settlement: s86(2) LRA 1925.

b) The rights of a tenant arising from a notice under the Leasehold Reform Act 1967 of his desire to have the freehold or an extended lease: s5(5) Leasehold Reform Act 1967.

c) The rights of occupation of a spouse under Matrimonial Homes Act 1983, see (e) above.

This confirmed the rejection by the House of Lords in *National Provincial Bank* v *Ainsworth* [1965] AC 1175 of the Court of Appeal view that a deserted spouse's right of occupation was a 'right' within s70(1)(g).

Such a right was created by the Matrimonial Homes Act 1967, but it can be protected against third parties only by registration of a notice of matrimonial homes right in the charges register of registered land: s2(8)(a) Matrimonial Homes Act 1983 and r3 Land Registration (Matrimonial Home Rights) Rules 1997 (SI 1997/1964).

d) An access order under the Access to Neighbouring Land Act 1992. This order was not an overriding interest and had to be protected by a notice or caution. See s5 of the Access to Neighbouring Land Act 1992 which added a new s49(1) to the LRA 1925. The effect of the access order was to enable a landowner to go onto adjoining land to carry out work which was reasonably necessary to preserve his land.

A question arose whether contractual licences or licences protected in equity or by estoppel (see Chapter 13) were capable of being rights falling within s70(1)(g). On strict land law principles the answer should probably have been no. However, the decision in *Re Sharpe (A Bankrupt)* [1980] 1 All ER 198 did suggest that the equitable proprietary rights of a licensee which arose from expenditure on the land (the estoppel factor) were capable of falling within s70(1)(g) LRA 1925 when accompanied by actual occupation.

2. The owner of the right had to be in actual occupation of the land or in receipt of the rents or profits therefrom affected by the right.

'Actual occupation' was not defined by the Act. It was held to mean physical presence on the land, not some entitlement in law to occupy the land: *Williams & Glyn's Bank* v *Boland* (above).

A tenant under an unregistered registrable lease who did not occupy the premises himself and allowed someone else to live there rent-free, under a licence or a tenancy at will, did not qualify under either head (*Strand Securities* v *Caswell* [1965] Ch 958) even though he had a right to possession. The physical presence had to be reasonably continuous: *Epps* v *Esso Petroleum Co* [1973] 1 WLR 1071.

A person might have been in actual occupation even though this was not readily ascertainable from inspection of the property: *Hodgson* v *Marks* [1971] Ch 892.

The date when the owner had to be in occupation was said to be the date of the mortgage in *Paddington Building Society* v *Mendelsohn* (1985) 50 P & CR 244. This excluded from the protection of s70(1)(g) many purchasers who did not occupy until after the mortgage was completed which was usual in the case of many purchases of residential premises.

This point was confirmed by the House of Lords in *Abbey National Building Society* v *Cann* [1990] 2 WLR 832. There Lord Oliver confirmed that the relevant date for determining the existence of an overriding interest under s70(1)(g) LRA 1925 was the date of registration *but* the relevant date for determining whether the claimant was in actual occupation for the purposes of s70(1)(g) was the date of completion.

The brief facts of *Cann* were that in May 1984 George Cann (the son) applied for a loan of £25,000 on a flat. Contracts were exchanged in July 1984, a legal charge was executed on 6 August 1984 and the money was advanced. Completion took place on 13 August 1984 and on 13 September 1984 George was registered as proprietor and the building society was registered as proprietor of the charge.

Mrs Cann was the mother of George and she claimed the benefit of an overriding interest under s70(1)(g). She relied on the fact that on 13 August 1984 carpet layers began to lay her carpets and her son started to bring her furniture into the house from about 11.45 am on that day. Completion took place at about 12.20 pm on 13 August so there was a period of about 35 minutes in which she claimed to be in occupation vicariously (through her son and the carpet layers) prior to completion. The House of Lords rejected her claim. Mrs Cann knew that George would need a mortgage for the balance of the purchase money, and as she impliedly authorised raising the mortgage, Lord Oliver said that:

> '... she must necessarily have authorised him to that extent to create a charge ... having priority to her interest'.

The society was an equitable chargee for money actually advanced with priority over Mrs Cann's expectation of an interest if and when the property was acquired. Mrs Cann raised the question of the gap between occupation and completion which she said fed the estoppel against the society on the basis of *Church of England Building Society* v *Piskor* [1954] Ch 553. The House of Lords also rejected this claim. There was no *scintilla temporis* on 13 August between the acquisition of the property and the creation of the charge which could feed any estoppel in Mrs Cann. In the words of Lord Oliver they were '... precisely simultaneous ... [and] ... indissolubly bound up together'. Any purchaser who relied on such a mortgage acquired an equity of redemption and Lord Oliver described the effect of this as follows:

> '... from the very inception [land] charged with the ... loan without which it could never have been transferred at all'.

The House of Lords concluded that *Church of England Building Society* v

Piskor was wrongly decided. Finally, the acts of moving in Mrs Cann's furniture and laying her carpets prior to completion were not sufficient to amount to 'actual occupation' for the purpose of s70(1)(g). Rather, they were acts preparatory to occupation.

After *Cann* the appropriate date for ascertaining the existence of an overriding interest under the LRA 1925 was the date of registration, but the date for determining whether the claimant was in actual occupation was the date of completion.

This rule was applied by the House of Lords in *Lloyds Bank plc v Rosset* [1990] 2 WLR 867 where the majority decision of the Court of Appeal was reversed. Mrs Rosset and her builders had commenced renovation work on the property in early November 1982. Contracts were exchanged for the purchase on 23 November 1982. Mr Rosset took out a loan by way of overdraft on 14 December 1982 and completion in the name of Mr Rosset alone took place on 17 December with the bank taking a charge to secure the loan. The charge was registered on 7 February 1983.

Mrs Rosset claimed she had a beneficial interest in the property by way of a constructive trust which qualified as an overriding interest and which was binding on the bank under s70(1)(g) because she was in actual occupation both at the charge and registration. She claimed a significant contribution in kind to the acquisition because of the work done towards renovation and this gave rise to the constructive trust in her favour. No evidence was produced to show that Mrs Rosset would eventually have an interest in the property. The purchase was from Mr Rosset's resources and made in his name alone. The House of Lords said there was no constructive trust in favour of Mrs Rosset. Lord Bridge expressed the decision in a very forthright manner. The amount of renovation work

> '... expressed as a contribution to a property ... exceeding £70,000 ... [was] ... so trifling as to be almost de minimis'.

Lord Bridge went on say:

> 'If Courts must rely on conduct of parties to infer a common intention to share property beneficially and to give rise to a constructive trust direct contributions to ... purchase price by ... partner ... not the legal owner whether initially or by payment of mortgage instalments, would readily justify ... the creation of a constructive trust ... extremely doubtful whether anything less would do.'

The work done by Mrs Rosset in the renovation of the future matrimonial home which was then bought by Mr Rosset in his own name with his own finance was not sufficient to justify any inference of a common intention that she should have a beneficial interest in the property. As a consequence she had no 'right' within the terms of s70(1)(g) LRA 1925.

3. The saving clause to s70(1)(g) required that the purchaser had to have made inquiry of the owner of the right, and not been told of the right – 'save where inquiry is made of such person and the rights are not disclosed'.

Inquiry of the vendor alone would not suffice, it had to be of the person in 'actual occupation' (*Hodgson* v *Marks* (above)), nor would an inquiry made for another purpose suffice, eg under s40 Landlord and Tenant Act 1954: see *London and Cheshire Insurance* v *Laplagrene* [1971] Ch 499.

It could have been argued that this saving clause introduced some further element of 'notice' into registered land.

Effect of s70(1)(g)

If the three requirements were satisfied, the right claimed was converted by actual occupation from a minor interest into an overriding interest – which, of course, did not have to be protected by registration. See *Williams & Glyn's Bank* v *Boland* [1981] AC 487.

The date at which there must be actual occupation was the date of the conveyance to a purchaser. If the owner of the right subsequently ceased occupation, the right remained an overriding interest. It was not converted back into a minor interest. See *London and Cheshire Insurance* v *Laplagrene* (above).

Where land was registered, the conveyance was effected by the registration of the registered disposition. Any disposition of registered land was subject to all overriding interests existing at the date of registration, which was of necessity later than the date of the disposition.

The effect of the decision in *Williams & Glyn's Bank* v *Boland* must now be read in the light of the decision of the House of Lords in *City of London Building Society* v *Flegg* [1987] 2 WLR 1266.

If a legal charge is granted by trustees of registered land holding for tenants in common who remain in occupation, but with no knowledge of the creation of the charge, the interest of the tenants in common is transferred to the equity of redemption held by the trustees and the capital monies raised by the charge (the trustees in *Flegg* held the land on a trust for sale). The tenants in common could not claim an overriding interest under s70(1)(g) LRA 1925 to enable them to remain in occupation because their beneficial interest in the land was overreached by the legal charge, leaving nothing to which a right of occupation could attach. The payment to two trustees distinguishes this case from the *Boland* decision. The distinction was expressed by Lord Templeman. He referred to *Boland* and continued:

'There the husband was sole proprietor who was trustee for himself and his wife as tenants in common. The wife's beneficial interest coupled with actual occupation constituted an overriding interest to which the husband's mortgagee took subject. But in that case the interest of the wife was not overreached or overridden because the mortgagee advanced capital moneys to a sole trustee. If the mortgagee's interest had been overreached by advancing capital moneys to two trustees there would have been nothing to justify the wife in remaining in occupation as against the mortgagee.

There had to be a combination of an interest which justified continuing occupation plus actual occupation to constitute an overriding interest. Actual occupation was not an interest in itself.'

In considering s70(1)(g) the actual occupation was only the initial basis for the claim. Such occupation had to be regarded as the 'key to the door' (ie use the key to open the door to discover what 'rights' the occupier had claim to). It was only these rights which could satisfy the overriding interest provisions of s70(1)(g) LRA 1925.

The decision in *Abbey National Building Society* v *Cann* [1990] 2 WLR 832 had an important limiting effect on attempts to establish a s70(1)(g) overriding interest. The need for occupation at completion restricted most claims under s70(1)(g) to cases of later or second mortgages since it was unusual for a purchaser to be in occupation before completion. Accordingly, s70(1)(g) would have applied in the following situation: matrimonial home in husband's name alone; wife with an equitable interest; no mortgage initially, thereafter husband takes out a loan for his business secured on the matrimonial home and the lender failed to make enquiries of the wife.

Conclusion

Overriding interests, particularly s70(1)(g), were the subject of much litigation and an almost ever present feature in land law examination papers over the years. However, under the Land Registration Act 2002 the role of such interests has been significantly reduced and s70(1) LRA 1925 has been replaced by a new statutory regime (see section 7.8 below).

7.7 Other aspects of registration under the Land Registration Act 1925

In this section, brief consideration is afforded to the following:

- Classes of rights
- Minor interests
- Protection of minor interests
- Official search certificate
- Rectification of the register
- Compensation

Classes of rights

Under the LRA 1925 all estates and interests in land were divided into three categories – registrable interests, overriding interests and minor interests.

Registrable interests did not wholly equate to legal estates under s1(1) LPA 1925 because not all legal leases were registrable dispositions. Overriding interests were rights that bound a purchaser even though they could not be registered. They consisted of:

1. Legal estates or interests which were not registered dispositions.
2. Equitable or legal interests which were registrable as minor interests but protected as overriding interests under s70(1) LRA 1925, if not so registered.

All interests which were neither registered interests nor overriding interests were minor interests and had to be registered. Failure to register rendered a minor interest void against a purchaser unless it was protected under s70(1)(g). Accordingly, under the LRA 1925 all interests had to fit into one of the three categories.

Minor interests

As stated above, all interests which were neither registered dispositions nor overriding interests were minor interests and had to be protected by registration. A full definition of 'minor interest' was contained in s3(xv) LRA 1925 as:

'... the interests not capable of being disposed of by registered dispositions and capable of being overridden (whether or not a purchaser has notice thereof) by the proprietors unless protected as provided by this Act and all rights and interests which are not registered or protected on the register and are not overriding interests, and include:
(a) In the case of land subject to a trust of land, all interests and powers which are under the Law of Property Act 1925 capable of being overridden by the trustees, whether or not such interests and powers are so protected: and
(b) In the case of settled land, and interests and powers which are under the Settled Land Act 1925, and the Law of Property Act 1925, or either of them, capable of being overridden by the tenant for life or statutory owner, whether or not such interests and powers are so protected as aforesaid.'

Thus minor interests formed a residuary group.
There were two classes of minor interest:

1. Interests capable of being overreached on a proper sale. These were the interests of the beneficiaries under a trust of land or a strict settlement.
2. Interests which would not bind a purchaser unless registered. These included equitable interests registrable under the LCA 1972 for unregistered land and the miscellaneous equitable interests which were not registrable under that Act, eg beneficial interests under resulting trusts. Legal interests arising under a lease for 21 years or less, granted rent-free or at a fine, had also to be registered as minor interests.

However, under the Land Registration Act 2002 there is no category of interest known as 'minor interest' (see section 7.8 below).

Protection of minor interests

There were four methods of protecting minor interests. Protection was effective from the date of registration.

Notice
This was entered in the charges register, and ensured that any future dealings with the land took place subject to the interest protected by the notice. It could only be entered if the land certificate was produced, and so in general it could only be entered if the registered proprietor agreed.

Under the LRA 1925, the estate owner was given a copy of the entry in the land register, called a land certificate, provided there was no mortgage – this was merely a copy of the entries in the register and was not a document of title.

Caution
A caution merely gave the person entering it a right to be warned of any impending transaction with the land and gave him time to object. When the land was unregistered a caution against first registration might be entered, but the more usual caution was one against dealings. A caution was used when a notice could not be entered because the land certificate could not be obtained. It was weaker protection than a registered land charge in unregistered land because:

1. It put the onus on the cautioner to take steps to protect his interests.
2. It could be 'warned off' at any time by the registered proprietor requiring notice to be given to the cautioner that he must defend his claim within a given time.

The entry of a caution to protect an interest in land did not confer priority on that interest over a subsequently registered charge. This was established by the Court of Appeal in *Clark and Another* v *Chief Land Registrar and Another* [1994] 4 All ER 96.

Finally, it was important to remember that if the land certificate could not be obtained (ie it was not available to the applicant) a caution had to be used.

Inhibitions
An inhibition was an order of the court or the Registrar forbidding all dealings with the land either for a specified time period or until a specified event or until further notice. This was usually a last resort, although it was used routinely when a sole registered individual proprietor became bankrupt.

Restrictions
A restriction prevented dealing with the land until some condition was complied with, but unlike an inhibition it was not hostile to the registered proprietor. It was used, for example, when land was held on a trust of land or was settled land, to ensure that the overreaching mechanism was gone through.

Official search certificate
A bona fide purchaser for value could protect himself against interests which were registered *after* he had purchased the land but before he had been registered as

proprietor by obtaining an official search certificate. This gave the purchaser a temporary 30 working days 'priority period' so that, provided that he registered within that time, he was not bound by any minor interests which might be registered during the 30 working days. If the purchaser's application to register was correct and was delivered to the appropriate office of the Land Registry within the 30 working days, any entries on the register made during that 'priority period' would be postponed to this application of the purchaser (see Administration of Justice Act 1982).

Note: the Land Registration Act 2002 abolishes (subject to transitional arrangements) cautions and inhibitions with the result that the only ways of protecting rights and interests in registered land are by notice or restriction.

Rectification of the register

Need for rectification
Because mistakes can be made on registration, particularly on first registration, and because the registered title may become incorrect over a period, for instance if a person acquires squatter's title, provision is made for correcting entries on the register; this is known as rectification. The court has confirmed that there is no general discretion to order rectification of the register in any case in which it might be thought just to do so. See *Norwich and Peterborough Building Society* v *Steed* [1993] Ch 116. Corresponding provision is made for compensating those who suffer loss through rectification.

Power to rectify
Section 82(1) LRA 1925 conferred upon the High Court and the Chief Land Registrar a discretionary power to rectify the register if the circumstances of a given case came within certain specified gounds (eg where two or more persons were by mistake registered as proprietors of the same registered estate or of the same charge or where a mortgagee had been registered as proprietor of the land instead of as proprietor of a charge and a right of redemption was subsisting).

However, s82(3) of that Act placed restrictions on the circumstances in which the register might be rectified against 'the proprietor who is in possession' by providing that rectification could only be ordered against such a person in the following four situations.

The rectification gave effect to an overriding interest or an order of the court. These first two situations followed from the fact that the registered proprietor took subject to such interests existing at the date of registration. See *Chowood* v *Lyall* [1930] 2 Ch 156.

The registered proprietor had caused or substantially contributed to the error or omission by fraud or lack of proper care. This ground applied when the mistake was made by the first registered proprietor and rectification was claimed against him.

Where for any other reason it would have been unjust not to rectify the register against the proprietor. This gave a wide residuary discretion. The provisions were considered in *Re 139 High Street, Deptford* [1951] Ch 884 and in *Epps* v *Esso Petroleum Co* [1973] 1 WLR 1071.

In every case the remedy of rectification was discretionary. See *Re Sea View Gardens* [1967] 1 WLR 134; *Epps* v *Esso Petroleum Co* (above).

Compensation

Need for indemnity

By s83 LRA 1925 (as substituted by s2 of the Land Registration Act 1997) a person who *suffered loss* by reason of rectification or non-rectification of the register, or 'by reason of the loss or destruction of any document lodged at the registry for inspection or safe custody' (s83(3)) or inaccurate searches, *could* claim compensation.

At least five main points could be made about the substituted s83:

1. An indemnity was not payable where the loss was due wholly or partly to the claimant's fraud or wholly due to his own lack of proper care (s83(5)(a)).
2. An indemnity could be claimed if the loss suffered was partly a result of the claimants own lack of proper care. However, in such a situation the indemnity would be reduced to reflect the claimant's contributory negligence (s83(6)).
3. No indemnity was payable in respect of any costs or expenses (of whatever nature) incurred without the Registrar's consent except in cases of urgency (ie it was not practicable to seek the Registrar's consent before they were incurred) or retrospective consent (s83(5)(c)).
4. The rights of the Land Registry to recoup indemnities were widened (s83(10)). In particular, it could pursue any claim which could have been pursued by the person indemnified.
5. The claim for an indemnity had to be made within the limitation period. See *Epps* v *Esso Petroleum Co* (above).

The substituted s83 applied to indemnity claims made after 27 April 1997. Finally, no compensation was payable when the rectification was to give effect to an overriding interest because no loss had been suffered by the rectification. The proprietor's title had been subject to the overriding interest all the time and the rectification merely formalised the position. See *Re Chowood's Registered Land* [1933] Ch 574.

Amount of compensation

Compensation was calculated in accordance with the following principles:

1. Where the register was rectified, the value of the lost interest at the date of rectification.
2. Where the register was not rectified, the value of the lost interest at the date the mistake was made. See *Epps* v *Esso Petroleum Co* (above).

7.8 Land Registration Act 2002

Background

In September 1998, the Law Commission and the Land Registry jointly issued a consultative paper *Land Registration for the Twenty-First Century* (Cm 4027, Law Com No 254). The purpose of the paper was to seek views on a number of proposals for making dealings in land simpler, quicker and cheaper. There were two main driving forces behind this initiative. First, it was anticipated that during the first decade of the new millennium conveyancing would switch to electronic form. Second, there was a desire to place land registration on a new basis rather than as a mirror of the system of unregistered conveyancing (the approach of the 1925 legislation). A new Act was envisaged. The Joint Working Group recognised that if there was a move to electronic conveyancing the current 'registration gap' between completion of a sale or other transaction and its registration would disappear.

The paper put forward for discussion a wide range of proposals of which the following three were particularly noteworthy. First, there was a proposal to reduce the duration of registrable leases from 21 years to 14, with a possible alternative of permitting voluntary registration by lessees of those of the shorter duration. Second, in relation to overriding interests, significant reform of s70(1)(g) LRA 1925 was proposed, together with abolition of some of the more obsolete categories of such interests. Third, there was a proposal to replace the current law on adverse possession (which was deemed to be unsatisfactory) with an entirely new substantive system applicable only to registered land. In particular there was a proposal to protect a registered title against squatters. The Joint Working Group hoped that the reform could be integrated easily into the current system without undue expense – indeed they stated quite clearly that changes involving unquantifiable costs should be avoided.

Commencement and effect

The Act received the Royal Assent on the 26 February 2002. The Act came into force on 13 October 2003. However, not all of its provisions took effect immediately. In particular the electronic conveyancing regime is unlikely to become operative until 2007 at the earliest. The Act repeals the Land Registration Act (LRA) 1925 and confers wide rule-making powers. The Act fundamentally changes the system of registered title in England and Wales. It is divided into twelve parts. In the ensuing paragraphs an outline of the Act's objectives, and of the main changes it makes, are given.

Objectives

The principal objective of the Act 'is that, under the system of electronic dealing with land that it seeks to create, the register should be a complete and accurate reflection of the state of the title of the land at any given time, so that it is possible to investigate title to land on line, with the absolute minimum of additional enquiries and inspections': para 1.5 *Land Registration for the Twenty-First Century: A Conveyancing Revolution* (2001) Law Com No 271. In essence the Act advocates the principle of the 'conclusive register'.

The rationale for the aforementioned objective is to make conveyancing 'quicker, easier and cheaper' (which was the rationale for the introduction of the system of registered title in the first instance). However, it is recognised that this principal objective cannot be fully achieved because the law allows certain rights and interests in land to be created informally, eg rights arising by estoppel, leases granted for three years or less. Nevertheless, much of the Act is designed to secure the principal objective and it deals with some of the main obstacles to achieving that objective under the current system of registered title. For example, an overriding interest binds a purchaser without appearing on the register and even though the purchaser had no knowledge of it: see s70(1) LRA 1925. As such they are a significant impediment to the 'mirror principle' (ie the register is designed to operate as a mirror accurately reflecting the totality of estates and interests affecting the registered land) and are often referred to as a 'crack in the mirror'. While it is not feasible to abolish all overriding interests, the Act significantly reduces the overall importance of such interests (see below).

Main changes

Electronic conveyancing. The Act establishes the requisite framework to move from the current paper-based system of conveyancing to one which is wholly electronic (ie paperless). The electronic conveyancing regime is set out in Part 8 of the Act. The Land Registry will provide an electronic communications network so that the whole conveyancing procedure can be conducted on line. The network will be a secure one and limited to solicitors and licensed conveyancers authorised to have access to it under a network access agreement (the criteria to be satisfied in order to gain such authorisation has still to be decided). Whilst the Land Registry is required to enter into a network access agreement with professionals who meet the relevant criteria, those who do not satisfy it or who display consistently poor conveyancing standards will be excluded. Anyone denied such access will have a right to appeal to the Adjudicator with a further right of appeal to the High Court. The terms of the network access agreement may require an authorised professional to provide monitoring information, eg confirming that a pre-completion stage such as obtaining a mortgage offer has been completed. This is designed to better help the Land

Registry manage a chain of transactions. The Land Registry could charge for access to this network.

An important consequence of electronic conveyancing is that it is anticipated that registration will take place at the same time as completion (currently registration can be up to three months after completion). Simultaneous registration will involve authorised solicitors/licensed conveyancers actually changing the register and will constitute a significant departure from the current arrangements which involve applications for changes being made to the Land Registry.

Private individuals carrying out their own conveyancing are not excluded from electronic conveyancing since the Act imposes a duty on the Land Registry to provide assistance to such individuals. In practice this will invariably involve such individuals travelling to a district land registry where the Registrar will carry out the transaction electronically on their behalf. Further, the Act gives the Lord Chancellor the power to make the use of electronic conveyancing compulsory. However, the provisions on e-conveyancing did not come into force on 13 October 2003. Rather it is anticipated that they will only be brought into force after the Lord Chancellor has consulted widely and the necessary structures (both technological and administrative) are in place. What will be crucial will be keeping on top of the IT issues. The expectation is that the introduction of e-conveyancing will take place in 2007 or 2008. The reality is that initially there will be both a paper and an electronic system for conveyancing, with the latter gradually replacing the former.

First registration. The Land Registration Act 1997 made first registration compulsory in a number of new situations (ie over and above registration on sale or on the grant or assignment of a lease for more than 21 years), including conveyances by way of gift and first legal mortgages of freeholds or leaseholds having more than 21 years to run. The Act makes some further changes in this area (see Part 2 of the Act). In particular, it extends compulsory first registration to leases with more than seven years to run (rather than 21 years as previously) and to the assignment of leases with more than seven years to run (rather than 21 years as previously). This change will undoubtedly increase the administrative burden on the Land Registry. Under the 2002 Act, voluntary registration is available as widely as it was under the LRA 1925 – namely that a person with an unregistered legal estate can apply for registration at any time. However, some new interests are available for voluntary registration, namely profits à prendre in gross (eg shooting or fishing rights) and franchises provided they are held for an interest equivalent to a fee simple absolute in possession or a lease with at least seven years to run. A franchise is a grant of a right (say to hold a market or fair) to a person by the Crown out of the Royal prerogative. However, the view of both the Law Commission and the Land Registry is that it is not yet feasible to introduce compulsory registration for all remaining unregistered land.

Registered dispositions. The range of such dispositions is extended to include the grant of leases for a term of more than seven years.

The Act gives the Lord Chancellor the power to further reduce the length of registrable leases. The expectation is that the length of registrable leases will be further reduced to three years once it is clear that the Land Registry and the 'conveyancing industry' can cope with such a change.

Overriding interests. As previously noted, the role of such interests is significantly reduced. Some overriding interests are abolished outright, some will lose their overriding status after ten years (in the case of such interests they will at the end of this period have to be entered on the register in order to be protected) and some others are narrowed in scope. The guiding principle of the new regime is that an interest should only rank as an overriding one if it is not reasonable for it to be protected in the register.

Under the new regime what has to be determined is whether the transaction said to be affected is a *first registration of title* (in which case Schedule 1 of the Act applies) or a *disposition of an already registered title* (in which case Schedule 3 of the Act applies). There are some differences as between these two Schedules.

1. *First registration – Schedule 1*
    Schedule 1 contains a list of these interests which override the effect of first registration and subject to which first registration is affected and which do not have to appear on the register. They are as follows:

    a) leases of under seven years;
    b) interest of a person in actual occupation except for an interest under the SLA;
    c) legal easement or profit;
    d) local land charge.

2. *Disposition of already registered title – Schedule 3*
    Schedule 3 contains a list of unregistered interests which override a registered disposition and subject to which a *registered disposition* takes effect. They are as follows:

    a) lease granted for less than seven years;
    b) interest of a person in actual occupation relating to land of which he is in actual occupation except:

    • an interest under SLA;
    • an interest of a person of whom inquiry was made before the disposition and who failed to disclose the right when he could reasonably be expected to do so; and
    • an interest belonging to a person whose occupation would not have been obvious on a reasonably careful inspection of the land and of which the person to whom the disposition was made *did not have actual knowledge.*

c) Legal easement or profit *except* for an easement or profit à prendre which is not registered under the Commons Registration Act 1965 and which at the time of the disposition is not within the actual knowledge of the transferee and would not have been obvious on a reasonably careful inspection of the land in question (para 3(i)). However, the exception in para 3(i) does not apply if the person entitled to the easement or profit can prove that it has been exercised in the period of one year prior to the day of the disposition.

At least four key points can be made about these Schedules. First, Schedule 3 interests are more precisely and narrowly defined than those in Schedule 1. This means that more 'interests that override' will bind on a first registration of title under Schedule 1. An explanation as to why Schedule 3 interests are narrower in scope than those in Schedule 1 may well be that more interests that override will fall into place at the disposition of registered title (Schedule 3) stage than at first registration (Schedule 1), which is in essence a process of discovery. And since the aim of the Act is to reduce the significance of interests that override, Schedule 3 interests are accordingly narrower in scope. Second, equitable easements and profits are excluded from both Schedules (thus nullifying the judgment of Scott J in *Celsteel Ltd* v *Alton House Holdings Ltd* [1985] 1 WLR 204 – see section 7.6). Third, Schedule 3 denies overriding status to certain legal easements, eg those not exercised within one year before the transaction: see para 3 above. Fourth, an obvious difference between them and s70(1)(g) LRA 1925 is that in contrast to the latter and the 'old regime' the 'receipt of rent and profits' does not give rise to overriding status under either Schedule.

Under both Schedule 1 and 3 some overriding interests will lose their overriding status after ten years – franchises, manorial rights, rights in respect of embankments, sea or river walls etc. As previously noted, at the end of this ten-year period they will have to be entered on the register in order to be protected.

Adverse possession. The pre Act law on adverse possession which was considered to be unsatisfactory is replaced with an entirely new substantive system applicable only to *registered land* (see Part 9 of the Act). The effect of the new arrangements is to make it much more difficult for a squatter to obtain title to registered land than it was under the old law. This is achieved by stipulating that a registered proprietor's title is not lost through mere lapse of time. Rather, the onus is on the squatter to take action if he wants to obtain title to registered land. The new regime is in keeping with the principle that, where registered land is concerned, registration should confer title rather than possession. This can be done by way of an application to be registered as proprietor after a period of ten years' adverse possession (ie there is a separate limitation period of ten years for registered land). Upon receipt of such an application the Land Registry will notify the registered proprietor and other interested parties of it and such persons will be able to object by serving a counter-notice within a prescribed period. In the event of no counter-notice being served the squatter is registered as proprietor. However, if a counter-notice is served the squatter's application is dismissed unless he can establish one of three limited grounds what could entitle him to be registered. The three grounds are as follows (see para 5 of Schedule 6 to the Act):

1. It would be unconscionable because of an equity by estoppel for the proprietor to seek to dispossess the applicant and the circumstances are such that the applicant ought to be registered as proprietor.
2. The applicant is for some other reason entitled to be registered as proprietor.
3. The land to which the application relates is adjacent to land belonging to the applicant, the exact boundary line has not been determined and for at least ten years the applicant or a predecessor reasonably believed the land belonged to him and the land was registered more than a year before the application.

It will be interesting to see if the judges construe these exceptions broadly (thus facilitating adverse possession) or narrowly. Where an application is rejected a further application can be made if the applicant is in adverse possession for a further period of two years.

Finally, the law relating to unregistered land would not be affected. The distinction between registered and unregistered land in this regard is justified on the basis that title to unregistered land depends on possession and also because unregistered land probably has a very limited future.

Protection of rights and interests. Subject to transitional arrangements, the Act abolishes cautions and inhibitions with the result that the only ways of protecting rights and interests in registered land are by notice or restriction.

As with the scheme under the LRA 1925, interests under trusts of land and strict settlements cannot be registered nor can leases for less than three years nor restrictive covenants in a lease. As previously noted, there is no category of interest known as 'minor interest' under the Act. Rather there are interests that need to be protected by an entry on the register by way of the new style notice.

A notice (ie 'new notice') can be either an *agreed notice* or a *unilateral notice*. It is an entry in the register in respect of the burden of an interest affecting registered land. An *agreed notice* is one which is registered either by the registered proprietor with his consent or where the Registrar is satisfied as to the validity of the entry. If one of these is not satisfied then the notice is a *unilateral one*. If a unilateral notice is registered the Registrar has to give notice to the proprietor and any other prescribed person. A unilateral notice must indicate it is such and identify the beneficiary of the notice. The proprietor or a person entitled to be so registered may apply to the Registrar for the cancellation of the notice. The Registrar must then give notice of that application to the beneficiary of the notice. If the beneficiary does not object within the prescribed period the Registrar must cancel the notice.

Restrictions still exist. They are similar to those under the LRA 1925. A restriction can prohibit the making of an entry relating to a disposition or a disposition of a specified kind or prohibit the making of an entry indefinitely, for a specified period or until a specified event. Where a restriction is registered no entry can be made on the register except in accordance with its terms. A person can apply for a restriction if he is the proprietor, has the proprietor's consent or has sufficient interest. The Registrar may enter a restriction if it is necessary or desirable to do so to:

1. prevent unlawfulness in relation to dispositions;
2. secure that overreachable interests are overreached;
3. protect a right or claim in relation to a registered estate.

No restriction can be entered to protect an interest which could be the subject of a notice. Finally, notice of the entry must be given to the proprietor.

Proprietary interest in land. Rights established by proprietary estoppel and 'mere equities' are regarded as proprietary interests in land for the purposes of the Act.

Rectification of the register. The law in this regard is substantially revised with the new designation being 'alteration' (see s65 and Schedule 4 of the Act).

When the person successfully claiming rectification/alteration is replaced as the registered proprietor, he will normally take free of incumbrances created by the wrongfully registered proprietor unless he is by his conduct estopped from taking priority. See *Argyle Building Society* v *Hammond* (1984) 49 P & CR 148; see also *Re Dances Way, West Town, Hayling Island* [1962] Ch 490.

The effective date is the date of the application for registration. Where the rectification results in the entry of a notice on the register, earlier dispositions will not be affected by the interest, the subject of the notice.

This ability to seek rectification is one of the dangers in registered land. It can have a serious effect on the claims of certainty of title which are made on behalf of registered land as a supposed advantage over land with unregistered title. Megarry and Wade put the matter thus:

'The first English Act for the registration of title proclaimed its intention "to give certainty to the title to real property". However, the reality is that registration does not confer an indefeasible title, for there is a discretion to rectify the register in cases of error, omission or mistake' (at p290).

Crown land. Prior to the Act coming into force a considerable amount of Crown land could not be registered. This was because only an estate in land could be registered and Crown land was not held for any estate because in consequence of the Norman Conquest in 1066 all land in England and Wales belonged to the Crown by virtue of conquest (ie estates are held of the Crown). However, the Act enables the Crown to grant itself a freehold estate so as to register it (see Part 7 of the Act). The rationale for this change is to better protect Crown land from adverse possession. There are also provisions to ensure that where a registered freehold escheats to the Crown it remains in the register.

Independent adjudication. The Lord Chancellor is to appoint a new independent adjudicator (Adjudicator to HM Land Registry) to deal with disputes between individuals and the Land Registry concerning land registration matters (see Part 11 of the Act).

Under the old regime such matters were dealt with by the Solicitor to the Land Registry. However, the latter was not seen as independent (this is an example of the Human Rights Act 1998 having an impact upon the new legislation).

Conclusion
The move to electronic conveyancing is an inevitable consequence of the technological advancements that have been taken place in recent years. In providing a framework for on line conveyancing, the opportunity has been taken to reform and develop a number of other areas of the law relating to registration of title. Given that all existing legislation has been replaced, all conveyancers would be advised to start familiarising themselves with the new set of provisions as soon as possible. Even after the new provisions become law, full electronic conveyancing will still be some years away as there are still several important matters that need to be addressed, eg how will the government collect stamp duty (currently 4 per cent of purchase price on property sales in excess of £500,000, 3 per cent on transactions between £250,000 and £500,000 and 1 per cent on transactions between £60,000 and £250,000) if a transaction takes place on line. The success or otherwise of on line conveyancing will in reality depend upon whether paperless conveyancing commands the support and confidence of conveyancers and property purchasers.

The Lord Chancellor, Lord Irvine, in giving the government's response to the Land Registry's Quinquennial Review published in June 2001 (many of the Review's recommendations are anticipated by the Act), concluded that:

> '... the development of electronic conveyancing services will bring major benefits to both homebuyers and businesses in their dealings in land and property. They will make the property market more transparent and the property transaction process faster, cheaper and more efficient.'

As previously noted, a key aim of the Law Commission and the Land Registry in their September 1998 consultative paper was to put land registration on a new basis rather than as a mirror of the system of unregistered conveyancing which was the approach of the 1925 Act. The need for a new basis is because society at the start of the twenty-first century is vastly different in social, economic and technological terms from that which existed at the start of the twentieth century. In essence, putting land registration on a new basis is essential. Nevertheless, despite the obvious merits of the new Act, one thing that land lawyers and conveyancers can be sure of is that like any new legislation which effects comprehensive reform it will not be without its problems.

8

Settlements of Land

8.1   Introduction

8.2   Settlements under the Settled Land Act 1925

8.3   How is a settlement created?

8.4   Who is the tenant for life?

8.5   When there is no tenant for life

8.6   Who are the trustees of the settlement?

8.7   Powers of the tenant for life

8.8   Personal nature of the statutory powers: s108

8.9   Protection of the statutory powers: s106

8.10 Powers remain with the tenant for life: s104

8.11 Death of the tenant for life

8.12 Acquisition by the tenant for life of the settled land: s68

8.13 Dispositions by the tenant for life and protection of purchasers

8.14 Capital money

8.15 Functions of Settled Land Act trustees

8.16 Trusts for sale under Law of Property Act 1925

8.17 Position of trustees for sale

8.18 Position of the beneficiaries

8.19 Ad hoc settlements and trusts for sale

8.20 Strict settlements and registered land

8.21 Comparison of the strict settlement and the trust for sale

8.22 Trusts of Land and Appointment of Trustees Act 1996

8.1 Introduction

As has already been noted, under the 1925 legislation there were two methods of creating a succession of interests in land, settlements under the Settled Land Act 1925 and trusts for sale which were generally controlled by the Law of Property Act 1925.

The main difference between the two methods of settlement was that in the case of the strict settlement the legal ownership and the powers of dealing with the land are vested in the tenant for life, who will normally be the beneficiary who is at present entitled to possession of the land. He has a dual role and is in the position of a trustee as well as being a beneficiary. The onus is upon him to exercise his powers (see section 8.7) in the best interests of all the beneficiaries including himself. The trustees of the settlement will oversee the exercise of these powers and will either be told of the tenant for life's intention to use them or give their consent to his doing so. Any money received as a result of exercising these powers will be paid to the trustees of the settlement.

In the case of the trust for sale, the legal ownership and the powers of dealing with the property were vested in separate trustees for sale. It was the trustees for sale who would receive any money derived from the exercise of their powers.

On 1 January 1997 a new unitary system of holding land on trust was introduced with the coming into force on that date of the Trusts of Land and Appointment of Trustees Act 1996. Henceforward all land held on trust is held by the new concept of the *trust of land*. The only exceptions to this regime are: (1) strict settlements in existence before the coming into force of the 1996 Act; and (2) land to which the Universities and College Estates Act 1925 applies. Under the 1996 Act, all existing trusts for sale (ie those in existence before 1 January 1997) are automatically trusts of land. It is still possible to create an express trust for sale albeit as one type of the new trust of land. Further, it provides that no new strict settlement can be created under the Settled Land Acts after the commencement date. Accordingly, since pre 1996 Act strict settlements are still in existence it is necessary (at least in the short term) for students to have an appreciation of the Settled Land Act regime.

8.2 Settlements under the Settled Land Act 1925

What constituted settled land prior to 1 January 1997? By s1(1) of the Settled Land Act 1925 a settlement is created by any document or documents which deal with land in one of the ways set out in the subsection. The most important of these are:

1. Where the land stands for the time being limited in trust for any persons by way of succession. The most common example of such a limitation is 'to A for life and then to B in fee simple'. There are certain special sorts of succession which are included in separate heads in s1(1). They include:

2. Entails, eg 'to A for an entailed interest'.
3. An estate subject to a gift over on the failure of issue or other event (but see Chapter 4, section 4.4, for conditional fees, for example 'to A in fee simple but if A dies without issue then over to B').
4. A determinable fee (see, again, Chapter 4, section 4.4), for example 'to A in fee simple until A commits some act of bankruptcy'.
5. Where land is given to an infant.
6. Where the land is subject to a family rentcharge (such charges are not affected by the Rentcharges Act 1977), for example 'to A in fee simple but charged with the payment of £1,000 per annum to A's widow during her lifetime'.

It is important to emphasise that these were the main situations prior to the coming into force of the Trusts of Land and Appointment of Trustees Act 1996 when a strict settlement would have arisen. The effect of s2(1) of the 1996 Act is to prevent new strict settlements being created after 31 December 1996. Today all new successive interests in land fall under the new trust of land system – although as noted previously entailed interests are abolished by the 1996 Act (see Schedule 1 para 5).

8.3 How is a settlement created?

By s4(1) SLA 1925 every settlement must be effected by *two documents*, a trust instrument and a vesting deed. The latter contains all that a purchaser of the settled land needs to know, while the details of the trust are contained in the trust instrument which the purchaser is not entitled to see. These details are said to be *'behind the veil'* or to be subject to the *'curtain principle'*. The object is to enable the land to be sold easily in spite of the beneficial interests of the settlement.

Contents of the vesting deed – the public document

The vesting deed must (s5(1)):

1. Describe the settled land.
2. Declare that the settled land is vested in the person named as tenant for life on the trusts contained in the trust instrument.
3. Contain the names of the trustees of the settlement.
4. Contain any additional powers of the tenant for life.
5. Name the persons with power to appoint new trustees.

The purpose of the vesting deed is to vest the legal fee simple in the person who for the time being is to have the enjoyment of the land itself. The tenant for life obtains the legal estate which is held on the trusts of the settlement.

Contents of the trust instrument – the private document

The trust instrument must (s4(3)):

1. Declare the trusts affecting the settled land.
2. Appoint or constitute trustees of the settlement.
3. Contain the power, if any, to appoint new trustees of the settlement.
4. Set out any additional powers.
5. Bear any stamp duty payable.

This trust instrument declares the beneficial interests of the tenant for life and successors and is said to be 'behind the curtain'.

Where the settlement is made by will, the will itself is the trust instrument. The testator's personal representatives must vest the legal estate in the tenant for life by means of a vesting assent, which acts as the vesting deed.

If after the execution of the principal vesting deed more land is acquired within the settlement, it will be conveyed to the tenant for life by a subsidiary vesting deed.

Pre-1926 settlements

Before the SLA 1925 settlements could be created by a single document. To bring pre-1926 settlements into line with the new legislation it was provided that the single document should be treated as the trust instrument, and that as soon as was practicable the trustees of the settlement should, and, if so requested by the tenant for life, must, execute a vesting deed. However, it was also provided that in such cases a purchaser is entitled to look at the trust instrument as well as the vesting deed.

Incompletely constituted settlements

If an *inter vivos* settlement is not made by means of these two documents, a vesting deed and a trust instrument, then by s4(1) the legal estate is not transferred and therefore remains in the settlor. The only way this can be put right is by the trustees executing a vesting deed (s9(2)) (a rare example of a legal estate being conveyed by a person who does not have it himself).

Furthermore, until there are two documents, s13 (the so-called 'paralysing' section) operates. This provides that a tenant for life can make no disposition of the legal estate in the land until a vesting deed has been executed in accordance with the Act. Any purported disposition before this has been done operates as a contract to carry out the transaction after the vesting deed has been executed. This, of course, would be a registrable estate contract. There are exceptions to the paralysing effect of s13:

1. Where the disposition is made by a personal representative.
2. Where the disposition is made to a purchaser of a legal estate without notice of

the settlement – although after 1925 this must be registered as a land charge Class C(iv).

3. Where the settlement has come to an end. A settlement will end where one person becomes solely and absolutely entitled and the trusts set out in the trust instrument are concluded. *Re Alefounders' WT* [1927] 1 Ch 360.

4. Where s1 Law of Property (Amendment) Act 1926 applies. This provides that where a person of full age is entitled to land subject to family charges (which make the land settled land by s1(1)(v)), the person entitled may sell the land subject to those charges without going through the SLA 1925 formalities. This only applies where the only reason that the land is settled is because of the charges, and gives the estate owner the choice of going through the SLA procedure and selling free of the charges which are overreached, or conveying subject to the charges without the SLA formalities. The latter is not attractive to a purchaser because he only has the protection of a personal indemnity from the vendor.

When there has been an incompletely constituted settlement a purchaser may look at the trust instrument.

8.4 Who is the tenant for life?

The tenant for life is the key person in a strict settlement because by s16(1) the legal estate is vested in him, and by s108 all the powers of management of the settled land are exercisable by him. The person who is tenant for life is defined by ss19 and 20 SLA 1925.

Section 19 contains the general definition which applies to most settlements:

'The person of full age who is for the time being beneficially entitled under a settlement to possession of the settled land for his life is for the purposes of this Act the tenant for life of that land ...'

However, because of the wide definition of settled land in s1(1) SLA 1925, it is necessary to define 'tenant for life' in special cases with more particularity. This is done by s20 which provides that each of the following persons being of full age shall, when his estate or interest is in possession, have the powers of a tenant for life under the Act:

1. A tenant in tail (with the coming into force of the Trusts of Land and Appointment of Trustees Act 1996 no new entailed interests can be created in real or personal property – Schedule 1 para 5).
2. A person with a conditional fee.
3. A person entitled to a base or determinable fee.
4. A tenant for years determinable on life, not holding merely under a lease at a rent. This definition excludes a person paying even a nominal rent.

5. A person entitled to the income of land under a trust during his own or any other life.
6. A person entitled in fee simple subject to family charges (this class of tenant for life can sell the land subject to the charge, see above).

8.5 When there is no tenant for life

There are certain circumstances in which, although the land is settled land, there is no tenant for life. The most common of these are:

1. Where the person entitled is an infant.
2. Where no person is entitled to the whole income, for example, where only a definite fraction of the income is to be paid to the person entitled, the remainder to be accumulated (*Re Frewen* [1926] Ch 580), or where a fixed annual amount (an annuity) is to be paid.
3. Where no person is entitled to the income, that is, where there is a discretionary trust.

When there is no tenant for life, then by s23 the powers of the tenant for life are vested in the statutory owner, defined in s117(1)(xxvi) as either:

1. The person of full age on whom the settlement expressly conveys the powers of a tenant for life ; *or*
2. (more commonly) the trustees of the settlement.

8.6 Who are the trustees of the settlement?

Section 30 SLA 1925 sets out five definitions, each of which must be applied in turn; in other words, if there is no person within head (1) then head (2) must be examined, but if there are persons within head (1) then they will be trustees of the settlement and there is no need to look at head (2). The sequence should be noted carefully with particular reference to the first two heads.

The various heads are:

1. The persons who under the settlement are trustees with power to sell or to consent to or to approve sale. In any event such power of sale will only be exercised by the tenant for life, but the attempt is enough to make such persons the trustees of the settlement.
2. The persons expressly declared by the settlement to be 'trustees for the purposes of the Settled Land Act'. The appointment must be declared to be 'for the purposes' of the SLA 1925.
3. Persons who under the settlement are trustees with a power or duty to sell other land comprised in the settlement.

4. Persons who under the settlement are trustees with a future power or duty to sell the settled land.
5. Persons appointed by deed by those able to dispose of the whole equitable interest in the settled land.

When a settlement arises under a will or intestacy, and there are no trustees under any other provisions, the personal representatives are trustees of the settlement until others are appointed (s30(3)).

Where none of the above provisions apply, or where it is in any other case expedient, an application can be made to the court under s34 by the tenant for life, statutory owner or any other person having under the settlement an estate or interest in the settled land. In such a case the court will not appoint the tenant for life as trustee of the settlement. See *Re Harrop* (1883) 24 Ch D 617. Otherwise there is no general restriction on the tenant for life becoming a trustee of the settlement, although such an appointment may not always be practicable. See s68(3) SLA 1925.

8.7 Powers of the tenant for life

In *Re Mundy and Roper's Contract* [1899] 1 Ch 275 Chitty LJ described the powers of the tenant for life as follows:

'The object is to render land a marketable article, notwithstanding the settlement. Its main purpose is the welfare of the land itself and of all interested therein, including the tenants and not merely the persons taking under the settlement ... The scheme adopted is to facilitate the striking off from the land of the fetters imposed by the settlement; and this is accomplished by conferring on tenants for life in possession and others considered to stand in a like relation to the land, large powers of dealing with the land by way of sale, exchange, lease and otherwise and by jealously guarding those powers from attempts to defeat them or to hamper this exercise.'

This jealous 'guarding' is now supported by s106 SLA 1925 which provides that these powers given by the SLA to the tenant for life cannot be excluded, restricted or modified by the settlement or by any contract made by the tenant for life.

The various powers of the tenant for life may be demonstrated by the following diagram relating to the authorisations necessary before the respective powers are exercised.

Powers exercisable on giving notice to the trustees	Powers exercisable (A) *With the consent of the trustees*	Powers exercisable without either notice to or consent of the trustees or the court
1. Sale, ss38–39	1. Compromise or settle disputes, s58(1)	1. Make improvements, ss83–89
2. Lease, ss41–48	2. Release rights imposed on other land for benefit of settled land, s58(2)	2. Accept surrenders of leases, s52
3. Exchange, ss38–40		3. To take leases of other lands, s53
4. Grant Options, s51	(B) *With the consent of the trustees or the court*	
(all the above require *general notice* which states the intention to exercise a power but without being specific)	1. To cut and sell timber, s66	4. To make leases of less than 21 years, s42(5)
5. Mortgage, s71	2. To dispose of the principal mansion house, s65(1)	
(following the giving of *specific notice*)	(C) *With the consent of the court*	
	1. To sell heirlooms, s67	
	2. To effect any transaction not otherwise authorised by the Act or settlement if it is for the benefit of the land or beneficiaries, s64	
	3. To grant building/mining leases for terms longer than in the Act, s46	

There is no statutory system of controlling the exercise by the tenant for life of his powers in respect of the legal estate nor can the settlor impose controls (see below), but there are certain *safeguards* against his abusing them. These are:

1. His position as trustee for all the beneficiaries under the settlement (s107). He is therefore liable to an action for breach of trust if he abuses those powers which he holds both for his own benefit and as trustee for all the beneficiaries under the settlement.

2. In the case of the most important of the powers he has to give notice to the trustees of the settlement. The notice must be in writing and must be given at least one month before the transaction in question to no fewer than two trustees. However this requirement does not give much protection because:

   a) The trustees are under no duty to interfere with an improper transaction.

b) In most cases a general notice is sufficient – except in the case of mortgages where specific notice is required – s101 SLA 1925.

c) Any trustee may in writing accept less than one month's notice or waive it altogether.

d) A person dealing in good faith with a tenant for life is not concerned to inquire whether notice has been given.

3. In some cases he must obtain the consent of the trustees or an order of the court before he exercises his powers. The tenant for life is free to deal with his own beneficial interest as he pleases and his right to do so is inherent and not given by statute.

Powers exercisable on notice

Power of sale: ss38–39

The tenant for life may sell all or any part of the settled land or any easement, right or privilege of any kind over the land. However, as well as giving notice he must obtain the best consideration in money that can reasonably be obtained and the purchase money must be paid to at least two trustees (unless a trust corporation is trustee when the money can be paid to the trust corporation). See *Wheelwright* v *Walker* (1883) 23 Ch D 752. (For provisions protecting a purchaser from a tenant for life see section 8.13.)

Power to exchange: ss38–40

Settled land, or any part of it, or any easement right or privilege over it may be exchanged for other land etc. Any adjustment in money for difference in value, 'equality of exchange' capital money, may be paid and received.

Power to lease: ss41–48

The settled land, or any part of it, or any easement right or privilege over it, may be leased for periods not exceeding:

1. 999 years for building or forestry.
2. 100 years for mining.
3. 50 years for any other purpose eg a residential lease.

Every lease must comply with the following conditions:

1. It must be made by deed.
2. It must take effect in possession not more than one year after its date, or in reversion after an existing lease with not more than seven years to run at the date of the new lease.
3. It must reserve the best rent obtainable in the circumstances, regard being had to any fine taken and to any money to be spent by the tenant in improving the land. Any fine is capital money.

4. It must contain a covenant by the lessee for payment of rent and a condition of re-entry on rent not being paid within a specified time not exceeding 30 days.
5. A copy (known as a counterpart) of the lease must be executed by the lessee and given to the tenant for life. There is an exception to these rules where the lease is for not more than 21 years and is for the best rent without taking a fine and does not exempt the lessee from liability for waste. Then the lease:
6. May be made without giving notice to the trustees.
7. If the lease is for not more than three years it may be made by writing provided that there is an agreement to pay the rent.

A lease which does not comply with these requirements is void, except so far as it binds the equitable interest of the tenant for life. However, by s152 LPA 1925, if the lease was made in good faith and the lessee has taken possession, the lease will be effective in equity as a contract for a lease.

Power to mortgage: s71
If the tenant for life wishes to raise money for his own benefit, in the absence of a special provision in the settlement, he can only do so by mortgaging his *beneficial interest*. This will necessarily be an equitable mortgage as the security, the tenant for life's own life interest, can only be equitable. The legal estate can only be mortgaged for the following purposes:

1. To provide money required to be raised under the provisions of the settlement.
2. To provide money where reasonably required for specified purposes. These are all concerned with the settled land and the most important are:
3. To discharge an incumbrance.
4. To pay for authorised (ie by the SLA 1925 or by the settlement) improvements to the land (the most common purpose).
5. Equality of exchange.
6. Payment of the costs of the above and certain other transactions.

In creating such a mortgage, specific notice must be given to the trustees of the settlement.

Power to grant options: ss90(1)(i) and 51
A tenant for life may grant an option in writing to purchase or take a lease of all or any part of the settled land or of any easement, right or privilege over it, provided that:

1. The price or rent must be the best reasonably available and must be fixed at the time of granting the option.
2. The option must be exercisable within an agreed number of years not exceeding ten.
3. The option may be granted with or without any consideration being paid, but if it is paid it is capital money.

Powers exercisable only with consent

Consent of the trustees

Power to dispose of the principal mansion house: s65. If either the settlement was made before 1926 and does not expressly dispense with consent, or the settlement was made after 1925 and expressly requires consent, then consent is required before the tenant for life can sell or lease the principal mansion house. If the house is usually occupied as a farmhouse, or if the site of the house together with its grounds is less than 25 acres, then it is not a principal mansion house within the section. In all other cases, it is a question of fact.

Power to cut and sell timber: s66. Consent is only required where the tenant for life is impeachable for waste. If consent is required, three-quarters of the proceeds are capital money and the remaining one-quarter will go to the tenant for life as income.

Power to compromise claims: s58(1)

Consent of the court

Power to sell settled chattels (known as 'heirlooms'): s67. Such a sale of heirlooms requires the order of the court – consent of the trustees will not suffice.

Power to effect any proper transactions: s64. This section gives the court a residual power to permit any other transaction with the settled land or capital money which would be for the benefit of the land or the beneficiaries.

In *Hambro* v *Duke of Marlborough* [1994] 3 All ER 332, the court gave the widest possible meaning to its power under s64 by concluding that under this provision it could approve a scheme which would have the effect of removing the land from the Settled Land Act 1925 by creating a trust for sale. The case concerned Blenheim Palace and estate which was given to the first Duke of Marlborough and his issue by the nation as a reward for his military services. The conveyance established a strict settlement. The eleventh Duke was tenant for life and the Marquess of Blandford, his eldest son, would become tenant for life in due course. However, owing to the irresponsible behaviour of the Marquess, the plaintiffs (settlement trustees) sought an order under s64 which in effect would have limited the right of the Marquess to manage the Blenheim estate. Under the scheme put forward by the trustees the trust fund was to be held to pay the income to the eleventh Duke for life and subject thereto on protective trusts for the Marquess for his life and capital on the trusts of the existing settlement. Furthermore, the Duke was to execute a conveyance of substantially all the land comprised in the settlement to the trustees of the new trust to be held by them on trust for sale. This scheme would have taken the land out of the Settled Land Act by creating a trust for sale and it would have varied the beneficial interest of the Marquess without his consent. The Marquess opposed the application of the trustees. The court held that it had jurisdiction under s64 to approve the scheme. By virtue of s64 it could approve any transaction which was for the benefit of the settled land even if thereafter the land ceased to be settled land within the Settled Land Act 1925. Furthermore, the court held that it could approve a transaction which varied the beneficial interest of an ascertained beneficiary of full age and capacity who did not consent, provided that the variation was for the benefit of the settled land, or all the beneficiaries under the settlement. Accordingly, the person whose beneficial interest was affected would obtain some countervailing advantage either as one of the beneficiaries or as someone interested in the settled land which was being benefited.

Powers exercisable without either giving notice or obtaining consent

Powers to effect improvements: ss83–89 and Schedule 3
Improvements are special operations of a capital nature, as opposed to current repairs which must be paid out of income. If the improvements are to be paid out of the capital money or money raised by a mortgage of the settled land, the tenant for life must comply with the provisions of ss83–89 and Schedule 3. Improvements are classified as follows according to their place in Schedule 3 SLA 1925:

Part I. There are 25 heads, including drainage, building bridges and putting a hard surface on the track leading from the farm to the main road. The tenant for life *cannot be required* to pay for such improvements and the estate itself pays for them.

Part II. There are six heads, including the restoration of buildings damaged by dry rot and additions to existing buildings. The tenant for life *may* be required by the trustees to repay the capital by up to 50 half-yearly instalments. Any such repayment will be by way of a rentcharge paid by the tenant for life.

Part III. There are three heads, including the provision of heating or lighting or vehicles used on the estate for farming purposes, eg combine harvesters. The trustees *must* require repayment by the tenant for life by not more than 50 half-yearly instalments.

8.8 Personal nature of the statutory powers: s108

No powers over settled land can be given to anyone other than the tenant for life. A settlement may confer powers in addition to the statutory powers on the tenant for life, but any attempt by the settlor to give these additional powers to any other person or to provide that the statutory powers should be exercised by some person other than the tenant for life is invalidated by s108 SLA 1925, and the additional powers contained in the settlement are by that section conferred on the tenant for life.

8.9 Protection of the statutory powers: s106

The statutory powers cannot be ousted, curtailed or hampered, and s106 makes void any provision in the settlement which has the effect of preventing or discouraging the tenant for life from exercising the statutory powers. Thus:

1. A provision requiring him to obtain the consent of some person to the sale or lease of land is void.
2. A provision which provides that he should forfeit his beneficial interest if he should exercise any of his powers is void.

However, such conditions must be carefully construed as they are only invalid so far as they attempt to fetter exercise of the statutory powers. For example, a provision that the tenant for life will forfeit his interest if he ceases to reside on the settled land will be void if he ceases to reside because he has exercised a statutory power, eg sold or leased the land, but valid if he ceases to reside for some other reason; for instance, if he voluntarily decides to emigrate, and so leaves the property, the forfeiture clause will be valid. See *Re Trenchard* [1902] 1 Ch 378 and *Re Acklom* [1929] 1 Ch 195.

Where a fund is provided by the settlor for the upkeep of the property during the tenant for life's residence, it has been held that he can still claim for payments after letting the land but not after selling. See *Re Burden, Mitchell* v *St Luke's Hostel Trustees* [1948] Ch 160 and *Re Aberconway's Settlement Trusts* [1953] Ch 647.

Romer J expressed the general principle in these words in *Re Burden*:

> '... there is nothing whatever in the section (s106) to convert the trust from a direction to pay outgoings into a direction to pay money out to the tenant for life.'

8.10 Powers remain with the tenant for life: s104

A tenant for life cannot assign, release or contract not to exercise his powers in respect of the legal estate even though he has disposed of his entire beneficial interest. There are, however, three cases in which the powers may become exercisable by someone other than the tenant for life:

1. If he assigns his beneficial interest to the person next entitled under the settlement with intent to extinguish it, then the statutory powers become exercisable by the assignee (provided that he is of full age). The tenant for life is treated as if he were dead (s105). The assignment must be to the person next entitled for the section to apply. See *Re Maryon-Wilson's Instruments* [1971] Ch 789.
2. If he ceases to have a substantial interest in the land and either consents to an order being made or has unreasonably refused to exercise his powers, the court may make an order authorising the trustees of the settlement to exercise the

statutory powers in his name (s24). For this provision to apply there must be more than neglect and a clear refusal by the tenant for life to exercise his powers.
3. Where the tenant for life is a mental patient, his statutory powers may be exercised under an order of the Court of Protection.

The consent of an assignee of the tenant for life's beneficial interest is not required for the exercise of any of the statutory powers, but he must be given notice of any intended transaction.

8.11 Death of the tenant for life

If the land remains settled, the deceased tenant for life's special personal representatives, the SLA trustees, must take out a grant of probate or letters of administration limited to the settled land, and then convey the land by vesting assent to the person entitled. If, on the other hand, the land ceases to be settled land, then the land will vest in the deceased tenant for life's ordinary personal representatives who will then convey it by simple assent to the person next entitled.

8.12 Acquisition by the tenant for life of the settled land: s68

If the tenant for life wants to acquire the fee simple, s68 SLA 1925 permits this if a prescribed procedure is followed. He must inform the settlement trustees of his wish to purchase and they must take over the powers of tenant for life with regard to that transaction.

8.13 Dispositions by the tenant for life and protection of purchasers

There are several provisions regulating dispositions and protecting purchasers.
Section 13 SLA 1925 both regulates dispositions and protects purchasers (see section 8.3). However, s13 does contain an exception in favour of a purchaser of a legal estate without notice.
Section 18 states that any disposition other than one authorised by the SLA 1925 is void except in so far as it binds the tenant for life's equitable interest. A purchaser would therefore take subject to the beneficial interests whether he had notice or not. Further, even if the disposition is authorised, any capital money must be paid to at least two trustees of the settlement (or a trust corporation) or the beneficial interests will not be overreached.

Protection under s95

If the money arising under a transaction is paid to the trustees the payer is not concerned to see that the money is properly applied. This is particularly important when settled land is mortgaged, as if the money is used improperly the mortgage is unauthorised and, without the effect of this section, would be void by s18.

Protection under s110

Section 110(1) provides that a purchaser dealing in good faith with a tenant for life shall be deemed to have given the best price etc, and to have complied with the provisions of the SLA. Section 110(2) also provides that a purchaser shall not be entitled to inspect the trust instrument, but is entitled to assume that the particulars given in the vesting deed are correct. Section 110(3) protects the purchaser from personal representatives.

Conflict between s18 and s110

Problems have arisen when a purchaser has dealt in good faith with a person he thought was an absolute owner, but who was in fact a tenant for life making an unauthorised transaction. In the first instance case of *Weston* v *Henshaw* [1950] Ch 510, it was held by Danckwerts J that the protection of s110 only applied to a purchaser dealing with a person whom he knew to be a tenant for life. Cheshire points out at page 888 that this decision seems to be

'the only decision in unregistered land which is an exception to the immunity of the bona fide purchaser for value of the legal estate without notice'.

In the later case of *Re Morgan's Lease* [1972] Ch 1 (also at first instance), Ungoed-Thomas J, relying on the Court of Appeal decision on the equivalent provision in the Settled Land Act 1882, in *Mogridge* v *Clapp* [1892] 3 Ch 382, which was not cited in the earlier case, decided that s110 did apply to a purchaser who was in fact dealing with a tenant for life even though he did not know it. Ungoed-Thomas J stated:

'Thus my conclusion is that s110 applies whether or not the purchaser knows that the other party to the transaction is a tenant for life.'

Most authors appear to favour this latter decision. Megarry and Wade remind their readers at page 397 that s110 does require the purchaser to be acting in good faith, and this aspect must always be applied to problems relating to the conflict between ss18 and 110 SLA 1925.

When the settlement has come to an end

A problem could arise when a settlement has come to an end because a tenant for life has forfeited his beneficial interest, but the tenant for life has not vested the legal estate in the person entitled and deals with the land as if the settlement were continuing. The purchaser would not appear to be protected by s110(2) as this applies to a 'purchaser of a legal estate in settled land'.

While there is no authority on this point, it would seem probable that the purchaser would acquire the legal estate, as this was still vested in the tenant for life, but take it subject to the equitable interests.

8.14 Capital money

Capital money, which may either have been provided by the settlor or arise from disposition of the settled land, eg sale or three-quarters of the sum received upon the sale of timber, must be invested in one or more of the ways specified in s73 SLA 1925, including trustee securities, paying for authorised improvements, or purchase of land held on fee simple or on a lease with 60 years or more still to run. The tenant for life may select the mode of investment (s75(3)), even though he does not have direct control of the capital money.

8.15 Functions of Settled Land Act trustees

1. To receive and hold capital money – see section 8.14.
2. To receive notice from the tenant for life when required.
3. To give consent when required.
4. To act as special personal representatives on the death of the tenant for life when the settlement continues.
5. To act as statutory owner when there is no tenant for life.
6. To exercise the powers of the tenant for life when he wishes to acquire the settled land for his own benefit.
7. To execute the vesting deed when the settlement is imperfectly constituted.
8. To exercise the powers of the tenant for life where the tenant for life has ceased to have a substantial interest and has either consented or the court has made an order. See s24.
9. To execute a deed of discharge when necessary on the determination of the settlement. See s17 SLA 1925. Such a deed is not necessary:

   a) If the settlement has come to an end by the death of the tenant for life, because the ordinary PRs' simple assent is sufficient to show the land has ceased to be settled. See *Re Bridgett and Hayes' Contract* [1928] Ch 163.
   b) If the settlement has come to an end before a vesting instrument has been executed. See *Re Alefounders' WT* [1927] 1 Ch 360.

10. To exercise a general supervision. This function is neatly summarised by Cheshire at page 211:

    'The role of the trustees is to manage and protect the money that is paid to them.'

8.16 Trusts for sale under Law of Property Act 1925

Distinction between settlements under the Settled Land Act 1925 and trusts for sale

Trusts for sale, were expressly excluded from the SLA 1925 (see s1(7) SLA 1925: 'this section does not apply to land held upon trust for sale'). They were defined by s205(1)(xxix) LPA 1925 and s117(1)(xxx) SLA 1925 as 'an immediate binding trust for sale', and the most important distinction was that when land was held on trust for sale the legal estate and powers of dealing with the land were vested in the trustees, as opposed to a strict settlement when they are vested in the tenant for life.

Definition – 'immediate binding trust for sale'

Trust for sale. This meant that there had to be a duty to sell and thus a true trust for sale, and not just a mere power to sell. If the settlor did not impose a duty to sell the settlement came within the SLA 1925. See *Re Newbould* (1913) 110 LT 6.

Immediate. This meant that if the trust for sale arose in the future there would be a settlement rather than a trust for sale. But s25(1) LPA 1925 did provide a power to postpone sale. Thus the trust for sale could be effective immediately even though the duty to sell could then be postponed.

Binding. It is not altogether clear why this word was included in the definition. The most obvious explanation was to stress the mandatory nature of the trust for sale (ie that the land must be sold) as distinct from a discretionary mere power of sale. However, given that the word 'trust' itself imports a mandatory duty it might well have been appropriate to regard 'binding' as an unnecessary addition to the definition.

Types of trust for sale under LPA 1925

A trust for sale could arise:

1. *Expressly* by the wording of the settlement. There was no requirement of two documents as there was for settlements under the SLA. As a matter of practice it was often found that two documents had been used for precisely the same reason as in the SLA, in order to keep the trusts off the title.
2. *By statute.* The most common examples of trusts for sale imposed by statute were:

   a) When two or more persons were jointly entitled to land (see Chapter 9).
   b) When a person died intestate, then a trust for sale was imposed on his estate by s33 of the Administration of Estates Act 1925. From 1 July 1995, where a person dies intestate his property passes to the Public Trustee until the grant

of administration (s14 of the Law of Property (Miscellaneous Provisions) Act 1994), whereas before that date it vested in the President of the Family Division. Section 33 of the Administration of Estates Act 1925 imposed an implied trust for sale on any land or personal property in an intestate estate. The section has been amended by the Trusts of Land and Appointment of Trustees Act 1996 (see Schedule 2 para 5). Now whenever the death occurred or occurs if there is land in the estate it is held by the trustees on a trust of land with a power of sale.

c) If trustees lent money on mortgage and the property became vested in them, eg by foreclosure.

8.17 Position of trustees for sale

Power to postpone sale

Unless a contrary intention appeared, a power to postpone sale was implied in every trust for sale by s25 LPA 1925 (repealed by the 1996 Act). However, because there was a trust for sale, there was a duty to sell, and the rule was that any trustee could compel his co-trustees to do their duty but they had to be unanimous if they wanted to exercise a power. Therefore the land had to be sold unless all trustees agreed to postpone. See *Re Mayo* [1943] Ch 302. However, the court would not enforce a sale if that would defeat the object of the trust or if it would be in breach of a contractual obligation on the trustees. See *Re Buchanan-Wollaston's Conveyance* [1939] Ch 738.

This rule had particular application in respect of the family home. See *Jones* v *Challenger* [1961] 1 QB 176; *Bedson* v *Bedson* [1965] 2 QB 666; *Re Evers' Trust* [1980] 1 WLR 1327; *Bernard* v *Josephs* [1982] 3 All ER 162; *Dennis* v *McDonald* [1982] Fam 63; *Burns* v *Burns* [1984] 1 All ER 244; and *Grant* v *Edwards* [1986] 3 WLR 114.

The above cases on family home matters also illustrate the conflict which could arise between the statutory power to postpone sale under s25 LPA 1925 and the wide discretion given to the court under s30 LPA 1925 (repealed by ss14 and 15 of the 1996 Act) to 'make such order as it thinks fit' on an application by 'any person interested' (in the property). The court had to decide not only on the duty or power dichotomy, but also whether the purpose of the trust could still be achieved.

Upon an application for a s30 order for sale, the court looked for any 'secondary' or 'collateral' purposes to the trust – that was, any reason for the purchase of the land other than sale. A common example of a secondary purpose was the purchase of the property as a family home.

Where the court found the existence of a secondary purpose and where that purpose was still subsisting the court would not usually grant the order. In *Jones* v *Challenger* (above) the secondary purpose had come to an end. There a house had been purchased jointly by a married couple for a matrimonial and family home and at the relevant time the children had grown up and left and the marriage had ended in divorce. Accordingly, a s30 order was made compelling the reluctant ex-spouse to join in a sale of the property.

The court took into account the need for a roof over a family, particularly where there were young children involved. In *Re Evers' Trust* (above) the court refused on these grounds to order a sale in spite of the fact that the land was subject to a duty to sell.

In *Re Citro, Domenico (A Bankrupt)* [1991] Ch 142 the Court of Appeal held that a collateral purpose would not be treated as subsisting when that purpose was to provide a matrimonial home and one of the parties ceased through bankruptcy to own his share. There a husband was adjudicated bankrupt, his only asset being a half share of the beneficial interest in the matrimonial home. His wife had a beneficial interest in the matrimonial home and lived in it with their children. The trustee in bankruptcy applied under s30 LPA 1925 for possession in order to sell the house. In granting the orders sought, the Court of Appeal concluded that the interest of the creditors prevailed over those of the wife and children, although they did postpone sale for six months.

These issues were considered by the Court of Appeal in *Abbey National plc* v *Moss* [1993] 1 FLR 307. There a mother owned the property in question outright. She was persuaded by her daughter to transfer the property into their joint names in order to simplify the passing of the property on the mother's death. However, the transfer was on condition that the house would never be sold during the mother's lifetime without her consent. Subsequently the daughter borrowed £30,000 from the plaintiff on the security of the house. The mother and daughter then fell out, the daughter left the country having defaulted on the mortgage, and the plaintiff sought possession of the house under s30 LPA 1925.

The Court of Appeal concluded that the trust for sale could not be implemented without the mother's consent (that is, she had to consent before a sale of the property took place). Until she consented, a secondary or collateral purpose was in existence (that the mother should remain in the property during her lifetime). The court emphasised that it would not usually allow a trust for sale to defeat a secondary or collateral purpose just because one of the original parties to the trust assigned her interest. Here it could not have been within the contemplation of either the mother or the daughter that the assignment (whether voluntary or involuntary) by the daughter of her interest could lead to the house being sold against her mother's wishes. Further, in the court's view it was impossible to conclude that the secondary purpose had come to an end just because the daughter had lost her beneficial interest through the mortgage, because the secondary purpose was completely unaffected by that event (it would have been different if the secondary purpose had been that both mother and daughter were to have lived together in the house). Finally, the court said that *Re Citro* (above) was limited to situations where one of the parties ceased to have an interest by reason of bankruptcy or insolvency. Accordingly, it was inapplicable here and the mother's appeal against a sale order was allowed.

Given that s30 LPA 1925 has been repealed by the 1996 Act, is the case law developed by the courts under that provision of any continuing value? The view of the Law Commission is that there is much of value in that body of case law. Accordingly, it seems that it will remain influential despite the demise of s30 LPA 1925. Further, in *TSB Bank plc* v *Marshall* [1998] 39 EG 208 the court concluded that the case law developed under s30 LPA 1925 was still relevant to the successor provisions (ss14 and 15) of the 1996 Act. However, in *Mortgage Corporation* v *Shaire & Others* [2001] Ch 743 the Court of Appeal concluded that the pre-1996 Act authorities (ie cases decided under the now repealed s30 LPA 1925), whilst still useful, should be treated 'with caution': see section 8.22 below.

Other powers

By s28(1) LPA 1925 (repealed by the 1996 Act) the trustees for sale had all the powers of a tenant for life of settled land and of Settled Land Act trustees. If, however, the consent of any person was required for sale, these powers could only be exercised subject to the same consent.

Curtailment of the powers

Trusts for sale could be made subject to a condition that the land should not be sold without the consent of the named person or persons (s28(1)). If the trustees failed to obtain such consent they would be in breach of trust, but by s26(1) LPA 1925 (repealed by the 1996 Act) a purchaser for value had only to ensure that the consent of two such persons was obtained and he was then protected. The consent of an infant could be given by his parent or guardian, and of a mental patient by the Court of Protection. The court had power to dispense with consents that could not be obtained by s30 LPA 1925 (repealed by the 1996 Act).

The effect of allowing such consent (compare the position under the Settled Land Act) was that the powers of the trustees could be effectively curtailed. In *Re Inns* [1947] Ch 576 the person whose consent was required was a contingent remainderman who would only benefit if the land remained unsold, but the court said, obiter, that this was a valid requirement. This helped answer the following question which was frequently asked after 1925 – what was the most effective method of keeping land unsold? It appeared from *Re Inns* that the combined effect of the power to postpone sale in s25(1) LPA 1925 and the need for consents under s28(1) LPA 1925 might be to keep the land unsold. This led to the conclusion that to achieve the original intention of a strict settlement to retain land within the family prior to the coming into force of TOLATA 1996 it would have been better to create a trust for sale rather than a strict settlement under the SLA 1925. The problem with the latter, of course, is that the SLA gives the tenant for life a power of sale and this cannot be taken away from him because of the provisions of s106 SLA 1925.

8.18 Position of the beneficiaries

A person with an immediate life interest in the whole property could be permitted to occupy it himself.

Delegation

By s29 (repealed by the 1996 Act) the trustees could in writing revocably delegate to such a person certain powers, including those of leasing and management. If they refused to delegate these powers the court could direct them to do so under s30.

Consultation

By s26(3) (repealed by the 1996 Act) the trustees had, so far as was practicable, to consult the persons of full age for the time being beneficially interested in possession and had, so far as was consistent with the general interests of the trust, to give effect to their wishes or to the wishes of the majority in terms of value. A purchaser was not concerned to see that such wishes were complied with. However, this provision only applied to statutory trusts for sale (see section 8.16) and to express trusts which expressly indicated that the section should apply.

Powers of the court

If the trustees refused to sell or exercise any of their powers or if any requisite consent could not be obtained, 'any person interested' could apply to the court under s30 for an order giving effect to the proposed transaction and the court could make such an order as it thought fit. The operation of s30 LPA 1925 was the subject of much litigation (see section 8.17).

Doctrine of conversion

Theoretically there was no overreaching in a trust for sale because of the effect of the doctrine of conversion, ie that from the very creation of the trust the beneficiary's rights were rights in money not in land. However, the same overreaching provisions applied to trusts for sale: the purchase money had to be paid to at least two trustees or a trust corporation in order for the purchaser to take free of the rights of the beneficiaries.

The doctrine was designed to simplify conveyancing. Since the interests were not in the land but in the proceeds of sale a purchaser could take free of them. The doctrine was abolished by s3 TOLATA 1996.

8.19 Ad hoc settlements and trusts for sale

A complicated and little-used machinery was set up in order to overreach certain prior equitable interests which were not overreached by the usual methods in both settlements and trusts for sale. An ad hoc settlement or trust for sale could be used, with special trustees approved by the court or a trust corporation.

8.20 Strict settlements and registered land

Strict settlements under the SLA 1925

1. The title will be registered in the name of the tenant for life.
2. Prior to the Land Registration Act 2002, the existence of the settlement would be revealed by a restriction entered as a minor interest in the proprietorship register. It would take the following form:

> 'Restriction registered on the ... day of ... 1986.
>
>   No disposition by the proprietor of the land under which capital money arises is to be registered unless the money is paid to A of ... and B of ... (the trustees of the settlement of whom there must be not less than two nor more than four unless a trust corporation is the sole trustee) or into court. Except under an order of the registrar no disposition by the proprietor is to be registered unless authorised by the Settled Land Act 1925.'

3. If the tenant for life of a strict settlement of registered land mortgages his life interest, how can the mortgagee preserve his priority? This was formerly achieved by the entry of a priority caution in the Minor Interests Index under s102(2) LRA 1925.

    This procedure was ended by the Land Registration Act 1986 by the repeal of s102(2) LRA 1925. The result was to abolish the Minor Interests Index and provide that priority between dealings with equitable interests in registered land is to be determined by the rule in *Dearle* v *Hall* (1828) 3 Russ 1. This means that the order of priority is the order in which notices are received by the trustees of the settlement.

    As a consequence the rules of priority for equitable mortgages are now the same in both registered and unregistered land by the application of this rule.

8.21 Comparison of the strict settlement and the trust for sale

Feature	Strict settlement	Trust for sale
1. Controlling Act	Settled Land Act 1925	Law of Property Act 1925
2. Legal Estate	Vested in tenant for life or statutory owners, s19(1)	Vested in trustees for sale, s28(1)
3. Documents	Two documents must be used – the vesting deed and the trust instrument, s4(1)	Only one document required but two were often used to keep the trusts off the title
4. Sale	Tenant for life has a power to sell, s38	Trustees for sale were under a duty to sell, s205(1)(xxix)
5. Conversion	No application to a strict settlement	Converted land held on trust for sale into personalty
6. Restrictions on powers	Settlor cannot restrict the powers of the tenant for life, s106	Settlor could place restrictions by way of consents and there was a power to postpone sale, s25, s26(1), and *Re Inns* (1947)
7. Application of capital money	Decided by the tenant for life on the basis of the settlement, s73 and s75(2)	Decided by the trustees for sale, s28(1)

8.22 Trusts of Land and Appointment of Trustees Act 1996

The Trusts of Land and Appointment of Trustees Act 1996 received the Royal Assent on 24 July 1996 and came into force on 1 January 1997. It effects some of the most important reforms to real property law since the 1925 legislation and it forms part of a clear programme to review and revise the trust system which has remained substantially unaltered since the 1925 legislation. Except where otherwise specified, all references are to the 1996 Act.

Background

The effectiveness of a strict settlement in keeping land within a family was broken by the Settled Land Acts (SLA) 1882 and 1925 which, as a general rule, vest the legal estate to the settled land in the tenant for life (s16(1) SLA 1925); give the tenant for life the power to sell the land (ss38 and 39 SLA 1925); and stipulate that this and other powers of the tenant for life could not be expressly excluded by a trust instrument (s106 SLA 1925). Accordingly, following the coming into force of the Settled Land Acts 1882 and 1925 you would not have created a strict settlement if your aim was to keep land within the family because you could not prevent a tenant for life possessed of the legal estate from selling it if he wanted to. However, strict settlements still arose – usually unintentionally, eg where a will was drawn up without professional advice.

In contrast, a trust for sale was used to convert property into cash which in turn could easily be distributed amongst the beneficiaries. Under a trust for sale, the beneficiaries were deemed to have an interest in the proceeds of sale into which the estate was to be converted, rather than in the property itself (the doctrine of conversion). This was the position even before the land had been sold. Accordingly, in the case of a trust for sale land was held as an investment asset rather than for long term occupation (this explained why the trustees were under a *duty* to sell).

In addition to the fact that the strict settlement and the trust for sale each had a different rationale (the former was traditionally used to keep ownership of land within a given family, while under the latter land was held as an investment asset), there were also significant differences between the two systems as to how the legal estate was held and who had powers of management. For example, in the case of a strict settlement the legal estate was usually vested in the tenant for life (with the settlement trustees in a more peripheral role) whereas in the case of a trust for sale the legal estate was vested in the trustees.

A primary catalyst for the new legislation was the 1989 Law Commission Report *Transfer of Land: Trusts of Land* (Law Com No 181). The Law Commission concluded that there was a need for 'an entirely new system' in order to clarify and rationalise the law and that any new system should be based upon a new type of trust. They identified a number of weaknesses with the then system including the following five:

1. The existence of a dual system gave rise to a number of difficulties.
2. The settled land regime was unnecessarily complicated.
3. It was possible to create a strict settlement unintentionally, eg a will drawn up without professional advice which left a house to the testator's wife for her life and then to the testator's children absolutely.
4. The trust for sale mechanism was not appropriate to the conditions of modern home ownership. In particular the duty to sell was artificial and inconsistent with the wishes of the majority of co-owners.
5. It was entirely artificial to maintain that equitable joint tenants or equitable tenants in common had no interest in a house or flat held on trust for sale but had only an interest in the sale proceeds (the doctrine of conversion) when no sale was actually contemplated.

Finally, one of the Commission's aims was to achieve greater parity between trusts of real and personal property.

Introduction

The Act is in three parts. Part I deals with Trusts of Land and derives substantially from the Law Commission Report. Part II deals with Appointment of New Trustees and Part III is a collection of supplementary provisions usually found at the conclusion of an Act.

Key Points

1. A new concept, the *trust of land*, is created.
2. Generally speaking no new strict settlement can be created under the Settled Land Act.
3. All existing trusts for sale are automatically trusts of land.
4. It is still possible to create an express trust for sale albeit as one type of the new trust of land.
5. In relation to trusts created on or after 1 January 1997, it is provided that where there would have been a trust for sale imposed by *statute* there is now a trust of land.
6. The doctrine of conversion is abolished.
7. Trustees are no longer under a duty to sell land. Rather they have a power to sell and a power to retain the land.
8. Additional rights for beneficiaries are created.
9. Wider powers for the court are provided.
10. Part II applies to trusts of personalty as well as those of land.

Part I – Trusts of Land

It introduces a new unitary system of holding land on trust.

Trust of Land

The 'trust of land' is defined widely and includes any trust of property which consists of or includes land: s1(1)(a). The new regime applies as follows:

1. to all trusts of land whether the trust is created expressly or implied by statute;
2. to both concurrent and successive interests in land; and
3. whenever equitable interests in land arise by way of resulting or constructive trusts.

Before the 1996 Act, the strict settlement related to successive interests in land, while the trust for sale related principally to concurrent interests in land, although it could also relate to successive interests in land.

No new strict settlement can be created after the Act comes into force: s2(1). However, pre-Act settlements and resettlements of settlements in existence at the commencement date will still be governed by the SLA regime (in the case of such resettlements, the conclusion that they are to continue to be subject to the SLA regime can be avoided by an express statement in the creating instrument to the effect that this result is not intended, ie they can be converted to trusts of land).

Accordingly, the scheme of the Act applies to nearly all *existing* trusts and nearly all *new* trusts which include land. The exceptions to this clear picture are pre-Act strict settlements, as noted above, and land to which the Universities and College Estates Act 1925 applies.

Abolition of doctrine of conversion

The effect of the doctrine of conversion was that where land was held on a trust for sale the interests of the beneficiaries were deemed to be in the proceeds of sale of the land even before it had been sold. Historically the aim of the doctrine was to ease conveyancing – since the beneficiaries had an interest in the proceeds of sale rather than in the land itself, a purchaser of the land took free of such beneficial interests.

The Law Commission, as previously noted, concluded that the doctrine of conversion was artificial. Accordingly, s3 abolishes it for all trusts for sale. However, the overreaching of the equitable interests of beneficiaries on a sale of land remains unchanged (ie the conveyancing advantage is not lost). In *Birmingham Midshires Mortgage Services Ltd* v *Sabherwal* (2000) 80 P & CR 256 the Court of Appeal made clear that the abolition of the doctrine of conversion had not, in respect of registered land, overruled the principle laid down in *City of London Building Society* v *Flegg* [1987] 2 WLR 1266 (ie that overreaching takes place where the mortgagee has paid the capital monies to two trustees of land). There S had argued, inter alia, that the abolition of the doctrine of conversion by s3 of the 1996 Act had rendered s2(1)(ii) of the 1925 Act (the overreaching provision) ineffective. In concluding that this argument could not be sustained, the Court emphasised that the 1996 Act contained nothing to exclude the essential overreaching provisions set out in s2(1)(ii) of the 1925 Act. On the contrary, that provision had been amended so as to reflect the new terminology of the 1996 Act, and so was in effect confirmed (with that new terminology) by the 1996 Act. Accordingly, 'two trustee' overreaching has survived the 1996 Act.

There is one exception to the abolition of the doctrine – a trust created by will where the testator died before the commencement of the Act: s3(2).

Power of sale and power to postpone sale

Before the Act, trustees for sale of land were under a *duty* to sell land. Further, such trustees had an implied power to postpone sale (s25 Law of Property Act (LPA) 1925), although it was possible to expressly exclude the power to postpone sale. This regime, as previously noted, was consistent with land being held as an investment asset rather than for long term occupation.

Under the Act, trustees of land are to hold the legal estate in land on trust with a power to sell and a power to retain the land: s4. Accordingly, the trust of land places no duty to sell the land on the trustees. The Act implies into every trust of land a power for the trustees to postpone sale, and they are not to be liable even if they postpone selling for an indefinite period. This power to postpone sale prevails over any wording in the trust instrument to the contrary (this reverses the pre-Act position).

It seems that it will continue to be possible to create a trust for sale expressly. However, as just noted, a power to postpone sale is implied into all such trusts and cannot be excluded by the trust instrument.

General powers of trustees

Section 6 confers two general powers upon trustees of land in relation to the discharge of their functions:

1. They can convey land to beneficiaries (provided they are of full age, capacity and absolutely entitled to the land), even if such a conveyance has not been requested by the beneficiaries: s6(2). Further, if necessary, the court can make an order requiring the beneficiaries to take the land. The consultation requirement of the Act (see below) does not apply in relation to this power.
2. They have a specific power to acquire land under the power conferred by s8 of the Trustee Act 2000 (para 45 of Schedule 2 of the 2000 Act amending s6(3)). Under s8 of the Trustee Act 2000 trustees are entitled to purchase freehold or leasehold land in the UK (not restricted to England and Wales) as an investment; or for occupation by a beneficiary or for any other reason. This provision mirrors s6(4) of the 1996 Act which has now been repealed. This power can be used for purposes of investment, to house the beneficiary or for any other reason.

The Law Commission concluded that trustees of land ought to be put in much the same position as an absolute owner (they reached this conclusion because the circumstances of most trusts of land are such that the people who are trustees invariably regard themselves as the owners of the trust land). Section 6 is a fulfilment of the Commission's goal.

Section 7 gives trustees of land a specific power to partition trust land where the beneficiaries are of full age, capacity and absolutely entitled to the land. The provision is a substantial reenactment of s28(3) LPA 1925. Before exercising this power the trustees must obtain the consent of each of the beneficiaries.

Only the trustees can give a valid receipt for purchase money, hence their role in overreaching is preserved.

Finally, the powers conferred upon trustees of land by ss6 and 7 can be excluded or restricted. This may be done either by the trust instrument expressly restricting them (s8(1)) or by the trust instrument requiring the consent of a stated person or persons to be obtained before they are exercised: s8(2).

Power of delegation

Under s29 LPA 1925, trustees for sale could only delegate powers of management of the land to the beneficiaries. The Law Commission concluded that trustees of land ought to have much wider powers of delegation than that. Accordingly, s9 enables trustees to delegate any of their functions relating to the land to any beneficiaries of full age, capacity and entitled in possession to the land. Such a delegation may be for any period or indefinite: s9(5). The delegation may be effected by a non-enduring power of attorney (the legal estate remains with the trustees).

Where trustees delegate any of their functions under s9 they are not liable for any consequent acts or defaults by the beneficiaries *unless* they failed to exercise reasonable care in making the delegation. Further, any liability arising from the operation of s9 will be *prospective* only.

Section 9 constitutes a significant change from the pre-Act law (it supersedes s29 LPA 1925). It enables beneficiaries under a trust of land to be given much the same powers as those enjoyed by a tenant for life under a strict settlement. However, a delegation can only be made to a beneficiary who is entitled in possession to the land (ie trust powers in relation to land cannot, for example, be delegated to a beneficiary with a future or contingent interest in land).

Consents and consultation

Where a trust instrument requires the consent of two or more persons to the exercise by the trustees of any function (ie power) relating to the land, the consent of any *two* such persons will suffice in favour of a purchaser: s10.

Under the SLA 1925 the statutory powers cannot be ousted, curtailed or hampered, and s106 SLA 1925 makes void any provision in a settlement which has the effect of preventing or discouraging the tenant for life from exercising the statutory powers. Accordingly, a provision requiring the tenant for life to obtain the consent of some person to the sale of land is void. However, trusts for sale could have been made subject to a condition that the land should not be sold without the consent of a named person or persons: s28(1) LPA 1925. If trustees failed to obtain such consent they would have been in breach of trust, but by s26(1) LPA 1925 a purchaser for value needed only to ensure that the consent of two such persons was obtained and he was then protected.

Section 10 is modelled to some extent on s26 LPA 1925. However, there are significant differences between the two provisions. For example, s10 does not apply to charitable, ecclesiastical or public trusts (ie in such cases purchasers are required to ensure that *all* consents are obtained).

Section 10 applies to *any* disposition creating a trust of land which stipulates that the exercise by the trustees of any of their powers is subject to the consent of others. This means that under the new regime a trust instrument can stipulate that trustees must obtain such consent whether the interests under the trust are *concurrent or successive*. This represents a clear departure from the SLA position in respect of successive interests where, as previously noted, the statutory powers cannot be ousted or curtailed. The existence of a consent requirement may affect the ability of the trustees to sell the land.

Finally, it is not possible to exclude the operation of s10 (s26 LPA 1925 is repealed by it).

Trustees of land are required to *consult* with beneficiaries of full age and beneficially entitled to an interest *in possession in the land* before exercising any of their powers: s11. The obligation applies whether the interests are concurrent or successive. The duty to consult can be expressly excluded by the trust instrument (ie the possibility of exclusion does not apply to resulting or constructive trusts). Further, the requirement is only to consult 'so far as practicable' and only to act in accordance with the beneficiaries' wishes 'so far as consistent with the general interest of the trust'. In the event of there being a dispute between the beneficiaries as to what should be done then the trustees must follow the wishes of the majority (according to the value of their combined interests).

As noted previously, the duty to consult does not apply in relation to the power of trustees to convey land to beneficiaries absolutely entitled to the land irrespective of whether they want it: s6(2). The application of s11 to an existing trust (ie a pre-Act trust) depends upon whether it was created by will or by deed. Section 11 never applies to trusts arising under a *will* made before the Act. Existing trusts created by *deed* are also exempt from the obligation unless the settlor or surviving settlors execute a deed stipulating that it is to apply.

The effect of s11 is to extend to express trusts a rule which under the pre-Act law only applied to implied trusts for sale (see s26(3) LPA 1925, which is now repealed).

Beneficiaries and occupation

Before the 1996 Act there was considerable uncertainty as to whether a person with a beneficial interest in land subject to a trust for sale had a right to occupy the land.

The Act addresses this problem. Section 12 gives a right of occupation to certain beneficiaries. A beneficiary entitled to an interest in possession in land has a right to occupy the property subject to a trust of land where: (a) the purpose of the trust includes making the land available for the beneficiary's occupation (s12(1)(a)); or (b) the land is held by the trustees so as to be so available (s12(1)(b)).

There are two hurdles for a beneficiary to surmount in order to have a right to occupy property subject to a trust of land:

1. The beneficiary must be entitled to an interest in possession in land. The right only extends to a beneficiary with a present vested interest in land. A beneficiary with a purely monetary interest or with a future or contingent interest is excluded. 'Possession' for the purposes of the Act has the same meaning as for the LPA 1925 (ie it is defined as including not only physical possession of the land but also the receipt of rents and profits or the right to receive them, if any). Whether a given beneficiary is entitled to an interest in possession in land under

a trust depends upon the nature of his interest. For example, where a trust of land comes into being by operation of law (ie a resulting or constructive trust or a statutory trust coming into effect because the land is conveyed to more than one person) the beneficiary of such a trust will have an interest in land. This is because the Act repeals s35 LPA 1925, which imposed upon such trusts the statutory trusts under which the interests of beneficiaries would be interests in the proceeds of sale. In contrast an annuitant is not a person with an interest in possession in land subject to a trust: s22(3).

2. A beneficiary is only entitled to this right of occupation if either s12(1)(a) or (b) is satisfied. Given the wording of s12(1)(a), consideration should be given by trusts draftsmen to spelling out the purpose of the trust in the trust instrument. As to s12(1)(b), where land is not intended to be available for occupation it might be prudent to make this clear in the trust instrument.

Section 13 details the exclusions and restrictions which operate to restrict the right to occupation given by s12. It deals primarily with the situation where more than one beneficiary claims the statutory right of occupation. Where there is more than one beneficiary eligible to occupy the land the trustees have a discretionary power to exclude or restrict the right of occupation of any one or more, but not of all, of them. The matters which the trustees are to have regard to in exercising this discretion include the intention of the person who created the trust, the purpose for which the land is held and the circumstances and wishes of each of the eligible beneficiaries: s13(4). The trustees may impose 'reasonable conditions' on any beneficiaries occupying land under s12 (s13(3)), including the payment of compensation to any beneficiary whose right to occupy land under s12 has been excluded or restricted (s13(6)).

Finally, the aim of s13 is to help in co-ownership trusts of residential properties where there are frequent disputes as to occupation.

Powers of the court

A trustee or any person with an interest in property subject to a trust of land can apply to the court for an order under s14. On such an application the court can make any order it thinks fit:

1. Relating to the exercise by the trustees of any of their powers (s14(2)(a)); or
2. Declaring the nature or extent of any person's beneficial interest in the property subject to the trust: s14(2)(b).

Under s14 the court can make orders for sale, preventing sale, overriding a consent requirement, etc. In *Bank of Baroda* v *Dhillon & Another* (1997) The Times 4 November the Court of Appeal concluded that the wording of s14 of the 1996 Act (and its predecessor s30 LPA 1925) was sufficiently wide in a bankruptcy situation to enable a court to order a sale of a house subject to a possession order in favour of a mortgagee even though another party had a right to occupy the house by virtue of an old s70(1)(g) LRA 1925 overriding interest which ranked before that of the mortgagee. There a matrimonial home was registered in the husband's name alone. The wife had a beneficial interest. The husband took out a bank loan which was secured by a legal charge over the matrimonial home in favour of the bank. Subsequently, the husband fell into arrears with the repayments and the bank obtained judgment and a possession order against him. The husband was then adjudicated bankrupt. However, before the warrant for possession was executed the wife applied to be joined as second defendant claiming she had an equitable interest in the house which overrode the bank's legal charge of which she had no knowledge. The county court judge held that the wife had an overriding interest under s70(1)(g) LRA 1925 but after weighing the various considerations he concluded that the bank should be granted a sale order under s30 LPA 1925 because there was no prospect that it would receive payment in the foreseeable future unless there was a sale. The wife appealed. By the time the appeal was heard, s30 LPA 1925 had been repealed by s14 TOLATA 1996. In dismissing the wife's appeal, the Court of Appeal concluded that the court had a wide discretion under s14 of the 1996 Act to order a sale of property held on trust on the application of an interested party under s14 even though another party had a right to occupy the property by virtue of a s70(1)(g) LRA 1925 overriding interest ranking before that of the applicant.

This decision was not entirely unexpected. In *Re Domenico Citro (A Bankrupt)* [1991] Ch 142 there was no suggestion that the wife's half share in the beneficial interest of the matrimonial home precluded the trustee in bankruptcy making an application under s30 LPA 1925. Further, in *Abbey National plc* v *Moss* [1993] 1 FLR 307 there was no suggestion that an application under s30 LPA 1925 was defeated by an overriding interest. Finally, it is important to note that in a *Bank of Baroda* v *Dhillon* situation the holder of the overriding interest would be paid first. The court has no jurisdiction under s14 to make any order as to the appointment or removal of trustees.

In two respects, the powers of the court under s14 are wider than those it enjoyed under s30 LPA 1925. First, it can declare the nature or extent of a person's interest in the property subject to the trust: s14(2)(b). Secondly, the wording of s14(2)(a) is sufficiently wide to allow it to sanction a transaction which would otherwise be a breach of trust. The very wide jurisdiction given to the court to make orders relating to the trustees' powers is in line with the conclusion of the Law Commission that the 'courts should be able to intervene in any dispute relating to a trust of land'.

Section 15(1) contains a statement of factors which the court is to have regard to in making an order under s14. These factors include:

1. the settlor's intention;
2. the purposes for which the property subject to the trust is held;
3. the welfare of any minor who occupies or might reasonably be expected to occupy the trust land; and
4. the interests of secured creditors.

The use of the word 'include' in s15(1) demonstrates that the list is not intended to be exhaustive. Section 15(1) is based on how the courts have interpreted s30 LPA 1925. There is no order of priority as to the matters listed. Accordingly, it is unclear as to what will happen if there is a conflict between two of the matters listed, eg when the welfare of a minor conflicts with the interests of a secured creditor (under the pre-1996 Act case law, priority would have been given to the interests of the secured creditor: see *Re Citro (A Bankrupt)* [1990] 2 WLR 880. Where the s14 application is by a trustee in bankruptcy s15 is inapplicable: s15(4).

Section 30 LPA 1925 is replaced by ss14 and 15. Accordingly, it is pertinent to consider whether the case law developed under s30 LPA 1925 is still relevant today. At first sight it would seem to have little relevance to applications under s14 because s15(1) prescribes the matters that the court must take into account in exercising its discretion in determining applications under s14. However, the view of the Law Commission was that there was much of value in that body of case law – suggesting that it would remain influential despite the demise of s30 LPA 1925. The question whether the s30 LPA 1925 case law is still relevant today fell to be determined in *TSB Bank plc* v *Marshall* [1998] 39 EG 208. There the court decided that the principles laid down in that case law were applicable to applications under s14 of the 1996 Act. The court concluded that three principles could be derived from the authorities decided under s30 LPA 1925. First, the court should as a matter of discretion do what was equitable, fair and just. Second, where the interests of the chargee and an innocent spouse in the matrimonial home differed the former ought to prevail unless there were exceptional circumstances. Third, where there was a subsisting collateral purpose of the trust for sale the court should not defeat that purpose by ordering a sale. However, it is important to emphasise that this is a decision of a county court and as such is not binding.

This 'positive' view of the s30 LPA case law must now be set against the more cautious view taken of the matter by the Court of Appeal in *Mortgage Corporation* v *Shaire & Others* [2001] Ch 743. There MC (the chargee) sought possession of the home (in order to sell it) as against S (the defendant) pursuant to s14 TOLATA 1996. S argued that any order under s14 would be to the detriment of her family contrary to s15(1) of the 1996 Act. Although it was well established under the pre-TOLATA 1996 case law (see *Re Citro (A Bankrupt)* and *Lloyds Bank plc* v *Byrne* [1993] 1 FLR 369) that save in exceptional circumstances the will of the person seeking a sale, be they a trustee in bankruptcy or a chargee, would prevail over the interest of children and families, since the replacement of trusts for sale with the 'less arcane' trusts of land under the 1996 Act the following question had to be addressed, namely 'had the law relating to the way in which the court would exercise its power to order a sale at the suit of a chargee changed?' In concluding that it had, the Court made four main points. First, Parliament must have intended a change in the law in specifically setting out in s15 of the 1996 Act the matters that the court had to have regard to when exercising its jurisdiction to order a sale. Second, s15(1) of the 1996 Act made clear that the interests of the chargee were just one of four specified factors that the court was to consider in the exercise of its powers. Further, there was nothing to suggest that those interests were to be given any more weight than the interests of children residing in the home (another of the four specified factors). Third, the concept of trust for sale and the law as it had been developed by the courts suggested that, in the absence of a good reason to the contrary, the court should order a sale, whereas there was nothing in the language of the 1996 Act to suggest that it upheld the old concept of the trust for sale. Fourth, while *Lloyds Bank plc* v *Byrne* supported the reasoning in s30 LPA 1925 that a case involving a bankrupt co-owner should be treated precisely the same way as one involving an application for possession by a chargee, it was quite clear that Parliament now regarded it as appropriate to have a different approach in these two situations. Accordingly, there was ample evidence to support the conclusion that the 1996 Act had been drafted with the aim of relaxing the old law so as to enable the court to have a greater discretion which could be exercised in favour of families and against banks and other chargees. In view of that conclusion, pre-1996 Act authorities (ie cases decided under the now repealed s30), whilst still useful, should be treated 'with caution'. This was a case which called for the exercise of the court's discretion in favour of S's family and, accordingly, no order would be made.

Protection of purchasers

Section 16 deals with the protection of purchasers of *unregistered* land which is or has been held on trust. It absolves such a purchaser from the need to enquire whether there has been a breach of trust in various circumstances, eg he does not have to investigate whether the trustees have obtained the consent of beneficiaries to a partition (s7(3)) or consulted the beneficiaries (s11(1)). Further, it is provided that where trustees convey land to persons they believe to be beneficiaries of full age and capacity absolutely entitled to the land under trust, they are to execute a deed declaring that they are discharged from the trust in relation to the land: s16(4).

The effect of s16 is to confirm the protection that was in place before the commencement of the Act. The provision does *not apply to registered land* because purchasers of such land can rely upon the state of the register. If in the case of registered land it is intended to limit the trustees' powers or to require the consent of two or more persons to the exercise by the trustees of any power relating to the land then the settlor will want to ensure that appropriate restrictions are placed on the register of title.

Part II – Appointment and retirement of trustees

This Part of the Act applies to all trusts (whether of land or personalty) whenever created. Its aim is to give beneficiaries greater powers over the appointment of trustees.

Background

The pre-Act position was that trustees did not have to consult the beneficiaries when appointing new trustees: *Re Brockbank* [1948] Ch 206. Further, beneficiaries could not (except in the case of maladministration of the trust) force the trustees to retire.

The aim of the new law is to provide an alternative to the only option formerly available to beneficiaries who wanted to control the appointment of trustees, namely to bring the trust to an end under the rule in *Saunders* v *Vautier* (1841) 4 Beav 115 and then reconstitute it with their own candidates as trustees (this option was unattractive from a tax perspective).

Sections 19–22

The Act establishes a new right for beneficiaries: s19. They can now give trustees a written direction to retire from the trust or to appoint a particular person as a trustee (ie the decision in *Re Brockbank* is reversed). This right can be exercised at any time (not just when the existing trustees have to make an appointment to augment their number). However, there are a number of qualifying conditions to this right. The new right is only available if:

1. there is no person who is given the power to appoint trustees in the trust instrument (this condition falls to be determined at the time when s19 is under construction);
2. the beneficiaries are of full age and capacity; and
3. it has not been expressly excluded by the trust instrument.

The effect of condition 2 is to make Part II inapplicable to discretionary trusts or where there are infant beneficiaries. The right can be excluded in respect of trusts created before the commencement of the Act. Further, s19 takes effect subject to the restrictions imposed by the Trustee Act 1925 on the number of trustees: s19(5).

The effect of these provisions is clearly to pass more control to the beneficiaries. Further, the fact that Part II applies both to trusts of land and trusts of personalty is in line with the Law Commission's goal of achieving greater parity (in this instance greater standardisation of beneficiaries' rights) between both types of trust. It is anticipated that many settlors or testators will want to exclude the operation of Part II. Accordingly, it is most likely to apply in relation to a resulting or constructive trust (usually in respect of a family home) where the legal title is held by one person on trust for another who has contributed to the purchase price.

Conclusion

The Act is an amending rather than a consolidating statute. It removes the complication of the pre-Act system of two distinct ways of holding land in trust. It is retrospective except as regard pre-Act strict settlements. Accordingly, the Settled Land Act regime still remains (with some amendments) part of English land law – at least in the short term. However, strict settlements will be phased out. The timescale in this regard is uncertain (for example it will depend upon how frequently on a resettlement of a pre-Act settlement advantage is taken of the facility to convert to a trust of land).

Finally, like the Law of Property (Miscellaneous Provisions) Act 1994 the Act aims to make the law more comprehensible to lay people. However, time alone will tell whether that goal will be achieved.

9

Co-ownership

9.1 Introduction

9.2 Creation of a joint tenancy

9.3 Creation of a tenancy in common

9.4 Resulting trusts and co-ownership

9.5 Aspects of co-ownership under the 1925 legislation

9.6 Co-ownership under the Trusts of Land and Appointment of Trustees Act 1996

9.7 House deposit and co-ownership

9.8 Ending of co-ownership

9.9 Rights between co-owners

9.10 Other forms of co-ownership

9.11 Worked example

9.1 Introduction

Creation

Co-ownership arises when two or more persons hold an interest in land at the same time. Their interests in land must be *concurrent* rather than consecutive. If land is conveyed to A and B in fee simple in possession, then A and B are co-owners. If land is conveyed to A for life, the remainder to B, then A and B both have an interest in the same land, but their interests are consecutive, not concurrent, and they are not co-owners.

Where land is held by co-owners, then during their lifetimes each is entitled to live on or share in the proceeds of the land. See *Bull* v *Bull* [1955] 1 QB 234. But on the death of a co-owner (say A), there are two possible ways in which his interest in the land could devolve. It could pass to the remaining co-owner (B), so that B becomes the sole owner of the land. Alternatively, the interest could pass under A's will or intestacy to a third party, eg two children C and D, so that B and C and D then become co-owners of the land. The problems arise as to their respective shares.

124

This may be illustrated by the following diagram, assuming A and B make an equal contribution to the purchase price.

Joint tenancy	*Tenancy in common*
A–B	A–B
A dies leaving two children C and D. The result is: B takes all as survivor.	A dies leaving two children C and D. The result is: C – D – B
	1/4 1/4 1/2

Where the first arrangement exists, A and B hold the land as 'joint tenants', and B's entitlement to A's share on A's death is known as the 'right of survivorship'. Under the second arrangement, A and B hold the land as 'tenants in common' and B, C and D continue to hold as tenants in common.

Co-owners must hold their land either as joint tenants or as tenants in common. The main distinction between the two means of holding the land is that the right of survivorship applies only to joint tenancies and that only the joint tenancy can exist at *law* after 1925.

Note:

1. The word 'tenant' in the context of co-ownership has nothing to do with a tenant under a lease. It is derived from tenure and describes how the land is held.
2. The right of survivorship is also known by its Latin form, as the *jus accrescendi*.
3. By the Bodies Corporate (Joint Tenancy) Act 1899 a corporation may acquire and hold any property in joint tenancy in the same manner as if it were an individual.

Joint tenancy

Under a joint tenancy the joint tenants are considered to be a single composite person who is the land owner. All the joint tenants own all the land and no single joint tenant can point to any part of the land as his alone. However, each joint tenant has a potential share in the land equal to that of all the other joint tenants. If there are four joint tenants, each has a potential quarter share. This word 'potential' should always be used to describe the prospective interest of the surviving joint tenants at any time.

The right of survivorship follows logically from the concept of a single composite owner. The loss (through the death of a joint tenant) of part of the composite owner does not prevent the continued existence of the composite owner so long as there are at least two surviving co-owners. If A, B, C and D hold land as joint tenants, the joint tenancy will continue until there is only one survivor who will be solely entitled to the land. This may generally be referred to as the 'lottery effect' with the prize going to the person who lives the longest.

A joint tenant *cannot* dispose of his interest *by will*. The right of survivorship will take precedence over any attempted disposition by will and over the usual rules of intestacy. This rule is expressed in Latin as *jus accrescendi praefertur ultimae voluntati*. But a joint tenant can dispose of his interest during his lifetime. His interest will consist of his potential share, and the person to whom it is granted will hold that interest as a tenant in common, not as a joint tenant, and so will not be affected by the jus accrescendi. But such disposition can only take place *in equity* because s1(6) LPA 1925 provides that:

> 'A legal estate is not capable of subsisting or of being created in an undivided share in land.'

Alternatively, a joint tenant can avoid the jus accrescendi by transforming his joint tenancy into a tenancy in common during his lifetime. This is called 'severance' and is dealt with in detail in section 9.9.

Tenancy in common

A tenancy in common arises where land is limited to two or more persons with words of severance, which indicate an intention that the parties are to take separate shares.

Under a tenancy in common each co-owner remains an individual land owner with a distinct share in the land. These shares need not be equal. If A and B are tenants in common, their shares could be half each or three-quarters and one quarter. While the size of each co-owner's share is known, the share does not represent any particular piece of land. Each tenant has a share in all the land. Hence these shares are known as '*undivided shares*' in land, the phrase used in the LPA 1925 to describe tenancies in common.

When the land is sold, the proceeds of sale are divided according to the tenants' respective shares. The right of survivorship does not apply, and so a tenant in common can dispose of his interest both inter vivos and by will.

Severance

A joint tenant who wishes his interest to pass to a person other than the remaining joint tenants cannot give effect to his wishes by will. Any attempt to dispose of his interest by will is ineffective, as the right of survivorship comes into operation on his death. However, he can avoid the right of survivorship by converting his joint tenancy into a tenancy in common during his lifetime. This process is called severance (see section 9.9).

If A, B and C are joint tenants and A severs his interest, B and C remain as joint tenants, with mutual rights of survivorship, while A's interest becomes a tenancy in common of one-third of the equitable interest. A no longer has any rights of survivorship, but he can dispose of his interest by will. At the same time A will remain a joint tenant at law, and A, B and C will hold the legal estate as joint tenants for A as a tenant in common in equity and B and C as joint tenants in equity.

Where there are only two joint tenants, severance by one converts the interest of the other into a tenancy in common, as there cannot be a sole joint tenant. Again such effect only applies in equity; while the two will continue as joint tenants at law, they will both become tenants in common in equity: *Williams* v *Hensman* (1861) 1 J & H 546.

Severance can be effected by:

1. Alienation *inter vivos* by a joint tenant.
2. Acquisition of another estate in land.
3. Homicide.
4. Notice in writing (s36(2) LPA 1925).
5. Bankruptcy.
6. Course of dealing.

These methods are dealt with in detail in section 9.9.

Legal and equitable interests under co-ownership

There is no requirement that the legal and equitable interests in land held under co-ownership should be identical, and frequently they differ. A key to the proper understanding of co-ownership is always to consider the legal estate separately from the equitable interest. This is an area where the drawing of diagrams to illustrate the respective interests is an invaluable aid to understanding the principles.

Prior to the 1925 legislation joint tenancies and tenancies in common could exist both at *law* and *in equity*. Now *only a joint tenancy can exist at law* and a tenancy in common must be held behind a trust. Hence the legal title of land held under co-ownership must always be held as a joint tenancy. The equitable interest can be held as a joint tenancy or as a tenancy in common or as a mixture of both.

The separation of the legal and equitable interests

The following examples show the importance of considering the legal and equitable interests separately.

If A, B and C are co-owners as joint tenants, then they hold the legal estate on trust for themselves as joint tenants in equity.

Legal estate	*Equitable interest*
A, B, C as joint tenants	A, B, C as joint tenants

If C dies, the jus accrescendi (the right of survivorship between joint tenants) operates both at law and in equity, so that A and B are left as legal and equitable joint tenants.

A, B   A, B
as joint tenants   as joint tenants

The combined effect of the above two examples may be illustrated as:

A B C   –   joint tenants at law
A B C   –   joint tenants in equity

Death of C and the effect of the right of survivorship:

A B   –   joint tenants at law
A B   –   joint tenants in equity

Alternatively, where A, B and C are joint tenants both at law and in equity, C can sever his equitable joint tenancy. The effect of this is that A, B and C remain joint tenants at law, holding the equitable interest on trust for A and B as joint tenants and C as a tenant in common.

Legal estate   *Equitable interest*

A, B, C   A, B as joint tenants of two-thirds
as joint tenants   C as tenant in common of one-third

The effect of this may be shown as:

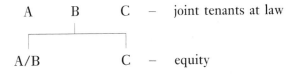

A   B   C   –   joint tenants at law

A/B   C   –   equity

joint tenants   tenant in common
two-thirds   one-third

If A, B and C are co-owners as tenants in common, they hold the legal estate as joint tenants on trust for themselves as equitable tenants in common.

Legal estate   *Equitable interest*

A, B, C   A, B, C
as joint tenants   as tenants in common

If C dies, the jus accrescendi operates on the legal estate so that A and B acquire C's legal estate and remain joint tenants, but they hold C's equitable interest under his tenancy in common on trust for his personal representatives.

Legal estate	*Equitable interest*
A, B	A, B, C's personal representatives as tenants in common

The combined effect of the last two examples may be illustrated as:

A   B   C   –   joint tenants at law

A   B   C   –   tenants in common in equity

Death of C and assuming each contributed an equal share to the purchase price.

A   B   –   joint tenants at law

A   B   PRs of C   –   tenants in common in equity

one-   one-   one-
third third third

It should be noted that the legal owner(s) need not be the same person(s) as the equitable co-owners. A and B can jointly hold the legal estate on trust for C and D as equitable joint tenants or equitable tenants in common.

Determination of the type of co-ownership

As the legal estate must always be held under a joint tenancy, it is the equitable interest that reflects whether land is held under a joint tenancy or a tenancy in common.

How the equitable interest is held will depend upon the means by which the co-ownership came into existence, and whether there has been severance of any or all of the equitable interests after the creation of a joint tenancy.

9.2 Creation of a joint tenancy

The essence of the joint tenancy is that the joint tenants do not have separate interests in the property. Together they are entitled to the same interest. A joint tenancy can be created expressly or impliedly. In either case the 'four unities' must be present before there can be a joint tenancy.

The four unities (PITT)

These are:

1. *Unity of possession.* This means that each co-owner is equally entitled to possession of the whole land and can sue if excluded from any part of the land. The essential feature is described by Megarry and Wade at page 477:

   '... each co-owner is as much entitled to possession of any part of the land as the others.'

2. *Unity of interest.* The interest of each co-owner must be identical with regard to the extent, duration and nature of the interest held in the land. None of the individual co-owners can dispose of the interest by himself because he does not have the whole estate, as seen in *Thames Guaranty Ltd* v *Campbell* [1984] 2 All ER 585.

3. *Unity of title.* Each co-owner must claim title under the same document or act; for instance, all the co-owners acquired their interest from the same conveyance.

4. *Unity of time.* The interest of each co-owner must vest at the same time.

If there is no unity of possession there is no co-ownership; if one of the other three unities (interest, title or time) is missing there may be a tenancy in common but not a joint tenancy.

Express creation

This occurs when a grant to co-owners expressly states that the land is to be held jointly and the four unities are present.

Implied or presumed creation

Where a grant of land to co-owners is silent as to how the land is to be held, there is a presumption at law that the land will be held as a joint tenancy provided that:

1. the four unities are present; and
2. the presumption of a joint tenancy is not rebutted by:

   a) words of severance; or
   b) factors showing that a tenancy in common was intended; or
   c) factors giving rise to an equitable presumption of a tenancy in common.
   (See below.)

9.3 Creation of a tenancy in common

As with a joint tenancy, a tenancy in common can be created expressly or impliedly.

In either case there must be *unity of possession*, without which there cannot be any form of co-ownership. But there is no requirement for the other unities to be present.

Express creation

A grant to co-owners stating that they are to hold as tenants in common creates an equitable tenancy in common, provided that there is unity of possession.

Implied or presumed creation

A grant of land to more than one person where the grant is silent as to how the land is to be held will take effect in equity as a tenancy in common if:

1. Any of the four unities (apart from unity of possession) is missing; or
2. Words of severance were used in the grant. These are words showing an intention on the part of the grantor that the co-owners were each to have distinct, but undivided, shares in the land, rather than to hold the land as a notional composite person. Words that have been held to give co-owners undivided shares in land and so create a tenancy in common are:

    To A and B equally
    To A and B in equal shares
    To be divided among A and B
    Among A and B

    The words must be clear.
3. The grant as a whole showed that a tenancy in common was intended.

Equitable presumptions in favour of a tenancy in common

A rebuttable equitable presumption which overrides the presumption at law of a joint tenancy arises in certain circumstances. In general, these are circumstances where it would be inequitable for there to be a joint tenancy with the consequent right of survivorship and equal division of the proceeds of sale.

First, where the purchase money for land conveyed into the names of more than one person was provided by those persons in *unequal shares*, the legal estate will be held by the owners as joint tenants on trust for themselves as equitable tenants in common holding undivided shares proportionate to their respective contributions. See *Bull* v *Bull* [1955] 1 QB 234. But no such presumption arises in the case of equal shares where they will be presumed to be joint tenants.

Secondly, where two or more persons advance money on mortgage, whether in equal or unequal shares.

Thirdly, where the land is partnership property. See *Lake* v *Craddock* (1732) 3 P Wms 158 where it was held that the right of survivorship is incompatible with a commercial undertaking – *jus accrescendi inter mercatores pro beneficio commerci locum.*

It is clear that this is only a presumption which may be subject to any express declaration to the contrary in favour of a joint tenancy. A good example of the presumption being so rebutted is *Barton v Morris* [1985] 2 All ER 1032. There a farm was conveyed to two people *expressly* as joint tenants with the bulk of the purchase money being provided by one of them. The property was run as a guest house and small farm, and the person who provided the bulk of the purchase money kept partnership accounts showing the farm as a partnership asset. Nicholls J held that in view of the express declaration in the conveyance that the property was to be held on joint tenancy, he could not accept that there had been any course of dealing with the property from which a severance of the joint tenancy could be inferred. Thus the presumption of a tenancy in common derived from the fact of the partnership accounts could not prevail over the express words of the conveyance.

The Privy Council has indicated that the list is not exhaustive and, in particular, has added a fourth category of presumption in favour of a tenancy in common in equity: where the grantees hold the premises for their several individual business purposes. The case in which this arose was *Malayan Credit Ltd v Jack Chia MPH Ltd* [1986] 1 All ER 711, which concerned a five-year lease of one floor of an office block in Singapore. The floor area and responsibility for outgoings was apportioned between tenants as to 62 per cent and 38 per cent respectively, and each tenant used the accommodation for their separate commercial activities. Sale of the property was ordered with a division of the proceeds of sale in the above proportions.

Lord Brightman said:

'Where premises are held by two persons as joint tenants at law for their several business purposes, it is improbable that they would intend to hold as joint tenants in equity.'

He was of the opinion that the equitable presumptions in favour of a tenancy in common should not be restricted to the usual three (above) and concluded:

'There are other circumstances in which equity may infer that the beneficial interest is intended to be held as – tenants in common – one such case is where the grantees hold the premises for their several individual business purposes.'

This new presumption fits neatly between the first and third existing presumptions discussed above: where the purchase money is provided in unequal shares, and in the case of partnership property.

9.4 Resulting trusts and co-ownership

A presumed equitable joint tenancy or tenancy in common can arise where land is conveyed into the name of one person. Where two or more persons contribute to the purchase money of land which is conveyed into the name of only one of them (or into the names of fewer than contributed), there is a rebuttable equitable presumption that they were all intended to share ownership of the land. To give effect to this presumption, equity imposes a resulting trust on the person(s) in whom the legal estate is vested, to hold the equitable interest on trust for all the contributors as equitable co-owners. If the purchase money was contributed in equal shares, the equitable interest will be held as a joint tenancy. Otherwise the equitable presumption of a tenancy in common will prevail. See *Williams & Glyn's Bank* v *Boland* [1980] 3 WLR 138.

The context in which such resulting trusts arise must be emphasised – legal title in the name of one co-owner with another or more persons (not on the legal title) having contributed to the acquisition of the land.

Many of the cases in this area concern the family home. In this regard it is important to distinguish between the case of a married couple involved in *matrimonial proceedings* (divorce, nullity or judicial separation) and other situations. In the former situation where for example a co-owning married couple are divorcing the court can invoke its discretionary powers under ss23–25 of the Matrimonial Causes Act 1973 to order a distribution of the property of the spouses. In other situations the principles of property law apply to disputes as to the family home between co-owners. In particular, they will apply to the following three situations where the legal title is in the name of one co-owner and the other party not on the legal title has made a contribution to the acquisition of the property. First, in the case of an unmarried couple (co-habitees) if the relationship breaks down the court has no statutory powers (like the Matrimonial Causes Act for married couples) to adjust their property interests. Secondly, in the case of a married couple whose relationship is over but who are not seeking a divorce etc and there is a dispute as to their respective beneficial entitlements. Thirdly, in cases concerning the right to possession where for example the co-owner on the legal title defaults on his mortgage and the other co-owner is trying to prevent the bank/building society gaining possession with a view to sale. Under the old s70(1)(g) of the Land Registration Act 1925 the party not on the legal title had to have a proprietary interest (eg a beneficial interest) in the property and had to be in actual occupation prior to completion of the transaction (eg the mortgage).

Also of note in this regard is the Civil Partnership Act 2004 which establishes civil partnership as a legal relationship between two people of the same sex and provides that such a partnership only ends on death, dissolution or annulment. By virtue of s65 of the 2004 Act, where a civil partner has made a substantial contribution in money or money's worth to the improvement of property in which either or both the civil partners have an interest, he or she is treated as having acquired a share or an enlarged share in that property. Further, s66 enables civil partners to refer disputes over property to court. The Act received the Royal Assent on 18 November 2004 and some of its provisions came into force on that day.

Where the legal title to a property is in the name of only one party (usually the husband/man) he will prima facie be deemed to own the entire equitable interest in the property. However, if the conveyance contains an express declaration as to beneficial ownership that, in the absence of fraud or mistake, will be conclusive. If the conveyance contains no such express declaration then the party not on the legal title (usually the wife/woman) can claim a beneficial interest in the property in a variety of ways *including* the following:

1. express declaration;
2. direct contribution to acquisition; and
3. indirect contribution to acquisition.

Express declaration

If there is an express declaration as to beneficial ownership, but *not* in the conveyance, then provided such declaration is evidenced in writing (ie complies with s53(1)(b) LPA 1925) it is enforceable.

Direct contribution

Where the party not on the legal title makes a direct contribution in money or money's worth to the acquisition of the property this will give rise to a resulting trust (ie the co-owner in whom the legal title is vested holds the property on trust for himself and the other co-owner in equity). Direct contributions to acquisition include payment of legal costs, providing a cash deposit on purchase or payment of or substantial contributions to the mortgage instalments.

Where the non-owning party has made a direct contribution to acquisition beneficial ownership will be shared in proportion to that contribution. For example, if H and W buy a house for £50,000 with H providing £40,000 and W £10,000 with the legal title being vested in H's name alone, H will be holding the property on resulting trust for himself and W in equity as to ⅘ and ⅕ respectively. However, in *Midland Bank plc* v *Cooke & Another* [1995] 4 All ER 562 the Court of Appeal held that where a partner in a matrimonial home not on the legal title established an equitable interest through direct contribution to the purchase price of the property, the court would (in the absence of express evidence of intention) assess the proportions the parties were to be assumed to have intended for their beneficial ownership by looking at the whole course of dealing between them relevant to their ownership and occupation of the property and would not be bound *solely* to the financial contribution of the parties when the circumstances suggested that some other agreement as to shares in the property was appropriate. This decision is out of line with established authorities on the point (see for example, *Bull* v *Bull* [1955] 1 QB 234 and *Sekhon* v *Alissa* [1989] 2 FLR 94) and it is submitted that the better view is that the non-owning party who makes a direct contribution to acquisition will have a share in the beneficial interest proportionate to her financial contribution.

A direct contribution by the non-owning spouse to the acquisition of the property will give rise to a purchase money resulting trust. In *Lloyds Bank plc* v

Rosset [1991] 1 AC 107 the House of Lords seems to regard direct contributions as giving rise to a constructive trust. Lord Bridge put the matter thus:

> 'Direct contributions to ... purchase price by [a] partner ... not the legal owner whether initially or by payment of mortgage instalments, would readily justify ... the creation of a constructive trust ... extremely doubtful whether anything less would do'. (at p133)

However, this is contrary to established principles.

A potent source of confusion in property disputes between co-owners (where only one is on the legal title) has been caused by the suggestion made by a number of judges that it was irrelevant whether the terminology used was that of a resulting trust or of a constructive trust (see eg Lord Denning MR in *Hussey* v *Palmer* [1972] 1 WLR 1286 at pp1289, 1290). However, such confusion is less likely now. In *Drake* v *Whipp* [1996] 1 FLR 826, the Court of Appeal emphasised that there was a difference between acquiring a beneficial interest under a resulting trust as opposed to a constructive trust. In a resulting trust, the claimant's share was directly related to the cost of acquisition. In a constructive trust what was needed was a common intention that the party not on the legal title would have a beneficial interest and that that party had acted to his or her detriment in reliance on that intention. Further, the court made clear that in the case of a constructive trust the court could adopt a 'broad brush' to the proportions (in respect of the beneficial interest) awarded. Accordingly, it is submitted that these two types of trust have different origins and consequences. This clear judicial recognition for the fact that resulting and constructive trusts are not the same is most welcome. In this regard, it is interesting to note that the distinction between resulting and constructive trusts has been maintained in Canada (see *Pettkus* v *Becker* (1980) 117 DLR (3rd) 257).

Finally, in the case of a direct contribution it seems that no actual intention to share has to be proved.

Indirect contribution

Where the party not on the legal title makes an indirect contribution to the acquisition of the property this may give that party a beneficial interest in the property. This is a highly volatile area of the 'family home' and a substantial number of the cases come within the constructive trust category. In *Eves* v *Eves* [1975] 1 WLR 1338, for example, the case concerned an unmarried couple who bought a house as a joint home. However, the conveyance was taken in the man's name alone and he gave as an excuse for not putting it in joint names the fact that at the relevant time the woman was under 21 years of age. The woman made a substantial work contribution in relation to both the house and garden (way beyond ordinary housework) including breaking up the concrete surface with a sledge hammer and disposing of the rubble into a skip. Further, she also prepared the front garden for turfing. When the couple separated, she successfully claimed a share of the house. Lord Denning MR put the matter thus: '[it would be] most inequitable for him to deny her any share in the house. The law will impute or impose a *constructive trust* by which he was to hold it in trust for both of them' (at p1341). Further, in *Hazell* v *Hazell* [1972] 1 WLR 301 the court found a beneficial interest for a wife based upon her contributions towards housekeeping expenses.

The way in which the constructive trust has been used in cases concerning indirect contributions has changed over the years. During the 1970s a broad principle emerged to the effect that a constructive trust might be imposed irrespective of established legal rules in order to reach the result required by justice and good conscience (the 'justice approach'). The trust was styled as the new model constructive trust and Lord Denning MR its principal exponent described it in *Hussey* v *Palmer* [1972] 3 All ER 744 as 'a trust imposed by law whenever justice and good conscience require it. It is a liberal process, founded on large principles of equity, to be applied in cases where the defendant cannot conscientiously keep the property for himself alone, but ought to allow another to have the property or a share in it.' R H Maudsley explained the emergence 'of the new model constructive trust' as follows: 'It is possible to read into recent decisions a rule that in cases in which the plaintiff ought to win, but has no legal doctrine or authority to support him, a constructive trust in his favour will do the trick' (1977) 28 NILQ 123.

Three main criticisms were made of the new model constructive trust and the 'justice approach' taken to its imposition. First, it was at variance with the House of Lords decision in *Pettitt* v *Pettitt* [1969] 2 WLR 996. Secondly, the concept of justice on its own was too vague to be used as the basis for determining property rights and the imposition of a constructive trust on this basis was difficult to predict – all turned on the views of an individual judge. Thirdly, this system of 'palm tree justice' between the litigating parties could result in injustice to others in particular mortgagees.

Since the retirement of Lord Denning MR there has been a clear retreat by the Court of Appeal from the new model constructive trust and the 'justice approach'. In *Burns* v *Burns* [1984] Ch 317, for example, the woman looked after the children of the family, performed domestic duties, paid telephone bills, bought domestic chattels for the house and redecorated the interior ie she had made no financial contribution referable to its acquisition. Even though this had been going on over a period of 17 years the woman failed in her claim to a share of the beneficial interest. Further, in *Passee* v *Passee* [1983] 1 FLR 263 the Court of Appeal held that contributions towards running costs of a house did not give rise to any interest in it.

It is now clear that the courts do not enjoy a broad adjustive discretion (like the one articulated by Lord Denning MR in *Hussey* v *Palmer*) to impose a constructive trust in order to achieve a 'fair result' (see eg *Sekhon* v *Alissa* [1989] 2 FLR 94).

At present a new approach – 'the intention approach' – governs the imposition of a constructive trust to give a party not on the legal title who has made an indirect contribution to the acquisition of property a share of the beneficial interest. Under this approach what is needed is a common intention that the party not on the legal title will have a beneficial interest and that that party has acted to his or her detriment in reliance on that intention. In *Grant* v *Edwards* [1986] 3 WLR 114 where the court was considering whether a co-habitee should have a beneficial interest in a home, Nourse LJ put the matter thus:

> '... where there is no written declaration or agreement, nor any direct provision by the plaintiff of part of the purchase price so as to give rise to a resulting trust in her favour, she had to establish a common intention between her and the defendant, acted upon by her, that she should have a beneficial interest in the property. If she could do that equity would not allow the defendant to deny that interest and would construct a trust to give effect to it.'

There is case authority for the view that there needs to be an *express common intention* (see *Hammond* v *Mitchell* [1991] 1 WLR 1127). In *Lloyds Bank plc* v *Rosset* [1991] 1 AC 107, the House of Lords considered, inter alia, the question of common intention. Their Lordships concluded that the work done by the wife was insufficient to justify an inference of a common intention that she should have a beneficial interest in it. Neither common intention by spouses that a house was to be renovated as a joint venture nor a common intention that it was to be shared by them and their children as the family home threw any light on their intention with respect to the beneficial ownership of the property.

Finally, it seems that any beneficial interest arising under a constructive trust crystallises as soon as there is a sufficient act of detrimental reliance on the part of the claimant (ie it arises before its confirmation by the court and therefore it can effect third parties).

Conclusion

Where a person not on the legal title has made a direct contribution to the acquisition of the property, as noted above, he/she will acquire a beneficial interest under a resulting trust. However, case law demonstrates that such a person can claim an enlarged share of the beneficial interest beyond his/her contribution proportion (eg by also making an indirect contribution to acquisition) provided that it is based on the *real intention* of the parties. The conclusion of the Court of Appeal in *Midland Bank plc* v *Cooke* [1995] 4 All ER 562 that the presumed intention of the parties could be sufficient to bring about an enlargement of the claimant's beneficial interest is out of step with established case law (see eg *Lloyds Bank plc* v *Rosset*).

Finally, the equitable presumption of a resulting trust can be rebutted by evidence showing that the contribution was intended as a loan or gift. In *Re Sharpe (A Bankrupt)* [1980] 1 All ER 198 (see Chapter 13) Browne-Wilkinson J put the matter thus:

> 'In my judgment, if, as in this case, moneys are advanced by way of loan there can be no question of the lender being entitled to an interest in the property under a resulting trust. If he were to take such an interest, he would get his money twice; once on repayment of the loan and once on taking his share of the proceeds of sale of the property.'

9.5 Aspects of co-ownership under the 1925 legislation

Before 1926 both joint tenancies and tenancies in common could exist as legal estates. Considerable conveyancing problems could arise with legal tenancies in common as the conveyance had to be signed by all the legal tenants in common, who could be numerous and whose names would not necessarily be on the original deed.

For example, if prior to 1 January 1926 Blackacre was held on a legal tenancy in common by A, B, C and D and each co-owner had, say, four children to whom A, B, C and D on death by will passed legal title in Blackacre to, this would have resulted in there being 16 legal tenants in common (prior to the aforementioned date there was no restriction on the number of persons who could be on the legal title to land). In such a situation all 16 co-owners had to agree to sell and sign a conveyance to that effect before Blackacre could be sold. Such a state of affairs militated against ease of sale and conveyance of land and usually added to conveyancing costs (especially if difficulties were encountered in finding all the legal tenants in common).

As part of the general ruling of the 1925 legislation and specifically in order to remedy the above problem (for land other than settled land), the following principles were laid down by ss34–36 LPA 1925:

1. Tenancies in common *cannot* exist as legal estates, but only as equitable interests.
2. A joint tenant cannot convert his joint tenancy to a tenancy in common (ie sever his joint tenancy) at law, but only in equity.
3. The legal estate of land held in equity by co-owners is always held as a joint tenancy.
4. The legal joint tenancy was held by trustees on trust for sale for the equitable co-owners, who might be tenants in common or joint tenants.

Abolition of a legal tenancy in common (for land other than settled land)

This is recognised by s1(6) LPA 1925:

'A legal estate is not capable of subsisting or of being created in an undivided share in land.'

This was achieved by two provisions:

1. A legal tenancy in common cannot exist or be created after 1925 (s34 LPA 1925). Section 34(1) provides:

'An undivided share in land shall not be capable of being created except ... as hereinafter mentioned.'

The detailed provisions are to be found in s34(2) LPA 1925. The effect is that any attempt to create a legal tenancy in common takes effect as a joint tenancy at law and a tenancy in common in equity. It is important to note that the 1925 legislation refers to tenancies in common as 'undivided shares in land'.

As a consequence, if land is conveyed to A and B to hold as legal tenants in common, A and B will hold the legal estate as joint tenants on trust for themselves as tenants in common in equity.

2. A legal joint tenancy cannot be severed after 1925 (s36(2) LPA 1925). Section 36(2) provides:

'No severance of a joint tenancy of a legal estate, so as to create a tenancy in common in land, shall be permissible.'

Where land is held under a joint tenancy both at law and in equity only the equitable interest can be converted to a tenancy in common.

If A, B and C are joint tenants at law and in equity, C's severance of his joint tenancy can only take effect in *equity*. He will remain a joint tenant at law, and because he holds the legal estate as a trustee, he will continue to hold the legal estate until he dies or resigns as trustee, even though he may have severed his equitable interest by selling it to D. This is a particular point of many co-ownership degree examination questions and emphasises the need for separation of the legal estate from the equitable interest when answering such questions.

Imposition of a trust for sale

Whenever there was beneficial co-ownership in possession of land (other than settled land) the legal estate had to be held on a trust for sale (ss34 and 36 LPA 1925). If the conveyance did not expressly provide for a trust, a statutory trust was imposed. The terms were set out in s35 LPA 1925 (repealed by the Trusts of Land and Appointment of Trustees Act 1996). All the usual rules that applied to trusts for sale applied to the statutory trusts.

In the case of equitable joint tenancies, the trust for sale was imposed by s36 LPA 1925. In the case of tenancies in common, the trust for sale was imposed by s34 LPA 1925 and the trustees for sale held the legal estate as joint tenants for the co-owners as beneficial (equitable) tenants in common.

9.6 Co-ownership under the Trusts of Land and Appointment of Trustees Act 1996

The main consequences for land law of the coming into force on 1 January 1997 of the Trusts of Land and Appointment of Trustees Act 1996 have already been noted (see Chapter 8, section 8.22). However, it is useful to re-emphasise three of them. First, no new strict settlement can be created after 31 December 1996. Secondly, all trusts for sale in existence prior to 1 January 1997 are automatically converted into trusts of land. Thirdly, nearly all new trusts which include land will come within the new regime. However, it is still possible to create a trust for sale of land *expressly* after 31 December 1996 albeit as one type of the new trust of land (ss1(2), 4). A power to postpone sale is implied into all such trusts.

What is the effect of the 1996 Act on co-ownership? Schedule 2 of the Act deals with cases where under the 1925 legislation a trust for sale was imposed. In all such situations they are converted to trusts of land.

Joint tenancies

Section 36 LPA 1925 has been amended. It now provides as follows:

'Where a legal estate (not being settled land) is beneficially limited to or held in trust for any persons as joint tenants, the same shall be held *in trust*, in like manner as if the person beneficially entitled were tenants in common, but not so as to sever their joint tenancy in equity.'

The amendments to s36 have no practical significance. When land is, or was, conveyed to joint tenants they hold it upon a trust of land. The severance rules are unaffected. A legal joint tenancy cannot be severed. However, when an equitable joint tenancy is severed inter vivos the equitable interests are now held on a trust of land.

Tenancies in common

Section 34 LPA 1925 has been amended. It now provides as follows:

'(2) Where, after the commencement of this Act, land is expressed to be conveyed to any persons in undivided shares and those persons are of full age, the conveyance shall (notwithstanding anything to the contrary in this Act) operate as if the land had been expressed to be conveyed to the grantees, or, if there are more than four grantees, to the four first named in the conveyance, as joint tenants *in trust* for the persons interested in the land ...'

As with s36 LPA 1925, the amendments to s34 LPA 1925 have little practical effect. It is still the case that a legal estate cannot be conveyed to tenants in common. Wherever land is, or was, expressed to be conveyed to persons as tenants in common the conveyance takes affect as a conveyance to them (or if more than four to the first four named who are able and willing to take) as joint tenants upon a trust of land for themselves as tenants in common.

9.7 House deposit and co-ownership

The effect of a parent paying the deposit on a first matrimonial home as a wedding present has been considered by the courts. In *McHardy & Sons* v *Warren* [1994] 2 FLR 338 the husband held the legal title to the matrimonial home (which was unregistered) in his sole name. The wife's claim to a beneficial interest arose because her father-in-law had paid the deposit (£650) on the first matrimonial home as a wedding present to his son and daughter-in-law (the defendants). The court held that where a parent so acts then the bride and groom are to have equal interests in the home and not an interest by reference to the percentage which the deposit bore to the full price. Further, it was irrelevant that the property was in the husband's name alone. Accordingly, the home was held by the husband on an implied trust for sale for himself and his wife in equal shares.

This is a somewhat doubtful decision as to the allocation of beneficial interest. Why should half of a deposit give the spouse not on the legal title half the beneficial interest without consideration as to who paid the rest of the purchase price subsequently?

In similar vein is *Midland Bank plc* v *Cooke & Another* [1995] 4 All ER 562. There C and his wife moved into a house after they married which C had purchased just before their marriage in his sole name. The house cost £8,500 and it was financed by way of a mortgage of £6,450 with the balance coming out of C's savings and a wedding gift of £1,100 from C's parents. It was held that the wife had a beneficial interest in the property based on her contribution represented by her half share of the wedding gift from C's parents (ie she had made a direct contribution to the purchase price). At first instance she was awarded a beneficial interest of 6.47 per cent in the property being the proportion represented by her half share of the wedding gift (£550) to the total purchase price of the property (£8,500). However, on appeal she controversially obtained a half share of the beneficial interest (see section 9.4 above).

These cases demonstrate that a spouse not on the legal title can acquire a beneficial interest in a house through a share of a wedding gift used to assist in acquiring the matrimonial home and that such a contribution to acquisition will rank as a *direct* one.

9.8 Ending of co-ownership

Joint tenancy and tenancy in common both come to an end

First, if the land is divided physically between the co-owners or the land sold and the proceeds divided: this is known as partition. Section 28(3) of the Law of Property Act 1925 gave trustees for sale the power to partition the land. This provision has now been replaced by s7 of the Trusts of Land and Appointment of Trustees Act 1996 which applies the aforementioned power to the new trust of land regime. The power to partition land is an alternative to selling it. For co-owned land to be partitioned into separate shares the beneficiaries must be of full age and be absolutely entitled in individual shares to the land subject to the trust (s7 TOLATA 1996).

Secondly, if the entirety of the land becomes vested in one person: this is known as union. By the Law of Property (Joint Tenants) Act 1964 a purchaser from a sole surviving joint tenant is bound to assume that the survivor is solely and beneficially entitled if he conveys 'as beneficial owner' unless a memorandum of severance is endorsed on the conveyance which created the joint tenancy.

Thirdly, the problem of making title by the surviving joint tenant has created difficulties since 1925. By the Law of Property (Amendment) Act 1926 it was provided that the surviving joint tenant who is solely and beneficially entitled to the land could deal with the legal estate as if it were not held on trust for sale. This did not satisfy conveyancers because the deceased tenant – without the knowledge of the survivor – could have severed his interest. To overcome this rule many purchasers insisted that a second trustee be appointed in order to make title.

This is no longer necessary because s1(1) Law of Property (Joint Tenants) Act 1964 provides that the survivor of joint tenants shall, in favour of the purchaser, be deemed to be solely and beneficially interested if he conveys as beneficial owner.

This provision is subject to two major exceptions:

1. where a memorandum of severance has been endorsed on the conveyance by which the legal estate was vested in the joint tenants;
2. where the title to the land is registered (s3 1964 Act). This recognises the paramount position of the land register and the fact that the purchaser can rely upon the entries in the register. The purchaser will then only be affected by any severance of the joint equitable interest which has been entered on the register.

A joint tenancy may be severed and converted into a tenancy in common

It is possible to sever the *equitable joint tenancy* without disturbing the joint tenancy of the legal estate. Severance, to be effective, must be done during the joint tenant's lifetime. There are a variety of ways in which an equitable joint tenancy can be severed. In the ensuing paragraphs the following are considered:

1. alienation;
2. acquisition of another estate in land;
3. homicide;
4. notice in writing;
5. bankruptcy;
6. course of dealing.

It is important to emphasise that severance can only effect the equitable interest, not the legal estate. First, severance can be effected by a joint tenant alienating his interest *inter vivos*. The assignee becomes a tenant in common, although the other co-owners remain joint tenants as between themselves. A partial alienation, such as a mortgage, is sufficient to sever a joint tenancy, but a mere incumbrance is not.

Secondly, severance can be effected by a joint tenant acquiring another estate in the land. This destroys the unity of interest.

Thirdly, severance can be effected by homicide. The rule that no-one may benefit from his crime means that one joint tenant who kills another cannot benefit from that other's death by the operation of the principle of survivorship.

Fourthly, by virtue of s36(2) LPA 1925 an equitable joint tenancy can be severed by a joint tenant giving written notice to the other joint tenants. Any form of written notice will suffice provided it is given to all the other joint tenants and it shows a sufficient wish to effect an immediate severance. In *Re 88 Berkley Road London NW9* [1971] Ch 648 it was held that a notice had been properly served if it was sent by recorded delivery even if it was not received by the addressee. This was confirmed in *Kinch* v *Bullard* (1998) The Times 16 September. There Neuberger J concluded that a notice of severance of an equitable joint tenancy sent pursuant to s36(2) LPA 1925 was validly served within s196(3) LPA 1925 if it was posted to and delivered at the last known place of abode of the addressee even though he did not actually receive it. The court rejected the contention that there could not be a valid service where the sender had prevented the addressee from learning of the notice. However, it was suggested that the position might be different if the *sender* had informed the *addressee* of his wish to revoke the notice while it was still in the post. A point of difference between *Kinch* and *Re 88 Berkeley Road, London NW9* is that because the latter involved recorded delivery it concerned s196(4) LPA 1925, whereas the former concerned s196(3) LPA 1925. An unequivocal intention is sufficient. This was satisfied in *Re Draper's Conveyance* [1969] 1 Ch 486 where a wife who was a joint tenant of the matrimonial home asked the court (by way of issuing a summons) for an order granting her share in the property as soon as possible. However, in *Harris* v *Goddard* [1983] 1 WLR 1203 a mere prayer in a divorce petition under s24 Matrimonial Causes Act 1973 relating to the former matrimonial home was held not to be a notice of a desire to sever the joint tenancy under s36(2) LPA 1925. This was because in contrast to *Re Draper's Conveyance* (above) there was held to be no sufficient immediate intention to receive a specific share. Rather it was simply a request for the future.

Fifthly, an equitable joint tenancy can be severed by an act of bankruptcy by one joint tenant. Such severance occurs on the date of the act of bankruptcy and not on the later date of adjudication of bankruptcy. This was established in *Re Dennis (A Bankrupt)* [1995] 3 All ER 171. There D and his wife owned two properties as beneficial joint tenants. In September 1982, D committed an act of bankruptcy (he failed to comply with a bankruptcy notice) and so a bankruptcy petition was presented against him. D's wife died in February 1983, leaving her estate to her two children in her will. In May 1983 a receiving order was made against D, and in November 1983 he was adjudicated bankrupt. The question arose whether the vesting of D's property in the trustee, which severed the joint tenancies, occurred at the date of the act of bankruptcy by retrospective effect of the adjudication, or at the date of adjudication of bankruptcy. If the former, the joint tenancies were severed before the wife's death and her share as a tenant-in-common would devolve under her will. If the latter, the joint tenancies were not severed before the wife's death and the wife's share would pass on her death to D as survivor, with the result that on adjudication the whole interest in the properties vested in the trustee and was available to D's creditors. The Court of Appeal held that where a joint tenant of property was adjudged bankrupt under the Bankruptcy Act 1914, the title of the trustee in bankruptcy to that property related back to the first act of bankruptcy even though the debtor was not adjudged bankrupt until some later date. Consequently, in this case the joint tenancies had been severed on D's act of bankruptcy in September 1982 (ie before the wife's death) and therefore the wife's share devolved under her will. Accordingly, the court declared that a one-half share in the properties formed part of the wife's estate. (See also *Re Palmer (Deceased) (A Debtor)* [1994] 3 All ER 835.)

Finally, severance can be effected by a course of dealing. In *Burgess* v *Rawnsley* [1975] Ch 429 a widow, R, met a widower, H. They became good friends and bought a house together in which to live. Each paid half of the purchase price and held both the legal title and equitable interest as joint tenants. Subsequently, the relationship broke down and the elderly couple reached a verbal agreement whereby H was to buy R out. However, before this was reduced to writing H died. The Court of Appeal unanimously held that severance had occurred. Although the contract to sell was unenforceable because of the lack of written evidence required by s40 LPA 1925, there was a course of dealing which was sufficient to effect a severance. Lord Denning MR considered how far a course of dealing might provide the necessary evidence of severance and stated at pp438, 439:

'The thing to remember today is that equity leans against joint tenants and favours tenancies in common ... It is sufficient if there is a course of dealing in which one party makes clear to the other that he desires that their shares should no longer be held jointly but in common. Similarly it is sufficient if both parties enter on a course of dealing which evinces an intention by both of them that their shares shall henceforth be held in common and not jointly.'

The mutual agreement need not be specifically enforceable. The significance of the agreement is not that it binds the parties, but that it serves as an indication of a common intention to sever. Since *Burgess* v *Rawnsley* (above) was decided, s40 LPA 1925 has been repealed by s2 Law of Property (Miscellaneous Provisions) Act 1989 (contracts for the sale or disposition of an interest in land have to be 'made in writing': see Chapter 10, section 10.4). It is not clear what impact this will have on *Burgess* v *Rawnsley* and it is possible that the decision will be unaffected by the legislative change. In *Gore and Snell* v *Carpenter* (1990) 61 P & CR 456 it was held that mere negotiations were not sufficient for severance where there was no express agreement to sever and the negotiations did not amount to a sufficient course of dealing for severance.

The burden of proof is on the person seeking to establish a severance. A memorandum of severance should, for the protection of the severed interest, be endorsed upon the conveyance which created the joint tenancy.

9.9 Rights between co-owners

Where prior to the Trusts of Land and Appointment of Trustees Act 1996 a trust for sale arose by statute or by implication, the beneficiaries were entitled to possession of the land pending sale: see *Bull* v *Bull* [1955] 1 QB 234.

In *Jones* v *Jones* [1977] 1 WLR 438 it was held that one tenant in common who was not in occupation was not entitled to rent from another tenant in common, even though that other occupied the whole. But see *Dennis* v *McDonald* [1982] Fam 63 which showed that payments between the parties might be ordered. Here an occupation rent was ordered to be paid.

Under the Trusts of Land and Appointment of Trustees Act 1996 the position is governed by ss12 and 13 (see Chapter 8, section 8.22).

In a landlord and tenant context, notice to determine a joint periodic tenancy served on the landlord by one of two joint periodic tenants will determine the tenancy even if the other joint tenant does not concur: *Hammersmith and Fulham London Borough Council* v *Monk* [1991] 3 WLR 1144 (HL).

9.10 Other forms of co-ownership

Coparcenary

When a person died intestate before 1926 his realty descended to his heir, who could in certain circumstances be more than one person; for example, where the deceased had no sons but two or more daughters, the daughters were the heir. These persons held the realty as coparceners. Coparcenary resembled tenancy in common in that there was no right of survivorship, but for some purposes it was treated as a joint tenancy. Since s45 AEA 1925 coparcenary could arise only in the case of entailed interests and had necessarily to be equitable. However, the Trusts of Land and Appointment of Trustees Act 1996 prevents the creation of any more entailed interests (Schedule 1, para 5 of the 1996 Act).

Tenancy by entireties

Before the Married Women's Property Act 1882, if land was granted to a husband and wife in such circumstances that they would ordinarily take as joint tenants they took as tenants by entireties and there was no right of severance. The tenants were one person (the husband!). The MWPA 1882 prevented the creation of such tenancies after 1882 and made it possible for a woman to own her own property. However, under the rule in *Re Jupp* (1888) 39 Ch D 148, if land was granted to H and W and X, H and W were still regarded as only one person in relation to X, who therefore took half, and H and W took the other half. This rule was abolished by s37 LPA 1925, which provides that:

'A husband and wife shall for all purposes of acquisition of any interest in property … be treated as two persons.'

9.11 Worked example

Q Albert, Boris, Charles and David are all married men with families, and in 1994 they buy a seaside cottage for holidays, each putting up a quarter of the price. It is conveyed to all four of them jointly. In 1995 Charles is killed in a car crash, and in 1996 Albert sells his share to Edward. David has recently become unemployed and wants the cottage sold in order to get some money; he is unable to sell his share. Can David force a sale, and if so who can sell and what share in the proceeds will David get?

A In answering this kind of question the student is advised to use the following type of diagram to help him sort out the legal and equitable situation. Although much of the facts pre date the coming into force of the Trusts of Land and Appointment of Trustees Act 1996 on 1 January 1997, the answer reflects that Act in particular the fact that all trusts for sale in existence prior to that date are automatically converted into trusts of land.

Legal		*Equitable*	
1994	A, B, C, D	A, B, C, D	
	in trust	joint tenants – price in equal shares	
1995	A, B, D	A, B, D	
1996	A, B, D	E	B, D
		tenant in common	joint tenants
		of one-third	of two-thirds

Or this form of diagram may be used in the alternative:

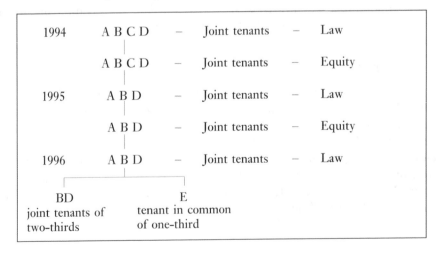

This shows that the effect of the conveyance was to vest the legal estate in the four purchasers (assuming them all to be of full age) in trust for themselves as beneficial joint tenants. It is arguable that this property is a form of 'partnership' property, so they would take as tenants in common, but probably the presumption only applies when there is a legal partnership.

On Charles' death in 1995 the jus accrescendi operates on both sides of the line, leaving Albert, Boris and David holding on a trust of land for themselves as beneficial joint tenants.

The effect of the sale by Albert of his share is to sever his equitable interest. Edward therefore takes a one-third share as tenant in common, with Boris and David the remaining joint tenants having two-thirds. Albert's act has no effect on the legal estate unless he formally retires as trustee.

Prior to the coming into force of the Trusts of Land and Appointment of Trustees Act 1996 on 1 January 1997, the trustees would have had a duty to sell with a statutory power to postpone sale, and unless they all agreed on postponement the property would have had to have been sold: *Re Mayo* (1943). Therefore, prima facie, David could have compelled his co-trustees to have sold the legal estate. However, if they had not been willing to do so he could have applied to the court for an order of sale under s30 LPA 1925 and the court might have refused to grant such an order if to do so would have been a breach of contract or would have defeated a continuing purpose of the trust. See *Jones* v *Challenger* (1961); and *Re Buchanan-Wollaston's Conveyance* (1939). The purpose for which the cottage was purchased in 1994 was to provide a holiday home which purpose was continuing prior to 1 January 1997, and so David might not have got an order for sale.

With the coming into force of the Trusts of Land and Appointment of Trustees Act 1996, the trustees have a power to sell and a power to postpone sale (s4 of the 1996 Act). Section 30 LPA 1925 has been repealed and replaced by ss14 and 15 of the 1996 Act. Any person with an interest in property subject to a trust of land (eg David) can apply to the court for an order under s14. The court can, under s14, make orders for sale, preventing sale etc. The aim of the provision is to enable the courts to intervene in any dispute relating to a trust of land.

Section 15(1) contains a statement of factors which the court is to have regard to in making an order under s14 (it is based on how the courts have interpreted s30 LPA 1925). These factors include:

1. The settlor's intention;
2. The purposes for which the property subject to the trust is held;
3. The welfare of any minor who occupies or might reasonably be expected to occupy the trust land; and
4. The interests of secured creditors.

The use of the word 'include' in s15(1) demonstrates that the list is not intended to be exhaustive. As noted above, if David's application had been heard under the repealed s30 LPA 1925 he might not have got an order of sale because of the state of caselaw developed under that provision. How might he fare today under s14 of the 1996 Act? The Law Commission in its 1989 Report *Transfer of Land: Trusts of Land* (which was a primary catalyst for the 1996 Act) took the view that s30 LPA 1925 case law would remain influential despite the demise of that provision. The Law Commission took this view because it saw its proposals for the replacement of s30 LPA 1925 (ie ss14 and 15 TOLATA 1996) as a consolidation of the case law developed under the former provision. Support for the Law Commissioin view was given by the county court in *TSB Bank plc* v *Marshall* [1998] 39 EG 208. There the court in the first reported case on ss14 and 15 of the 1996 Act concluded that the case law developed under s30 LPA 1925 was still relevant to the successor provisions. However, it is important to emphasise that a decision of the county court is not binding. Further, a more cautious view of the matter was taken by the Court of Appeal in *Mortgage Corporation* v *Shaire & Others* [2001] Ch 743. Nevertheless, it seems that even if David's application was heard under s14 of the 1996 Act the outcome could well be the same as if it had been heard under the old s30 LPA 1925.

10

Leases and Tenancies

10.1 Introduction

10.2 Definitions

10.3 Assignments and subtenancies ⌒ sub-letting

10.4 The essentials of a lease

10.5 Distinction between a lease and a licence

10.6 Types of tenancy

10.7 Terms implied into leases

10.8 Express covenants in leases

10.9 Determination of tenancies

10.10 Forfeiture

10.11 Enforceability of covenants in leases

10.12 Statutory protection of tenants

10.13 Residential tenancies

10.14 Agricultural tenancies

10.15 Business tenancies

10.1 Introduction

Land held under a lease or tenancy is held for a legal estate, 'a term of years absolute' as defined in ss1(1)(b) and 205(1)(xxvii) LPA 1925. The complete definition in s205(1)(xxvii) LPA 1925 should be perused and understood:

> ' "Term of years absolute" means a term of years (taking effect either in possession or in reversion whether or not at a rent) with or without impeachment for waste, subject or not to another legal estate, and either certain or liable to determination by notice, re-entry, operation of law or by a provision for cesser on redemption, or in any other event (other than the dropping of a life, or the determination of a determinable life interest), but does

149

not include any term of years determinable with life or lives or with the cesser of a determinable life interest, nor, if created after the commencement of this Act, a term of years which is not expressed to take effect in possession within twenty-one years after the creation thereof where required by this Act to take effect within that period; [see s149(3) LPA 1925] and in this definition the expression "term of years" includes a term for less than a year, or for a year or years and a fraction of a year or from year to year.'

Section 1(5) LPA 1925 provides:

'A legal estate may subsist concurrently with or subject to any other legal estate in the same land.'

Hence the same land may be held both as a legal freehold estate and as a legal leasehold estate at the same time, and there may be two or more leasehold estates subsisting in the land at the same time.

Both landlords and tenants have legal estates in possession, because 'possession' is defined by s205(1)(xix) LPA 1925 as including 'receipt of rents and profits or the right to receive the same, if any'.

The effect of the grant of a leasehold estate is that the fee simple owner grants to the leaseholder, for a fixed or ascertainable length of time, the right to deal with the land as though he owned it (subject to certain limitations). Until and unless the lease ends, the fee simple owner is no longer entitled to physical possession of the land, but only to the 'reversion' on the lease, which amounts to legal possession of the land.

L's fee simple absolute in possession is illustrated below:

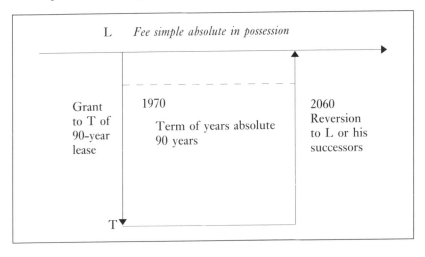

10.2 Definitions

Lease: a contract either in writing or by deed granting a leasehold estate in land.

Tenancy: the interest held under a lease. A tenancy can be granted orally, or by a tenancy agreement.

Demise: the grant of a tenancy.

Covenant: a promise expressly made in a lease, or implied into a lease or tenancy agreement by statute or at common law.

Rent: the consideration given by a tenant to his landlord in return for the grant of a tenancy. Rent is paid throughout the term. It usually takes the form of money, but need not.

Fine or premium: a lump sum paid by a tenant at the beginning of the term. If a fine is paid, usually it is only very low, or no rent is payable for the remainder of the term.

Determination: the coming to an end of a tenancy.

Reversion: the interest in the land held by a landlord during the subsistence of a lease.

A number of words are used interchangeably for 'landlord' and 'tenant'.

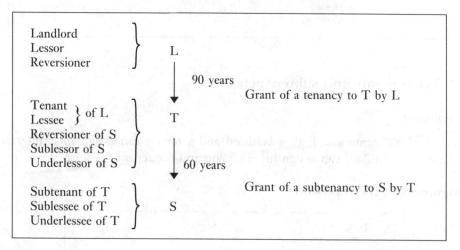

This may also be demonstrated by adapting the earlier style of diagram:

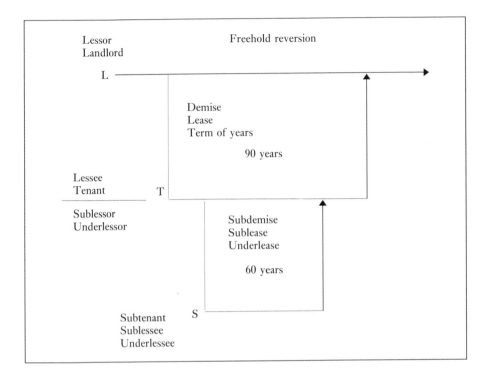

10.3 Assignments and subtenancies

Assignment

While the lease continues, both a landlord and a tenant can assign their interest in the land. The landlord can assign his reversion and the tenant his lease.

Assignment of the reversion

The landlord assigns his reversion by selling his fee simple estate to R during the term of the lease. R steps into L's shoes and becomes T's landlord. L no longer has any rights in the land, or any rights under the lease.

Assignment of the lease

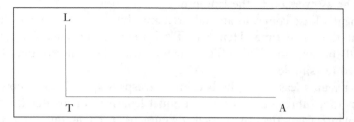

An assignment of a lease is the grant by the tenant to the assignee of the whole *remaining interest under the lease*. The assignee (A) steps into T's shoes, and the original tenant no longer has any rights to possession of the land comprised in the lease.

If the original tenant, T, has granted any subtenancies prior to the assignment, then so far as the subtenants are concerned T's assignment is an assignment of his reversion on their subtenancies, and the assignee, A, becomes their landlord.

Subtenancy

Care must be taken to distinguish the effect of an assignment of the residue of the lease from the creation of a subtenancy. A subtenancy is the grant by the tenant of *less* than his whole interest under the lease. This can be achieved by either a grant to the subtenant of only part of the land comprised in the tenancy, or a grant of all the land to the subtenant for a term shorter than that held by the tenant.

The subtenant holds his land of the tenant. So far as the subtenant is concerned, the tenant is his landlord, and the tenant holds the reversion on the subtenant's interest; see diagram below:

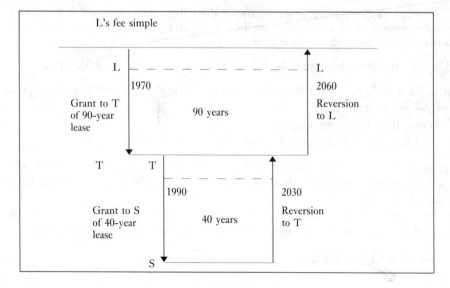

It is important to note that in all cases where leases or subleases are created there must always be a reversion to the landlord.

If the tenant's lease comes to an end prematurely, then all subtenancies also come to an end at the same time. Hence if T's lease is determined by forfeiture (see section 10.10 below) in 2000, S's tenancy also determines and L holds an unencumbered fee simple.

Once the tenant's lease ends, he becomes a trespasser, as do any subtenants.

The grant to a subtenant of a term of equal length to or greater length than that held by a tenant takes effect as a legal assignment, even in the absence of a deed. The supposed subtenant steps into the tenant's shoes and holds the land for the same term and on the same conditions as the tenant.

10.4 The essentials of a lease

In order to grant a valid *legal estate*, a lease must comply with three requirements: it must be in the correct form; it must be certain in duration; and the tenant must have exclusive possession. These will be dealt with in turn.

The formal requirements must be met

Section 52(1) LPA 1925 provides:

> 'All conveyances of land or any interest therein are void for the purposes of conveying or creating a legal estate unless made by deed.'

Hence legal leases must be made by deed. This is the general rule to which one exception exists. Section 54(2) LPA 1925 provides the exception:

> 'Nothing in the foregoing provisions ... shall affect the creation by parol of leases taking effect in possession for a term not exceeding three years ... at the best rent which can be reasonably obtained without taking a fine.'

Thus a valid legal lease may be made orally or in writing provided that:

1. It is for a term not exceeding three years, whether or not the lessee has power to extend the term; and
2. It takes effect in possession; and
3. It is at the best rent reasonably obtainable without taking a fine.

All periodic tenancies (see section 10.6 below) and terms certain of three years or less fall within this exception. It should be noted that s54(2) does include leases for precisely three years.

A lease for more than three years not made by deed is void at *law*, but can take effect in *equity* as a specifically enforceable contract for a lease provided that:

1. It was granted for value; and

2. It was made in writing to satisfy s2(1) of the Law of Property (Miscellaneous Provisions) Act 1989.

This contract must incorporate all the agreed terms and, instead of being signed by the potential defendant alone, must now be signed by or on behalf of each party to the contract: s2(3) of the 1989 Act.

The effect is to repeal s40 LPA 1925 in total. No longer can a contract merely be evidenced in writing, it must be *made in writing*. Section 40(2) LPA 1925 is also repealed, and this sees the end of the doctrine of part performance so far as it relates to land law. The raison d'être of s2 of the 1989 Act is to simplify conveyancing by requiring the certainty of a written document. In the debate leading up to the enactment of the 1989 Act, the view was that the void created by the abolition of part performance could be filled by the rules of estoppel. In particular, the Law Commission suggested that estoppel could 'achieve very similar results where appropriate to those of part performance'. In *Yaxley* v *Gotts & Gotts* [1999] 3 WLR 1217 the Court of Appeal endorsed that view. Robert Walker LJ emphasised 'that any general assertion of s2 as a "no-go" area' for estoppel would be unsustainable. There it was established that proprietary estoppel could operate to give effect to an agreement rendered void by s2 of the 1989 Act in circumstances when to do otherwise would be to allow unconscionable conduct or equitable fraud to prevail.

The exceptions to s2 LP(MP)A 1989 are set out in s2(5) as:

1. a contract to grant a lease not exceeding three years under s54(2) LPA 1925;
2. a contract made at public auction;
3. a contract regulated under the Financial Services Act 1986;
4. contracts creating resulting, implied or constructive trusts.

Section 2 LP(MP)A 1989 came into force on 27 September 1989 and does not relate to contracts made *before* that date. It provides as follows:

'2(1) A contract for the sale or other disposition of an interest in land can only be made in writing and only by incorporating all the terms which the parties have expressly agreed in one document or, where contracts are exchanged, in each.

(2) The terms may be incorporated in a document either by being set out in it or by reference to some other document.

(3) The document incorporating the terms or, where contracts are exchanged, one of the documents incorporating them (but not necessarily the same one) must be signed by or on behalf of each party to the contract.

(4) Where a contract for the sale or other disposition of an interest in land satisfies the conditions of this section by reason only of the rectification of one or more documents in pursuance of an order of a court, the contract shall come into being, or be deemed to have come into being, at such time as may be specified in the order.

(5) This section does not apply in relation to:

a) a contract to grant such a lease as is mentioned in s54(2) of the Law of Property Act 1925 (short leases);

(b) a contract made in the course of a public auction; or

(c) a contract regulated under the Financial Services Act 1986;

and nothing in this section affects the creation or operation of resulting, implied or constructive trusts.

(6) In this section:

"disposition" has the same meaning as in the Law of Property Act 1925;

"interest in land" means any estate, interest or charge in or over land or in or over the proceeds of sale of land.

(7) Nothing in this section shall apply in relation to contracts made before this section comes into force.

(8) Section 40 of the Law of Property Act 1925 (which is superseded by this section) shall cease to have effect.'

An example of the application of s2(5) of the Act is *Yaxley* v *Gotts & Gotts* [1999] 3 WLR 1217. There Y asked G2 for financial help in buying a property. After viewing the property, G2 decided to buy it himself. G2 offered to give Y the ground floor flat in return for him carrying out renovation work on the other floors and thereafter acting as his managing agent for the upstairs flats. The agreement was an *oral* one. Subsequent to the agreement, G2 arranged for the house to be bought by his son G1 and he was named as the registered proprietor. Y only discovered this later. Y duly carried out the renovation work and thereafter acted as managing agent. Following a dispute between the parties G2 excluded Y from the property and denied the existence of any agreement. Y argued that he was entitled by virtue of proprietary estoppel to a long lease of the ground floor. The county court judge found for Y and granted him a 99-year lease of the ground floor. On appeal the court concluded that although the judge had not made any findings as to the existence of a constructive trust, on the findings of fact that he had made it was not disputed that a proprietary estoppel arose and those findings could equally provide the basis for a conclusion that Y was entitled to an equitable interest in the property under a constructive trust. The significance of this was that the creation or operation of a constructive trust was saved from the requirement of writing by virtue of s2(5) of the 1989 Act. Accordingly, the appeal would be dismissed and the judge's order affirmed.

One of the points of controversy surrounding s2 LP(MP)A 1989 is whether an exchange of correspondence regarding an oral agreement concerning land can meet the requirements of s2. In *Hooper* v *Sherman* [1994] NPC 153 the Court of Appeal, in a case not concerning leases, held (by a majority) that an exchange of letters could create an enforceable contract within s2. In *Commission for the New Towns* v *Cooper (GB) Ltd* [1995] 2 All ER 929 a different Court of Appeal reached a contrary decision. There the court held that the closing stages of correspondence by which an agreement was reached, ie the final offer or counter-offer and an unqualified acceptance of it, could not also constitute the 'exchange of contracts' which was required by s2 before a contract could be made. An additional exchange of documents setting out or incorporating all 'the terms which the parties have agreed' must take place or the parties must sign a simple document which sets them out. An obvious consequence of these conflicting decisions is uncertainty for conveyancing practitioners. A definitive decision on the point from the House of Lords would be welcome.

All legal leases must be assigned by deed, even if created orally: *Crago* v *Julian* [1992] 1 All ER 744.

An incidental change effected by s1 LP(MP)A 1989 is that deeds no longer have to be 'signed, sealed and delivered'. Section 1(3) removes the need for sealing the deed, which will now be valid if it is merely signed and delivered.

Differences between legal and equitable leases

A specifically enforceable lease is regarded as a valid *equitable lease* under the rule in *Walsh* v *Lonsdale* (1882) 21 Ch D 9 on the principle that 'equity regards as done, that which ought to be done'. As a consequence undergraduate law examiners frequently ask candidates to consider whether an equitable lease is as good as a legal lease. It is true that an equitable lease is as good as a legal lease for many purposes *except* that an equitable lease:

1. depends for its validity on the discretionary remedy of specific performance, which may not be available – for example, if the tenant is in breach of a covenant. See *Cornish* v *Brook Green Laundry Ltd* [1959] 1 QB 394.
2. does not carry with it easements and other rights under s62 LPA 1925 (see Chapter 12) because it is not a conveyance;
3. is void against a subsequent purchaser of the land if:

   a) the land is unregistered and the agreement is not registered as an estate contract (Class C(iv) land charge). See *Hollington Bros Ltd* v *Rhodes* [1951] 2 All ER 578;

   b) the land is registered and the lessee is not in actual occupation or has not protected his interest by an entry on the register.

In addition, there is no privity of estate (see section 10.11) between the landlord and an assignee of the tenant under an equitable lease.

The commencement date and duration of the term must be certain

In order to comply with the definition of term of years absolute in s205(1)(xxvii) LPA 1925 both the commencement date and the duration of the term must be certain or capable of being ascertained at the outset of the term. A lease which does not comply with this requirement is void, and leases which are therefore void under this rule are:

1. leases for life: see s149(6) LPA 1925, section 10.6 (below) and *Binions* v *Evans* [1972] Ch 359;
2. leases for perpetuity: see section 10.6;

3. leases for an uncertain period (eg 'a lease for the duration of the war'): see *Lace* v *Chantler* [1944] KB 368.

The decision in *Lace* v *Chantler* was reviewed and applied by the House of Lords in *Prudential Assurance Co Ltd* v *London Residuary Body* [1992] 3 WLR 279. A brief review of the facts will help to show how this question of uncertainty can arise.

In 1930 land fronting a highway was sold to the then London County Council for future road widening. It was leased back to the plaintiffs' predecessors in title at a yearly rent of £30.00. The agreement stated that

'the tenancy shall continue until ... the land is required by the Council for the purposes of ... [road widening]'.

Sixty years later the highway had still not been widened, and the reversion was now with the London Residuary Body (LRB) which was not a highway authority. The LRB served a six months' notice to quit purporting to end the tenancy. The current rental value of the land was estimated to be over £10,000 per annum. The plaintiffs sought a declaration that the notice to quit was null and void because the tenancy could only be determined if the land was required for road widening purposes.

The House of Lords reversed the decision of the Court of Appeal and held that all leases and tenancy agreements must be certain in duration. Here the lease was for an uncertain period and was void. The land was held on a yearly tenancy created by the tenants' possession plus the payment of a yearly rent, and only those terms in the agreement which were consistent with a yearly tenancy would apply. The term relating to road widening was inconsistent with the ability of either party to determine a yearly tenancy on six months' notice, and as a result the tenancy had been lawfully determined.

Lord Templeman (at p283) gave a most useful description of how such a yearly tenancy can come into existence:

'When the agreement in the present case was made, it failed to grant an estate in land. The tenant however entered into possession and paid the yearly rent of £30 reserved by the agreement. The tenant entering under a void lease became by virtue of possession and the payment of a yearly rent, a yearly tenant holding on the terms of the agreement so far as those terms were consistent with the yearly tenancy.

A yearly tenancy is determinable by the landlord or the tenant at the end of the first or any subsequent year of the tenancy by six months' notice ...'

He went on to consider how a periodic tenancy of this nature can be said to be certain, and continued (at p285):

'A tenancy from year to year is saved from being uncertain because each party has power by notice to determine at the end of any year. The term continues until determined as if both parties made a new agreement at the end of each year for a new term for the ensuing year.'

This confirms that the existing rule that the lease must be certain or capable of being made certain at the outset of the term does apply to periodic tenancies.

Lord Templeman then said:

'A power for nobody to determine or for one party only to be able to determine is inconsistent with the concept of a term from year to year.'

This was a reference to the decision in *Re Midland Railway Co's Agreement* [1971] Ch 725 which had been applied by the Court of Appeal in *Ashburn Anstalt* v *Arnold* [1989] Ch 1. These cases had decided that the landlord could bar himself from determining the lease. As Lord Templeman observed:

'That case, if it was correct, would make it unnecessary for a lease to be of a certain duration.'

In the circumstances it was held that both of these cases were wrongly decided, and they were overruled. Lord Templeman concluded:

'A grant for an uncertain term does not create a lease. A grant for an uncertain term which takes the form of a yearly tenancy which cannot be determined by the landlord does not create a lease.'

The rule is now much clearer. If the lease is void but a periodic tenancy then arises from the payment and acceptance of rent, such periodic tenancy will not incorporate any provisions for determination set out in the void lease which are inconsistent with the periodic tenancy.

Exclusive possession

The tenant must be given exclusive possession, that is the right to exclude other persons including the landlord from the premises.

If exclusive possession is not given then the grantee is only a licensee; for example, a lodger or hotel guest has only a licence to use his room. The significance of exclusive possession as an essential feature in identifying a lease has been emphasised by the House of Lords in *Street* v *Mountford* [1985] 2 WLR 877. See section 10.5.

10.5 Distinction between a lease and a licence

If exclusive possession is not granted, the agreement can only be a licence. The grant of exclusive possession is a factor indicating that a lease has been granted, but it is not a decisive factor as it is possible for the grantee to be given exclusive possession and still not have a lease. Whether an agreement constitutes a lease or a licence depends on the true intention of the parties.

This intention must now be considered in the light of the decision by the House of Lords in *Street* v *Mountford* (above). Tests used by the courts in determining the intention to create a licence include:

1. The words used: the way the parties describe their agreement is evidence of their intention but is not conclusive: see *Addiscombe Garden Estates* v *Crabbe* [1958] 1 QB 513.
2. Concurrent rights of possession: where the landlord reserves concurrent rights of possession there is only a licence: see *Shell-Mex and BP* v *Manchester Garages* [1971] 1 WLR 612. But the reservation of a right of access for specific purposes does not prevent the grant of a lease: see *Heath* v *Drown* [1973] AC 498.
3. Family arrangements: family and similar arrangements are usually regarded as licences, there being no intention to create a formal landlord-tenant relationship: see *Errington* v *Errington and Woods* [1952] 1 KB 290.
4. Employees: employees who are required to reside in premises as a necessary part of their duties (eg caretakers, house surgeons) are licensees.
5. Mistresses: where a mistress occupies premises provided by her lover, the courts have tended to regard her as a licensee: see *Tanner* v *Tanner* [1975] 1 WLR 1346 and *Horrocks* v *Forray* [1976] 1 WLR 230.
6. Circumstances: the court will in all cases look at the circumstances in which the agreement was reached, and this is the ultimate test: see *Abbeyfield (Harpenden) Society Ltd* v *Woods* [1968] 1 WLR 374; *Marchant* v *Charters* [1977] 1 WLR 1181.

The Rent Act 1977 does not apply to licences, and so landlords attempt to avoid the protection of the Act by granting licences, just as the occupier seeks to create a lease in order to obtain security of tenure.

In *Somma* v *Hazelhurst* [1978] 1 WLR 1014 a landlord did succeed in establishing that he had granted a licence of a bed-sitting room. The important factors were that the written agreement reserved to the licensor the right to designate who should share the room with the licensee, and also made each licensee occupying the room separately responsible for paying a proportion of the rent. See also *Buchmann* v *May* [1978] 2 All ER 993.

The decision in *Somma* v *Hazelhurst* was expressly disapproved by the House of Lords in *Street* v *Mountford* (above). Lord Templeman concluded with these words:

'My Lords the only intention which is relevant is the intention demonstrated by the agreement to grant exclusive possession for a term at a rent. Sometimes it may be difficult to discover whether on the true construction of an agreement, exclusive possession is conferred. Sometimes it may appear from the surrounding circumstances that there was no intention to create legal relationships. Sometimes it may appear from the surrounding circumstances that the right to exclusive possession is referable to a legal relationship other than a tenancy. Legal relationships to which a grant of exclusive possession might be referable and which would or might negative the grant of an estate or interest in the land include occupancy under a contract for the sale of the land, occupancy pursuant to a contract of employment or occupancy referable to the holding of an office. But whereas in the present case the only circumstances are that residential accommodation is offered and accepted with exclusive possession for a term at a rent, the result is a tenancy ... Henceforth, the courts which deal with these problems will, save in exceptional circumstances, only be concerned to inquire whether as a result of an agreement relating to residential accommodation the occupier is a lodger or a tenant. In the present case I am satisfied that Mrs Mountford is a tenant.'

From this decision it is clear that exclusive possession leads to a presumption of a lease which has to be rebutted by the landlord (in this regard it helpfully identifies several exceptional situations where 'exclusive possession' will not give rise to a lease). Exclusive possession is now crucial in establishing the evidence of a tenancy and the absence of a licence. The only relevant general test in relation to residential accommodation is to establish whether the occupier is a lodger or a tenant. See also *Royal Philanthropic Society* v *County* (1985) 276 EG 1068; *Bretherton* v *Paton* (1986) 278 EG 615.

In the opening sentence of the above quotation from Lord Templeman in *Street* v *Mountford*, reference was made to 'a term at a rent'. The need for rent was challenged by Fox LJ in *Ashburn Anstalt* v *Arnold* [1988] 2 All ER 147 on the basis that the need for rent was negatived by the definition of 'term of years absolute' in s205(1)(xxvii) LPA 1925 as

' ... a term of years (taking effect either in possession or in reversion whether or nor at a rent)'.

Fox LJ went on to say:

'In the circumstances I conclude that the reservation of a rent is not necessary for the creation of a tenancy. That conclusion involves no departure from Lord Templeman's proposition ... We are saying only that we do not think that Lord Templeman was stating the quite different proposition that you cannot have a tenancy without a rent.'

It is submitted that this argument will not be affected by the overruling of *Ashburn Anstalt* v *Arnold* by the House of Lords in *Prudential Assurance Co Ltd* v *London Residuary Body* [1992] 3 WLR 279.

The non-exclusive possession agreement

The problem whether exclusive possession has been granted was further considered in *Hadjiloucas* v *Crean* [1987] 3 All ER 1008, where the Court of Appeal concluded that the words of Lord Templeman may be too wide to cover some non-exclusive possession agreements, and do not necessarily cover certain examples of multiple occupation. Purchas LJ suggested that the circumstances must be considered against the factual background, the factual matrix, and as a result: each occupier is a licensee if he cannot exclude others; or there may be parallel leases where each tenant has a right to exclude all others; or the agreement may produce a joint tenancy with a collective form of exclusive possession in all the co-owners.

The joint tenancy approach

This solution was adopted by the Court of Appeal in *AG Securities* v *Vaughan* [1988] 2 All ER 173 where a majority of the Court held that, even though the separate agreements of each of four occupiers expressly excluded a right for that occupant to have exclusive possession of a four-bedroom flat, nevertheless the four occupants had between them a collective form of exclusive possession of the whole flat. This meant that together they had a lease as co-owners even though there was no joint liability to pay a single rent. The majority in the Court of Appeal was satisfied that the four unities of possession, interest, title and time existed as pre-conditions of such a joint tenancy. The existence of the four unities, and in particular the unities of title and time, was challenged in a dissenting judgment by Sir George Waller in which he concluded

'... there cannot be a joint tenancy where there are serious doubts about each of the four unities.'

The cases of *AG Securities* v *Vaughan* and *Antoniades* v *Villiers* were heard by the House of Lords as a joint appeal and reported together at [1988] 3 WLR 1205. In *AG Securities* v *Vaughan* the appellants owned a block of flats, one of which contained six rooms in addition to a kitchen and bathroom. They furnished four rooms as bedrooms, a fifth as a lounge and the sixth as a sitting room and entered into short-term agreements with four individuals, each referred to in the relevant agreement as 'Licensee'. The agreements were made at different times and on different terms and were normally for six months' duration. Each agreement provided that the licensee had

'the right to use [the flat] in common with others who have or may from time to time be granted the like right ... but without the right to exclusive possession of any part of the ... flat'.

When a licensee left, a new occupant was mutually agreed by the appellants and the remaining licensees. Their Lordships held that the occupants were indeed licensees.
Lord Bridge of Harwich concluded as follows:

'These rights and obligations having initially been several, I do not understand by what legal alchemy they could ever become joint. Each occupant had a contractual right, enforceable against the appellants, to prevent the number of persons permitted to occupy the flat at any one time exceeding four. But this did not give them exclusive possession of the kind which is distinctive of a leasehold interest. Having no estate in land, they could not sue in trespass. Their remedy against intruders would have been to persuade the appellants to sue as plaintiffs or to join the appellants as defendants by way of enforcement of their contractual rights.

The arrangement seems to have been a sensible and realistic one to provide accommodation for a shifting population of individuals who were genuinely prepared to share the flat with others introduced from time to time who would, at least initially, be strangers to them. There was no artificiality in the contracts concluded to give effect to this arrangement. On the contrary, it seems to me to require the highest degree of artificiality to force these contracts into the mould of a joint tenancy.'

In similar vein Lord Oliver of Aylmerton stated:

'The respondents are compelled to support their claims by a strange and unnatural theory that, as each occupant terminates his agreement, there is an implied surrender by the other three and an implied grant of a new joint tenancy to them together with the new incumbent when he enters under his individual agreement ... this appears to me to be entirely unreal. For my part, I (find) no unity of interest, no unity of title, certainly no unity of time and, as I think, no unity of possession. I find it impossible to say that the agreements entered into with the respondents created either individually or collectively a single tenancy either of the entire flat or of any part of it.'

In *Antoniades* v *Villiers* the attic of the respondent's house was converted into furnished residential accommodation comprising one bedroom. Wishing to live together there, the appellants signed identical agreements called 'licences' which were executed at the same time and stressed that they were not to have exclusive possession. In particular, the agreements provided that

'The licensor shall be entitled at any time to use the rooms together with the licensee and permit other persons to use all of the rooms together with the licensee.'

No attempt was made by the respondent to use the rooms or to have them used by others. Stressing, too, that the real intention of the parties was to create a licence not coming under the Rent Acts, the agreements provided for a monthly payment of £87 and stated that they were determinable by one month's notice by either party. The court held that the agreements created a joint tenancy.

Lord Bridge of Harwich put the matter thus:

'Here the artificiality was in the pretence that two contemporaneous and identical agreements entered into by a man and a woman who were going to live together in a one-bedroom flat and share a double bed created rights and obligations which were several rather than joint. As to the nature of those rights and obligations, the provisions of the joint agreement purporting to retain the right in the respondent to share the occupation of the flat with the young couple himself or to introduce an indefinite number of third parties to do so could be seen, in all the relevant circumstances, to be repugnant to the true purpose of the agreement. No one could have supposed that those provisions were ever intended to be acted on. They were introduced into the agreement for no other purpose than as an attempt to disguise the true character of the agreement which it was hoped would deceive the court and prevent the appellants enjoying the protection of the Rent Acts. As your Lordships all agree, the attempt fails.'

Lord Templeman continued:

'My Lords, in *Street* v *Mountford* this House stipulated with reiterated emphasis that an express statement of intention is not decisive and that the court must pay attention to the facts and surrounding circumstances and to what people do as well as to what people say ...

... My Lords, in the second appeal now under consideration, there was, in my opinion, the grant of a joint tenancy for the following reasons. (1) The applicants for the flat applied to rent the flat jointly and to enjoy exclusive occupation. (2) The landlord allowed the applicants jointly to enjoy exclusive occupation and accepted rent. A tenancy was created. (3) The power reserved to the landlord to deprive the applicants of exclusive occupation was inconsistent with the provisions of the Rent Acts. (4) Moreover, in all the circumstances the power which the landlord insisted on to deprive the applicants of exclusive occupation was a pretence only intended to deprive the applicants of the protection of the Rent Acts.'

The lease-licence debate continues, and the courts can now take advantage of the two decisions of the House of Lords in *AG Securities* v *Vaughan* and *Street* v *Mountford* [1985] 2 WLR 877. These decisions were applied by the Court of Appeal in *Aslan* v *Murphy* [1989] 3 All ER 130 and *Mikeover* v *Brady* [1989] 3 All ER 618. (See also *Norris* v *Checksfield* [1991] 1 WLR 1241.)

The debate also arises in the context of the provision of accommodation for the homeless. In *Family Housing Association* v *Jones* [1990] 1 WLR 779, a tenancy was confirmed even though the Association retained a key, but this was overruled by the House of Lords in *Westminster City Council* v *Clarke* [1992] 2 WLR 229. It was held that an agreement known as a 'licence to occupy' did not grant exclusive possession of any particular room and did not create a landlord and tenant relationship. The council could change the hotel accommodation, and the occupier could be required to share a room with other persons. This degree of control was necessary to ensure the smooth running of the hotel.

In *Stribling* v *Wickham* (1989) 27 EG 81 the Court of Appeal had a further opportunity to consider whether a number of agreements, each purporting to grant an individual licence, also created a joint tenancy. The court held that the separate agreements genuinely represented the reality of the transaction, and, as none of the sharers could be regarded as a tenant of any individual part, they must be licensees. The following points were suggested by way of guidance:

1. All the circumstances surrounding the creation of the agreements must be considered, including the relationship between the prospective occupiers and the intended and actual mode of occupation.
2. The actual mode of accommodation may not be used to construe documents, but may be used to determine whether any parts of the documents should be ignored as being parts which the parties never intended to act upon.
3. The court must determine the true nature of the transaction. This agreement was said to be 'a genuine and sensible arrangement for the benefit of both sides'.
4. The fact that the agreements were all entered into at one time as replacements of earlier agreements was not significant if the earlier agreements were entered into separately.

Street v *Mountford* (above) was decided in the context of residential occupation, and the courts must decide whether to apply the decision by analogy in the case of commercial leases.

10.6 Types of tenancy

Terms certain

These are leases for a fixed period of time. The length of time can vary from a few weeks to thousands of years, but it cannot be unending because every lease must have a reversion.

A term certain comes to an end at the end of the fixed term. No notice to quit is required to determine this type of tenancy; it is said to end by effluxion of time.

A term certain can be brought to an end before the expiry of the term by:

1. forfeiture: where the tenant is in breach of an obligation in the lease (see section 10.7).
2. notice to quit: provided that provision for determination by notice to quit is made in the lease. In the absence of express provision, notice to quit cannot be used to determine terms certain.

Yearly tenancies

These may be created expressly or by implication of law. A tenancy by implication arises when there is no express agreement as to the nature of the tenancy, but rent is paid and accepted with reference to an annual sum. See Lord Templeman's speech in *Prudential Assurance Co Ltd* v *London Residuary Body* [1992] 3 WLR 279 at p283, discussed in section 10.4 above. At common law, in the absence of agreement to the contrary, at least half a year's notice is required to determine a yearly tenancy, such notice expiring at the end of a completed year of the tenancy. If the tenancy began on one of the 'usual quarter days' (25 December, 25 March, 24 June, 29 September) two quarters' notice is required. In all other cases six calendar months' notice must be given. The rent may be paid at more frequent intervals than one year; it is common in yearly tenancies to provide for the rent to be paid quarterly.

Other periodic tenancies

These can be created in the same way as a yearly tenancy, in other words expressly or by implication. The notice period, however, is a full period expiring at the end of one of the periods of the tenancy. This is subject to any contrary agreement. When the tenancy is that of premises used as a dwelling, at least four weeks' notice is required by statute, and this notice must be given in the form required by statute (see s5 Protection from Eviction Act 1977). The Court of Appeal had held in *Re Midland Railway Co's Agreement* [1971] Ch 725 that the landlord could limit his ability to serve notice to determine the lease. This decision was overruled by the House of Lords in *Prudential Assurance Co Ltd* v *London Residuary Body* (above). As a consequence, any provision which either grants a power to determine an uncertain lease, *or* prevents the termination of an uncertain lease during a period of uncertainty, will itself be void.

In *Centaploy Ltd* v *Matlodge Ltd* [1974] Ch 1, Whitford J expressed the principle in these words:

> ' ... it must be basic to a tenancy that at some stage the person granting the tenancy shall have the right to determine and a tenancy in which the landlord is never going to have the right to determine at all is, as I see it, a complete contradiction in terms.'

Tenancy at will

A tenancy at will arises whenever a tenant, *with the landlord's consent*, occupies land on terms that either party may determine the tenancy at any time. It usually arises where a lease has come to an end and the tenant with the landlord's consent stays on the land because the parties are negotiating for a new lease. Unless the landlord has agreed that the occupation should be rent free compensation must be paid by the tenant for his period of occupation. If there was no agreement as to rent, and subsequently the tenant commences to tender rent on a regular basis and the rent is accepted, the tenancy is converted into a periodical tenancy, the period being related to the period of payment of rent. Since the 'tenancy' has no definite time span it cannot be a legal lease. Rather, it is a personal licence.

Tenancy at sufferance

This can only arise when a tenant holds over after the expiry of a valid tenancy *without the landlord either consenting or objecting*. The tenant is liable to pay a reasonable sum for use and occupation, and the tenancy may be determined at any time or may be converted into a periodical tenancy in similar circumstances to the tenancy at will above. As with a 'tenancy at will', the 'tenancy at sufferance' has no definite time span and therefore it cannot be a legal lease. However, it is not a personal licence because there is no permission from the landlord. Rather, a tenant at sufferance is akin to a squatter. Finally, it differs from trespass in that the occupant's original entry was lawful.

Leases for lives

A lease, whether made before 1926 or after 1925, for a life or lives, or for a term of years determinable with life or lives or on the marriage of the lessee, is by s149(6) LPA 1925 converted into a lease for 90 years determinable after the end of the life or lives or on the marriage of the lessee, as the case may be, by the giving by either party of not less than one month's notice expiring on one of the quarter days, applicable to the tenancy. This provision applies only to a lease at a rent or fine. A term determinable with life at no rent or fine could prior to the coming into force of the Trusts of Land and Appointment of Trustees Act 1996 have come within s20(1)(iv) SLA 1925, creating a strict settlement. See *Binions* v *Evans* [1972] Ch 359.

In *Bass Holdings Ltd* v *Lewis* (1986) 280 EG 771 Lewis was the tenant of a public house. His three-year lease included a provision for termination after the three years 'on six months' notice or on the death of the tenant by notice of not less than 14 days'. The Court of Appeal was not impressed by the tenant's argument that this provision brought the lease within s149(6) LPA 1925. This was not a lease for life or lives within s149(6). For the Act to apply the lease must be granted either for a term limited by reference to a life or lives, or for a term of years conditionally upon the survival of a life or lives. Nourse LJ concluded as follows:

'I add by way of illustration that the simplest example of a term of years limited conditionally upon the survival of a life or lives is a lease to A for a term of 20 years if he shall so long live.'

Perpetually renewable leases

These are leases which give the lessee the right to renew the lease for another period as often as it expires. They are converted by s145 and Schedule 15 LPA 1922 into terms of 2,000 years determinable only by the lessee by not less than ten days' notice expiring on any of the old renewal dates. If the lease provides for the payment of a fine on renewal then:

1. If the lease was granted before 1926 the fine was converted into additional rent spread over the period between the renewal dates.
2. If the lease was granted after 1925 the provision for payment of a fine is void.

The lessee is bound to notify the lessor of any assignment of the term, and if the lessee does assign he ceases to be liable on the covenants in the lease (even though privity of contract still exists between him and the lessor. See section 10.11). A perpetually renewable lease may be inadvertently created by unrestricted renewal clauses, eg 'on the same terms and conditions, including this clause'. See *Re Hopkin's Lease, Caerphilly Concrete Products Ltd* v *Owen* [1972] 1 WLR 372 and compare with *Marjorie Burnett Ltd* v *Barclay* (1980) 258 EG 642.

The essence of the perpetually renewable lease is that the renewal clause itself is included. In *Parkus* v *Greenwood* [1950] Ch 644 a lease for three years included a clause that:

'... the lessor will on the request of the tenant grant him a tenancy at the same rent containing the like provisions as are herein contained including the present covenant for renewal.'

The courts lean against perpetual renewability. This was demonstrated by Nourse J in *Marjorie Burnett Ltd* v *Barclay* (above) who put the matter thus:

'It seems clear, therefore, that the court must bear in mind the leaning against perpetually renewable leases and must find expressed in the lease an express covenant or obligation for perpetual renewal. The court must look ahead to see what the second lease would contain when the requirements of the first lease had been duly complied with.'

Reversionary leases

The grant of a lease at a rent or a fine is void if it is to commence more than 21 years after the date of the grant (s149(3) LPA 1925), as is a contract to grant a lease if the lease is to commence more than 21 years after the grant.

10.7 Terms implied into leases

Obligations are implied into leases both at common law and by statute. These obligations can be expressly excluded from leases (obligations imposed upon a landlord by s11 Landlord and Tenant Act 1985 cannot be excluded but can be modified by County Court order if it is considered reasonable in the circumstances) but in the absence of express provision, both landlords and tenants are subject to implied covenants. There are two situations to consider:

1. the position in the absence of express provision; and
2. usual covenants.

Position in the absence of express provision

Where a lease has *actually been granted* and it does not contain covenants concerning certain matters these matters will be regulated by implied covenants (see below). However, as Lord Cozens Hardy MR stated in *Malzy* v *Eichholz* [1916] 2 KB 308 at pp313 and 314, if the lease does contain an express covenant 'there is no room for an implied covenant covering the same ground or any part of it'.

The landlord's obligations
Covenant for quiet enjoyment. This means that the landlord undertakes that the tenant shall be free from disturbance by adverse claims or physical interference with the tenant's enjoyment of the demised premises by the landlord himself or by persons claiming under him. Harassment and intimidation of the tenant is a breach of this covenant (as well as being a criminal offence under s1 Protection from Eviction Act 1977). In *Perera* v *Vandiyar* [1953] 1 WLR 672 a landlord who caused physical discomfort to the tenant by cutting off his gas and electricity was held to be in breach of this covenant. However, interference with privacy by erecting a staircase giving a view into the demised premises was not: see *Browne* v *Flower* [1911] 1 Ch 219.

The covenant does not extend to the acts of persons having title paramount, *Jones* v *Lavington* [1903] 1 KB 253, nor to the wrongful acts of persons claiming under them.

For the remedies available for breach, see later and *Sampson* v *Hodson-Pressinger* [1981] 3 All ER 710.

The landlord is not in breach of his covenant for quiet enjoyment where the acts which constitute the interruption of the tenant's rights are due to the exercise of rights created by a title which is superior to that of landlord. See *Celsteel Ltd* v *Alton House Holdings Ltd (No 2)* [1987] 1 WLR 291.

Not to derogate from the grant. This prevents the landlord from doing anything or permitting anything to be done which would render the premises unsuitable for the purpose for which they were let. In *Newman* v *Real Estate Debenture Corporation* [1940] 1 All ER 131 a flat was let in a building which was intended to be let for residential purposes. It was held that the landlord had derogated from his grant when he let a large part of the same building for business purposes. But this does not extend to acts merely making the lease less profitable (*Port* v *Griffith* [1938] 1 All ER 295), or to a mere invasion of privacy. See *Browne* v *Flower* (above).

Obligations as to repairs and fitness for occupation. At common law there is no general obligation imposed on a landlord to repair premises, nor is there any term implied into the lease that the premises should be suitable, either physically or legally, for the purposes for which they are let. See *Hill* v *Harris* [1965] 2 QB 601.

There are five exceptions to this general rule:

FURNISHED DWELLING HOUSES. Under the rule in *Smith* v *Marrable* (1843) 11 M & W 5 there is an implied condition in the letting of a furnished dwelling house that it should be reasonably fit for human habitation at the beginning of the tenancy. The obligation does not continue thereafter to require the landlord to maintain the dwelling in a habitable condition.

Failure to comply with this condition is a repudiatory breach of contract, which allows the tenant to treat the contract of tenancy as at an end.

BLOCKS OF FLATS. There is an implied condition in every lease of a flat in a block of flats that the landlord will take reasonable steps to keep the common parts (lifts, staircases, etc) retained by him in repair. See *Liverpool City Council* v *Irwin* [1977] AC 239.

DWELLING HOUSES LET FOR LESS THAN SEVEN YEARS. Section 32 Housing Act 1961, which has now been consolidated in ss11–16 Landlord and Tenant Act 1985, implies into the leases of dwelling houses let for less than seven years, granted after 24 October 1961, a covenant by the landlord:

1. to keep in repair the structure and exterior of the dwelling house, including drains, pipes and gutters; and
2. to keep in repair and proper working order the installations in the house:

a) for the supply of water, gas and electricity and for sanitation (including basins, sinks, baths and sanitary conveniences, but not other fixtures, fittings and appliances for making use of water, gas and electricity); and
b) for space heating or heating water.

This covenant overrides any express covenant to repair by the tenant, and the landlord cannot make the tenant pay for repairs he is obliged to do under this covenant. See *Brikom Investments Ltd* v *Seaford* [1981] 2 All ER 783.

In deciding whether a landlord is in breach of his obligation as to the structure and exterior of a dwelling house, the test seems to be whether the area in disrepair is essential to the reasonable use of the house.

The duty on the landlord under s11 Landlord and Tenant Act 1985 is to carry out the repairs within a reasonable time of receiving notice of the need for repair. In *Morris* v *Liverpool City Council* (1988) 14 EG 59 it was held that failure to carry out permanent repairs within a week of notification where temporary repairs had been made was not unreasonable.

For the purposes of s11 Landlord and Tenant Act 1985, knowledge of the need of repairs may be obtained in various ways. In *Hall* v *Howard* (1989) 57 P & CR 226 a valuation report had been sent to the landlord during unsuccessful negotiations for the purchase of the reversion. This report identified certain structural defects within s11. The Court of Appeal held that the valuation report, in spite of the different context, would put a reasonable landlord on notice of a possible breach of the repairing covenant implied by s11. Notice in respect of a s11 obligation need not be in writing nor need it be given by the tenant to the landlord so that liability can arise as a result of information given to the landlord by a third party: see *McGreal* v *Wake* [1984] 1 EGLR 42.

HOUSES LET AT LOW RENT. By ss8–10 Landlord and Tenant Act 1985 (replacing s6 Housing Act 1957) when a house is let on or after 6 July 1957 at a rent not exceeding £80 pa in Greater London and £52 pa elsewhere, there is an implied condition that the house is fit for human habitation at the commencement of the tenancy, and an implied obligation on the landlord to keep it in such a condition throughout the tenancy. The obligation only extends to defects of which the landlord has notice. In determining whether the house is unfit for human habitation regard must be had to the matters set out in s10 Landlord and Tenant Act 1985, including repair, natural lighting, ventilation and water supply. The implied covenant has little (if any) application today. This is because the rental sums have remained virtually unchanged since 1957. So while a not insignificant amount of property came within the covenant in 1957 it is virtually redundant in today's altogether different rental marketplace.

DEFECTIVE PREMISES ACT 1972. The landlord may also be under an obligation under s4 of this Act to all persons who might be affected by defects in the premises to take reasonable care to see that they and their property are reasonably safe from injury or damage.

The tenant's obligations

To pay the rent. At common law a landowner has a right to recover from any person occupying his land as a tenant a reasonable sum for use and occupation unless the circumstances indicate otherwise.

To pay rates and taxes. This means usual local authority rates, council tax and other rates assessed in respect of the premises except such as are imposed expressly upon the landlord. The obligation will normally arise due to the occupation of the premises by the tenant.

Not to commit waste. The tenant commits waste if he causes any alteration or damage to the premises which injures the reversion. If the lease is for a fixed term, the tenant is liable for both permissive and voluntary waste and he must therefore keep the premises in repair. See *Yellowly* v *Gower* (1855) 11 Exch 274.

In the case of a periodic tenancy the tenant is liable for voluntary waste only, and he must use the premises in a 'tenant-like manner'. See *Warren* v *Keen* [1954] 1 QB 15.

To permit the landlord to enter and view the premises. This is required when the landlord is obliged to repair them.

Usual covenants

The parties may have agreed to be bound by the 'usual covenants'. They are a species of implied term. The phrase 'usual covenants' is generally taken to refer to the following covenants:

By the tenant   –   to pay tenant's rates and taxes;
to pay rent;
to keep the premises in repair and deliver them up in repair;
if the landlord has undertaken to repair, to permit the landlord to enter and view the state of repair;
a condition for re-entry on non-payment of rent.

By the landlord   –   for quiet enjoyment.

But in *Chester* v *Buckingham Travel Ltd* [1981] 1 All ER 386 it was decided that this list was not exhaustive and the decision as to whether any covenant is 'usual' must depend upon the circumstances of each case. The research will include the practice in any particular area and the character of the property.

10.8 Express covenants in leases

A carefully drafted lease may contain a large number of express covenants, some by the landlord, but most of them by the tenant, which regulate in detail the parties' conduct under the lease.

In all cases it is necessary to decide whether any alleged breach falls within the precise wording of the covenant. Some of the most common express covenants are discussed below.

Covenant to pay rent

This should stipulate the rent and the dates on which it is payable. If it is not expressly made payable in advance it is payable in arrear. It remains payable even though the premises are destroyed or rendered uninhabitable, unless the lease expressly stipulates otherwise. See *Cricklewood Property and Investment Trust Ltd* v *Leightons Investment Trust Ltd* [1945] AC 211.

The application of the doctrine of frustration to leases was further considered in *National Carriers Ltd* v *Panalpina Northern Ltd* [1981] AC 675. In general the amount payable cannot be altered while the tenancy subsists unless the lease so provides or the parties agree. Modern commercial leases do contain rent review clauses.

The landlord can enforce payment of rent by:

1. Suing in contract for the money.
2. Distress. This is an ancient remedy which is governed by archaic and technical rules, and is little used today.
3. Forfeiture (see section 10.10).

In *P & A Swift Investments* v *Combined English Stores Group plc* [1988] 2 All ER 885 the House of Lords had to consider whether a covenant by a surety guaranteeing the payment of rent and the observance of covenants was a covenant which touched and concerned the land. The test for establishing whether a covenant does touch and concern was confirmed under three propositions:

1. Does it only benefit the reversioner for the time being?
2. Does it affect the nature, quality mode or user or value of the land?
3. It is not expressed to be personal.

If all these three propositions are satisfied, a covenant to pay a sum of money can be a covenant touching and concerning the land if it is connected with something to be done on, to or in relation to that land. When these propositions are applied, a covenant by a surety which guarantees performance of the tenant's covenants touching and concerning the land itself touches and concerns the land and is enforceable by an assignee of the reversion against the surety without express assignment.

Covenant to insure

Such a covenant, which may be given by either party, is breached if the premises are at any time uninsured, even if no fire occurs. The covenant may be to insure with a named company, or one approved by the landlord. If the tenant has covenanted to repair and the premises are destroyed or damaged by fire he is bound to restore in any case, but if there is no such covenant he is only obliged to restore if the fire was caused by his negligence. See *Beacon Carpets Ltd* v *Kirby* [1984] 2 All ER 726.

Covenants as to user

It is common for the landlord to restrict the use to which the tenant may put the demised premises.

Covenants not to assign, underlet or part with possession of the demised premises

A breach of this covenant is not capable of remedy, and the notice served under s146(1) need not require the breach to be remedied. See *Scala House and District Property Co Ltd* v *Forbes* [1974] QB 575. However, in such a situation reasonable notice (14 days will suffice) must be given to the tenant so that he can consider his position and consult his solicitor. There are two types of such a covenant.

1. An *absolute covenant*: in such a case the tenant may not assign etc the demised premises. The landlord may, of course, waive the covenant.
2. A *qualified covenant* not to assign etc without the landlord's consent: by s19(1) Landlord and Tenant Act 1927 such consent is not to be unreasonably withheld. If the landlord gives reasons for refusal the burden of proving unreasonableness is on the tenant, otherwise it is on the landlord.

A requirement in a lease that a tenant must offer to surrender his lease before he can seek consent to an assignment is valid, despite s19 LTA 1927. See *Adler* v *Upper Grosvenor Street Investments Ltd* [1957] 1 WLR 227; *Bocardo SA* v *S & M Hotels Ltd* [1980] 1 WLR 17.

In many of the cases on this topic it is a question of construction on the terms of the lease.

Reasonableness

This is a question of fact, but a refusal must relate to the proposed assignee as tenant rather than as an individual, or to the nature of the property. Examples of *reasonable refusal* are:

1. where the proposed assignee's references are unsatisfactory *Shanly* v *Ward* (1913) 29 TLR 714;

2. where the proposed subletting was at a high premium and a low rent which devalued the landlord's interest in the property;
3. where the proposed assignee was a development company interested only in sharing in development to take place after the end of the lease to the detriment of the landlord: see *Pimms Ltd v Tallow Chandlers Co* [1964] 2 QB 547;
4. where the assignee would acquire a statutory protection that the assignor did not have: see *Bookman (Thomas) v Nathan* [1955] 1 WLR 815;
5. where the assignee would acquire a right to buy the freehold under the Leasehold Reform Act 1967 which the assignor did not have: see *Bickel v Duke of Westminster* [1976] 3 WLR 805; *Norfolk Capital Group v Kitway* [1977] QB 506.
6. Where the proposed assignee would use the property for trade competition detrimental to other property of the landlord: see *Premier Confectionary (London) Co Ltd v London Commercial Sale Rooms Ltd* [1933] Ch 904.

Examples of *unreasonable refusal* are:

1. where the landlord wished to recover the premises for himself: see *Bates v Donaldson* [1896] 2 QB 241;
2. where the assignee was a diplomat with diplomatic immunity: see *Parker v Boggon* [1947] KB 346;
3. if the refusal is aimed to achieve some collateral purpose not connected with the terms of the tenancy: see *Bromley Park Garden Estates Ltd v Moss* [1982] 1 WLR 1019.

By statute (s24 Race Relations Act 1976 and Sex Discrimination Act 1975), consent to assignment is unreasonably withheld if it is on the basis of race, colour, creed or sex. There is an exception for small premises where the person withholding consent will continue to reside on the premises. By s19 LTA 1927 no fine shall be payable in respect of a licence to assign unless the lease expressly provides for it.

If the tenant assigns or sublets without consent he is in breach of the covenant. If consent is unreasonably refused the tenant can:

1. go ahead with the transaction, wait for the landlord to sue and then set up the unreasonable refusal by way of defence; or
2. apply to the county court under s53 LTA 1954 (as amended by s148(1) County Courts Act 1984) for a declaration that consent has been unreasonably withheld.

The question of reasonableness for the purposes of s19(1) Landlord and Tenant Act 1927 was reviewed in *International Drilling Fluids Ltd v Louisville Investments (Uxbridge) Ltd* [1986] 2 WLR 581, and Balcombe LJ deduced the following propositions from the authorities:

1. The purpose of the covenant was to protect the lessor from having his premises used or occupied in an undesirable way or occupied by an undesirable tenant or assignee.

2. As a corollary a landlord was not entitled to refuse his consent to an assignment on grounds which had nothing whatever to do with the relationship of landlord and tenant.

3. The onus of proving consent had been unreasonably withheld was on the tenant (but see the Landlord and Tenant Act 1988 below).

4. It is not necessary for the landlord to prove that the conclusions which led him to refuse consent were justified, if they were such as a reasonable man would have so concluded.

5. It might be reasonable to refuse consent on the grounds of the proposed user even though that purpose was not forbidden by the lease.

6. There were conflicting authorities as to whether it was right to have regard to the consequences for the tenant if consent is refused. The two streams of authority could be reconciled by showing that while a landlord usually considers his own relevant interests, there might be cases where there was such a disproportion between the benefit to the landlord and the detriment to the tenant if consent is refused that it became unreasonable for the landlord to refuse consent.

7. Subject to these propositions it was a question of fact, depending on all the circumstances, as to whether the landlord's consent to an assignment was being unreasonably withheld.

If the landlord is slow in giving consent the tenant may lose his potential assignee.

The Landlord and Tenant Act 1988 introduced new statutory duties from 29 September 1988. The effect is that in the case of a qualified covenant against assignment, subletting, or parting with possession, certain additional obligations are imposed on the person who is to give approval. By virtue of s1 of the Landlord and Tenant Act 1988 the onus of proof of reasonableness is now placed on the landlord. If a landlord receives a written application for consent from the tenant a duty is then owed to the tenant within a reasonable time to give that consent unless the landlord can reasonably refuse and to serve a notice on the tenant of that decision (s1(3)). Any conditions of that consent must be set out in the notice. Reasons for refusal must be specified in the notice, and although the emphasis is still on reasonableness the burden of proof has now shifted from the tenant to the landlord. This reverses proposition three propounded by Balcombe LJ in *International Drilling Fluids* (above).

In *Go West Ltd* v *Spigarolo and Another* [2003] 2 All ER 141 the Court of Appeal provided valuable guidance as to s1(3) of the 1988 Act. There GW (the claimant) had been granted a lease of premises by S (the defendant). The lease contained a covenant which prohibited the tenant from assigning the lease without obtaining the landlord's written consent which was not to be unreasonably withheld or delayed. In March 2001, GW wrote to S seeking permission to assign the lease and in May 2001 S wrote back refusing consent. Correspondence between the parties continued until July 2001 when GW commenced proceedings for a declaration that S had unreasonably withheld his consent. The county court judge found for S (the landlord) on the basis that although S's refusal of consent was unreasonable, the correspondence between the parties subsequent to S's letter of refusal demonstrated that they had treated it as having no real effect and that by July 2001 when GW commenced proceedings consent was not still being unreasonably withheld. GW appealed, submitting that the effect of S's letter of refusal was to bring to an end the 'reasonable time' allowed by s1(3) of the 1988 Act. In response, S submitted that the correspondence after his letter of refusal of May 2001 amounted to an ongoing request by GW for a licence to assign.

The Court of Appeal made three main points in respect of s1(3) of the 1988 Act. First, in assessing what length of time was reasonable regard had to be had to all the circumstances of the case, not just the circumstances known at the date of the tenant's application but also any subsequent events. Reasonable time was the time reasonably required by the landlord to do the things the 1988 Act required him to do. Second, once a landlord served his written notice of the decision under s1(3)(b) of the 1988 Act that brought to an end the reasonable time he was given for deciding whether to grant or withhold consent to the proposed assignment. Thereafter S could not claim that it was open to him to reconsider the request of GW during the remainder of what might otherwise have been a reasonable period. Third, a landlord could not rely on reasons for withholding consent that were not specified in his written notice of the decision. Upon an examination of the parties' correspondence, it was clear that there had never been an unequivocal withdrawal by S of his refusal to consent or by GW of its assertion that S's refusal to consent was unreasonable. Further, there was no factual support for any waiver or estoppel. S was in breach of his duty under s1(3) because he had failed with a reasonable time (ie within the period leading up to the sending of his letter of refusal) to consent to the assignment which, as the judge found, he had unreasonably withheld. S had been in breach of this duty on the day his letter of refusal was sent. The judge should have granted the declaration sought and assessed damages. Accordingly, the appeal would be allowed and the case remitted to the county court.

Where property is let on an assured periodic tenancy under the Housing Act 1988, and nothing is said about assignment or subletting, then s15 implies a qualified covenant against assignment, subletting or parting with possession. In this case there is no implied provision that the landlord must not unreasonably withhold consent.

Where a qualified covenant exists not to assign, underlet or part with possession of the demised premises without the consent of the landlord, this is already subject to the qualification that such consent shall not be unreasonably withheld (s19(1) Landlord and Tenant Act 1927).

Covenants to repair

The fact that one party to a lease does not covenant to repair does not mean that the other party is impliedly obliged to.

Scope of the covenant

Many of the leading cases explaining the meaning of 'repair' were reviewed in *Elite Investments Ltd* v *T I Bainbridge Silencers Ltd* (1986) 280 EG 1001. The courts continue to face the problem of repair in the context of inherent defects to the premises. The following cases should be noted:

Ravenseft Properties Ltd v Davstone (Holdings) Ltd [1979] 1 All ER 929. The insertion of expansion joints into the concrete cladding of a building did not change the character of the building and fell within the express covenant to repair. The joints formed a relatively minor part of the whole building and the tenant was liable under the covenant to repair.

Elmcroft Developments Ltd v *Tankersley Sawyer* (1984) 270 EG 140. The landlords were required to insert a damp-proof course in the performance of their repairing covenant. This did not require the landlord to provide a new or wholly different thing from that demised, nor did it change the nature or character of the premises.

Quick v *Taff-Ely Borough Council* [1985] 3 All ER 321. If the damage caused to property falls outside the repairing covenant, then remedying an inherent defect is *not* within the covenant to repair. Thus condensation due to faulty design and construction of the windows in a council house did not mean that the building was in need of repair.

Post Office v *Aquarius Properties Ltd* [1987] 1 All ER 1055. The defect was in the structure of the basement of an office. This did not get worse but continued to allow water into the basement. The tenant was not liable, on the covenant to repair, to remedy these defects in the original construction of the building.

Stent v *Monmouth Borough Council* (1987) 282 EG 705. A defective front door to a council house let in water which caused damage to the tenant's carpets. The landlord was held liable to remedy the defective door. There was actual damage which was sufficient to establish a breach of the landlord's repairing obligation.

It is possible to establish the following general principles from the above case law:

1. If the problem is caused by an inherent defect then remedial work is not within the covenant to repair unless the defect has caused some damage to the building or its contents.
2. If the inherent defect causes deterioration to the building, this does not justify carrying out remedial work beyond the terms of the repairing covenant.
3. If it is found that remedial work is necessary within the terms of the covenant to repair, then this may extend to the remedy of the inherent defect itself.
4. There is no 'disrepair' within the covenant to repair if there is no proof of physical deterioration to the building.

If the tenant covenants to do all the inside repairs and permits the landlord access for any reasonable purpose, problems may arise if no express obligation is imposed on either party to keep the outside of the premises in repair. This problem arose in *Barrett* v *Lounova (1982) Ltd* [1989] 1 All ER 351 where the outside of the property was in a bad state of repair and the tenant claimed that the landlord was in breach of an implied covenant to keep the outside of the premises in reasonable repair.

The Court of Appeal confirmed that such a repairing covenant could be implied against the landlord if a tenant's covenant as to inside repairs becomes impossible to perform where there was no equivalent obligation on the landlord to execute outside repairs. The imposition of such an obligation to execute outside repairs would be necessary in order to give business efficacy to the tenancy agreement.

Repairs and estoppel

If occupiers of property carry out repairs and improvements which enhance the value of the property, they do not acquire an interest in the property by way of proprietary estoppel unless they can show that they had acted in the belief that they would acquire an interest in the property. Such a belief must have been encouraged by the landlord. See in this regard *Brinnand* v *Ewens* (1987) The Times 4 June.

Whether or not a defect is within the scope of a covenant to repair is a question of fact and a question of degree.

A party who covenants to repair is not obliged to renew (ie entirely reconstruct the premises). See *Lurcott* v *Wakeley* [1911] 1 KB 505; *Lister* v *Lane and Nesham* [1893] 2 QB 212; *Brew Bros* v *Snax* [1970] 1 QB 612. Nor is he obliged to make improvements.

Often 'fair wear and tear' is excepted. This exempts the covenantor from liability for the normal action of time and weather, and the normal and reasonable use for which the premises were let. In *Regis Property Co Ltd* v *Dudley* [1959] AC 370 Lord Denning described the extent of this exclusion as follows:

> 'It exempts a tenant from liability for repairs that are decorative and for remedying parts that wear out or come adrift in the course of reasonable use, but it does not exempt him from anything else.'

Standard of repair

The standard of repair required depends on the character of the demised premises and their locality at the time the lease was granted. See *Proudfoot* v *Hart* (1890) 25 QBD 42; *Anstruther-Gough-Calthorpe* v *McOscar* [1924] 1 KB 716. This standard of repair is expressed as such repairs as having regard to the age, character and locality of the premises would make them reasonably fit for occupation by a reasonably minded tenant of the class which would be likely to take it.

Damages for breach

Normally an injunction or decree of specific performance cannot be obtained for a breach of a repairing covenant. If, however, the landlord is in breach and the tenant is unable to repair because the breach concerns property not demised to him, specific performance may be decreed. See *Jeune* v *Queens Cross Properties Ltd* [1974] Ch 97.

By s18(1) of the Landlord and Tenant Act 1927 damages for breach of a tenant's covenant may not exceed the damage to the reversion. If the premises are to be demolished or structurally altered in such a way as to make the repairs useless, no damages are payable. For the right to serve a counter-notice under the Leasehold Property (Repairs) Act 1938 see section 10.10 below. If the landlord is in breach of his repairing covenant, although the tenant cannot repudiate the tenancy he can carry out the repairs himself after giving notice and set off the cost against future rent. See *Lee-Parker* v *Izzet* [1971] 1 WLR 1688 for this self-help remedy.

The measure of damages suffered by the landlord in the diminution of value of the reversion will usually be equivalent to the cost of repairs.

10.9 Determination of tenancies

There are eight ways in which a lease or tenancy may come to an end: expiry, notice to quit, forfeiture, merger, surrender, frustration, enlargement and disclaimer.

Expiry

This applies only to terms certain, which come to an end on the expiry of the term granted. There are statutory exceptions to this rule, which allow certain terms to continue after the end of the term until the tenancy is determined according to the methods laid down by statute: for business tenancies, Landlord and Tenant Act 1954 Part II, and for agricultural tenancies, Agricultural Holdings Acts 1948 and 1984 (see sections 10.14 and 10.15 below). Where the statutes do not apply, a tenant holding under a term certain becomes a trespasser when the term ends, and the landlord is entitled to possession.

Notice to quit

This is the method by which *all periodic tenancies* can be determined. Terms certain can be determined by notice to quit, but only where the right to do so is expressly stated in the lease.

A notice to quit is a notice served on the tenant by the landlord requiring the tenant to quit the premises and give up possession at the end of the next period of the tenancy. There is no need to show any reason for the notice to quit. The landlord under a periodic tenancy has a right to recover possession in this way.

The length of the notice is dependent on the type of periodic tenancy. In all cases the notice must expire on the anniversary of the day on which the tenancy commenced. See *Dodds* v *Walker* [1981] 2 All ER 609.

Weekly tenancy	–	one week's notice (for dwelling houses, by s5 Protection from Eviction Act 1977, there must be four weeks' written notice).
Monthly tenancy	–	one month's notice.
Half-yearly/yearly tenancy	–	six months' notice.

Forfeiture

A landlord can forfeit a tenancy at any time where the tenant is in breach of covenant, so long as the right to forfeit (or re-enter) is reserved in the lease. This is normally known as a 'proviso for re-entry'. Every lease should contain such a right of re-entry as a matter of course.

Forfeiture is normally used to determine terms certain, where the term still has some time to run. Periodic tenancies can be forfeit, but the procedure would be appropriate only for longer periodic tenancies.

Merger

Where a tenant acquires his landlord's interest in the land, the tenancy merges with the reversion and determines. Merger may also take place where both interests become vested in a third party.

Surrender

Where a tenant gives up his interest under a tenancy to his landlord, the tenancy ends. Surrender can occur expressly or by operation of law, where a tenant accepts a new tenancy during the currency of an existing one.

Frustration

It used to be thought that a contract of tenancy could never be frustrated. Hence the liability to pay rent continued, even though the demised premises no longer existed, having been burnt down or bombed.

In *National Carriers Ltd* v *Panalpina (Northern) Ltd* [1981] AC 675 the House of Lords held that leases were capable of frustration, but only in very special circumstances: 'Not never, but hardly ever.' Their Lordships unanimously held that a 10 year lease of a warehouse was not in fact frustrated when it was made unusable for 20 months by the closing of an access road to it.

Enlargement

The lease can be enlarged into the fee simple under s153 LPA 1925. For a term of years to be enlarged under this provision a number of conditions must be satisfied. First, the lease originally must have been granted for a period of 300 years or more and at the date of enlargement 200 years must still be left to run. Second, the term must not be affected by any trust or right of redemption in favour of the freeholder or other person entitled in reversion expectant on the term (this excludes mortgages). Third, the term which it is proposed to enlarge must not be liable to be terminated by 're-entry for condition broken'. Fourth, no rent of any money value must be payable. Fifth, the enlargement must be effected by deed. Finally, if the term was created by subdemise from a superior term, both must be enlargeable.

However, the difficulties involved in utilising this device are considerable. The combination of conditions which must be present in order to invoke s153 are rarely encountered in practice. Further, the statutory power has been rarely invoked and its possibilities are somewhat uncertain (in particular there is uncertainty as to the effect of enlargement upon the reversion).

Disclaimer

Finally, disclaimer arises where the tenant denies the landlord's title, for example by tendering rent to a third party.

10.10 Forfeiture

Before a landlord can forfeit a lease he must:

1. Establish that he has the right to forfeit the lease by ensuring the lease contains the necessary forfeiture clause.
2. Ensure that there is no waiver of that right.
3. Comply with s146 LPA 1925 (for all breaches except breach of a covenant to pay rent).
4. Bring possession proceedings in court.

A lease is not forfeited until the proceedings are served on the tenant. Once the lease has been declared forfeited by a court, the tenant and any subtenants may apply for relief from forfeiture.

The right to forfeit

The right to determine a tenancy by re-entry arises where:

1. The lease expressly provides for a right of forfeiture on breach of a covenant by a tenant and the tenant is in breach. A typical forfeiture clause reads as follows:

   'Provided always and it is hereby agreed:

   That if the rent hereby reserved or any part thereof shall at any time be in arrear for twenty-one days after becoming payable (whether formally demanded or not) or there shall be any breach of the foregoing covenants on the part of the Tenant ... then the Landlord may ... re-enter upon the premises and determine the tenancy.'

2. The tenant denies the landlord's title by operation of law.
3. The demise is made conditional upon performance by the tenant of his obligations under it.

At common law a landlord is entitled to re-enter and take possession if he can do it peaceably. Section 6 of the Criminal Law Act 1977 makes it an offence to use any force, and so it is advisable to enforce forfeiture by legal proceedings. In the case of premises let as a dwelling, s3 Protection from Eviction Act 1977 makes legal proceedings compulsory.

It is important to show that the conduct complained of does constitute a breach of covenant.

The exercise of the right of re-entry does not depend on rent being owed to the landlord actually exercising the right so long as rent is owed under the lease. This was established in *Kataria* v *Safeland plc* [1998] 1 EGLR 39. There S agreed to purchase the freehold of a shop let to K. Under the terms of the sale agreement S assigned the right to recover rent arrears to his predecessor in title (ie the former landlord). At the relevant time K owed rent of some £10,000. The lease contained a forfeiture clause for non-payment of rent. S re-entered the premises in accordance with the aforementioned clause (ie he forfeited the lease by peaceable re-entry on the ground of non-payment of rent). K argued that the purported forfeiture was unlawful because the rent arrears had to be owed to the landlord who sought to enforce the right of re-entry and here S was not personally owed rent since he had assigned the right to recover rent arrears to the former landlord. In finding for S, the Court of Appeal emphasised that a right of re-entry was a proprietary right which was available to a landlord as a landlord and that it was independent of any covenant it supported. So long as rent was owing under the lease an incoming landlord was entitled as a matter of law to exercise its right to re-enter the premises even though it might have assigned the right to recover rent arrears to its predecessor in title. The decision also highlights an important difference between residential tenancies and business tenancies. In the case of the former, Parliament enacted legislation over 40 years ago requiring a landlord to obtain a court order before dispossessing a tenant. In the case of the latter, there is no such requirement and that is why S was able to act as he did (ie forfeit by peaceable re-entry).

Waiver

The landlord may lose his right to forfeit by expressly or impliedly waiving the breach of covenant. Waiver will be implied if the landlord, with knowledge of the tenant's breach, does some act which shows that he regards the tenancy as continuing. The most common form of waiver is the demand and acceptance of rent. See *Central Estates (Belgravia) Ltd* v *Woolgar (No 2)* [1972] 1 WLR 1048.

The effect of waiver depends on the type of breach. Breaches are divided into two categories:

1. Once and for all breaches: breach of a covenant not to sublet or assign; possibly a very serious breach of an immoral use covenant.
2. Continuing breaches: all other breaches, eg repairs.

Waiver of a once and for all breach waives the right to forfeit altogether. Waiver of a continuing breach operates only for the period in relation to which rent was accepted.

Section 146 notice

Section 146(1) LPA 1925 provides a preliminary procedure designed to protect tenants from forfeiture for breach of covenant, without first being given a chance to remedy the breach.

For all breaches other than a failure to pay rent, a landlord cannot forfeit a lease unless he has served a s146 notice on the tenant and the tenant has failed to comply with the notice within a reasonable time.

Section 146(1) provides that a notice must be served on the tenant and that the notice must:

1. specify the breach complained of;
2. require the tenant to remedy the breach (if it is capable of remedy) within a reasonable time;
3. require monetary compensation for the breach.

The landlord must give the tenant a reasonable time to comply with the notice. What is a reasonable time depends on the nature of the breach. Breaches are divided into:

Irremediable breaches

These are of two types:

1. Parting with possession to a subtenant: see *Scala House and District Property Co Ltd* v *Forbes* [1974] QB 575.
2. Serious immoral use: see *Rugby School Governors* v *Tannahill* [1935] 1 KB 87; compare with *Glass* v *Kencakes* [1966] 1 QB 611.

As noted above, even where the breach is irremediable, the tenant must be given reasonable notice (14 days will suffice) so that the tenant can consider his position and consult a solicitor.

Remediable breaches

These include most other kinds of breach.

Only a short period of time need be given to the tenant before commencing proceedings. For breach of a covenant to repair, three months is reasonable.

The importance of a s146 notice requiring a tenant to remedy a breach if it is capable of remedy was demonstrated by *Savva & Savva* v *Hussein* (1997) 73 P & CR 150. There the tenant (H) covenanted not to erect signs or carry out alterations to the premises without the consent of the landlords (S & S). In breach of that covenant, H, inter alia, changed a sign at the front of the premises and altered part of its facia. Thereafter S & S served a s146 notice purporting to forfeit the lease for breach of covenant. However, the notice did not require H to remedy the alleged breaches of covenant (ie S & S were claiming that the breaches were incapable of remedy). The Court of Appeal concluded that the breaches of covenant complained of were capable of remedy – the mischief here could be removed by removing the sign and restoring the premises to the state they were in prior to the alteration. Accordingly, the s146 notice should have required them to be remedied (ie it should have stated what remedial action was required of H in order to remedy the mischief) and it was invalid for not doing so. Hence the lease could not be forfeited.

Breach of covenant to repair

The Leasehold Property (Repairs) Act 1938, as amended by s51 Landlord and Tenant Act 1954, applies where:

1. The breach is of a repairing covenant.
2. The lease was for at least seven years.
3. There are at least three years of the lease left to run
4. The lease is not an agricultural tenancy.

The 1938 Act, where it applies, requires the landlord's s146 notice to inform the tenant of his rights under that Act. Under it the tenant, by serving a counter-notice within 28 days, can require the landlord to obtain the sanction of the court before commencing possession proceedings. See *Land Securities plc* v *Receiver for the Metropolitan Police District* [1983] 1 WLR 439.

In order for the court to give the landlord leave to proceed he must prove:

1. The immediate remedying of the breach is necessary to prevent substantial diminution in the value of his reversion.
2. The immediate remedying is to give effect to some enactment or by-law.
3. The immediate remedying is in the interests of the occupier.
4. A small expense to remedy compared with greater expense if the necessary work is postponed.
5. Special circumstances render it just and equitable in the opinion of the court that leave should be given. See s1(5) Leasehold Property (Repairs) Act 1938.

In *SEDAC Investments Ltd* v *Tanner* [1982] 3 All ER 646 it was held that if the landlord effects the repairs as an emergency then the court cannot subsequently give him leave to proceed under the 1938 Act because the repairs have by then been carried out. Judge Michael Wheeler QC put the matter thus

'The whole scheme of s1 of the [1938] Act appeared to hinge upon the service of a valid notice by the lessor and if therefore to be effective, the s146 notice had to be served before the breach was remedied, the conclusion could only be that if a lessor remedied a breach and then attempted to serve on the lessee a notice under s146(1) and so deprived the lessee of his right to serve a counter-notice, the court had no jurisdiction to give the lessor leave to commence proceedings for damages.'

However, the courts may have found a solution to this situation, namely that instead of suing for breach of the covenant to repair the landlord should claim for the debt due, as this action is not caught by the 1938 Act. This was the method used successfully in *Hamilton* v *Martell Securities Ltd* [1984] 1 All ER 665. There, Vinelott J held that where the landlord had carried out repairs, the claim for the cost against the tenant was for a debt due under the lease rather than a claim for damages for breach of the covenant to repair, and so no leave under the 1938 Act was required in order to bring the action against the tenant.

Exceptions to s146(1)

A s146 notice need not be served in the following cases:

1. breach of covenant to pay rent;
2. breach of covenant to allow inspection in mining leases;
3. bankruptcy of the lessee of any of the following:

   a) agricultural land;
   b) mining lease;
   c) public house;
   d) furnished house;
   e) any property where the personal qualifications of the tenant are important. See *Bathurst (Earl)* v *Fine* [1974] 1 WLR 905.

In such cases the landlord can forfeit immediately when bankruptcy occurs.

In any other lease where there is a proviso for re-entry on bankruptcy, s146(10) LPA 1925 provides that:

1. If the trustee in bankruptcy sells within a year, despite proceedings for forfeiture, he can claim relief even after the year has expired and the court can confirm the title of the purchaser.
2. If the trustee in bankruptcy does not sell within the year, although the landlord cannot forfeit without serving a statutory notice during the year, he may forfeit without serving a notice after the expiration of a year.

Relief from forfeiture

Tenants

Where a tenant is in breach of covenant, the court must allow the landlord to forfeit the lease and order possession. Section 146(2) LPA 1925 gives the court a wide discretion to allow the tenant relief from forfeiture, on terms that the breach ceases. Where the breach is irremediable (see 'Section 146 notice' above) the court will not allow relief from forfeiture. Nor will relief be allowed where the landlord has already re-entered. Section 146(2) only applies while the landlord is 'proceeding' to enforce his rights and not where he has in fact entered before the tenant seeks relief.

Where the breach relates to only one part of the demised premises, that part alone may be forfeited. See *GMS Syndicate Ltd* v *Gary Elliott Ltd* [1982] Ch 1.

Subtenants and mortgagees

If the head lease is forfeited, any sublease or mortgage falls with it. However, s146(4) LPA 1925 gives the sublessee (or mortgagee or chargee) a right to apply to the court for relief against forfeiture of the head lease, whatever the ground of forfeiture and even if the head lessee could not himself have applied for relief. If relief is granted the court may make an order vesting the whole or any part of the demised premises in the subtenant for a term not longer than the sublease and on such conditions as the court thinks fit. In *Bland* v *Ingram's Estate Ltd* (2001) The Times 18 January the Court of Appeal held that an equitable chargee could not succeed under s146(4) LPA 1925 as that provision only allowed an application for relief from forfeiture to be made by 'a person claiming as under-lessee (ie a person with a derivative interest in the land) and an equitable chargee was not such a person.'

Forfeiture for non-payment of rent

At common law a landlord cannot exercise a right of re-entry unless he has first made a *formal demand*, that is, he or his agent have demanded the exact sum due in the demised premises on the day it is due at such convenient hour before sunset as will give time to count out the money. This requirement can be dispensed with:

1. if expressly excluded by the lease (which it is in all standard form leases);
2. under the Common Law Procedure Act 1852 if half a year's rent is in arrear, and insufficient goods to satisfy the arrears are available for distress.

If the landlord brings an action for possession the tenant has the right under s212 Common Law Procedure Act 1852 to have the action discontinued if he pays all arrears and costs at any time before the trial. However, it was held in *Standard Pattern Co Ltd* v *Ivey* [1962] Ch 432 that this section is confined to cases where at least half a year's rent is due.

Even after judgment has been given the court can give the tenant relief from forfeiture. The power to do so was originally equitable but is now governed by ss210–212 Common Law Procedure Act 1852. The tenant must apply within six months of the judgment, and relief will be granted if he pays the rent due and the landlord's costs, and if it is equitable in the circumstances to grant it.

The six-month time limit does not apply if the landlord re-entered other than by an action for possession. Relief may be granted on terms, eg that the tenant should do outstanding repairs. Given that a tenant can apply for relief within six months of execution of the judgment, what happens if after recovering possession the landlord re-lets the premises and then the old tenant claims relief against forfeiture within the six month period? Will the court grant relief? The general rule is that where the landlord has forfeited for non-payment of rent the court will grant the tenant relief from forfeiture. However, an exception to this rule is often made where the parties have altered their position prior to the application for relief. In *Gill* v *Lewis* [1956] 2 QB 1 Jenkins LJ put the matter thus:

'... where parties have altered their position in the meantime, and in particular where the rights of third parties have intervened, relief ought not to be granted where the effect of it would be to defeat the new rights of third parties or be unfair to the landlord having regard to the way in which he has altered his position' (at p10).

In line with this dicta the Court of Appeal in *Silverman* v *Afco (UK) Ltd* [1988] 1 EGLR 51 refused relief where the landlord had in the meantime granted a new tenancy to a third party.

However, there are cases where the courts have been prepared to grant relief despite the fact that the landlord has granted a new tenancy to a third party (see eg *Fuller* v *Judy Properties Ltd* [1992] 1 EGLR 75). If a court decides to so act it seems that the original tenant will either get (1) the lease back but subject to the new tenancy (ie the old tenant becomes the new tenant's immediate landlord) or (2) the lease back unencumbered by the new tenancy.

A subtenant where the head tenancy is forfeit for failure to pay rent can seek relief from forfeiture under s146(4) LPA 1925.

Alternative jurisdiction is in the county court. If the tenant begins proceedings for relief in the county court under s138 County Courts Act 1984, then this excludes any possible relief against forfeiture through the High Court. This was established in *Di Palma* v *Victoria Square Property Co Ltd* [1985] 3 WLR 207, where the Court of Appeal confirmed the decision of Scott J at first instance. Lawton LJ concluded:

'It followed that on the plain meaning of the words used in the section Parliament intended that a tenant who did not do the acts specified should not later be able to apply to the High Court for relief from forfeiture.'

Section 55 of the Administration of Justice Act 1985 has amended s138 County Courts Act 1984 following the decision of the Court of Appeal in *Di Palma* v *Victoria Square Property Co Ltd* [1985] 3 WLR 207. The effect of s55 of the Administration of Justice Act 1985 is to allow a tenant to apply for relief against forfeiture in the county court at any time during the six months following re-entry of the landlord. This right of relief is also available to a sublessee or a mortgagee. This amendment effectively gives the tenant the same rights to relief as were already available in the High Court and should avoid the anomalies – which were highlighted in this decision and in *Jones* v *Barnett* [1984] Ch 500 – of the choice of court in which to commence proceedings.

Evaluation

The current law of forfeiture of leases has a number of shortcomings. The Law Commission has described the current law as 'complex and confused' (Law Com No 142, March 1985 at para 3.2). A number of reasons can be advanced in support of such a conclusion. First, the fact that there are separate procedures depending upon whether the landlord is proposing to forfeit for non-payment of rent or for breach of some other covenant is a complication in itself. Second, the present law is both statutory and non-statutory. Originally the court used its inherent equitable jurisdiction to grant relief from forfeiture. Since those early days there have been major statutory incursions into the law of forfeiture, with the result that there is some uncertainty as to the extent to which the inherent equitable jurisdiction has survived these legislative developments (see *Abbey National Building Society* v *Maybeech Ltd* [1984] 3 All ER 262 and *Official Custodian for Charities* v *Parway Estates Developments Ltd* [1984] 3 All ER 679). In *Bland* v *Ingram's Estate Ltd* (2001) The Times 18 January the Court of Appeal had an opportunity to consider the court's inherent jurisdiction. There a lease was forfeited for non-payment of rent. The tenant made no claim for relief from forfeiture. However, previous tenants with an equitable charge over the lease claimed relief from forfeiture under the inherent jurisdiction of the court. The issue to be determined was whether they could so proceed. The Court made two main findings. First, it could not entertain a claim for *direct relief*. Second, an equitable chargee of a lease in these circumstances (forfeiture for non-payment of rent with tenant himself not seeking relief) could claim relief from forfeiture *indirectly* under the inherent jurisdiction by the chargee joining the tenant as defendant and claiming in his shoes. Third, there are different schemes for relief in relation to non-payment of rent between the High Court and county court, which is difficult to justify. Fourth, under the present regime a landlord has to guess accurately whether a given breach is remediable, and also decide how much time to give a tenant to remedy the breach before serving a writ. Finally, waiver is technical and operates irrespective of the merits of the case.

In 1985 the Law Commission published its Report on Forfeitire of Tenancies (Law Com No 142). It recommended that the current law of forfeiture, both statutory and non-statutory, should be abolished and with it the doctrine of re-entry. It was proposed that a landlord should have the right to bring termination order proceedings which would not depend on any clause in the lease (ie no need for a right of re-entry). Such a right could be expressly excluded. Under the new scheme there would be no distinction between termination for non-payment of rent and termination for other reasons. In termination order proceedings the landlord would have to establish a 'termination order event' in order to be successful. These would be: (i) a breach of covenant by the tenant; or (ii) a disguised breach of covenant (broadly a breach by the tenant of an obligation imposed on him otherwise than by covenant); or (iii) the tenant's insolvency. A successful application by a landlord for a termination order would result in either an 'absolute order' (to terminate the tenancy unconditionally on a date specified), or a 'remedial order' (to terminate the tenancy on a date specified unless the tenant has remedied the breach of covenant in conformity with the order of the court by that time). In both cases, the court would have a discretion to grant or refuse to grant an order in accordance with certain guidelines.

In 1994, the Law Commission published a further report which is, in reality, a republication of the 1985 Report with some small changes (Law Com No 221). The latest report includes a draft Termination of Tenancies Bill.

The enactment of the Law Commission's proposals would be advantageous in many respects and would remove much of the current complexity and confusion surrounding this particular area of the law. In particular, bringing to an end the separate procedures for termination for non-payment of rent and termination for other reasons would be a major advance.

10.11 Enforceability of covenants in leases

General principles

Definition of covenant

The strict definition of a covenant is a promise contained in a deed. However, promises contained in written documents or implied into tenancy agreements are also described as covenants, and are enforceable in the same way as covenants in a deed.

Methods of enforcement

Where covenants are enforceable between a landlord and a tenant, either party has a choice of methods of enforcement.

Where a landlord is in breach the tenant can either sue in contract for damages for breach of contract, or seek specific performance of the covenant (usual for a repairing covenant) or an injunction to restrain the landlord's breach (covenants other than repairing covenants) and damages. See *Sampson* v *Hodson-Pressinger* [1981] 3 All ER 710.

For breach of repairing covenants, the tenant is also entitled to do the repairs himself and withhold the cost from his rent.

Where the tenant is in breach the landlord can:

1. Sue in contract for damages for breach of contract.
2. Seek an injunction to restrain the breach and damages.
3. Forfeit the lease for breach of covenant, provided that:

   a) the lease contains a proviso for forfeiture (or re-entry) for breach of covenant by the tenant; and
   b) the landlord has not waived the breach; and

c) a s146 notice (if required) has been served on the tenant, and the tenant has not remedied the breach within a reasonable time of service of the notice.

Enforceability – two regimes

The law in this area was significantly reformed with the coming into force on 1 January 1996 of the Landlord and Tenant (Covenants) Act 1995. This Act applies a new enforcement regime to all new tenancies *granted* on or after 1 January 1996. Accordingly, the Act is not retrospective and therefore the old regime is still applicable in respect of leases *granted* before that date. In the ensuing paragraphs the law applicable to leases granted before 1 January 1996 and the law applicable to tenancies granted after 31 December 1995 is summarised.

Tenancies granted before 1 January 1996
Covenants in leases are enforceable between parties where there is privity of contract or privity of estate.

Privity of contract and estate. There is privity of contract between the original parties to a lease, and any third parties with whom the lease was said to be made (s56 LPA 1925). There is privity of estate between a tenant and his immediate landlord. Hence there is no privity of estate between a landlord and a subtenant.

Enforceability between original parties to lease. There is privity of contract between the original parties to the lease, so that all covenants are enforceable. Both landlord and tenant remain liable to each other for the whole term of the lease, even though either has assigned his whole interest in the land.

The only exception to this rule is that the tenant under a perpetually renewable lease is not liable after he has assigned his interest. See Schedule 15 paragraph 11(i) LPA 1922.

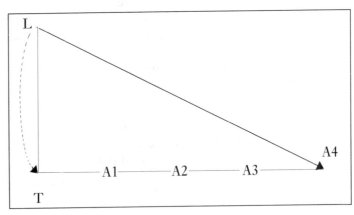

Where an assignee is in breach of covenant, L has a choice. He can sue either A4 (the assignee in possession) or T.

If T is sued for A4's breach, he has two remedies available to him. First, he can sue A1 under the covenant of indemnity implied into every assignment for value by s77 LPA 1925; A1 can then sue A2 and so on along this chain of indemnity covenants. Secondly, he can sue A4 directly in quasi-contract. See *Moule v Garrett* (1872) LR 7 Ex 101. This is based on the principles of quasi-contract and will only apply where the covenants touch and concern the land, and the liability of T and A4 is the same liability to L, the landlord. The law implies an obligation between joint debtors to repay money paid by one of them for the exclusive benefit of the other when both are legally liable to a common creditor. Under this rule, if T satisfies A4's debt he has the same right of indemnity as a surety.

Enforceability between assignees. When either the lease or the reversion or both have been assigned there is no privity of contract, but there is privity of estate arising out of the relationship of landlord and tenant. Covenants in the original lease are enforceable between persons standing in the relationship of landlord and tenant, even though one, or both, of them are not the original parties.

Where the tenant has assigned his interest

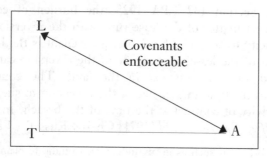

Covenants in the original lease are enforceable by and against the assignee of the tenant if:

1. the covenant *touches and concerns* the land, that is, it is related to the land itself or concerns the landlord as landlord and the tenant as tenant; and
2. the lease is a legal lease; and
3. the assignment is a legal assignment.

An assignee of the lease remains liable only so long as he remains a tenant, and is not liable for breaches committed after he has assigned the lease. Nor is an assignee liable for breaches committed prior to the assignment to him.

A tenant who suffers loss as a result of a breach of the landlord's covenant which was committed while he was, in fact, the tenant has a right to sue the landlord for loss after the tenant has assigned the residue of the lease. See *City and Metropolitan Properties Ltd* v *Greycroft Ltd* (1987) 283 EG 199.

Where the landlord has assigned the reversion

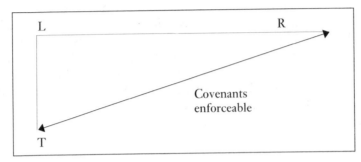

The assignee of the reversion, R, can enforce all covenants contained in the original lease against T provided that the covenants 'have reference to the subject matter of the lease'. This has the same meaning as 'touch and concern the land'.

At common law the assignee of the reversion had no power to enforce covenants in the original lease. This power was conferred by statute. Section 141 LPA 1925: the benefit of covenants that have reference to the subject matter of the lease runs with the reversion. Section 142 LPA 1925: the burden of covenants that have reference to the subject matter of the lease runs with the reversion. The benefit of a covenant is the capacity to sue. The burden of a covenant is the liability to be sued.

As with assignees of the lease, an assignee of the reversion cannot sue or be sued after he has parted with his interest in the land. The courts have, however, interpreted s141 so as to allow an assignee of the reversion to sue a tenant for breach when there is no privity of contract at the time of the breach. In *London and County (A & D) Ltd* v *Wilfred Sportsman Ltd* [1971] Ch 764 Russell LJ said:

> 'The language of s141 ... is such as in my judgment, to indicate plainly that an assignee of the reversion may sue and re-enter for rent in arrear at the date of the assignment when the right of re-entry has arisen before the assignment.'

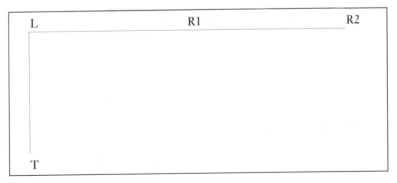

Thus R2 was held to be entitled to sue T for breaches committed by T even though the reversion was vested in R1 at the time of the breach.

Finally, it is important to note that ss141 and 142 LPA 1925 do not apply to new tenancies under the Landlord and Tenant (Covenants) Act 1995.

Tenancies granted after 31 December 1995

The Landlord and Tenant (Covenants) Act (LT(C)A) 1995 received the Royal Assent on 19 July 1995 and came into force on 1 January 1996. It reforms the doctrines of privity of contract and privity of estate so far as they relate to the relationship of landlord and tenant. The main catalyst for the legislation was the fact that during the early 1990s UK economic recession many former tenants were dismayed to discover that they could be required to settle the debts of their insolvent successors long after they had assigned their leases. Such a possibility made prospective tenants wary about taking long leases because of privity of contract (ie that an original tenant would remain liable for future rent and other covenants in the lease throughout the term even after he has parted with all interest in the property).

The need to reform this area of land law was identified by the Law Commission in their 1988 Report *Landlord and Tenant Law: Privity of Contract and Estate* (Law Com No 174). They concluded that 'it is intrinsically unfair that anyone should bear burdens under a contract in respect of which they derive no benefit and over which they have no control', with the proviso that 'the liability should be preserved where it is necessary but abandoned where it is not'. The Act gives effect to that conclusion. In the ensuing paragraphs an outline of some of the main changes introduced by the LT(C)A 1995 is given.

Key points

1. Applies to all new tenancies (both residential and commercial) granted on or after 1 January 1996.
2. Tenancies made pursuant to an agreement entered into before 1 January 1996 are exempt from the new provisions.
3. Makes provision for persons bound by covenants of a tenancy to be released from such covenants on the assignment of the tenancy.
4. Applies to all covenants in a tenancy apart from certain covenants arising by operation of statute under the Housing Act 1985 (covenants for repayment of discount on early disposals).
5. The LT(C)A 1995 differentiates between new tenancies (those granted after the Act came into force) and other tenancies.

Transmission of covenants. The LT(C)A 1995 introduces a statutory code for the transmission of the benefit and burden of leasehold covenants in respect of new tenancies. Under the Act the benefit and burden of all covenants pass upon assignment – whether it is the tenant who is assigning the leasehold interest or the landlord assigning the reversion. Accordingly, there is no longer any need to differentiate between covenants that 'touch and concern' the land and those that do not (s3). For example, on an assignment of a tenancy the assignee tenant becomes bound by the tenant covenants, to the extent that immediately before the assignment they bound the assignor, and becomes entitled to the benefit of the landlord covenants to a corresponding extent.

Release of former tenants. After a tenant assigns, he is released from his covenants and ceases to be entitled to the benefit of the landlord's covenants (s5). However, to this rule there are two categories of exception:

1. Excluded assignments – s11 provides that assignments that are either in breach of a covenant (ie unauthorised assignments) or by operation of law (ie following death or insolvency) cannot release the assigning landlord or tenant from his obligations under the covenants contained in the assigned tenancy. In these situations an assigning tenant or landlord cannot be released from the relevant covenants of the tenancy until there is a subsequent assignment that is lawful (ie not excluded).
2. Lease terms expressed to be made personal to a named person (s3(6)).

Landlord's right to release. It is not only tenants who can obtain release on assignment. Section 7 provides a new procedure whereby landlords can obtain release from their covenants under a lease when they sell their reversionary interest. However, it is important to note that the release of a landlord is not automatic. To obtain release, a landlord must serve a notice on the tenant as prescribed by s8 either before or within four weeks from completion of the reversionary assignment. If the tenant does not respond to the notice within the prescribed time the covenants in respect of which the notice is served are released. If the tenant responds in writing objecting to the release the landlord can apply to the county court for a declaration that the release sought is reasonable. In *BHP Petroleum GB Ltd* v *Chesterfield Properties Ltd* [2001] All ER (D) 451 the meaning of 'landlord covenant' fell to be addressed. There, following a transfer of the freehold reversion by the landlord, a s8 notice was served upon the tenant by the landlord. The covenant in question was a personal one to remedy building work defects. The issue was whether a s8 notice released the landlord from the personal covenant. The court held that a covenant could only rank as a landlord covenant for the purpose of the 1995 Act if it had to be complied with on an ongoing basis (s28 describes landlord as the person 'for the time being entitled to the reversion') and was transmissible. Accordingly, a personal obligation, as here, could not rank as a landlord covenant.

Section 24 somewhat restricts the scope of the release provisions. Any release arising under the LT(C)A 1995 does not affect any liability (of either landlord or tenant) arising from a breach of covenant occurring before the release.

Amendment to Landlord and Tenant Act 1927. Since the release of a former tenant can weaken a landlord's financial position, the Landlord and Tenant Act 1927 has been amended to give landlords more control over future assignments. Section 22 amends the 1927 Act by inserting a new s1A into it. This enables a landlord and tenant to detail in the lease what terms or conditions must be satisfied for the landlord to give his consent to an assignment. If thereafter the terms or conditions are not satisfied and the landlord does not consent to the assignment, his consent will not be regarded as having been unreasonably withheld. However, the amendment to s19 of the 1927 Act *cannot* apply to residential premises. It only applies to business premises.

Authorised guarantee agreement. A tenant who is released from a covenant on an assignment may be required by the landlord to enter into an 'authorised guarantee agreement' (s16). Such an agreement requires the assigning tenant to guarantee the performance by the assignee tenant (ie the person to whom he immediately assigns but not subsequent assignees) of the covenants from which he has been released by the assignment. Section 16(3) sets out the circumstances in which the landlord may require the tenant to enter into such an agreement. First, the lease must contain either an absolute prohibition against assignment or a qualified covenant (ie tenant cannot assign without the landlord's consent). Secondly, the landlord gave his consent to the assignment subject to a condition lawfully imposed that the tenant would enter into such an agreement. Thirdly, the agreement itself must be entered into by the tenant in pursuance of that condition.

New protection for former tenants. Since 1 January 1996, the only former tenants who can be held liable for debts of a successor are those holding under an 'old lease' (ie one executed before 1 January 1996) or former tenants under a 'new' lease who have entered into a s16 authorised guarantee agreement. In either case, a former tenant will not be liable to pay any amount (eg arrears of rent or fixed charges) unless a prescribed notice has been served on him by the landlord within six months of the debt becoming due (s17).

The aim of s17 is to protect a former tenant from arrears of rent etc accumulating against him without his knowledge. It is important to emphasise that s17 applies both to 'new' leases and to 'old' leases.

Finally, to guarantee the performance by the assignee tenant s19 strengthens the position of a former tenant who is obliged to pay the debts of a successor. Once such a former tenant has discharged his obligations under s17 he has the right to call upon the landlord to grant him an overriding lease (overriding the lease of the defaulting assignee). Such a lease is a tenancy of the landlord's reversion and puts the former tenant in the position of intermediate landlord in relation to the defaulting tenant. In the latter capacity the former tenant can exercise all the usual remedies available to a landlord, including the right to forfeit. This development is designed to meet the concerns of many original tenants who, in the early 1990s UK economic recession, found themselves powerless to control accruing liabilities due to the default of their successors in title.

Conclusion. The LT(C)A 1995 introduces some of the biggest reforms seen in the last 60 years. The way the property market operates will never be the same again. Any agreement restricting the operation of the LT(C)A 1995 is void: s25. It is important to emphasise that it is the date of the grant of the tenancy which is the determining factor and not the date when the term commences (ie it is the date of the grant which puts a tenancy either side of the cut off). The Act repeals ss141 and 142 LPA 1925 for the vast majority of leases granted on or after 1 January 1996. It is submitted that the Act has had at least three consequences. First, it creates a two-tier leasehold market – old leases subject to privity of contract and new tenancies with automatic tenant release. Accordingly, since it is not retrospective, practitioners dealing with leases have to distinguish carefully between a new tenancy to which the Act applies and an old lease covered by the privity of contract and estate regime. Second, given the amendment to s19 of the Landlord and Tenant Act 1927, it is submitted that the content of the assignment clause in new business tenancies is now a key area in leasehold negotiations, since it enables landlords to specify in that clause the security/creditworthiness criteria that a prospective assignee will have to meet. Third, it may result in an increased use of subletting to avoid the consequences of tenant release (the Act has no application to subletting).

Enforcement by and against subtenants

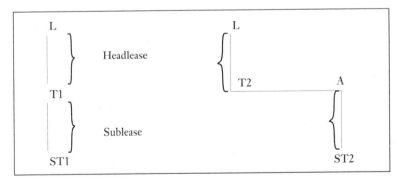

There is neither privity of estate nor privity of contract between a landlord and a subtenant. Privity of estate exists only between a landlord and his immediate tenant.

Liability of subtenants to head landlord
Hence, in *neither* of the examples given above, can L sue ST directly, under the rules dealing with the enforcement of covenants in leases, for conduct by ST that amounts to a breach of a covenant in the head lease. A subtenant is liable to his immediate landlord for breaches of covenants in the sublease (in the examples, T1 or A), but he is not liable at common law to the head landlord for breach of covenant.

A landlord can enforce a covenant against a subtenant either *indirectly* or *in equity*.

Indirect enforcement at common law

By s79 LPA 1925, a covenant relating to any land of a covenantor (the original tenant) is deemed to be made by the covenantor on behalf of himself, his successors in title (assignees) and persons deriving title under him or them (subtenants).

The effect of this provision is that a tenant is liable to his landlord if a subtenant is in breach of covenants contained in the head lease, so long as those covenants relate to the land. The landlord can therefore sue the tenant, or forfeit his lease for breach. Once the tenant's lease is forfeit, the subtenant's lease also comes to an end.

Both the subtenant and the tenant can seek relief from forfeiture, under ss146(4) and 146(2) LPA 1925 respectively.

Further, it is important to emphasise that in order to gain possession from a subtenant, a landlord must forfeit the tenant's lease. Both the tenant and the subtenant then become trespassers.

Enforcement in equity

A landlord can enforce a covenant directly against a subtenant in equity under the rule in *Tulk* v *Moxhay* (1848) 2 Ph 774 so long as:

1. The covenant is negative in substance; and
2. It touches and concerns the land held under the sublease; and
3. There was no intention expressed in the sublease that the subtenant should not be liable (subject to the burden); and
4. The subtenant has actual, constructive or imputed notice of the existence of the covenant. Covenants contained in leases are not registrable, so liability depends on notice.

If these conditions are satisfied a landlord can sue a subtenant for breach of a covenant in the head lease, and enforce the covenant by means of an injunction, or obtain damages in lieu. However, it is important to note that a landlord cannot forfeit a subtenant's lease, even though he can establish liability under the rule in *Tulk* v *Moxhay*. The reason a landlord can so enforce restrictive covenants in the head lease against subtenants is because his reversion is a sufficient interest in land (in this situation there is neither privity of contract nor privity of estate as between the parties). (For further details of restrictive covenants see Chapter 11.)

Liability of head landlords to subtenants

A subtenant cannot sue the head landlord directly for his breach of the covenants in the head lease under the rules relating to leasehold covenants, but under the rules relating to freehold land a subtenant may be able to sue the head landlord.

The original landlord. Where the original landlord has not assigned his reversion, a subtenant can enforce both positive and negative covenants directly against the landlord provided that:

1. The covenants relate to the land comprised in the sublease; and
2. The sublease does not state that the subtenant is to be deprived of the benefit of the covenants in the head lease.

The capacity of a subtenant to sue is based on s78(1) LPA 1925, which provides that a covenant relating to any land of the covenantee (the tenant) shall be deemed to be made with his successors in title (assignees) and the persons deriving title under him or them (subtenants).

In *Smith and Snipes Hall Farm* v *River Douglas Catchment Board* [1949] 2 KB 500 it was held that a covenant made with a freeholder could be enforced at common law by a tenant. This argument can be applied to subtenancies.

A successor in title of the original landlord. Where the original landlord has assigned his reversion, a subtenant can enforce only negative covenants against the assignee of the reversion under the rule in *Tulk* v *Moxhay*.

Contracts (Rights of Third Parties) Act 1999

The law in relation to the enforcement of leasehold covenants must now be considered in the light of the coming into force of the Contracts (Rights of Third Parties) Act 1999. The Act, which received the Royal Assent on 1 November 1999, applies to all contracts (including contracts concerning land) entered into on or after 11 May 2000 (in relation to contracts entered into between 1 November 1999 and 11 May 2000 the Act only applies if the contract expressly provides that it is to so apply). Since the Act applies to contracts concerning land a range of property transactions (sale, lease, etc) are potentially within its scope. In the ensuing paragraphs, the key provisions of the Act are outlined and its potential impact on leasehold covenant enforcement considered.

Background
The Act, which is a short one of only ten sections, is based upon the recommendations of the Law Commission in its report *Privity of Contract: Contracts for the Benefit of Third Parties* (Law Com No 242, 1996). It amends the doctrine of privity of contract. Prior to the Act, a third party could not enforce a benefit purported to be granted by the contract and a third party could not be made the subject of a burden imposed by the contract. Whilst the Act remains silent on the issue of imposing a burden on third parties it enables such parties to enforce contractual terms (ie the benefit) in certain situations.

Rights of third parties
The ways in which a third party (ie a non-contracting party) may have a right to

enforce a contractual term are set out in s1. A third party is given the right to enforce a contractual term in two situations. First, a third party has a right to enforce a term of a contract 'if the contract expressly provides that he may' (s1(1)(a)). Accordingly, the parties to a contract can expressly stipulate that a third party can enforce a contractual term. Second, a third party has a right to enforce a contractual term which 'purports to confer a benefit upon him' (s1(1)(b)). However, this second situation is subject to an important proviso. Section 1(2) provides that it does not apply 'if on a proper construction of the contract it appears that the parties did not intend the term to be enforceable by the third party'. This proviso constitutes an important qualification to third party rights, namely, if the contracting parties do not want any other persons to have a right to enforce any part of the contract they can expressly provide for this in the contract. In the absence of an express statement it is necessary to decide if the contract 'purports to confer a benefit' on a third party, and if it does, whether it appears as a matter of construction of the contract that the parties to the contract did not intend the third party to have rights of enforcement. Self evidently s1(1)(b) will be more difficult to apply than s1(1)(a).

In respect of both s1(1)(a) and (b), a third party can be expressly identified in a contract by name, as a member of a class or answering a particular description (s1(3)). Accordingly, a phrase like 'successors in title' would be capable of confirming rights of enforcement upon such persons in appropriate circumstances. Finally, s1 confers no right on a third party in respect of a contract on a bill of exchange, promissory note or other negotiable instrument.

Variation and rescission of contract

Where a third party has a right to enforce a term of the contract, the contracting parties cannot rescind the contract or vary it so as to extinguish or alter the third party's entitlement under it without his consent (unless the contract provides otherwise). The right of a third party 'crystallises' when he communicates his assent to the term to the promisor or has relied on the term (s2). The need for consent to a variation can be dispensed with by the court if the third party is incapable of giving consent or cannot be traced (s2(4)).

Enforcement

A third party enjoys the same remedies as would be open to him if he were a contracting party (s1(3)). In an action by a third party the promisor has available to him by way of defence or set off any matter arising from or in connection with the contract which would have been available to him if the proceedings had been brought by the promisee (s3).

Potential impact on leasehold covenants

It is submitted that the Act may potentially effect the enforcement of leasehold covenants in at least *three* respects.

First, the Act may effect the enforcement of covenants between a superior landlord (ie not an immediate landlord) and a sub-tenant. Prior to the Act a superior landlord could enforce covenants directly against a sub-tenant if, as was usual, the sub-tenant entered into a direct covenant with the superior landlord to observe the covenants in the sub-lease (this option remains after the Act). Further, prior to the Act it was established in *Amsprop Trading* v *Harris Distribution* [1997] 1 WLR 1025 that a superior landlord did not have direct rights of enforcement against a sub-tenant by virtue of s56 of the LPA 1925. Neuberger J concluded that the 'true aim of section 56 seems to be not to allow the third party to sue on a contract merely because it is made for his benefit; the contract must purport to be made with him'. What is the effect of the 1999 Act on the enforcement of covenants by a superior landlord? If an underlease is expressly drafted to give a superior landlord rights of enforcement then he will have a direct right to enforce under s1(1)(a). To so draft an underlease will give a superior landlord an easy way to achieve direct enforcement of covenants against an undertenant. However, if an underlease does not contain express rights of enforcement the covenant will have to 'confer a benefit' on the superior landlord for him to be able to enforce it (s1(1)(b)). A covenant which is frequently relevant in this context is one between the undertenant and the immediate landlord giving the superior landlord the right to enter upon the premises in order to view the condition of the property and to effect necessary repairs at the undertenant's expense (such a covenant was not enforceable by the superior landlord under s56 LPA 1925 in *Amsprop Trading* v *Harris Distribution* (above)).

Second, the Act may effect the enforcement of covenants *against* a superior landlord. Similar to the possibilities previously canvassed concerning enforcement of covenants by a superior landlord against a sub-tenant it may be possible for a sub-tenant to be able to sue a superior landlord directly for breach of a covenant to provide a given service. However, given that such a prospect is unlikely to appeal to superior landlords it is important to emphasise that the Act enables them to avoid such 'covenant exposure' by an appropriate use of express wording.

Third, the Act may facilitate the enforcement of covenants between tenants of a common landlord. For example, in the case of a multi-unit shopping centre owned by a landlord with units leased to shops/traders it is usual for each tenant to covenant with the landlord to keep his premises/unit open during usual shopping hours (the rationale for such a covenant is that the complex is perceived to be less attractive for shoppers if all the units are not usually open at the same time). Under the Act, mutual enforceability is possible under s1(1)(a) if the lease of each unit in the shopping centre expressly provides that other tenants can enforce the covenants. If the lease of each unit so provides, T1 who in breach of covenant does not open his shop unit during usual shopping hours may be liable to T2 who wishes to bring an action against him (for any loss to the trade of T2 arising from such closure) as well as being liable to the landlord. However, if the lease does not so provide enforcement under s1(1)(b) will depend upon whether the lease 'confers a benefit' on the other tenants and whether they are expressly identified in the lease (s1(3)).

What is difficult to predict is whether tenants would welcome the opportunity, if available, to sue each other (the tenant suing today may himself be in breach tomorrow and thus run the risk of being sued).

Conclusion

Whereas prior to the Act a third party could not enforce a benefit purported to be granted by the contract, now under the Act such a person can potentially enforce contractual terms in certain situations. The emphasis must, however, be on the word 'potentially' because the Act ensures that the main contracting parties are still in control by enabling them to exclude the application of the provisions of the Act. The potential impact of the Act on freehold covenants is considered in Chapter 11, section 11.11.

10.12 Statutory protection of tenants

Tenants are protected against their landlords by a complex and interrelated series of statutes. The type of protection depends upon the type of tenancy. Tenancies are divided into three types:

1. residential;
2. agricultural;
3. business.

Tenancies must fall within one of these categories, and cannot fall within more than one. The categories are mutually exclusive.

10.13 Residential tenancies

Residential tenancies are subject to various forms of protection afforded by legislation. This includes security of tenure afforded to a tenant (ie the limitation placed on a landlord to evict a tenant from his home), the amount of rent (including an amount in respect of service charges where relevant) payable by a tenant and in certain circumstances the right of a tenant to extend the period of the lease or even purchase the freehold. The protection varies according to the type of tenancy which the tenant enjoys, on the type of housing, whether social rented housing or private rented housing and whether the residence is a house or a flat (the latter is of particular importance in respect of lease extension and purchase of the freehold).

The summary on pages 204–205 sets out the main types of tenancy in the private sector. This is followed by a short outline of aspects of the Housing Act 2004.

Tenancies post Housing Act 1996

Current legislation

The Housing Act 1996 significantly amended the Housing Act 1988. It applies to *all* tenancies after 28 February 1997. Such tenancies, subject to those exceptions listed below, will be *assured shorthold* tenancies whether verbal or in writing. They can be for any period of time, either periodic (eg weekly or monthly) or for an fixed term (eg three months, six months or six years as there is no minimum period of time). Security of tenure is minimal the only restriction being that possession cannot be obtained by a landlord before the end of the first period of six months.

Exceptions

If circumstances exist, which are listed in Schedule 7 of the Housing Act 1996 an *assured* tenancy, rather than an assured shorthold, will be created. This has the effect of affording more security of tenure to tenants in that a landlord will have to establish a specific ground, such as non-payment of rent or breach of tenancy agreement, in order to obtain possession of the property. For a full list of grounds which can be relied upon reference will need to be made to the Housing Act 1988.

Some important circumstances when an assured tenancy will arise

1. Where the parties deliberately contract to create an *assured* tenancy. This must be done by notice in writing before the tenancy is entered into or be contained in the tenancy agreement;
2. Tenancies containing an exclusionary provision, for example an agreement that a tenancy is not a shorthold;
3. Where a tenant succeeds to the tenancy, perhaps due to the death of the former tenant, and is thus under the Housing Act 1988 entitled to an assured tenancy which in this case will be a periodic one.
4. Replacement tenancies, that is where an existing non-shorthold tenancy is being replaced by the original parties.

As regards rental levels tenants with either of the above tenancies are able to refer a demand by a landlord for an increase in the contractual rent to an independent Rent Assessment Committee when an *open market rent* will be determined.

In addition, in relation to assured shorthold tenancies, if a tenant feels that the agreed contractual rent is excessive an application can again be made to the Rent Assessment Committee. This must be done within the first six month period. For information on the composition of such committees see the Rent Act 1977 as amended.

Tenancies pre Housing Act 1996

A number of tenancies still exist which are regulated by the Housing Act 1988 and the Rent Act 1977 (as amended). The latter will continue for some time due to the succession provisions contained in the legislation.

Tenancies under the Housing Act 1988

Some tenancies created under this legislation, especially assured tenancies, are likely to be in existence for some time. In order for such a tenancy to exist it must have been created on or after 15 January 1989 and before 28 February 1997. Such tenancies will be *either assured shortholds* or *assureds*. The difference between their creation and the new, similarly named tenancies under the 1996 Act, is that to have created a shorthold tenancy under the 1988 Act the landlord would have had to give a *notice in writing* to the tenant prior to the tenancy agreement making it clear that what was being created was a shorthold. In the absence of such a notice the tenancy would become an assured one.

This requirement has been reversed in the Housing Act 1996 in that a notice is required to specifically create an assured tenancy otherwise the tenancy will be a shorthold.

Tenancies under the Rent Act 1977 (as amended by the Housing Acts 1980 and 1988)

Such tenancies, referred to as regulated or controlled tenancies, still exist and will have been created before 15 January 1989. They may have been succeeded to after that date (for succession provisions see both the Rent Act and amendments in the Housing Act 1980). In this regard it is interesting to note that in *Fitzpatrick* v *Sterling Housing Association Ltd* [1999] 3 WLR 1113 the House of Lords decided that same sex partners are eligible to succeed to a tenancy.

These tenancies have the benefit both of security of tenure and regulation of the rent payable so that a fair rent as opposed to an open market rent is payable. The advantage to a tenant of a fair rent, defined in s70 of the Rent Act 1977, is that such a rent is the open market rent less an amount attributable to scarcity, if any (scarcity being an unmeritous amount sought by the landlord where there is a shortage of accommodation). Hence a fair rent is normally less than a market rent, although due to more rented accommodation becoming available the scarcity factor is diminishing.

Other statutory protection

The following Acts are all relevant and provide information on the tenant's rights in various situations: The Housing Acts 1980, 1985, 1987, 1988 and 1996 the latter amending much of the legislation listed here; the Landlord and Tenant Act 1954, the Leasehold Reform Act 1967 and the Leasehold Reform, Housing and Urban Development Act 1993.

Conclusion

The largest gap in the legislation, however, is that it applies only to tenancies, not to licences. Over the years property owners have made wide use of this loophole and used ingenious devices for creating a licence which is a tenancy in all but name. In *Somma* v *Hazelhurst* [1978] 1 WLR 1014 a man and a woman who were not married were each granted a separate licence to occupy the same room in common with a person stipulated by the landlord. The landlord stipulated on the man's licence that the other occupant should be the woman, and vice versa. Both the occupants remained responsible only for their respective halves of the 'rent'. The Court of Appeal held that where both parties agree that there is to be a licence and not a tenancy, then they should be bound by that agreement, provided that the terms of the agreement are consistent with a licence. Here, neither of the two occupants had exclusive possession and they were not jointly liable for the whole 'rent'.

Therefore they were not joint tenants, but licensees, and outside the Rent Act 1977. This decision was expressly disapproved by the House of Lords in *Street* v *Mountford* [1985] 2 WLR 877. The fact that the distinction is now between tenant or lodger must curtail many of the former methods referred to above. It will not matter what name the parties give to the arrangement. See the earlier discussion at section 10.5 as to the joint decision of the House of Lords in *AG Securities* v *Vaughan* and *Antoniades* v *Villiers* [1988] 3 WLR 1205.

More recently in *Bruton* v *Quadrant Housing Trust* [1999] 3 WLR 150 the House of Lords held that an agreement to occupy a self-contained flat created a tenancy even though the grantor himself was only a licensee, the agreement was described as a licence and the occupier was required to vacate the premises on reasonable notice.

Summary of tenancies currently in existence

Post Housing Act 1996

Assured Shorthold

No notice requirement
Periodic or fixed term
For any period (no minimum)
No security at end of six months
Open market rent to be paid
Increase in rent may be referred to RAC *
Excessive rents may be referred to RAC

Assured

Prior notice required
or other exceptions listed in Act
Security of tenure provided by 1988 Act
Open market rental level
Increase in rent to RAC

Tenancies under Housing Act 1988

Assured Shorthold

Prior written notice required
Minimum six month fixed term
No security at end of term
Open market rental level
Excessive rent may be referred to RAC

Assured   No notice required

Periodic or fixed term

Security of tenure (see HA 1988)

Open market rental level

Increase in rent may be referred to RAC

Tenancies under Rent Act 1977 (as amended)

Regulated Tenancies   Can be fixed term or periodic at end of
which a statutory tenancy arises

No need for writing

Full security of tenure (see Act)

Only a fair rent may be charged

* RAC = Rent Assessment Committee (see Rent Act 1977 as amended)

Housing Act 2004

The Act makes provision for a range of housing matters, including giving local housing authorities new powers to deal with poor standard private housing, the licensing of houses in multiple occupation and the introduction of a new tenancy deposit scheme. The Act received the Royal Assent on 18 November 2004 and while some provisions are in force most are still to come into force. An outline of three aspects of the Act is set out below.

Housing Conditions (Part 1)

For many years, local housing authorities have had powers to deal with substandard housing. Under the Housing Act 1985 the focus is on the building itself and its fitness. In contrast, the 2004 Act introduces a new system for assessing housing conditions – the housing health and safety rating system – which puts the focus upon the effect on occupiers of hazards rather than on the building itself. It is the duty of a local housing authority to keep housing conditions in its district under review with a view to deciding whether any action needs to be taken.

There is a new enforcement regime to complement the new housing health and safety rating system. It includes local housing authorities being able to serve an improvement notice if a specified hazard exists on residential premises and to take remedial action. It is an offence for a person on whom an improvement notice is served not to comply with the same. Further, local housing authorities are given emergency powers to deal with urgent hazards. Finally, Part 1 of the Act is not yet in force.

Licensing of houses in multiple occupation (Part 2)

Under the Act the licensing of certain houses in multiple occupation in the private sector becomes mandatory – those over three storeys or housing five or more occupants. An application for a licence must be made to a local housing authority in accordance with its particular requirements, which may include the payment of a fee. In deciding whether or not to grant a licence a local housing authority must consider not just the conditions in the building but also whether the applicant is a fit and proper person to be a licence holder. A licence is valid for a maximum of five years and a person controlling or managing a house in multiple occupation must have a separate licence for each property. It is of course possible for an authority to revoke or vary a licence. It is an offence for a person to control or manage a house in multiple occupation without a licence. The Act provides a new definition of 'a house in multiple occupation' (see ss254–259). In essence, it is where a house is occupied by persons not forming a single household.

What is the rationale for mandatory licensing of certain houses in multiple occupation? It is designed to deal with the low standards which usually pertain in such properties and which in turn are usually occupied by young, low-earning single people. Appropriate enforcement powers have been given to local housing authorities. Part 2 of the Act is not yet in force.

Tenancy deposit schemes (Part 6)

A common feature of residential leases is the requirement from the tenant to provide the landlord with a deposit to cover possible damage to the premises. Further, tenants frequently complain that they encounter difficulty in getting the deposit back at the end of the lease. The Act addresses these realities.

Section 212 requires the Secretary of State to make arrangements to ensure that one or more tenancy deposit schemes are established to safeguard deposits paid to cover possible damage to the premises in respect of assured shorthold tenancies and to facilitate the resolution of disputes arising from such deposits. Landlords and their agents are required to ensure that any deposit so taken in respect of an assured shorthold tenancy is safeguarded by a tenancy deposit scheme. If a landlord does not comply with the tenancy deposit regime his power to seek possession of the assured shorthold is restricted in that he cannot recover possession under the mandatory two-month notice ground (see s21 of the Housing Act 1988).

All private landlords could be affected by this part of the Act when it comes into force.

Leasehold enfranchisement

The Leasehold Reform Acts 1967–79 (as amended by the Housing Act 1980) have further provisions which protect 'residential' tenants against eviction. If the tenant under a long lease, being a term of more than 21 years, of a home at a low rent has occupied the premises as his only or main residence for the last three years or three of the last ten years, then he may apply to the landlord either to purchase the freehold (ie enfranchise his lease) or to secure a 50-year extension of his lease. If the requisite conditions are satisfied, the landlord is bound to make a conveyance of the freehold at a price to be fixed in accordance with the relevant legislation. If the parties cannot agree the price it will be determined by the Leasehold Valuation Tribunal. If the tenant chooses lease extension rather than enfranchisement, once the extended term has commenced he must abide by this decision and cannot subsequently apply for enfranchisement. The benefit of a tenant's notice of his desire to purchase the freehold or obtain a 50-year extension of his lease under the Act can be assigned with the house. However, there is no right to enfranchise certain properties of particular historic interest or natural beauty. In *Tandon* v *Trustees of Spurgeon's Homes* [1982] AC 755 the House of Lords defined 'house' as a building designed or adapted for living in, ie for occupation as a residence, and then only exceptional circumstances would justify holding that the building could not be called a house.

Important changes to the Leasehold Reform Act 1967 were effected by the Leasehold Reform, Housing and Urban Development Act 1993. While the main innovation of the latter Act concerns flats, the changes to the 1967 Act are likely to be far-reaching. Four changes are particularly noteworthy. First, the right to enfranchise has been extended. Under the 1967 Act the right was restricted to houses having a rateable value limit of up to £1,500 in London and £750 elsewhere (this effectively excluded the owners of most higher-value houses from the provisions of the 1967 Act). The rateable value limits have now been abolished (s63 Leasehold Reform, Housing and Urban Development Act 1993). Accordingly, the tenants of higher-value houses who fulfil the remaining qualifying conditions (long lease at a low rent etc) now have the right to enfranchise under the 1993 Act. For many people that will be an attractive possibility. Secondly, an alternative low rent test has been introduced (s65 Leasehold Reform, Housing and Urban Development Act 1993). The new test, based as it is on the ground rent in the first year of the lease, should enable some leaseholders excluded by the existing test (which is based on the rent at the time of enfranchisement) to acquire the freehold. Thirdly, the price to be paid for enfranchisement of houses under the extended provisions has been revised (s66 of the 1993 Act). Fourthly, leaseholders who only qualify under the 1967 Act because of the 1993 Act only have the right to enfranchise – they cannot opt to extend the lease for a further period of 50 years. This is probably a reflection of the fact that enfranchisement has proved infinitely more attractive than lease extension.

As noted above, the right to enfranchise under the 1967 Act depends on a low rent test and the tenancy being let on a long lease, ie a lease 'granted for a term of certain years exceeding twenty-one years'. The definition of a low rent depended on the date the tenancy was entered into. It was complicated and meant that many tenants could not qualify and therefore did not have the benefit of the enfranchisement rights. The Housing Act 1996 attempts to remedy this. Section 105 of the 1996 Act (which came into force on 1 October 1996) effects amendments to the definition of low rent. In particular it provides that the date chosen for the low rent test is one on which the property does not have a nil rateable value. Further, the low rent test is removed in the case of the 1967 Act for tenancies of more than

35 years (ie the right to enfranchise has been extended by Schedule 9 of the 1996 Act to cases which do not fulfil the low rent requirement but which are let on a fixed term exceeding 35 years).

Harassment and unlawful eviction

In addition, all residential tenants are protected from harassment and unlawful eviction by s1 of the Protection from Eviction Act 1977. To be lawful, eviction must be by due process of law, following possession proceedings (s3). Where the tenancy is a periodic one, four weeks' written notice to quit must be given (s5).

Section 27 Housing Act 1988 widens damages available in tort if a landlord unlawfully deprives a residential occupier of occupation of the premises or does some act calculated to interfere with the peace or comfort of the occupier.

In addition the criminal offence of harassment has changed in that it is now necessary to prove that the landlord knew, or should have known, that his conduct would be likely to cause the occupier to give up his occupation.

10.14 Agricultural tenancies

The law in respect of agricultural tenancies was significantly reformed with the coming into force on 1 September 1995 of the Agricultural Tenancies Act 1995. The Act applies to agricultural tenancies created on or after that date. However, agricultural tenancies created before 1 September 1995 are still regulated by the Agricultural Holdings Act 1986. Given that there are a large number of agricultural tenancies in existence which were created before 1 September 1995 and that such tenancies are likely to be around for many years to come, a summary of both the 'old law' (ie pre 1 September 1995) and the 'new law' (post 31 August 1995) is set out below.

Pre 1 September 1995 tenancies

Agricultural tenancies created before 1 September 1995 are governed mainly by the Agricultural Holdings Act 1986. Agriculture has a wide meaning, including horticulture, seed growing, market gardening and grazing livestock.

The Act applies to most agricultural tenancies, except grazing or mowing agreements for less than a year and tenancies for more than one year but less than two. Where agricultural land is let with non-agricultural land, it is a question of fact whether the whole is an agricultural tenancy.

Protection is given by:

1. Converting all tenancies that fall within the Act into periodic yearly tenancies determinable by notice to quit.

2. Restricting the grounds on which a notice to quit may be served and in most cases giving the tenant the right to serve a counter-notice. This, in effect, gives the Agricultural Land Tribunal jurisdiction to adjudicate whether the notice should take effect or not.
3. Permitting rent increases only at three-yearly intervals, the increase to be agreed or submitted to an arbitrator.
4. Entitling a tenant who has received a valid notice to quit to compensation for improvements and disturbance.

Finally, any 'successor tenancies' arising out of these tenancies, even though arising after 31 August 1995, are still regulated under the 1986 Act.

Post 31 August 1995 tenancies

The Agricultural Tenancies Act 1995 fulfilled a commitment made by the Conservative Party in their 1992 General Election manifesto to liberalise agricultural tenancy laws. The pattern of agricultural land ownership and tenure has changed significantly during the course of the twentieth century. At the start of the last century about 90 per cent of agricultural land was rented, whereas by 1993 the percentage had declined to 35 per cent. The Government and much of the industry concluded that this decline had been hastened by the introduction of security of tenure. One of the aims of the Agricultural Tenancies Act 1995 is to tackle the decline in the number of agricultural tenancies being offered.

The Act replaces the former regime relating to agricultural tenancies with the concept of a *farm business tenancy* which must comply with a range of conditions, eg a tenancy cannot be a farm business tenancy if it began before 1 September 1995 or if it is a tenancy beginning on or after that date under the statutory succession provisions of the Agricultural Holdings Act 1986. The new 'farm business tenancy' introduces a greater measure of flexibility. In particular, landlords and tenants can now negotiate the tenancy's length, rent levels and, within certain limits, rent reviews and repair provisions, without statutory intervention.

In essence, the Agricultural Tenancies Act 1995 is a 'deregulating' one. It gives the opportunity for landlords and tenants to enter into agreements to suit their own particular needs. It should lead to many new agricultural tenancies being created. Evidence suggests that this began to happen immediately, and that a significant number of new tenancies were granted in the first six months after the Act came into force. However, this was undoubtedly due as much to the enhanced reliefs for inheritance tax purposes which were also made available to landowners granting such tenancies as to the terms of the Act itself. Subject to certain conditions being satisfied, the value of the landlord's interest in the land attracts 100 per cent relief for inheritance tax purposes where a new agricultural tenancy is granted on or after 1 September 1995. Before the passing of the new Act, relief was available at only 50 per cent.

10.15 Business tenancies

The main statutory provisions relating to business tenancies are contained in Part II of the Landlord and Tenant Act 1954. This applies to tenancies of premises which are

'... occupied by the tenant and are so occupied for the purposes of a business carried on by him',

and 'business' includes a trade, profession or employment (s23).

Personal occupation is not required where the tenant occupies by means of his servants/employees. Tenancy includes all tenancies except a tenancy at will. See *Manfield & Sons* v *Botchin* [1970] 2 QB 612.

Certain tenancies, however, are expressly excluded. They include agricultural tenancies, tenancies protected by the Rent Acts, etc, and service tenancies.

Security of tenure is given by providing that the tenancy can only be terminated by a notice in the prescribed form (s25). Unless the landlord stipulates in his notice one of the statutory grounds of opposition to a new tenancy set out in s30, the tenant may serve a counter-notice requiring the grant of a new tenancy. The House of Lords has confirmed that the 'corresponding date principle' applies to notices and applications under the 1954 Act: see *Dodds* v *Walker* [1981] 2 All ER 609. If one of the statutory grounds is stated the tenant may still apply to the court for a new tenancy, when the landlord must establish the ground relied upon.

If the parties cannot agree upon the terms of the new tenancy, they may apply to the court to determine the terms. See *O'May* v *City of London Real Property Co Ltd* [1982] 1 All ER 660.

Where the grounds of objection are that the landlord intends to demolish or reconstruct the premises, or intends to occupy them himself, the tenant is entitled to compensation. A tenant quitting the premises may also be entitled to compensation for improvements he has made.

11

Enforcement of Covenants between Freeholders

11.1 Introduction

11.2 Definitions

11.3 The creation of covenants

11.4 Enforcement of covenants at common law between original parties

11.5 Enforcement of covenants at common law by assignees

11.6 Example of the running of covenants at common law

11.7 Enforceability of covenants in equity

11.8 Enforceability in equity: original parties

11.9 Enforceability in equity by successors in title

11.10 Example of the running of covenants in equity

11.11 Effect of Contracts (Rights of Third Parties) Act 1999

11.12 Discharge of restrictive covenants

11.13 Reform

11.14 Worked example

11.1 Introduction

This chapter deals with the enforcement of covenants affecting land where there is no privity of estate between the covenantee and covenantor. In other words, that is the enforcement of covenants between parties who do not stand in the relationship of landlord and tenant. It is important to grasp the distinction between the rules governing covenants between landlord and tenant (dealt with in Chapter 10) and those governing whether or not covenants affecting land can be enforced by and against persons between whom there is no privity of estate. There are two distinct sets of rules – the common law and the equity rules.

11.2 Definitions

A covenant is a promise contained in a deed. The deed may be (and usually is) a conveyance of a freehold estate in land, but the covenant may be contained in a separate deed. The type of promise contained in such deeds usually concerns the land, for example:

1. a promise not to build a factory;
2. a promise to maintain a fence;
3. a promise to keep land as open space.

But there is nothing to stop the parties to the deed making any type of promise, although promises not concerning the land are limited in their enforceability. The person who makes the promise is the 'covenantor'. The person to whom it is made is the 'covenantee'. Hence the person seeking to enforce the covenant (the plaintiff) will be the covenantee and the defendant will be the covenantor.

The land owned by the covenantee will have the benefit of the covenant, and so far as the covenant is concerned will be the 'dominant tenement'. The land owned by the covenantor will have the burden of the covenant and will be the 'servient tenement'. This can be illustrated by the following diagram where X originally owned the whole of Greenacre and sold part to Y, taking from Y a covenant not to use the land for business purposes.

		X (Original owner of Greenacre)		
		Greenacre		
		Green 1/2 acre	Green – other 1/2 acre	
Benefit ←		X	Y	→ *Burden*
		Covenantee	*Covenantor* – not to use for business purposes	
		X	Y	
		Covenantee	*Covenantor*	
		Receives the benefit	Makes the covenant and becomes subject to the burden	
		Dominant land	*Servient land*	
Benefit Is the covenant enforceable by persons who subsequently acquire X's land – Green 1/2 acre?				*Burden* Can the covenant bind persons who subsequently acquire Y's land – Green – other 1/2 acre – so that later successors in title of the covenantor can be sued on the covenant?

Before a covenant can be enforced by X against Y, two conditions must be fulfilled:

1. The covenantee (X) must have the benefit of the covenant.
2. The covenantor (Y) must be subject to the burden of the covenant.

The 'benefit' means the capacity to sue. The 'burden' means the liability to be sued.

The key to a proper understanding of this subject is to consider the benefit and burden separately. Both conditions must be satisfied. It is quite possible for the covenantee, X, to have the benefit, but for the covenantor, Y, not to be subject to the burden, or vice versa. Unless X has the benefit and Y has the burden, X cannot enforce a covenant against Y.

11.3 The creation of covenants

A owns two adjoining pieces of land, Blackacre and Whiteacre. There is a large house on Whiteacre, and Blackacre is open country. B wants to buy Blackacre and build a house there. A is happy to sell provided that he can ensure that B does not build a factory or use the land in some other way that will reduce the value of the land retained by A.

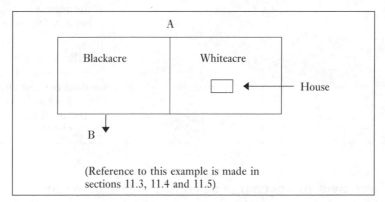

(Reference to this example is made in
sections 11.3, 11.4 and 11.5)

Therefore A makes it a condition of the sale to B that the conveyance of Blackacre to B contains a promise by B not to use Blackacre for any purpose except the building of one house. The covenant is made for the benefit of Whiteacre. As between A and B, the parties to the conveyance, this covenant remains enforceable under the normal rules of contract. The difficulties arise when either A or B sells the land as, though the covenant remains enforceable between them, B will no longer have any control over the land (if he has sold), so A's remedy will be limited to damages and he will be unable to ensure that the value of Whiteacre is not diminished by say the building of a factory on Blackacre.

To deal with this situation rules have been developed which ensure that, in some circumstances, covenants are enforceable by and against successors in title of the original parties. If this is the case, the covenant is said to 'run with the land'. That is, the burden of the covenant can run with the land of the covenantor and the benefit of the covenant can run with the land of the covenantee.

There are two sets of rules governing the running of covenants: the common law rules and the equity rules. The common law rules should be applied first, and then the equity rules if the covenant is not enforceable at law. This may be demonstrated by way of a basic flow chart:

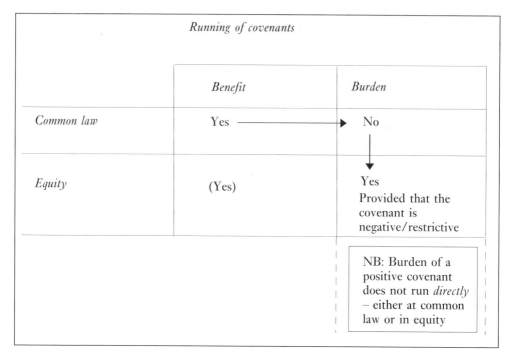

11.4 Enforcement of covenants at common law between original parties

Between original parties to the deed

The original covenantee can always enforce any express covenant against the original covenantor. But if the covenant was made for the benefit of land which the covenantee has parted with, then the covenantee may only recover nominal damages as he will not suffer any loss. The loss will be suffered by the present owner of the land. Hence if A sells Whiteacre to C, and B later builds four dwelling houses on Blackacre, A will be entitled to sue B for breach of covenant, but the loss will be suffered by C, so A will only be entitled to nominal damages.

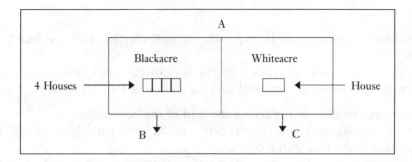

Extension of original parties by s56 LPA 1925

At common law it was a strict rule that no one could sue on a deed made inter partes who was not a party to the deed. This rule has been relaxed by s56(1) LPA 1925, which provides that:

> 'A person may take ... the benefit of any ... covenant over or respecting land ... although he may not be named as a party to the conveyance or other instrument.'

In order to qualify under s56 a person who was not a party to the original deed must show that the contract purported to be made with him (as covenantee), not just for his benefit. See *Beswick* v *Beswick* [1968] AC 58.

Hence, if in the conveyance of Blackacre B covenanted with A and with the owners for the time being of Redacre and Greenacre (plots of land adjoining Blackacre), then the persons who are owners of Redacre and Greenacre at the time of the covenant can sue B on the covenant, even though they are not named as parties to the conveyance, because the covenant was expressed to be made with them for the benefit of their land.

Section 56 can only benefit persons who are in existence and identifiable when the covenant is made. Hence if the conveyance stated that the covenant was made with the owner for the time being of Redacre and his heirs and assigns, the only person who can benefit directly is the present owner. Future owners will be able to enforce the covenant only if they can show that the benefit of the covenant has run with Redacre (see sections 11.5 and 11.6).

11.5 Enforcement of covenants at common law by assignees

The benefit and burden of a covenant must be considered separately. *Note*: in order to be enforceable the covenantee must have the benefit and the covenantor must be subject to the burden; *both conditions must be satisfied.*

Benefit

The benefit of a covenant can be expressly assigned together with the land to which it relates.

The benefit of a covenant runs with the land of the covenantee at common law, without express assignment, provided that the following four conditions are satisfied:

1. the covenant touches and concerns the land of the covenantee;
2. there is an intention that the benefit should run with land owned by the covenantee at the date of the covenant;
3. the covenantee must have the legal estate in the land which is to be benefited at the time of making the covenant; and
4. an assignee seeking to enforce the covenant must have the same legal estate in the land as the original covenantee.

The covenant must touch and concern the land

The rules here are the same as those governing pre-1996 leasehold covenants (see Chapter 10). The benefit of purely personal covenants will not run with the land eg B covenants to pay £150 per annum to A's son D. In *Smith and Snipes Hall Farm v River Douglas Catchment Board* [1949] 2 KB 500 Tucker LJ put the matter thus:

> 'The covenant must either affect the land as regards its mode of occupation or it must be such as per se, and not merely from collateral circumstances, affects the value of the land.'

The covenant must have been made for the benefit of land owned by the present covenantee

Hence, before C can enforce the covenant against B, he must show that the covenant was made for the benefit of Whiteacre and that he (C) is the present owner of Whiteacre. Once C assigns the land, he can no longer enforce the covenant. Only the original covenantee retains the right to enforce the covenant after he has assigned the land.

There is no requirement that the covenant has anything to do with any land owned by the covenantor. See *The Prior's Case* (1368) YB 42 Ed 3, Hil pl 14. Neither is it necessary to show that the assignee had notice of the existence of the covenant at the time of the assignment to him by the covenantee. Once the benefit is annexed to the land, it passes automatically. See *Rogers v Hosegood* [1900] 2 Ch 388.

The covenantee must have a legal estate in the land

Prior to 1875 the common law courts could not recognise the existence of equitable interests in land, so covenants could be enforced only by the owner of a legal estate.

Covenants made before 1926 can only be enforced at law where the assignee holds the *same* legal estate as the original covenantee. In *Smith and Snipes Hall Farm v River Douglas Catchment Board* (above) the Court of Appeal held that s78 LPA 1925 changed the law so that assignees did not need to have the same legal estate as the original covenantee so long as they derived title from the original covenantee. Hence both an assignee of the covenantee's freehold estate and the assignee's tenant could enforce a covenant – under s78 LPA 1925 the requirement is merely to be a 'successor in title'. In s78(2) this phrase is explained:

> '... to include the owners and occupiers for the time being of the land of the covenantee intended to be benefited'.

Note: the benefit of both positive and negative covenants can run at law.

The assignee seeking to enforce the covenant must have the same legal estate in the land as the original covenantee

Accordingly, if the original covenantee was an owner in fee simple, the benefit of the covenant could pass only to a third party who likewise owned the land in fee simple. There was limited authority for this requirement. The Court of Appeal decision in *Westhoughton UDC* v *Wigan Coal and Iron Co Ltd* [1919] 1 Ch 159 was frequently cited in support of this condition. However, in the opinion of some academics the point was not clearly decided on that occasion (see Megarry and Wade (5th edn) at p766 note 40, and Megarry and Wade (6th edn) at p100). Therefore, this final requirement constituted a rather doubtful feature of the common law rules on the passing of the benefit.

This rule, however, *has been abrogated for covenants made after 1925* by s78 Law of Property Act 1925. As a result of this provision it is now sufficient to show that the person seeking to enforce the covenant is a 'successor in title' of the covenantee.

Burden

The burden of a covenant cannot run with freehold land at law, even by express assignment. Hence, at law a covenant can be enforced only so long as the original covenantor retains the land. (See *Austerberry* v *Oldham Corporation* (1885) 29 Ch D 750; *E & G C Ltd* v *Bate* (1935) 79 LJ News 203.) However, there are several devices used by conveyancers to circumvent this rule in relation to positive covenants (the burden of a restrictive covenant can run in equity). The devices are intended to achieve *indirectly* what cannot be done directly. A number of such devices are considered below.

As the original covenantor remains liable on the covenant even though he has assigned the land, he may seek to protect himself by taking a covenant from his assignee that the assignee will observe the covenants. The covenantee may therefore be able to enforce the covenant by suing the original covenantor who will then sue the assignee ie the original covenantee should be able to secure the *indirect* enforcement of positive covenants against the current owner of the burdened land by initiating proceedings against the original covenantor. However, in practice the device is unsatisfactory for three main reasons. First, the person seeking to enforce the covenant must be able to locate the original covenantor. Secondly, there must be no break in the chain of indemnities. The chain is liable to be broken either because a party neglects to obtain a covenant of indemnity from its successor or because of the death, disappearance or insolvency of the covenantor or of one of the parties in the chain. Thirdly, even if the chain is not broken the only remedy available is an action in damages whereas the remedy usually wanted is an injunction or an order of specific performance. DJ Hayton criticises the device as follows:

> '[However, although] in theory liability can be maintained indefinitely in this way, with each sale of the land the chain of covenants for indemnity becomes longer, and more liable to be broken by the insolvency or disappearance of one of the parties to it. This indirect enforcement of covenants by means of indemnities is thus an imperfect substitute for the direct enforceability which the common law refuses to allow': Megarry's *Manual of the Law of Real Property* (8th ed 2002) at p462.

The disadvantage of this method is that once the chain of personal covenants becomes lengthy the chance that it will be broken by the disappearance or insolvency of one of the parties becomes greater.

A conveyancing device, as yet untested, is instead of conveying the land to grant a long lease at no rent containing the desired covenants. The lease is automatically enlarged by s153 LPA 1925 into a fee simple, but one made subject to all the obligations contained in the lease (see Chapter 10, section 10.9).

Under the so-called principle of benefit and burden as expressed in *Halsall* v *Brizell* [1957] Ch 169, where the burden (a covenant to contribute to the upkeep of a private road) was directly related to the benefit (the use by the covenantor of that road), the assignees of the covenantor could not take the benefit without taking the burden as well, even though the burden does not normally run at law. Upjohn J expressed the rule in these words:

> 'The defendants here cannot if they desire to use this house, as they do, take advantage of the trusts concerning the user of the roads contained in the deed and the other benefits created by it without undertaking the obligations thereunder. Upon that principle it seems to me that they are bound by this deed, if they desire to take its benefits.'

The use of the pure principle of benefit and burden was illustrated by Sir Robert Megarry VC in *Tito* v *Waddell (No 2)* [1977] Ch 106.

The extent of the principle was considered by the House of Lords in *Rhone* v *Stephens* [1994] 2 All ER 65 in which the issue was whether a positive covenant to maintain a roof was enforceable against a successor in title of the burdened land. Two clauses in the original conveyance were relevant to the litigation. Clause 2 imposed reciprocal benefits and burdens of support. Clause 3 imposed an obligation to repair the roof in question. The plaintiffs (who were seeking to enforce the positive covenant) argued that any party deriving any benefit from a conveyance had to accept any burden in the same conveyance. They submitted, in essence, that if a successor in title of the servient land took the benefit of clause 2 he had to accept the burden of clause 3. Lord Templeman rejected this contention in the following terms:

'The condition must be relevant to the exercise of the right. In *Halsall* v *Brizell* there were reciprocal benefits and burdens enjoyed by the users of the roads and sewers. In the present case clause 2 of the ... conveyance imposes reciprocal benefits and burdens of support but clause 3 which imposed an obligation to repair the roof is an independent provision. In *Halsall* v *Brizell* the defendant could, at least in theory, choose between enjoying the right and paying his proportion of the cost or alternatively giving up the right and saving his money. In the present case the owners of [the servient land] could not in theory or in practice be deprived of the benefit of the mutual rights of support if they failed to repair the roof.'

A covenant to pay money or to contribute to the upkeep of property may be construed as a rentcharge. The creation of a new rentcharge is prohibited by the Rentcharges Act 1977 (s2(1)). Section 2(3) of the 1977 Act details certain exceptions to this general rule. The creation of an 'estate rentcharge' is one of the very few exceptions to the general rule.

' "Estate rentcharge" is defined in s2(4) of the Rentcharges Act 1977 as
"a rentcharge created for the purpose
(a) of making covenants to be performed by the owner of the land affected by the rentcharge enforceable by the rent owner against the owner for the time being of the land;
or
(b) of meeting, or contributing towards, the cost of the performance by the rent owner of covenants for the provision of services, the carrying out of maintenance or repairs, the effecting of insurance or the making of any payment by him for the benefit of the land affected by the rentcharge or for the benefit of that and other land".'

The Wilberforce Committee in its 1965 Report (*Report of the Committee on Positive Covenants Affecting Land*), recommended that the burden of certain positive covenants should run with freehold land. The Law Commission has published three reports (in 1967, 1971 and 1984) dealing with the question of freehold covenants. The last report (Law Com No 127) entitled *Transfer of Land – The Law of Positive and Restrictive Covenants,* proposes fundamental changes in that both covenants and easements should be classified as land obligations, and the benefit and burden of a land obligation would run. The 1984 report of the Law Commission contains a draft Land Obligations Bill through which these proposals could be implemented.

Further, comments on the decision in *Austerberry* v *Oldham Corporation* (1885) 29 Ch D 750 were made by the House of Lords in *Rhone* v *Stephens* (above). There the issue, as noted above, was whether a covenant to maintain a roof was enforceable against successors in title. In holding that the burden of this positive covenant did not run their Lordships affirmed the rule in *Austerberry* v *Oldham Corporation*, that the burden of a positive covenant did not run with freehold land at law. They further affirmed that the burden of restrictive but not positive covenants could run with freehold land in equity so as to bind successors in title of the servient land. The case is noteworthy for the fact that the rule in *Austerberry* v *Oldham Corporation* was criticised by the Court of Appeal in *Rhone* v *Stephens* (1993) The Times 21 January, and while recognising that it was bound by it the court suggested that the House of Lords 'might feel able to abolish or modify it'. The fact that the House of

Lords has chosen not to do so means that once again we must wait to see what priority Parliament is prepared to allow for the important recommendations of the Law Commission in this regard.

Finally the covenant may be construed as an easement. In *Crow* v *Wood* [1971] 1 QB 77 a right to have a fence kept in repair was held to be capable of being an easement. This could have a dramatic effect on positive obligations which involve the expenditure of money.

11.6 Example of the running of covenants at common law

A sells the fee simple of Blackacre to B, retaining Whiteacre. In the conveyance B (as covenantor) covenanted with A (covenantee) to:

1. maintain the dividing fence (V);
2. build only one dwelling house (W).

A (covenantor) covenanted with B (covenantee) to:

1. not build on Whiteacre (X);
2. build an extension to the dividing wall (Y).

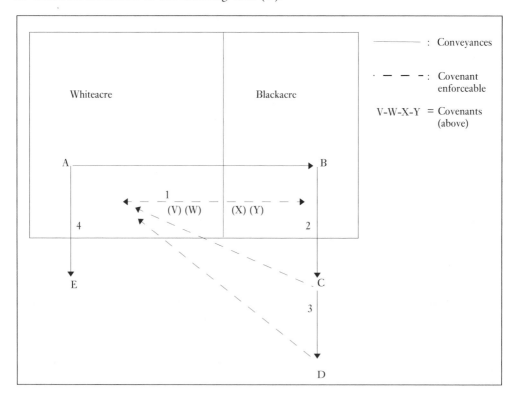

B subsequently conveys Blackacre to C.
C conveys it to D.
Later A conveys Whiteacre to E.

Enforceability of covenants in the above circumstances

Between A and B
All covenants are enforceable as A and B are original parties.

Between A and C
A is an original party, and so retains the benefit of covenants (V) and (W) and the burden of covenants (X) and (Y).

C is an assignee, so the burden of covenants (V) and (W) cannot pass to him. The benefit of covenants (X) and (Y) will pass to C provided that:

1. They touch and concern the land.
2. They were made for the benefit of Blackacre and C owns that land; and
3. C has a legal estate in Blackacre.

These conditions are fulfilled, and so C as covenantee has the benefit of covenants (X) and (Y). A as covenantor is subject to the burden, and so covenants (X) and (Y) are enforceable by C against A.

A has the benefit of covenants (V) and (W) but, as an assignee, C is not subject to the burden, and so C is not liable to A under covenants (V) and (W).

Between A and D
The position is identical to that between A and C (above).

Between E and D
Both E and D have the benefit of their respective covenants as covenantees, but as both are successors in title of the original covenantors, they are not subject to the burden. Hence neither can enforce a covenant against the other.

11.7 Enforceability of covenants in equity

Prior to the nineteenth century, covenants could not be enforced in equity. During that century the limitations on enforceability at common law led equity to develop rules allowing some covenants to be enforced in equity by means of an injunction. The starting point of the doctrine was that it was inequitable to allow a person to buy land subject to a covenant regulating its use of which he had notice, and which might have reduced the value of the land, and then to ignore the covenant because it was not enforceable at common law. Thus the original rule had its basis in the equitable doctrine of notice.

In *Tulk* v *Moxhay* (1848) 2 Ph 774 a restrictive covenant was enforced by equity against a successor in title who was not liable at common law, but who had purchased with *notice* of the covenant. There T (the plaintiff) owned a piece of open ground in Leicester Square and several houses located in the Square. When T sold the ground E covenanted with him as follows. The covenant stated:

> '... at all times thereafter at his own costs to keep and maintain the said piece or parcel of ground and square garden in its present form and in sufficient and proper repair as a square garden and pleasure ground in an open state and uncovered with any buildings in a neat and ornamental order.'

E covenanted on behalf of himself, his heirs and assigns with T and his heirs. The ownership of the relevant land eventually vested in M (the defendant). M's purchase deed contained a comparable covenant with his vendor but he conceded that he had purchased with notice of the original covenant. M wanted to change the character of the ground and T sought an injunction to restrain him. The injunction was granted. The court emphasised that the burden of a covenant could not run with freehold land at law. However, Lord Cottenham LC concluded that if a person bought land with *notice* of a covenant it would be inequitable to permit such a person to act in a manner inconsistent with the covenant. The salient features of the case may be obtained from the following diagram.

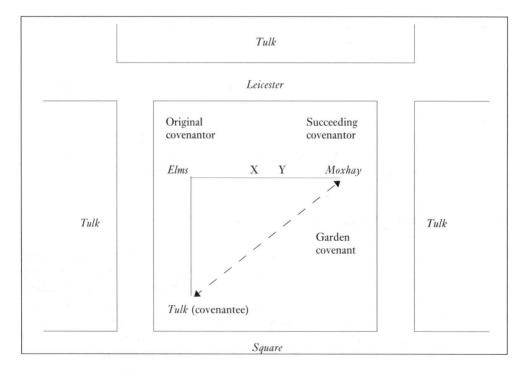

At first equity enforced both positive and negative covenants, but by 1881 it was decided that only negative covenants were appropriate for equitable enforcement. The reason for this limitation was the courts' reluctance to make orders requiring constant supervision by the courts, as would be the case for an injunction enforcing a positive covenant.

The rule in *Tulk* v *Moxhay* has developed beyond the original emphasis on notice, so restrictive covenants are now capable of being proprietary interests in land, analogous to equitable easements. The benefit of a restrictive covenant can run in equity with the dominant tenement, and the burden with the servient tenement, provided that the requirements set out below are satisfied, and the requirements as to registration have been complied with where the covenant was created after 1925.

Registration of restrictive covenants

In order to be enforceable against a successor in title of the original covenantor, restrictive covenants created after 1925 must have been registered prior to the assignment.

Covenants made after 1925
Where the land was *registered* under the Land Registration Act 1925, the covenant had to be registered as a minor interest, by the entry of a notice or a caution in the charges register of the land register. Under the Land Registration Act 2002, if it is a new restrictive covenant the servient owner would agree it could be recorded against his land (ie an agreed notice). However, in the case of an existing restrictive covenant under the 2002 Act, the dominant owner would apply to the Registry for a note to be made on the servient owner's title of the dominant owner's right. Where the land is *unregistered*, the covenant must be registered as a Class D(ii) land charge. Failure to register renders a restrictive covenant void against a purchaser for value of a legal estate in the land (s4(6) LCA 1972).

Covenants made before 1926
These are not registrable and the equitable doctrine of notice still applies. This is probably the best illustration of where the equitable rules of notice continue to apply today.

11.8 Enforceability in equity: original parties

The position in equity is the same as that at common law. The original covenantee can sue the original covenantor on the contract.

The original covenantee can sue successors in title of the original covenantor so long as the following conditions still apply:

1. He has retained land for the benefit of which the covenant was taken (ie the dominant tenement).
2. The burden has passed to the covenantor (see section 11.9).

The original covenantor remains liable even though he has parted with the land.

11.9 Enforceability in equity by successors in title

As at common law, a successor in title of an original covenantee will be able to enforce a covenant only if he has the benefit of the covenant and the covenantor is subject to the burden. Where both covenantee and covenantor are successors in title, the running of the benefit and the running of the burden must be considered separately.

The benefit of a covenant

A successor in title of the original covenantee will have the benefit of a covenant provided that *four* conditions are satisfied:

1. The covenant is negative in substance. The test is whether compliance with the covenant will require the expenditure of money by the covenantor, or some other active step. It is the substance of the covenant which matters and not the form. See *Haywood* v *Brunswick Permanent Benefit BS* (1881) 8 QBD 403.
2. The covenant touches and concerns the land of the covenantee. The benefit of purely personal covenants cannot run with the land of the covenantee. The test for whether the covenant touches and concerns the land is the same as for leasehold covenants (see Chapter 10). In *Rogers* v *Hosegood* [1900] 2 Ch 388 Farwell J put the matter thus:

   'The covenant must either affect the land as regards mode of occupation, or it must be such as per se, and not merely from collateral circumstances, affects the value of the land.'

3. The covenantee has retained land capable of benefiting from the covenant and the covenant was made for the benefit of that land. In *Formby* v *Barker* [1903] 2 Ch 539 an assignee of the original covenantee was held to be unable to enforce a covenant because she had sold all the land benefited by the covenant.

   As previously noted (see Chapter 10, section 10.11), a landlord's reversion is a sufficient interest in land to allow him to enforce restrictive covenants contained in the head lease against subtenants (under the rule in *Tulk* v *Moxhay*, see above), where there is neither privity of estate nor of contract between the parties. See *Regent Oil Co Ltd* v *J A Gregory (Hatch End) Ltd* [1966] Ch 402.

   It is a question of fact whether a covenant is capable of benefiting land retained by the covenantee. Some degree of physical proximity between the dominant and servient tenements is required.
4. The benefit of the covenant has passed to the covenantee (see section 11.9).

Passing of the benefit

The benefit may pass by annexation, assignment or a scheme of development (building scheme).

Annexation

Annexation confers the benefit of the covenant upon the *land* and not individuals. Whether the benefit is so annexed to the land depends upon the wording of the deed of covenant (this is *express annexation*). A classic formula is 'with intent that the covenant may enure to the benefit of the vendors, their successors and assigns and others claiming under them to all or any of their lands adjoining'. In *Rogers* v *Hosegood* [1900] 2 Ch 388 it was held that this was sufficient to annex the benefit to the land. However, in *Renals* v *Cowlishaw* (1878) 9 Ch D 125 a covenant merely with 'the vendors, their heirs, executors, administrators and assigns' was insufficient because no reference was made to the land. These cases demonstrate that wording which omits any reference to the land will be inadequate.

Where the benefited land is particularly extensive particular care is needed in trying to effect annexation. In *Re Ballard's Conveyance* [1937] Ch 473 it was held that there would be no effective annexation if the area of [alleged] benefited land was greater than could reasonably be benefited. There restrictive covenants were stated to be made for the benefit of the 'owners for the time being of the Childwickbury estate' (which was about 1,700 acres in extent). The Court held that the benefit of the covenant could not run with the estate even in favour of someone acquiring the entire estate. Although the land had been clearly identified it was greater than could reasonably be benefited by the covenant. In consequence of this decision it is usual for a conveyance to add the words 'or any part thereof' when identifying the benefited land. This enables the covenant to be enforced by a successor in title to any part of the land which the covenant *in fact benefits*.

The Court of Appeal decision in *Federated Homes Ltd* v *Mill Lodge Properties Ltd* [1980] 1 All ER 371 changed the law on annexation. It was held that where a restrictive covenant related to or touched and concerned the covenantee's land, s78(1) Law of Property Act 1925 annexed the benefit of the covenant to the covenantee's land. The covenant was enforceable at the suit of the covenantee and his successors in title, the person deriving title under him or them and the owner and occupier of the benefited land. The effect of s78(1) is that such a covenant ran with the covenantee's land and was annexed to it. The effect of this decision seems to be that the benefit of any covenant that touches and concerns the land of the covenantee is automatically annexed to the land of the covenantee when the covenant is made. It is important to note that while the decision in *Federated Homes* was good news for conveyancers (s78 could come to the rescue if the express annexation formula used by them turned out to be deficient), the reasoning used by the Court of Appeal on that occasion is not beyond criticism (see in particular the critical article by G H Newsom entitled 'Universal Annexation' in (1981) 97 LQR at page 32).

There is no doubt that the decision in *Federated Homes* remains a somewhat sensitive issue. Nevertheless, it is unlikely to be overruled. However, the landmark judgment in *Federated Homes* did leave two matters unresolved. First, it did not make clear whether it was necessary to identify the land intended to be benefited within the instrument containing the covenant in order to effect statutory annexation, or whether it sufficed that the covenant touched and concerned the land in the actual ownership of the covenantee. Second, it did not explain whether s78 was mandatory in nature.

The second matter fell to be considered at first instance in *Roake* v *Chadha* [1983] 3 All ER 503 where it was held that s78 LPA 1925 could not be used to annex the benefit of a covenant in the face of express wording in the transfer which precluded any annexation whatsoever. The precise words of the covenant were:

> '... this covenant shall not enure for the benefit of any one owner or subsequent purchaser ... unless the benefit of this covenant shall be expressly assigned.'

Judge Paul Baker QC held that even though s78 was not expressly made subject to a contrary intention the covenant had to be construed as a whole. The precise words that the benefit must be expressly assigned had to prevail and annexation of the benefit could not be implied under s78. He concluded as follows:

> 'The true position as I see it is that even where a covenant is deemed to be made with successors in title as s78 requires, one still has to construe the covenant as a whole to see whether the benefit of the covenant is annexed. Where one finds, as in the *Federated Homes* case, the covenant is not qualified in any way, annexation may be readily inferred, but where, as in the present case, it is expressly provided that "this covenant shall not enure for the benefit of any one owner or subsequent purchaser of any part of the Vendor's Sudbury Court Estate at Wembley unless the benefit of this covenant shall be expressly assigned", one cannot just ignore these words.'

The judge dealt with some of the comments on the *Federated Homes* decision and stated:

> 'I do not consider it to be my place either to criticise or to defend the decisions of the Court of Appeal. I conceive it my clear duty to accept the decision of the Court of Appeal as binding on me and apply it as best I can to the facts I find here.'

It was further held in *Federated Homes* that if a restrictive covenant is annexed to land then prima facie it is annexed to every part of the land without the need for express assignment in respect of a part of the land when the whole land has devolved through separate titles to the present covenantee.

No reference was made to *Re Ballard's Conveyance* [1937] Ch 473 or *Zetland* v *Driver* [1939] Ch 1, but to the extent that those decisions are based on the rule that a covenantee either must hold the whole of the land benefited by the covenant or show that the covenant was made for the 'whole or any part of the land', where he holds only a part of the land, they *appear* to have been overruled.

The effect of the decision in *Federated Homes Ltd* v *Mill Lodge Properties Ltd* is to create automatic annexation in most situations and therefore to significantly reduce the role of express annexation. However, in practice most conveyancers when drafting covenants will still seek to secure annexation expressly (ie the *Federated Homes* principle is used as a 'second line of attack').

Recently the Court of Appeal in *Crest Nicholson Residential (South) Ltd* v *McAllister* [2004] 2 All ER 991 gave authoritative guidance upon the two questions left unresolved by *Federated Homes* (see above). There in 1923 land bordering Claygate Common in Surrey was sold for building development to two brothers operating as a company. Thereafter the company sold the land in plots to individual purchasers by way of conveyances which imposed restrictive covenants on the land conveyed limiting the use of each plot to that of a private dwelling-house and prohibiting the erection of a building upon the land without the prior approval of the plans by the vendor. There were four groups of conveyances relevant to the litigation – the A, H, R and W conveyances. In 2000 CN (the appellant) entered into a conditional contract for the purchase of the land conveyed by the A, H and R conveyances with a view to development – the aim was to erect five new houses on it. The development was opposed by M (the respondent house owner) who was the successor in title to the land conveyed by the W conveyance. She argued that the proposed development breached the restrictive covenants contained within the A, H and R conveyances and that she was entitled to the benefit of them. CN sought declarations that the covenants did not prevent the erection of more than one dwelling on each plot. At first instance, Neuberger J held that the building restriction had become spent on the death of the two brothers or the dissolution of their company but that the effect of the user restrictions was to preclude CN from erecting more than one private dwelling-house. CN appealed and M cross-appealed.

The Court of Appeal held that a covenantor could restrict by express words the automatic annexation under s78 LPA 1925 of the benefit of the covenant to a successor in title. Although s78(1) made it unnecessary to state that a covenant was enforceable by persons deriving title under the covenantee or his successor in title and by the owner or the occupier of the land intended to be benefited, or that the covenant was to run with that land, the land to which it was intended to be benefited nevertheless had to be so described so as to be clearly identified. Here the benefit of the covenant was not annexed to the land owned by M and as such was not enforceable by her. In the case of three conveyances it was expressly stated that the benefit would subsist only as long as the original covenantee owned the retained land, ie the covenant was personal to the original covenantee and not annexed to the land at Claygate. In the case of the other conveyances, they did not include sufficient indication that the covenant had been taken for the benefit of the whole of the unsold land. This conclusion on annexation precluded the need for the court to reach a finding on the effect of the restrictions. Accordingly, the appeal was allowed, no order was made on the cross-appeal and the order of Neuberger J varied to declare that the covenants in the relevant conveyances were not enforceable by M.

The decision in *Crest Nicholson* is noteworthy for at least four main reasons.

First, it makes clear that statutory annexation under s78(1) LPA 1925 is always subject to the provisions in the instrument in which the covenant said to be annexed are contained. Accordingly, the court confirmed the first instance decision in *Roake v Chadha*. Second, if the benefit of the covenant is intended to be annexed to land then it is necessary to ensure that the benefited property is clearly identified. Third, Chadwick LJ made it clear that *Federated Homes* represented an accurate, if incomplete, statement of law. Finally, conveyancers drafting restrictive covenants need to know whether they are intended to be personal to the covenantee – if they are this should be made clear in the covenant.

The problem of pre-1926 covenants was considered in *J Sainsbury plc* v *Enfield London Borough Council* [1989] 2 All ER 817. There W purchased a house in 1881 and this was inherited by his son in 1882. Neither father nor son lived in the house. In 1894 the son sold part of the land with the benefit of a restrictive covenant from the purchasers preventing the use of the land by the purchasers or their successors in title for building purposes other than for houses. In due course all the remaining land was sold. In 1985 the plaintiff contracted to buy the land conveyed in 1894 conditional on a declaration being obtained that the land was no longer subject to the restrictive covenants of the 1894 conveyance.

The declaration was granted by Morritt J because it could not be inferred from the 1894 conveyance that the benefit of the covenants was intended to be annexed to the land retained by the son in 1894. Also the words of s58(1) Conveyancing and Law of Property Act 1881 which provided that covenants relating to land of inheritance are deemed to be made with the covenantee, his heirs and assignees and to have effect 'as if heirs and assignees were expressed' could not effect annexation of the benefit of the covenant. The court also emphasised the difference in wording between s58(1) 1881 Act and s78(1) LPA 1925 with the result that the decision in *Federated Homes Ltd* v *Mill Lodge Properties* (above) could not be applied by analogy to pre-1926 restrictive covenants.

Express assignment

The benefit may pass by express assignment at the time the covenantee acquired the land. It must be shown that the covenant was intended to benefit the land acquired, but this can be done by extrinsic evidence if the conveyance is not clear. See *Newton Abbot Co-operative Society Ltd* v *Williamson & Treadgold Ltd* [1952] Ch 286.

The assignment need not be made by the original covenantee. It can be made by anyone in whom the benefit of the covenant is vested. See, again, *Newton Abbot Co-operative Society*. An express assignment confers the benefit of a covenant on *persons*.

Finally, the scope and need for assignment has been significantly reduced by the 'revolutionary' effect on annexation of the Court of Appeal's decision in *Federated Homes*.

Building scheme

The benefit may also pass under a building scheme if certain requirements are satisfied. These requirements as originally laid down in *Elliston* v *Reacher* [1908] 2 Ch 374 were as follows:

1. The parties derived title from a common vendor.
2. There was a definite scheme of development.
3. The area affected was clearly defined.
4. There was an intention to impose a scheme of mutually enforceable restrictions on all purchasers of land in the development area and their successors in title.
5. Every purchaser bought his land knowing of the scheme of mutually enforceable restrictions.

Over the years, these requirements were modified by caselaw. In *Re Dolphin's Conveyance* [1970] 1 Ch 654, for example, the purchasers had not acquired their plots from a common vendor but a building scheme was still found to exist. Further, in *Baxter* v *Four Oaks Properties Ltd* [1965] Ch 816 the common vendor did not set out the land in lots before he began to sell it off. Despite this non-compliance with the second requirement of *Elliston* v *Reacher* Cross J concluded that there was a building scheme because there was sufficient evidence of common intention.

At present it seems two requirements are essential:

1. the area of the scheme must be defined; and
2. those who purchase from the creator of the scheme do so on the footing that all purchasers shall be mutually bound by and mutually entitled to enforce a defined set of restrictions. (Law Com No 127 at para 329)

In *Emile Elias & Co* v *Pine Groves* [1993] NPC 30 the conditions for a building scheme were not present. The area of the scheme was not defined, and there was no evidence that it was the intention of the parties to produce mutually enforceable covenants. Further, there was a lack of uniformity in the covenants imposed on lots of a similar nature (this was most unusual, given that the case concerned a high-class residential development).

Halsbury describes a building scheme as constituting:

'... a local law for the area over which it extends and has the practical effect of rendering each purchaser and his successors in title subject to the restrictions and of conferring upon them the benefit of the scheme, as between themselves and all other purchasers and their respective successors in title.'

Subschemes may be created within the building scheme.

In *Brunner* v *Greenslade* [1970] 3 All ER 833 Megarry J held that where there is a head scheme of development relating to an original plot, any subpurchasers are presumed to be bound *inter se* by the covenants of the head scheme even though they have entered into no direct covenants with the subvendor or each other:

'They are bound inter se by an equity independent of contractual obligation.'

The burden of a covenant

A successor in title of the original covenantor will be subject to the burden of the covenant provided that the following four conditions are satisfied:

1. the covenant is negative in substance;
2. the covenant was made for the benefit of land retained by the covenantee;
3. the covenant must touch and concern the dominant land;
4. the burden of the covenant was intended to run with the land of the covenantor.

The covenant is negative in substance

Since the decision of the Court of Appeal in *Haywood* v *Brunswick Permanent Benefit Building Society* (1881) 8 QBD 403 it has been clearly established that only the burden of a *negative covenant* can be enforced in equity. What is crucial is not whether the covenant is worded positively or negatively but whether it is negative in substance (a covenant could be worded positively but still be negative in substance). A useful test in deciding whether a covenant is positive or negative is to ask the question whether it requires the covenantor or his successor 'to put his hand in his pocket'. If the answer is yes, the covenant is positive, not negative.

The covenant was made for the benefit of land retained by the covenantee

The covenant must be made for the protection of land retained by the covenantee: see *London County Council* v *Allen* [1914] 3 KB 642. There are several exceptions and qualifications to this requirement. For example, the interest of a mortgagee in mortgaged land is a sufficiently 'real' interest to enable it to enforce a restrictive covenant concerning the land. Further, there are a number of statutory exceptions to this requirement: see, for example, s609 Housing Act 1985.

The covenant must touch and concern the dominant land

In general the test for deciding whether a covenant touches and concerns the land is comparable to that applicable to pre-1996 covenants in a lease. In essence the covenant must benefit the land as land.

The burden of the covenant was intended to run with the covenantor's land

In the absence of an express statement to the contrary in the original conveyance or the assignment, by virtue of s79 LPA 1925 a covenant is deemed to have been made by the original covenantor and persons deriving title through or under him.

It is also necessary to show either that the covenant was registered before the assignment, if made post-1925, or that the assignee of the covenantor had notice of the covenant for pre-1926 covenants.

Because the burden runs in equity, the appropriate remedy is an injunction, awarded at the discretion of the court. The court may award damages in lieu of an injunction. An injunction will be the usual remedy because to award damages would be altering the basic contract between the parties. See *Wakeham* v *Wood* (1981) 43 P & CR 40.

11.10 Example of the running of covenants in equity

A owns the fee simple in two adjoining pieces of land, Blackacre and Whiteacre. He sells Blackacre to B, retaining Whiteacre. In the conveyance to B:

1. B covenants with A for the benefit of any adjoining or adjacent property retained by A:

   a) to maintain the dividing fence (a);
   b) to build only one dwelling house on Blackacre (b).

2. A covenants with B for the benefit of Blackacre:

   a) to refrain from building on Whiteacre (c);
   b) to build an extension to the dividing fence (d).

B subsequently conveys Blackacre to C, who in turn conveys to D. Later A conveys Whiteacre to E. E conveys part of Whiteacre to F. Covenants (b) and (c) are registered as D(ii) land charges by A and B.

See diagram below.

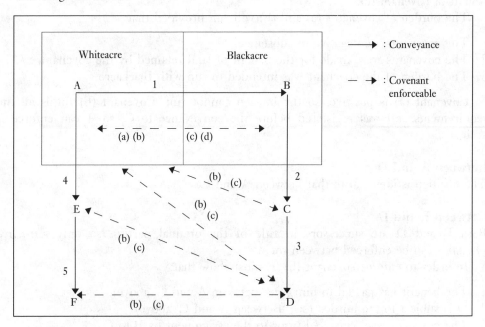

Enforceability of the covenants

Between A and B
All covenants are enforceable, as A and B are original parties.

Between A and C

A is an original party, so he retains the benefit of covenants (a) and (b) and the burden of covenants (c) and (d).

C is an assignee. He will be able to enforce covenants (c) and (d) if the benefit has passed to him, and covenants (a) and (b) will be enforceable against him if the burden has passed.

The *benefit* of covenants (c) and (d) will pass provided that:

1. The covenants are negative in substance.
2. The covenants touch and concern the land of the covenantee (C).
3. The covenantee (C) has retained land capable of benefiting and the covenant was made for the benefit of the land.
4. The benefit of the covenants has passed to C by express or implied annexation.

Covenant (d) is positive, so the burden cannot run. Covenant (c) is negative, and satisfies conditions (2) and (3). The wording of the original conveyance, which states that the covenant is for the benefit of Blackacre and identifies Blackacre is sufficient for the benefit to be annexed to Blackacre by s78 LPA 1925. C therefore has the benefit of covenant (c).

The burden of covenants (a) and (b) will run provided that:

1. The covenants are negative in substance.
2. The covenants were made for the benefit of land retained by the covenantee (A).
3. The burden of the covenant was intended to run with Blackacre.

Covenant (a) is positive, so the burden cannot run. Covenant (b) fulfils all the requirements and was registered before the conveyance to C, so A can enforce it against C.

Between A and D

The position is identical to that between A and C.

Between E and D

Both E and D are successors in title of the original parties, so only *restrictive covenants* can be enforced between them.

In order to enforce covenant (b), E must show that:

1. The benefit has passed to him (see 'Between A and C' above).
2. D is subject to the burden (see 'Between A and C' above).
3. The covenant was registered prior to the assignment by B to C.

These conditions are satisfied.

In the same way, in order to enforce covenant (c) against E, D must show that:

1. The benefit has passed to him.
2. The burden has passed to E.

3. The covenant was registered prior to the conveyance by A to E.

Again these conditions are satisfied.

Between F and D
Once the benefit and/or burden of a covenant becomes annexed to land, it is annexed to all or any part of that land. Hence both F and E can enforce covenant (b) against D, and D can enforce covenant (c) against F and E.

11.11 Effect of Contracts (Rights of Third Parties) Act 1999

The impact of the Act (an outline of the key provisions were given in Chapter 10, section 10.11) on freehold covenants is likely to be limited. There is no change to the rules concerning the passing of the *burden* of covenants. As to the running of the *benefit* of covenants, since the decision in *Federated Homes* v *Mill Lodge Properties Ltd* it is, as previously noted, comparatively easy to show that the benefit of a covenant has been automatically annexed to land by virtue of s78 LPA 1925.

However, the Act may be of assistance where the benefit does not run under the land law rules and the covenant in question is expressed to be made not only with the original covenantee but also with any 'successors in title' (see s1(3)). In particular, the Act may help in two situations. First, where there is no annexation or assignment of the benefit and there is difficulty in establishing that the covenant touches and concerns the land of the covenantee. Second, since *Crest Nicholson Residential (South) Ltd* v *McAllister* [2004] 2 All ER 991 it is clear that for the *Federated Homes* principle to apply it is necessary for the covenant to identify the benefited land, and if the land is not so identified, then it may be necessary to rely on the Act. Finally, it is important to emphasise that the Act cannot be invoked if the covenant in question does not identify any third party.

11.12 Discharge of restrictive covenants

In general a restrictive covenant remains enforceable indefinitely. There are various methods by which a restrictive covenant may be discharged:

The person entitled to the benefit expressly releases it, in other words waives his right to enforce it, by acquiescing to the breach of the covenant.

The person entitled to the benefit impliedly releases it by acting in such a way that it would be inequitable to enforce the covenant. In *Chatsworth Estates Co* v *Fewell* [1931] 1 Ch 224 Farwell J explained the jurisdiction as:

> '... in many ways analogous to the doctrine of estoppel ... have the plaintiffs by their acts or omissions represented to the defendant that the covenants are no longer enforceable?'

It may be discharged or modified by the Lands Tribunal on application made under s84 LPA 1925 as amended by s28 LPA 1969. See *Re Hughes' Application* [1983] JPL 318.

The grounds for application are:

1. The person entitled to the benefit (being of full age and capacity) has expressly or impliedly consented to the covenant being modified or discharged (s84(1)(b)). Self evidently in the absence of express consent there must be a presumption of consent to assist those seeking to rely upon the implied consent limb of ground (b). In *Re University of Westmister* [1998] 3 All ER 1014 the Court of Appeal shed important light on that presumption. There notice of the application was served on the persons entitled to the benefit of the covenants, none of whom responded by way of objection or otherwise. As to *implied* consent, for the purposes of s84(1)(b) the Court made two matters clear. First, there was no presumption that failure to respond to a notice of application by the persons entitled to the benefit of a restrictive covenant was sufficient evidence of agreement. Second, such a conclusion could only be drawn if the Lands Tribunal was satisfied on the balance of probabilities that:

   a) every person entitled to the benefit of the restriction had been made aware of the application;
   b) anyone who was not in agreement with the proposal to discharge or modify the restrictive covenant would have thought it necessary to object to safeguard his interest; and
   c) where necessary the notice made clear, beyond the possibility of misunderstanding, which covenants were being discharged and which were being modified and the respective consequences of each.

   The case dealt with an important practical matter. On the facts the Court concluded that the wording of the University's application did not satisfy (c) above.

2. The proposed discharge will not injuriously affect the person entitled to the benefit. In relation to this ground (s84(1)(aa)), the courts have accepted the 'thin end of the wedge' argument, ie that whilst the applicant's own proposal might not of itself cause harm to those entitled to the benefit of the restriction, harm might be caused to those persons either by similar proposals becoming generally permissible or from the existence of the modification order through the implication that the restrictive covenant was vulnerable to action by the Lands Tribunal. In *Re Snaith & Dolding's Application* (1996) 71 P & CR 104 Bernard Marder J emphasised that whilst each application should be determined on its own merits it was legitimate '... to have regard to the scheme of covenants as a whole and to assess the importance to the beneficiaries of maintaining the integrity of the scheme'. That approach was confirmed by the Judicial Committee of the Privy Council in *McMorris v Brown & Another* [1999] 1 AC

142. There the parties owned houses on two adjoining lots (each of three-quarters of an acre) in a development comprising six lots in a residential area of Kingston, Jamaica. All the lots were subject to, and enjoyed the benefit of, a restrictive covenant precluding subdivision of the land. B wanted to subdivide his lot into two and build another house on the second lot. He applied to modify the restrictive covenant under s3(1) of the Jamaican Restrictive Covenants (Discharge & Modification) Act 1960, which was modelled on s84(1) LPA 1925. The Privy Council held that the onus was on B to demonstrate that a *first relaxation* of the restrictive covenant would *not* constitute a real risk in terms of precedent to the scheme in question (six lots comprising family homes in very spacious grounds).

They concluded that that onus had not been discharged. The decision confirmed that when considering an application to modify or discharge a restrictive covenant under s84(1)(aa) LPA 1925 (the 'sister' provision of s3 of the Jamaican Act) it was a relevant matter that the granting of the application would have the effect of opening a breach in a carefully maintained and successful scheme of development and alter the context of future applications. A decision of the Judicial Committee of the Privy Council is not strictly speaking binding on courts in England. Nevertheless, such a decision is of strong persuasive authority since the Judicial Committee is comprised of law lords sitting 'with different hats on'.

3. The restrictions are obsolete due to changes in the neighbourhood. This will not be so if the restriction is of real value, or the value of property is affected. See *Re Truman, Hanbury, Buxton & Co Ltd's Application* [1956] 1 QB 261 and *Gilbert* v *Spoor* [1983] Ch 27.

The potential conflict between restrictive covenants and the obtaining of planning permission contrary to the covenants was considered by the Court of Appeal in *Re Martin's Application* (1989) 57 P & CR 119. There the restrictive covenant had been created under s37 Town and Country Planning Act 1962 (the predecessor of s52 Town and Country Planning Act 1971 which is now set out in s106 Town and Country Planning Act 1990). The covenant in question provided:

> '... that the said land ... shall not be used for any purpose other than as a private open space and that accordingly no building, structure or erection (other than fencing a summer house or garden shed if the owner shall so require) shall be placed thereon.'

In due course, and following an appeal to the Secretary of State for the Environment, an inspector granted outline planning permission for the erection of a two-storey detached house and garage on the protected land. Because of the existence of the covenant, the applicants applied to the Lands Tribunal to have the covenant discharged. The Tribunal dismissed the application, and this was confirmed by the Court of Appeal. The fact that planning permission had been obtained did not entitle the applicant to ignore the covenant. Fox LJ discussed the relationship between planning permission and covenants in these terms:

'... the applicants' contention is wrong in so far as it suggests that the granting of planning permission by the Secretary of State necessarily involves the result that the Lands Tribunal must discharge the covenant. The granting of planning permission is ... merely a circumstance which the Lands Tribunal can and should take into account when exercising its jurisdiction under s84. To give the grant of planning permission a wider effect is, I think, destructive of the express statutory jurisdiction conferred by s84. It is for the tribunal to make up its own mind whether the requirements of s84 are satisfied ... All the facts of the case have to be examined by the Lands Tribunal.'

4. The restrictions are of no substantial advantage or value.
5. The restrictions are contrary to the public interest.

By s28 LPA 1969 the Lands Tribunal may discharge or modify a restrictive covenant by awarding compensation where appropriate, or may impose an alternative restrictive covenant.

A defendant in an action to enforce a restrictive covenant may apply for a stay of proceedings to allow an application to be made to the Lands Tribunal.

By s610 Housing Act 1985, the county court may modify a restrictive covenant to allow the conversion of a single dwelling house into two or more dwellings if planning permission has been obtained or if, owing to changes in the neighbourhood, the house cannot readily be let as a single dwelling.

Section 237 Town and Country Planning Act 1990 allows the local planning authority to develop in accordance with a planning permission even if this infringes a restrictive covenant. Compensation will then be payable.

When the fee simple of the burdened and the benefited land becomes vested in the same person the restrictive covenants are discharged due to this 'unity of seisin'. See *Texaco Antilles Ltd* v *Kernochan* [1973] AC 609 and *Re Tiltwood, Sussex* [1978] Ch 269.

Section 84(2) LPA 1925 gives the court jurisdiction to declare whether land is affected by a restriction, the nature and extent of the restriction and by whom it is enforceable.

A recent illustration of the court granting a declaration is *Dano Ltd* v *Earl Cadogan and Others* [2004] 1 P & CR 169 which involved issues as to the construction of the restrictive covenant. There in 1929 the then Earl of Cadogan sold part of the *Cadogan Settled Estate* to Chelsea Metropolitan Council, with the remainder of the property remaining within the settlement. The conveyance to the Council contained a restrictive covenant which provided that the Council and its successors in title were restricted to using the sale land for no purpose other than the housing of the working classes 'so long as [the] adjoining or neighbouring property [to the sale land] or any part thereof forms part of the Cadogan Settled Estate'. Subsequent to the conveyance, a public house was built on the property with houses for the working classes being constructed on the rest of the sale land. In 1961 the Cadogan family re-arranged its affairs with the result that the strict settlement was terminated. In 1999, the property ceased to be used as a public house and in July 2000 the local authority sold the property to D Ltd who later that year obtained planning consent for the development of the property by demolishing the public house and constructing four private houses. In 2002, D Ltd (the claimant) sought a declaration to the effect that a covenant restricting the use of the property to 'the housing of the working classes' was not enforceable. They made two main submissions. First that since 1961 and the re-organisation of the Cadogan family affairs there was no longer an identifiable estate which continued to have the benefit of the restrictive covenant. Second, that the meaning of the words 'working classes' was so uncertain that the covenant could not be enforced by way of injunction. The C family (the defendants) claimed to be the owners of the land entitled to the benefit of the covenant and argued that the word 'settled' was merely descriptive of the nature of the estate in 1929 and that the covenant was for the benefit of all those interested in the land forming part of the Cadogan estate whether it was settled land or not. The judge at first instance found for D Ltd and C appealed.

The Court of Appeal concluded that D's interpretation accorded with the natural meaning of the words used, provided certainty as to the land to be benefited by the covenant and the duration of the benefit. In contrast, C's interpretation did not give the words of the restrictive covenant their ordinary meaning but involved a wholesale rewriting of the relevant provision and was at odds with the apparent intention of the parties that the restrictive covenant was only to be enforceable for the benefit of land continuing to form part of an identifiable estate – the Cadogan Settled Estate – which ceased to be settled in 1961. The inclusion the word 'settled' referred to the estate as it existed in 1929. Accordingly, the appeal would be dismissed and D Ltd were entitled to the declaration sought (ie that there was no adjoining or neighbouring property forming a part of the Cadogan Settled Estate within the meaning of the restrictive covenant and therefore no such adjoining or neighbouring property which the restrictive covenant was capable of benefiting. The litigation also determined that 'social housing' could be substituted for 'housing for the working classes'.

11.13 Reform

Commonhold and Leasehold Reform Act 2002

The Act received the Royal Assent in May 2002 and it is being brought into force on a piecemeal basis (a number of provisions were brought into force on 28 February 2005). It constitutes a radical reform of property ownership. The main reforms contained in the Act include a new system of 'commonhold' for the ownership of units in multi-unit structures, eg flat blocks. This will provide an alternative to the use of the leasehold system for such structures. In the ensuing paragraphs, an explanatory background to the commonhold proposals precedes an outline of the main provisions of the Act.

Background to the commonhold proposals

Since the latter part of the nineteenth century, it has been a clearly established principle of real property law that the burden of a positive covenant cannot run with freehold land either at law or in equity.

This principle gives rise to problems in a number of contexts, including, in particular, multi-unit structures, eg flat blocks. This is because the comfort and enjoyment which each unit (ie flat) owner derives from his home is dependent upon the rest of the building being properly maintained and repaired, the non-cessation of any services provided for his flat and the maintenance in good condition of any amenities (eg gardens, access roads and private drives) contained in the development. It is also crucially important to each flat owner that the common property of the building (entrance passages and stairs, etc) are properly repaired and maintained. Likewise, it is also vital that those parts of the structure, which although in the occupation of a single owner, provide support or shelter for the units of others, should not be allowed to deteriorate. These requirements in respect of services, amenities, common property, support and shelter all involve appropriate repair and maintenance work (ie positive action). If such work is not carried out, the comfort of people living in the structure will be adversely affected and the value of the individual flats will invariably fall. Accordingly, in a flat block it is crucial that certain positive covenants, eg repairing covenants and covenants to contribute to a common fund (in order to provide the finance for the upkeep of common property and amenities) are enforceable against the owners for the time being of all units. At present this goal can only be effectively secured by using leasehold schemes, which in turn means that there are very few freehold flats in England and Wales. Such freehold flats as there are tend to be found in certain coastal resorts, eg Worthing, Weston-Super-Mare, Scarborough, Filey and Bridlington. Most of them are located in large converted detached and semi-detached houses. Large purpose-built freehold flats are a rarity in England and Wales. Another reason why there are few freehold flats in England and Wales is because most banks and building societies are reluctant to advance money by way of mortgage on the security of a freehold flat because of the difficulties of ensuring the enforcement of positive covenants in a freehold flat complex (although as previously noted there are indirect devices used by conveyancers to circumvent the rule that the burden of a positive covenant cannot run directly with freehold land at law or in equity, none are foolproof – a reality well known to lending institutions). Further, even if a prospective purchaser of a freehold flat did not require mortgage finance in order to buy it, a prudent solicitor would advise him of the likely difficulty he would encounter in trying to find a buyer for his flat when he came to sell it (not many people can buy properties for cash).

The perpetuation in England of leasehold tenure in respect of multi-unit structures is both unnecessary and unpopular. It is unnecessary because condominium legislation exists in a number of common law jurisdictions (including the Bahamas, Bermuda, Jamaica, Trinidad and Tobago) while the strata titles system exists in New South Wales and other Australian states, and all the indications are that such legislation/schemes operate successfully and have done so in most cases for several decades now. It is unpopular because the clear preference of home seekers in England and Wales is for freehold, not leasehold, tenure.

Commonhold provisions

Not surprisingly, the provisions draw upon the established schemes in other parts of the common law world.

Under the commonhold regime, each unit in a multi-unit structure will be held on commonhold (in essence a freehold estate in the unit) with the common parts and facilities being owned by a commonhold association which will be a company limited by guarantee and registered at Companies House in the usual way. Membership of the association will be limited to the unit holders (for the time being) of the development in question. The company will have the standard set of memorandum and articles of association prescribed by regulations. Further, there will be a commonhold community statement setting out the rights and obligations of unit holders amongst themselves and between unit holders and the commonhold association. It will set out the voting rights of the unit holders, the necessary majorities, dispute handling procedures and the machinery for determining and collecting commonhold costs etc.

Accordingly, there will be no landlord. Rather, each unit holder will have two interests (ownership of his unit and an interest in the management company). The new regime will apply to both residential and non-residential multi-unit structures. However, the government has decided against a compulsory system of commonhold. It is anticipated that initially the main use for the new regime will be in respect of new residential developments. It will be possible for an existing multi-unit structure held on a leasehold basis to be converted to commonhold. For such a conversion to take place, the following consents will be required – every leaseholder agreeing to the surrender of their leases, that of the freeholder and any other third party who has an interest in the building. The Land Registry will be responsible for ensuring that such consents have been freely given. In view of the need to get such a range of consents, it may in practice be very difficult to convert an existing leasehold development into a commonhold one. Finally, disputes between unit holders and the commonhold association will be dealt with by way of an ombudsman scheme.

Conclusions

In a commonhold no one will have rights in the property superior to the unit holders. Further, the owner's interest in the property will not run out over time as it does in the case of a leasehold interest. Given that most people lay out considerable sums of money in acquiring a long lease of a flat, but have little control over the funding of the building in which it is located (the landlord usually has a monopoly over the supply of services with the tenant having to pay the cost) this will mean that the 'non-wasting asset' nature of a commonhold unit will be very attractive.

Although commonhold will not be compulsory for multi-unit structures, the clear anticipation of the government is that the attractions of commonhold will so outweigh that of leasehold tenure that the latter will inevitably decline. Whether or not such a scenario enfolds will depend upon the willingness of everyone who has an interest in the land consenting to an existing leasehold being converted into a commonhold and upon the attitude of the mortgage lenders. If they have confidence in the commonhold legislative framework, particularly the arrangements for ensuring the enforcement of positive covenants, then the new regime has every chance of achieving the goal of its proponents.

Finally, the Act is a comparatively straightforward piece of legislation which builds upon the legislative experience of a number of other common law countries.

11.14 Worked example

In answering questions concerning freehold covenants, the student should always keep two questions in mind:

1. Has the person seeking to enforce the covenant got the benefit of it?
2. Has the person against whom it is sought to enforce the covenant subject to the burden of it?

If the answer to both questions is 'yes' the covenant can be enforced. Both questions should *always* be considered in problems relating to restrictive covenants. In addition the dates of covenants should be considered to establish whether the rules of notice or registration apply.

Q   Victor is the owner in fee simple of the 'Old Hall' which is situated in a 20-acre estate in pleasant rural countryside. Title to the Old Hall is registered.

In 1998, he sold five acres of the estate as a building plot to Patrick. In the conveyance, Patrick covenanted with Victor, his heirs and assigns that he would:

1. erect and maintain a boundary wall between his plot and the rest of the Old Hall estate;
2. use the land solely for private residential purposes;
3. pay £100 pa to Victor's daughter Mary.

In 2001, Patrick sold the five-acre plot (which by then had a house on it) to Quintin, 'subject to' the covenants entered into by him with Victor. In 2002, Victor sold the 'Old Hall' and the remaining 15 acres to Robert without reference to the covenants contained in the 1998 conveyance.

The boundary wall is now in need of repair. Further, Quintin is proposing to use the building on his land as a guest house and restaurant, and has never paid any money to Mary.

    Advise Robert.

A The facts of the question can be represented diagrammatically as follows:

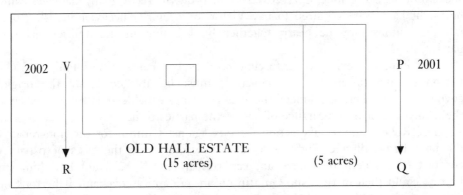

The Old Hall is the dominant land and the five-acre plot the servient land. Victor is the original covenantee and Patrick the original covenantor, and Robert and Quintin are their respective successors. In the ensuing paragraphs each covenant is dealt with separately.

1. *Erect and maintain a boundary wall – positive*

    Patrick's obligation to erect and maintain a boundary wall between his five-acre plot and the rest of the Old Hall estate ranks as a positive covenant. A positive covenant is one which obliges the owner to do something on his land (a work covenant) or to contribute money towards work to be done or services to be rendered for the benefit of his land (a money covenant, eg a covenant to contribute towards the construction or maintenance of a private road). Here Patrick's covenant is a work covenant.

    At common law the benefit but not the *burden* of a freehold covenant can run with the land, while in equity the benefit and burden of a restrictive (negative) covenant can also run with the land: *Austerberry* v *Oldham Corporation* (1885) and *Rhone* v *Stephens* (1994). It follows from this pre-emptive statement of the current law, that the burden of a *positive covenant* cannot run *directly* with freehold land either at law or in equity.

    The covenant is enforceable between Victor and Patrick on the basis of privity of contract. However, since Patrick sold the servient land to Quintin in 2001 the burden of the covenant cannot be enforced *directly* against Quintin by either Victor or Robert.

    However, the burden of the covenant may be enforced *indirectly* against Quintin. Because the original covenantor (Patrick) remains liable to the original covenantee (Victor) in respect of this covenant even if he subsequently sells the five-acre plot because of the privity of contract between them, it is advisable for an original covenantor to protect himself by taking a covenant of indemnity from the person to whom he sells the land (ie Patrick should have taken one from Quintin). If Patrick had taken a covenant of indemnity from Quintin it would mean that if he was then sued for any breach of the covenant by Victor he could sue Quintin on the indemnity covenant in order to recover any damages which he might have been required to pay Victor, or Victor's successor in title Robert (all the actions may be heard together by bringing in indemnifiers as third parties).

This indirect device for enforcing positive covenants is not foolproof. The person seeking to enforce the covenant must be able to locate the original covenantor. Further, the longer the chain the more liable it is to be broken by the insolvency or disappearance of one of the parties to it.

Here Robert cannot take action directly against Quintin for the non-repair of the boundary wall. He might be able to sue Patrick on the basis of privity of contract (the benefit of a covenant can run at law) if he could find him, and Patrick could then in turn sue Quintin on an indemnity covenant, if he took one from Quintin when he sold the five-acre plot to him.

The fact that the burden of a positive covenant cannot run *directly* with freehold land is one of the major weaknesses in English land law. It gives rise to difficulty in two contexts. First, as here, it causes difficulty in respect of covenants between neighbouring landowners as to such matters as fencing and boundary walls. Secondly, it also causes problems in relation to freehold flat blocks and other multi-unit developments (the fact that there is no *direct* enforcement of the burden of a positive covenant in relation to freehold land is one of the main reasons why most flat blocks in England and Wales are held on a leasehold basis). But NB Commonhold and Leasehold Reform Act 2002.

2. *Use the land solely for private residential purposes – negative*
   A restrictive covenant is one which restrains a landowner in some respect from the uninhibited use of his property, eg a covenant which prevents the covenantor from using his land for the purpose of conducting trade or business. Here covenant (2) (to use the land solely for private residential purposes) is a restrictive one. The fact that the covenant is expressed in a positive form of wording is not significant – it is negative in substance.

a) *Has Quintin got the burden?*
   As Quintin is not the original covenantor, he will only have the burden if certain conditions are satisfied. For the burden of a covenant to run in equity three conditions must be satisfied. First, the covenant must be a negative one: *Haywood* v *Brunswick Permanent Benefit Building Society* (1881). Here it is. Secondly, the covenant must have been made for the protection of land retained by the covenantee (Victor): *London County Council* v *Allen* (1914). Again this requirement would seem to be satisfied. Thirdly, the burden of the covenant must have been intended to run with the covenantor's (Patrick's)

land. By virtue of s79 LPA 1925, covenants relating to the covenantor's land which are made after 1925 are deemed to have been made by the covenantor on behalf of himself, his successors in title and the persons deriving title under him or them unless a contrary intention appears. Here the covenant was entered into post-1925 and there is no contrary intention. Accordingly, the third requirement is satisfied.

There is one final matter to consider in relation to the burden of the covenant – registration. Since the land in question is registered, to be binding on Quintin the restrictive covenant must prior to the Land Registration Act 2002 have been entered as a minor interest. For the purpose of the question it is assumed that the registration requirement has been satisfied. Accordingly, it seems that the burden of the covenant has passed to Quintin.

b) *Has Robert got the benefit?*

It is now necessary for Robert to show that the benefit of the covenant has passed to him. At common law the benefit of a covenant can run with freehold land if certain conditions are satisfied. However, since the burden of a covenant cannot run with freehold land directly at common law there is no real point in establishing whether the benefit of the covenant has passed to Robert at common law. Rather, it is crucial to consider whether the benefit has passed to him *in equity*.

For the benefit of a restrictive covenant to pass in equity to a successor in title of the covenantee (Robert) the covenant must 'touch and concern' or 'benefit' some land of the covenantee and the benefit must be transmitted in one or more of the ways prescribed by equity (annexation, assignment or scheme of development). Here, the covenant touches and concerns the remaining 15 acres of Old Hall estate. The key issue is whether the benefit has passed to Robert in one or more of the ways recognised by equity. On the facts, a scheme of development is not relevant.

Accordingly, it is necessary to consider annexation. Express annexation confers the benefit of the covenant upon the land and not individuals. Whether the benefit is so annexed to the land depends upon the wording of the covenants in the 1998 conveyance. In particular, it must be possible to identify the land to be benefited from such wording. In *Rogers* v *Hosegood* (1900) the covenant was deemed to be annexed since it referred to the dominant land. However, in *Renals* v *Cowlishaw* (1879) the covenant was not annexed because it only referred to 'the vendors, their heirs, executors, administrators and assigns' (ie no reference was made to any land). Here Patrick covenanted 'with Victor, his heirs and assigns'. This would not be enough for express annexation because there is no real identification of the benefited land.

However, statutory annexation is likely to be of help to Robert. In *Federated Homes Ltd* v *Mill Lodge Properties Ltd* (1980) the Court of Appeal held that where a restrictive covenant touches and concerns the covenantee's land, s78(1) LPA 1925 annexes the benefit of the covenant to the covenantee's land and the covenant is enforceable at the suit of the covenantee and his successors in title. On the strength of *Federated Homes* it would seem that Robert could show that the benefit of the covenant has passed to him. However, it is important to note that while the decision in *Federated Homes* was good news for conveyancers (s78 could come to the rescue if the express annexation formula used by them turned out to be deficient), the reasoning used by the Court of Appeal on that occasion is not beyond criticism.

Another consequence of *Federated Homes* has been to reduce the scope and need for assignment. An express assignment confers the benefit of a covenant on *persons*. Assignment involves passing the benefit of the covenant to each new owner by each conveyance of the benefited land. Here assignment is not available because in 2002 when Victor sold the Old Hall and remaining 15 acres to Robert he did so 'without reference to the covenants contained in the 1998 conveyance'.

Accordingly, provided that Robert can show statutory annexation (which seems likely), he will be able to enforce the restrictive covenant against Quintin. The remedy he would seek to stop Quintin using the building on his land as a guest house and restaurant would be an injunction.

3. *Pay £100 per annum to Mary – personal covenant*
This covenant is enforceable between Victor and Patrick on the basis of privity of contract. However, it cannot be enforced against Quintin because it does not touch and concern the land. It is personal to the original parties.

12

Easements and Profits

12.1 Introduction: examples of easements

12.2 Essentials of an easement

12.3 Legal and equitable easements

12.4 Acquisition of easements

12.5 Prescription

12.6 Extent of the easement

12.7 Remedies for infringement of easements

12.8 Extinguishment of easements

12.9 Access to Neighbouring Land Act 1992

12.10 Profits à prendre

12.11 Acquisition of profits à prendre

12.12 Remedies for infringement of profits

12.13 Extinguishment of profits

12.14 Worked example

12.1 Introduction: examples of easements

An easement is a right in the land of another which enables the landowner to restrict in some way the use of adjoining land by another party. Easements and profits are two kinds of rights which can be acquired over land belonging to another. Examples of easements are rights of light or of way; the extent of easements depends on how they are acquired.

The following feature among the most common rights which may or may not be easements:

Rights Capable of being Easements	*Rights not Capable of being Easements*
1. A right to receive light through a defined aperture in a building.	1. A right to a view: *Aldred's Case* (1610) (cf covenant in *Gilbert* v *Spoor* (1982))
2. A right to the passage of air through a defined channel: *Wong* v *Beaumont Property Trust* (1965).	2. A right of privacy: *Bernstein* v *Skyviews & General Ltd* (1977).
3. A right to have a building supported, eg by the wall of another building: *Dalton* v *Angus & Co* (1881).	3. A right to the general flow of air over land: *Chastey* v *Ackland* (1895).
4. A right to project a building over another person's land.	4. A right to have the wall of a separate building protected from the weather by an adjoining building: *Phipps* v *Pears* (1965).
5. A right to require the servient owner to fence his land: *Crow* v *Wood* (1971).	5. A right for the branches of a tree to overhang another person's land.
6. A right to store coal in another person's shed: *Wright* v *Macadam* (1949).	
7. A right to park a motor vehicle in a defined area: *Newman* v *Jones* (1982). Caveat – the use must not leave the servient owner without any reasonable use of his land: *London and Blenheim Estates Ltd* v *Ladbroke Retail Parks Ltd* (1992). But NB *Saeed* v *Plustrade Ltd* (2001).	
8. A right to the passage of piped water across another person's land: *Rance* v *Elvin* (1985).	
9. A right to fix a sign board on a neighbouring house: *Moody* v *Steggles* (1879).	
10. A right to store casks and trade produce on the servient land: *Att-Gen of Southern Nigeria* v *John Holt & Co (Liverpool) Ltd* (1915).	
11. A right to use a communal garden can exist as an easement: *Mulvaney* v *Jackson* (2002).	

In *Palmer and Another* v *Bowman and Another* [2000] 1 WLR 842 the Court of Appeal held that the drainage of natural water from higher land onto separately owned lower land could not exist as an easement because such drainage was an essential incident of land ownership. This is a contemporary example of a right not capable of being an easement. Easements can only belong to another landowner for the benefit of his land (compare restrictive covenants), but profits can exist 'in gross', that is, they can be held by people who are not landowners for their own benefit.

Right to park and right of storage

Two of the most controversial easements are the right to park and the right of storage.

A major impediment to the establishment of both these easements was the principle that, for a right to be an easement, it had to be a right against other land and not a right to possession of the other (ie servient) land: see, for example, *Copeland* v *Greenhalf* [1952] Ch 488 and section 12.2 below. It was felt that a right to park would contravene that principle. However, in the unreported decision of *Newman* v *Jones* (22 March 1982) Megarry V-C held that a right to park cars on the forecourt of a block of flats passed as an easement under s62 LPA 1925. Then, in *London and Blenheim Estates Ltd* v *Ladbroke Retail Parks Ltd* [1992] 1 WLR 1278 an easement of car parking was recognised in a reported case (although the Court made clear that the use must not leave the servient owner without any reasonable use of his land).

In *Batchelor* v *Marlow* (2001) 82 P & CR 36 the Court of Appeal held that a crucial factor in seeking to establish an easement of car parking was that the right granted/claimed must leave the servient owner with reasonable use of his land. There the court decided that an exclusive right to park six cars for 9.5 hours on each working day of the week rendered the servient owner without any reasonable use of his land. At first instance the court held that the right to park could be acquired by prescription, and in the Court of Appeal Tuckey LJ noted that that conclusion was 'not challenged' on appeal. In *Central Midlands Estates* v *Leicester Dyers* [2003] 2 P & CR D2 it was held that a right to park an unlimited number of cars upon a piece of land subject only to the limitations of available space could not amount to an easement. In so deciding, the court followed *Batchelor* v *Marlow*. However, in *Saeed* v *Plustrade Ltd* [2001] EWCA Civ 2011 the Court of Appeal surprisingly 'left open' the question whether a right to park cars could amount to an easement. The balance of authorities support an easement of car parking.

Despite the principle that for a right to be an easement it has to be a right against other land and not a right to possession of the other land, the Court of Appeal held in *Wright* v *Macadam* [1949] 2 KB 744 that a right to store goods on another's land could exist as an easement. This is a controversial decision, since storage seems, prima facie, to be very close to joint possession of the servient land.

An attempt to reconcile *Wright* v *Macadam* with the well-established principle confirmed in *Copeland* v *Greenhalf* was made in *Grigsby* v *Melville* [1974] 1 WLR 80. There, Brightman J suggested that a claim to the whole beneficial use of land could not be an easement, but that something less than exclusive use could be.

12.2 Essentials of an easement

In *Re Ellenborough Park* [1956] Ch 131 the Court of Appeal approved the classification made by Cheshire. There are four essentials:

1. There must be a dominant and a servient tenement.
2. The easement must accommodate the dominant tenement.
3. The dominant and servient owners must be different persons.
4. The right must be capable of forming the subject matter of a grant.

There must be a dominant and a servient tenement

This means that a right over land given to someone who does not own land capable of being benefited cannot be an easement. This is expressed in the statement that 'an easement cannot exist in gross'.

The easement must accommodate the dominant tenement

A right cannot be an easement unless it confers a benefit on the dominant tenement itself rather than its owner personally (compare 'touch and concern the land' in relation to covenants). In addition there must be some natural connection between the two tenements, although they need not be immediately adjacent. See *Hill* v *Tupper* (1863) 2 H & C 121.

The dominant and servient tenements must not be both owned and occupied by the same person

This derives from a basic principle that a man cannot have an easement over his own land. Rights habitually exercised by a man over part of his own land which would be easements if that part were separately owned and occupied are called 'quasi-easements'. An easement is a right 'in alieno solo' – in the land of another.

The right must be capable of forming the subject matter of a grant

This means that a right can only be an easement if it is of a kind that can be granted as an easement. The following tests are applied to determine whether the right is capable of being an easement:

1. The right must be of a kind already recognised as capable of being an easement. While this does not prevent new easements from being recognised as in *Re Ellenborough Park* (above), a right which does not resemble established easements will not in general be an easement, see *Phipps* v *Pears* [1965] 1 QB 76, and neither will a right which requires expenditure on the part of the servient owner: *Regis Property Co Ltd* v *Redman* [1956] 2 QB 612. But see *Crow* v *Wood* [1970] 3 WLR 516 where a right to have a fence or wall kept in repair was held to be capable of being an easement. (Compare this with positive covenants: see section 11.5.) There in spite of the expenditure of money required by such an easement Lord Denning said (at p521):

    > 'It seems to me that it is now sufficiently established, or at any rate, if not established hitherto, we should now declare, that a right to have your neighbour keep up the fences is a right in the nature of an easement which is capable of being granted by law so as to run with the land and to be binding on successors.'

    A right which amounts to a claim for joint possession of the servient tenement cannot be an easement. See *Copeland* v *Greenhalf* [1952] Ch 488; *Grigsby* v *Melville* [1974] 1 WLR 80.

    The statement of Lord St Leonards in *Dyce* v *Lady James Hay* (1852) 1 Macq 305 should be noted:

    > 'The category of servitudes and easements must alter and expand with the changes that take place in the circumstances of mankind.'

    This indicates that new easements may have to be recognised to keep pace with modern technology.

2. The right must be capable of reasonably exact definition. Thus there can be no easement of a vague kind such as a right to privacy (*Browne* v *Flower* [1911] 1 Ch 219), or a right to an unspoilt view (*Aldred's Case* (1610) 9 Co Rep 57b).

    But a right to a view may be protected by a restrictive covenant as in *Gilbert* v *Spoor* [1983] Ch 27, or to a general flow of air (*Harris* v *De Pinna* (1886) 33 Ch D 238).

3. There must be a capable grantor.
4. There must be a capable grantee.

These two rules mean that there can only be an easement if at the time it arose the servient tenement was owned by someone capable of granting an easement (for example, a tenant cannot bind the reversion and so cannot grant an easement) and the dominant tenement was owned by a legal person capable of receiving a grant.

12.3 Legal and equitable easements

An easement can only be a legal interest in land if it is held for an interest equivalent to a fee simple absolute in possession or a term of years absolute (s1(2)(a)

LPA 1925) and if it is created by statute, deed or prescription. A document which is not a deed cannot create a legal easement (s55 LPA 1925).

Any other easement is equitable

Where the servient tenement is *unregistered* land, an equitable easement created after 1925 is void against a purchaser of a legal estate for money or money's worth unless it is registered as a Class D(iii) land charge. See *Shiloh Spinners v Harding* [1973] AC 691.

Where the servient tenement was *registered* land, under the Land Registration Act 1925 (as amended) equitable interests were minor interests protected by entry of a notice or a caution on the register. Further, they might have been capable of being overriding interests under s70(1)(a) LRA 1925. Under the Land Registration Act 2002, if it is a new easement the servient owner would agree it could be recorded against his land (ie an agreed notice). However, in the case of an existing easement, under the 2002 Act the dominant owner would apply to the Registry for a note to be made on the servient owner's title of the dominant owner's right. In *Celsteel Ltd v Alton House Holdings Ltd* [1985] 1 WLR 204 an equitable easement was held to come within s70(1)(a) because it was 'a right enjoyed with the land' for the purpose of r258 of the Land Registration Rules 1925. It affected the registered title and so was an overriding interest which did not need to be protected by notice on the register as a minor interest.

12.4 Acquisition of easements

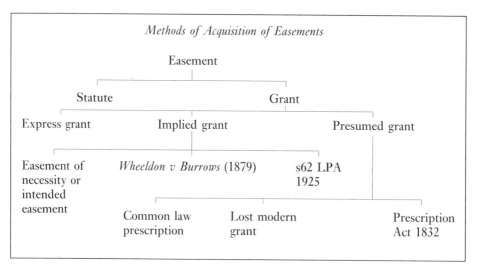

There are four ways in which an easement can be acquired:

Statute

Easements may be created by local Acts or may be given to public utilities, eg the early railway or canal companies.

Apart from statute, Cheshire expresses the rule at page 573 that the basic principle is that 'every easement must originate in a grant'.

Express grant or reservation

A grant is the giving of an easement by the servient owner to the dominant owner. A reservation is the reservation of rights by a landowner selling part of his land over the part sold. Before 1926 it was not possible to make a simple reservation; it had to be done by grant of the land to the purchaser and a regrant of the easement by the purchaser to the vendor. The effect of a grant or reservation is a matter of construction of the document, in the light of the general principles that a grant is construed against the grantor and a man may not derogate from his grant.

Implied grant or reservation

In favour of the grantor

As a grant is construed against the grantor, easements will only be impliedly reserved in favour of the grantor in *two* limited cases:

1. Easements of necessity. An easement of necessity is one without which the property retained cannot be used at all, and not one merely necessary to the reasonable enjoyment of the property. See *Union Lighterage Co* v *London Graving Dock Co* [1902] Ch 557 at 573.

   In *Nickerson* v *Barraclough* [1981] Ch 426 the Court of Appeal reversed in part Megarry V-C and held that a way of necessity could only exist in association with a grant of land. The right depended on the intention of the parties and the implication from the circumstances that unless some way was implied the land would be inaccessible. It was not a question of public policy, as the Vice-Chancellor had held at first instance.

   In *Titchmarsh* v *Royston Water Co Ltd* (1899) 81 LT 673 the court noted that 'the availability of an alternative route enjoyable as of right is, of course destructive of any claim of necessity, even though that alternative is inconvenient'. The way may be used for any purpose necessary to maintain that particular mode of enjoyment, but may not be used for subsequent additional purposes. See *London Corporation* v *Riggs* (1880) 13 Ch D 798. It is important to emphasise that easements of necessity are strictly limited to the circumstances of the necessity prevailing at the time of the grant.

   In *Sweet* v *Sommer* (2004) The Times 25 August the Chancery Division established that where on a transfer of part of land access to the property retained was only available either over the property transferred or by demolishing a building (which neither party anticipated doing) a right of way over the property transferred would be impliedly reserved as a matter of necessity. Prior to this case there was no direct authority on the matter. In essence the case demonstrated that the doctrine of implied reservation of an easement of necessity would 'be sensitive to physical as well as legal facts existing at the date of the relevant grant': per Hart J.

2. Intended easements. These are easements necessary to carry out the clear common intention of the parties; for example, the grant of one of a pair of semi-detached houses, the other being retained, implies the mutual grant and reservation of easements of support.

This was considered by the Court of Appeal in *Stafford* v *Lee* (1992) 65 P & CR 172, where it was held that a common intention must be shown between the parties that the land was to be used in some definite and particular manner and that the easement was necessary to give effect to that intention. The common intention could be proved on a balance of probabilities by, for example, reference to any plan available amongst the title deeds.

Nourse LJ quoted Lord Parker of Waddington in *Pwllbach Colliery Co Ltd* v *Woodman* [1915] AC 634:

'The law will readily imply the grant or reservation of such easements as may be necessary to give effect to the common intention of the parties to a grant of real property, with reference to the manner or purposes in and for which the land ... is to be used. But it is essential for this purpose that the parties should intend that the ... land ... should be used in some definite and particular manner.'

Nourse LJ concluded:

'In those circumstances, on the balance of probabilities, the parties could only have intended that the land should be used for residential purposes. No other intention could reasonably be imputed to them. It followed that the easement claimed by the plaintiffs was necessary to give effect to the intention so established.'

In favour of the grantee

In view of the fact that a grant is construed in favour of the grantee it is much easier for a grantee to acquire easements by implied grant. The types of easement which may be impliedly granted are:

1. Easements of necessity (see above).
2. Intended easements. These are more readily implied in the case of a grantee than of a grantor. See *Wong* v *Beaumont Property Trust* [1965] 1 QB 173; *Pwllbach Colliery Co* v *Woodman* (above).
3. Easements within the rule in *Wheeldon* v *Burrows* (1879) 12 Ch D 31. This case laid down that upon the grant of *part of a tenement* there would pass to the grantee as easements all quasi-easements over the land retained which:

a) were continuous and apparent; or

b) were necessary to the reasonable enjoyment of the land granted; and

c) had been, and were at the time of the grant, used by the grantor for the benefit of the part granted.

Continuous and apparent. There must be some feature which gives a permanence to the right. A continuous easement is one which is enjoyed passively, eg a right to light, rather than one requiring some activity for enjoyment, eg a right of way. An apparent easement is one which can be discovered by a careful inspection by a reasonably expert observer. Despite the apparent exclusion of rights of way as not being 'continuous', the courts have always held that they come within the rule in *Wheeldon* v *Burrows* (above).

Necessary to the reasonable enjoyment of the land granted. In *Wheeler and Another* v *J J Saunders Ltd and Others* [1995] 2 All ER 697, the Court of Appeal provided useful guidance on this requirement. While recognising that there had been some doubt as to whether the requirement that the easement should be continuous and apparent was an alternative to the requirement that the easement be necessary for the reasonable enjoyment of the property granted, the court, on reviewing *Wheeldon* v *Burrows*, concluded that the court on that occasion had treated the first requirement as synonymous with the second. The test of what was necessary for the reasonable enjoyment of land was not the same as the test for a way of necessity (one without which the property could not be used at all). Peter Gibson LJ noted (at p707) that in Cheshire and Burn's *Modern Law of Real Property* 'necessary' in the context of the doctrine of *Wheeldon* v *Burrows* indicated that the way 'conduces to the reasonable enjoyment of the property' (see p592 note 7). Further, Staughton LJ emphasised that the acquisition of easements under *Wheeldon* v *Burrows* was wider than acquisition of easements through the doctrine of necessity. Here, on the facts, access over the alleged servient land was not necessary for the reasonable enjoyment of the alleged dominant land.

The rule applies to a contract or a written or oral lease as well as to conveyances by deed.

This was established in *Borman* v *Griffith* [1930] 1 Ch 493. There, in 1923, the owner of a private car park containing two properties, known respectively as The Hall and The Gardens, made an agreement in writing to lease The Gardens to the plaintiff for seven years. The Gardens was approached by a drive which ran from the public road through the park to the plaintiff's premises, The Hall, and then on to the house known as The Gardens. Subsequently, the owner began to construct an alternative access to The Gardens, but this was impracticable for the plaintiff's trade as a poultry dealer and the plaintiff continued to use the drive. In 1926, The Hall was leased to the defendant, who obstructed the plaintiff's use of the drive. The plaintiff claimed a right of way over the drive relying on s62 of the Law of Property Act 1925 (see below).

The court held that the agreement for the lease was not a 'conveyance' within s205(1)(ii) LPA 1925, and therefore s62 did not apply. However, the right to use the drive passed under *Wheeldon* v *Burrows*. The plaintiff was entitled to specific performance of the agreement including such rights of way as would pass upon a conveyance or demise. The driveway was a feature permanently there and clearly suggesting that it was in use as a means of access from the road across the servient property – the park – to the property which was the subject of the agreement in writing. The drive was both plainly visible and necessary for the reasonable enjoyment of The Gardens.

The doctrine of *Wheeldon* v *Burrows* is not limited to situations where a common owner sells off part of his land to the person claiming the easement and retains the other part (the traditional factual scenario when the doctrine is invoked). It can also apply where the common owner sells the quasi dominant land to one person and the quasi servient land to another, provided the sales to the different persons are contemporaneous: see *Swansborough* v *Coventry* (1832) 2 M & S 362.

4. *Section 62 Law of Property Act 1925.* By this section, unless a contrary intention is expressed, every conveyance of land passes with it (inter alia) all liberties, privileges, easements, rights and advantages whatsoever, appertaining or reputed to appertain to the land, or any part thereof or, at the time of conveyance, enjoyed with the land or any part thereof. This section does not apply to contracts, only conveyances, and will not apply to an agreement for a lease. See *Borman* v *Griffith* (above). The section has the effect of creating new easements (and profits) out of all kinds of quasi-easements and profits, not just those covered by the rule in *Wheeldon* v *Burrows*, provided the rights are those capable of being an easement or profit. An example of its operation may occur if a landlord renews a lease, having previously allowed the tenant to enjoy certain additional privileges. Unless these privileges are expressly excluded, the grant of the new lease converts them into easements enjoyed as of right.

In *Wright* v *Macadam* [1949] 2 KB 744 the Court of Appeal held that a right to use a coal shed was a right capable of being granted at law. As the right was being enjoyed with the property at the date of the 'conveyance' (in fact the renewal of a lease) and no contrary intention was expressed in that document, the right to store coal in the shed passed as an easement under s62 LPA 1925. See also *Goldberg* v *Edwards* [1950] Ch 247.

It was held in *Long* v *Gowlett* [1923] 2 Ch 177 that the section did not operate where the quasi-dominant and quasi-servient tenements were in the same ownership and occupation prior to the conveyance. The House of Lords has now given its approval to *Long* v *Gowlett* in holding that s62 only applies where there has been some diversity of ownership or occupation of the quasi-dominant and quasi-servient tenements prior to the conveyance: see *Sovmots Investments Ltd* v *Secretary of State for the Environment* [1977] 2 WLR 951 HL.

This has a serious limiting effect on the application of s62, and where land in common ownership and occupation is divided, a claimant will have to use *Wheeldon* v *Burrows* (above) to support any claim for implied easements.

An easement of light may be implied under either s62 LPA 1925 or the common law rules for implied easements. See *Lyme Valley Squash Club Ltd* v *Newcastle under Lyme Borough Council* [1985] 2 All ER 405.

5. Presumed grant or prescription (see section 12.5).

12.5 Prescription

The basis of holding that an easement is acquired by prescription is that if long user as of right is proved, the court will presume that the user began lawfully, ie as a result of a grant. There are three methods of prescription (prescription at common law, by lost modern grant and under the Prescription Act 1832), but they all rely on proof of continuous user 'as of right':

User as of right

From the earliest times English law has followed the Roman tests of user as of right, which are that it must be:

1. Nec vi: no force must be used in order to enjoy the claimed right, nor must user take place under protest from the servient owner.
2. Nec clam: if the user is secret the servient owner has no chance to protest, and the user is not as of right. See *Liverpool Corporation* v *H Coghill & Son Ltd* [1918] 1 Ch 307. However, the servient owner cannot say that the user was secret if he would have discovered it by reasonable inspection.
3. Nec precario: user enjoyed by permission cannot be as of right, even if there is no written contract or periodical payment. See *Gardner* v *Hodgson's Kingston Brewery Co Ltd* [1903] AC 229. The advantage of such a payment for the servient owner is that it shows that the permission was renewed regularly; user after permission has lapsed may become user as of right if 'there is a change in circumstances from which revocation may fairly be implied': per Goff J in *Healey* v *Hawkins* [1968] 1 WLR 1967. This effect of permission was further considered by the Court of Appeal in *Jones* v *Price* (1992) 64 P & CR 404. It was held that oral permission during the prescriptive period would negative user as of right and this would continue to be so while the common understanding of the parties remained that the user was permissive.

There have been dicta in a number of cases (see in particular *R* v *Suffolk County Council, ex parte Steed* (1996) 75 P & CR 102) to the effect that for long use to have been 'as of right' the individuals exercising the right had to believe that they had a legal (ie enforceable) right to use the land in that way. However, the House of Lords in *R* v *Oxfordshire County Council, ex parte Sunningwell Parish Council* [1999] 3 WLR

160 unanimously concluded that such dicta was incorrect and that the state of mind of an individual using the property with consent was irrelevant. Their Lordships emphasised that to require an inquiry into the subjective state of mind of a user would be contrary to the entire concept of prescription, which required evidence that the landowner consented to the usage giving rise to an inference or presumption of a prior grant or dedication. This is an important decision on the meaning of the words 'as of right' in relation to the acquisition of rights over land by prescription. Their Lordships were clearly influenced by the fact that in the case of a 20 years' user it was inevitable that user in the initial years would have been without any very firm belief in the existence of a legal right to use.

User in fee simple

The user must be by or on behalf of a fee simple owner against a fee simple owner. However, provided that user began against a fee simple owner, it does not make it ineffective for the purposes of prescription if the land is later leased or becomes settled. A tenant cannot acquire an easement by prescription against his landlord. See *Kilgour* v *Gaddes* [1904] 1 KB 457. It has also been held that a tenant cannot acquire an easement by prescription at common law or by lost modern grant against another tenant holding from the same landlord. See *Simmons* v *Dobson* [1991] 1 WLR 720.

The user must be continuous

This does not mean ceaseless user, but there must not be excessive intervals between each user, nor must there be long periods of non-user between periods of user. Continuity of user is not broken by an agreed variation in the user (see *Davis* v *Whitby* [1974] Ch 186), but a claim to use a right of way every 12 years to remove cut timber was held not to be continuous in *Hollins* v *Verney* (1884) 13 QBD 304.

Prescription at common law

At common law a grant would be presumed if continuous user as of right could be shown to have continued from 'time immemorial', which is 1189 (the first year of the reign of Richard I). As it soon became impossible to prove user back to that date, the courts adopted the rule that user since 1189 would be presumed if user for 20 years or more could be shown. This presumption could, however, be rebutted by showing that the right must have arisen since 1189, for example a right of light claimed for a building built after 1189.

Prescription by lost modern grant

The second method by which an easement can be established by prescription is by the doctrine of lost modern grant. The doctrine is a legal fiction. The main catalyst for this development was the reality that as 1189 became further back in time it became very hard to prove that the right claimed as an easement had arisen since that date and therefore very difficult to establish common law prescription.

The way the doctrine works is as follows. If there is an obstacle to establishing an easement under common law prescription but user as of right for a sufficient period can be established (20 years' user is generally sufficient), the court *may* (ie it has a discretion) *presume* that there was an actual grant of the easement subsequent to 1189 but prior to the commencement of the period of user relied on and that the deed making the grant has subsequently been lost. It is a presumption which can be rebutted by the alleged servient owner, showing that during the entire period when the grant could have been made there was nobody who could lawfully have made it. However, it is assumed that the presumption cannot be rebutted by evidence to the effect that no grant in fact was made.

In *Palmer and Another* v *Bowman and Another* [2000] 1 WLR 842 the Court of Appeal stated that it was clear law that the subject matter of a presumed lost modern grant had to be a right capable of existing as an easement. In particular it had to be a benefit not enjoyed by the owner of the dominant land as an essential incident of ownership of his land. There the plaintiffs (P) and the defendants (B) owned adjoining farms. The ditches that ran along the boundary between the two farms had become blocked. The plaintiffs, relying solely on the *doctrine of lost modern grant,* claimed an easement allowing them to drain surface and percolating water from their higher land into the lower land of the defendants through the drainage ditches that belonged to the defendants and that the right had been wrongly interfered with. Further, they sought a declaration that they had the right to go onto the defendants' land in order to reopen and maintain those ditches. In giving judgment for the defendants the Court of Appeal concluded that there was no authority for the proposition that drainage of natural water from higher to lower land could form the subject matter of an easement because such drainage was an essential incident of land ownership.

To be able to claim an easement under the doctrine a plaintiff has to prove 20 years' user. Such user need not be continuous nor be the last 20 years immediately preceding the action (this provides some advantage compared with claims under the Prescription Act 1832, see below). Once such user is established the court may be prepared to infer a grant. Whether the court will do so depends on a number of factors, including all the circumstances of the case. This uncertainty is the major weakness with the device and a claimant can never be sure if the court will exercise its discretion in his favour. Further, the courts have refused to presume lost grants which would be contrary to statute or custom.

The question of tolerating a user of a track without objection from the owner of the land for sufficient years to support a claim for lost modern grant was considered by the Court of Appeal in *Mills* v *Silver* [1991] 2 WLR 324. Occasional use of a hill track by a neighbouring farmer without the permission of the landowner, but with his knowledge and acquiescence, was user as of right, creating the basis of a claim for an easement by presumption by lost modern grant. The case was lost on the basis that substantial improvement to the track was much more than repair to the track, and any prescriptive right did not authorise such work to the detriment of the landowner.

Prescription Act 1832

This Act was intended to simplify the acquisition of an easement by prescription, avoiding the difficulties of the common law and lost modern grant. Unfortunately it was drafted in very obscure terms. Rights to light and easements other than light are treated differently.

Easements other than light – s2 Prescription Act 1832

In order to establish a claim under the Prescription Act 1832 the claimant must show:

User as of right
This has the same meaning as for common law prescription except that there are rules relating to the effect of permission. These are:

1. Any consents, whether written or oral, given from time to time during the user defeat a claim under either of the statutory periods. See *Gardner* v *Hodgson's Kingston Brewery Co Ltd* [1903] AC 229.
2. A written consent given at the beginning of the user and extending throughout defeats a claim under either of the statutory periods.
3. An oral consent given at the beginning of the user and extending throughout defeats a claim under the shorter period but not the longer period.

User without interruption – s4 Prescription Act 1832
Interruption means some hostile obstruction and not merely non-user, although non-user may defeat a claim by showing insufficient enjoyment. The interruption is only effective in preventing an easement from being acquired if the claimant has acquiesced in the obstruction for a year after he has known of both the obstruction and the person responsible for it (s4). See *Davies* v *Du Paver* [1953] 1 QB 184, where Birkett LJ explained:

'Submission to or acquiescence in is a state of mind evidenced by the conduct of the parties ... it is a question of fact for the judge to decide on all the facts of the case ...'

This was echoed by Morris LJ:

'... the date when submission or acquiescence begins must be determined as a question of fact having regard to all the circumstances.'

This question of acquiescence/submission in an interruption for at least a year under s4 of the 1832 Act in the context of a claim to right of light was considered by the Court of Appeal in *Dance* v *Triplow* [1992] 1 EGLR 190. There D (the plaintiff) claimed that an extension built by T (the defendant) interfered with his right to light. He commenced his action in August 1984. The combined effect of ss3 and 4 of the 1832 Act was that P had to establish enjoyment for 20 years without interruption and that this period had to immediately precede D's action (ie the period between August 1964 and August 1984 was crucial). T's extension was completed in 1981. D complained to the council, had an officer of the council inspect the premises and in February 1982 he saw a solicitor and left the matter with him. T argued that D had acquiesced for more than one year after the interruption. The Court of Appeal held that D had submitted to the interruption for more than a year and therefore had no easement. Between February 1982 (when D passed the matter to his solicitor) and August 1984 (when a summons was served on T) – a period of 2.5 years – there had been no communication of any type between D or his solicitor and T. He had failed to make his opposition apparent to T and on these facts D had submitted to the interruption. His pre–February 1982 objections had ceased to be relevant long before August 1984 when the summons was served.

User for one of the statutory periods

There are two alternative periods on which the claim may be based:

1. The shorter period: this is 20 years for easements. This operates negatively, in that proof of user for the shorter period simply assists a claim at common law by preventing the defence that enjoyment must have begun after 1189.
2. The longer period: this is 40 years for easements. This operates positively, in that proof of user for the longer period makes the right absolute and indefeasible.

Both periods are measured backwards from the action in which the right is questioned, so that an easement can only be acquired under the Prescription Act by the bringing of legal proceedings. In *Reilly* v *Orange* [1955] 2 QB 112 Jenkins LJ concluded as follows:

> 'What the Prescription Act 1832 requires as appears from the combined effect of s2 and s4 is the full period of 20 years.'

Deductions

The Act has complicated provisions for the deduction of certain periods when computing whether user for the requisite period before action has been shown. The effect of these provisions is shown in the following table.

	Term of years	*Life tenancy*	*Infancy*	*Lunacy*
Shorter period	Not deductible but period cannot start to run against tenant	Deductible	Deductible	Deductible
Longer period	Deductible provided that reversioner resists claim within three years of determination of term	As for term of years	Not deductible	Not deductible

Easements of light – s3 Prescription Act 1832

The amount of light was considered by the House of Lords in *Colls* v *Home & Colonial Stores Ltd* [1904] AC 179 to be:

'such an amount as was required according to the ordinary notions of mankind for the beneficial use of premises'.

In the case of business premises the right to light is sufficient light for the use of the premises for its ordinary business uses. In *Carr-Saunders* v *Dick McNeil Associates Ltd* [1986] 1 WLR 922 the configuration of rooms behind the windows with an acknowledged right of light was changed. The test was propounded by Millett J:

'The extent of the dominant owner's rights is neither increased nor diminished by the actual use to which the dominant owner has chosen to put his premises or any of the rooms in them; for he is entitled to such access of light as will leave the premises adequately lit for all ordinary purposes for which they may reasonably be expected to be used. The Court must, therefore, take account not only of the present use, but also of other potential uses to which the dominant owner may reasonably be expected to put the premises in the future.'

The aforementioned principle included an alteration in the internal arrangements of the premises. Accordingly, development which restricted the dominant owner from subdividing the second floor of his premises as he wished was held to be an actionable nuisance:

'... because the second floor can no longer (as it formerly could) conveniently be subdivided in such a way that the subdivided areas each receive an adequate amount of light.'

This has now been further considered by the Court of Appeal in connection with the amount of light required for a greenhouse: see *Allen* v *Greenwood* [1979] 2 WLR 187 where, the court decided that the amount of light which may be acquired as an easement under s3 Prescription Act 1832 is the amount required for the use of a building for any ordinary purpose for which that building has been constructed or adapted. In this case, acquisition under s3 of an easement of light to a greenhouse must be sufficient for the cultivation of the plants. Goff LJ left the question of rights to light to activate solar heating panels for a future case, which will provide the opportunity to test in full the statement of Lord St Leonards in *Dyce* v *Lady James Hay* (1852) 1 Macq 305 that:

'... the category of servitudes and easements must alter and expand with the changes that take place in the circumstances of mankind.'

Section 3 of the Prescription Act 1832 provides that the actual enjoyment of the access of light to a dwelling house, workshop or other building for 20 years without interruption shall make the right indefeasible unless enjoyed by written consent or agreement. This has created the following differences from the provisions relating to other easements (see above).

1. User need not be of right, provided that it is not enjoyed by written permission.
2. An easement of light can be acquired by a tenant against his landlord.
3. There is only one period – 20 years.
4. There are no deductions.
5. There is no presumption of a grant, and so it may be acquired against an owner who is not a capable grantee.
6. Interruptions: 'interruption' has the same meaning as for other easements: see s4 Prescription Act 1832. Any interruption should be a physical obstruction of the light by means of a screen or similar erection. But, under the Rights of Light Act 1959, the interruption can be purely nominal, by registering a notice as a local land charge. The notice (known as a 'light obstruction notice') must identify the servient and dominant tenements and the size and position of the notional obstruction. This notice remains effective for one year unless previously cancelled. An aim of the Act is to provide an alternative to the erection of unsightly screens etc.

   Finally, it is important to emphasise that only access to light to a *building* can be acquired as an easement.

Conclusion

The question whether a period of time when land used without planning permission could count as part of the prescription period has been considered. In *Batchelor* v *Marlow* (2001) 82 P & CR 36 the court at first instance concluded that while the prescription period could not include any period of time during which the conduct relied upon to establish the right was illegal, a period of use of land without planning permission was not an 'illegal' use and therefore counted towards the prescription period. However, any period of time after the commencement of proceedings for injunctive relief would be discounted.

12.6 Extent of the easement

When the easement has been established, future questions may arise as to its content and extent. This would usually be a result of changes in the neighbourhood or of modernisation of methods of carriage over the years.

A straightforward increase in numbers may arise due to the success of a business. In *Woodhouse & Co Ltd* v *Kirkland (Derby) Ltd* [1970] 1 WLR 1185, Plowman J had to consider such an increase in custom and said this was 'a mere increase in user and not a user of a different kind or for a different purpose'.

The rule was effectively established in *British Railways Board* v *Glass* [1965] Ch 538. It was held that a general right of way is not limited to the user contemplated when the grant was made. An increase in the number of caravans using a site did not create an excessive user of a right of crossing in order to obtain access to the site which had been acquired by prescription. Harman LJ expressed the principle as follows:

> 'A right to use a way for this purpose or that has never been … limited to a right to use the way so many times a day or for such and such a number of vehicles so long as the dominant tenement does not change its identity.'

This question of the extent of the easement continues to create problems when the user is intensified or changed. If a user is a right of way, the intensification or change of user can have a dramatic effect on the quality of life of the servient owner. In the case of express grant of a right of way 'at all times and for all purposes', this can accommodate changes in user and the consequent intensification of use, as seen in *White* v *Grand Hotel, Eastbourne* [1913] 1 Ch 113.

Notwithstanding that a right of way is granted in wide terms, it may be restricted by the physical characteristics of the path over which it subsists. In *White* v *Richards* [1993] RTR 318 a right of way in respect of motor vehicles existed over a dirt track which was 2.7 metres wide and some 250 metres long, with the servient owners' house just under three metres away from the track. The Court of Appeal held that the physical characteristics of the track were such as to require the words 'motor vehicles' in the grant to be restricted to those of limited dimensions and width (thus stopping the dominant owner taking 15 juggernaut lorries a day over the track). An express grant of a right of way does not carry with it an implied grant to a right to park, even for loading and unloading vehicles using the right of way. See *London and Suburban Land and Building Co* v *Carey* (1991) 62 P & CR 480.

Finally, in *Groves and Another* v *Minor* (1997) The Times 20 November the Court of Appeal made clear that there was nothing to stop a servient owner from building right up to the edge of a right of way and the dominant owner was restricted in his use of a right of way to the exact width of the way.

Extent of easement of necessity

The above rule must be compared with that which applies in the case of an easement of necessity. There the extent of the implied right is strictly limited and depends on the 'mode of enjoyment' of the surrounding, servient, land at the time of the grant. The right may be used to maintain that 'mode of enjoyment' but for no other purpose.

Extent of easement acquired by prescription

The extent of an easement acquired by prescription depends on the extent of the user, and if the character or nature of the user remains constant there is no objection to an increase in its intensity.

Alteration to the dominant tenement

The fact that some land or another part of the building is added to the original dominant tenement will not necessarily destroy a right of way which was previously only appurtenant to the original dominant tenement. See *Graham* v *Philcox* [1984] 3 WLR 150, where it was held that the combining of a ground-floor and a first-floor flat into one dwelling where the right of way was only appurtenant to the first-floor flat did not affect the existence of the right.

Any such alteration must not, of course, make the user excessive.

Alteration to the servient tenement

In *Celsteel Ltd* v *Alton House Holdings Ltd* [1985] 1 WLR 204 an injunction was granted to restrain the building of a car-wash on the servient tenement which would restrict the width of access from nine metres to 4.14 metres. This would be a substantial interference with a right of way over the servient tenement.

Scott J identified two criteria: first, the interference would be actionable if it were substantial; and secondly, it would not be substantial if it did not interfere with the reasonable use of the right of way. The claim in this case satisfied the criteria, and an injunction was the appropriate remedy to restrain the construction of the car-wash, which would substantially interfere with the right of way.

12.7 Remedies for infringement of easements

Abatement

The owner of an easement may abate any obstruction to its exercise by removing it, provided that no more force is used than is reasonably necessary; there is no danger of injury to third parties; and there is no reasonable possibility of a breach of the peace occurring as a result. The law does not favour abatement.

Action

Possible remedies are an injunction, damages or a declaration. If damages are sought it is necessary to establish some substantial interference with the enjoyment of the easement. As to injunctions, a trivial or temporary infringement will not justify such a remedy.

In *B & Q plc* v *Liverpool and Lancashire Properties Ltd* (2000) 81 P & CR 246 the Chancery Division made two key points in respect of actionable interference with an easement. First, the fact that an interference was 'infrequent and relatively fleeting' did not prevent it from being actionable. Second, an interference was also actionable even if the access still remaining was reasonable. There B & Q took a lease from L of Unit 1 of its retail park in Merseyside. The lease gave B & Q a right of way over the Unit 2 service area (which provided the only means of access to Unit 1) and allowed their delivery vehicles to wait in the Unit 2 service area until allowed through the gates giving access to Unit 1. This was an ample right of way which was necessary because B & Q operated a 'one in, one out' policy whereby only one delivery vehicle at a time could be unloaded in the yard (the aim of the policy was to try to prevent drivers – often with the collusion of B & Q's staff – from stealing stock). L wanted to build an extension on land which formed part of the Unit 2 service area, the effect of which would have been that B & Q's right of way could not be exercised as conveniently as previously. B & Q sought an injunction to restrain L from building the extension, arguing that the proposed work constituted an actionable interference with the right of way granted to it by the lease over the Unit 2 service area. In granting B & Q an injunction the court emphasised that where a grantee had contracted for the relative luxury of an ample right he could not be deprived of it just because the reduced non ample right would be all that was reasonably required. This was because the test for actionable interference with an easement was whether the grantee's insistence on being able to continue to use the whole of what he contracted for was reasonable, not whether what he was left with was reasonable. Here B & Q's preferred modus operandi (ie the 'one in, one out' policy) was not unreasonable. Accordingly, there was an actionable interference with B & Q's right of way and an injunction would be granted.

Right of access – access order

By virtue of the Access to Neighbouring Land Act 1992 (see section 12.9) a landowner can apply to court for an 'access order' to give access to adjoining land. This could be obtained to enable a landowner to do work to preserve land in accordance with, for example, an easement, but is only available if the work cannot be carried out without entering the adjoining servient land.

12.8 Extinguishment of easements

There is no statutory procedure to discharge or modify easements as there is for restrictive covenants. Easements may be extinguished by:

1. Statute.
2. Express release.
3. Implied release.
4. Unity of ownership and possession.

These are dealt with in turn.

Statute

An Act of Parliament may extinguish an easement expressly or by implication.

Express release

A dominant owner can release the servient owner from the burden of an easement. Such release must be by deed in order to be effective at law.

Implied release

1. There must be an actual intention to abandon the right. Non-user is not by itself enough, although non-user for a long period raises a presumption of intention to abandon: see *Moore* v *Rawson* (1824) 3 B & C 332 where a wall containing windows was replaced by a blank wall; this was held to be an abandonment of any right of light to the windows after 17 years.

    In *Benn* v *Hardinge* (1992) The Times 13 October the Court of Appeal re-emphasised this requirement. There non-user of a right of way for 175 years was not by itself enough to indicate an intention in the proprietor of the right to abandon it. The non-use of the dominant owner and his predecessors was explained by the Court on the basis that they had an alternative means of access to the fields in question (in other words, there was no need for them to use the disputed right of way). Finally, the court emphasised that a right of way was a piece of property of latent value whose abandonment was not to be readily inferred.

2. Alteration of the dominant tenement making the easement impossible or unnecessary may show an intent to abandon.

Unity of ownership and possession

Unity of both ownership and possession of the dominant and servient tenements extinguishes the easement. If there is only unity of possession the easement is merely suspended. If there is unity of ownership the easement continues until there is unity of possession.

12.9 Access to Neighbouring Land Act 1992

The Act came into force on 31 January 1993. It deals with the situation of a person who needs to gain access to neighbouring land in order to carry out works on his own land, for example to enter a neighbour's land in order to erect a new fence.

Until the Act, in all but an exceptional case, if A's neighbour refused A access then A could do nothing. In many cases this resulted in the deterioration of property, for example if A needed to repair his guttering but could only do so by placing a ladder on his neighbour's land. The Act gives effect to recommendations made by the Law Commission in its report *Right of Access to Neighbouring Land* (Law Com No 151).

The Act allows a landowner to apply to court for an access order to give access to neighbouring land (the servient land) for the purpose of carrying out any works which are reasonably necessary for the preservation of any land (the dominant land), except where making an access order would be unreasonable to the person to whose land access is required (s1). To get an order the applicant has to show that the work is either impossible or substantially more difficult to carry out without access to the servient land (substantially greater expense of the work without access to servient land is not a good reason for an order).

The effect of an access order is to require the respondent (servient owner) to permit the applicant to enjoy the access specified in the order. The right of access extends to anyone reasonably assisting the applicant (s3). The county court has initial jurisdiction in access proceedings, with power for proceedings to be transferred to the High Court (s7).

An access order could be obtained to enable a landowner to do work to preserve land in accordance with an easement. The Act has in effect created a *statutory licence*. However, it should be seen as a remedy of last resort. Clearly it is always going to be better to secure a neighbour's agreement to the access needed.

An access order is binding on the respondent's successors in title, subject to registration. In the case of registered land, an access order is not an overriding interest and must therefore be protected by a notice or caution (s5). In the case of unregistered land, an access order has to be registered in the register of writs and orders affecting land (s6(1)(d) Land Charges Act 1972).

12.10 Profits à prendre

A profit à prendre is a right to take something from the land of another. A profit may be either a several profit, that is, enjoyed by one person only, or a profit in common, enjoyed by one person in common with others.

Unlike an easement, a profit is not necessarily annexed to a dominant tenement, but may be in one of the following forms:

1. A profit appurtenant: this is a profit annexed to a dominant tenement by the act of the parties, and runs with it. Such a profit complies with the same rules as apply to easements and must generally satisfy the same four essentials as apply to easements under *Re Ellenborough Park* [1956] Ch 131 above.
2. A profit appendant: this is a profit annexed to land by the operation of law; probably the only one is a common of pasture, and no such common could be created after Quia Emptores 1290.
3. A profit *pur cause de vicinage*: this only exists when there are two adjoining commons which are not fenced off from each other, and the cattle put on one common have always been allowed to stray onto the other and vice versa.
4. A profit in gross: this type of profit is exercised independently of the ownership of the land, hence there is no dominant tenement.

12.11 Acquisition of profits à prendre

Profits à prendre can be acquired in four ways:

1. By statute: this is illustrated by the effect of the Inclosure Acts or certain Local Acts of Parliament.
2. By express grant: the grant must be by deed to create a legal profit.
3. By implied grant: s62 LPA 1925 applies to profits but the rule in *Wheeldon* v *Burrows* (1879) Ch D 31 does not.
4. By prescription:

   a) At common law.
   b) Lost modern grant.
   c) Section 1 Prescription Act 1832. The periods are 30 and 60 years. By s16 Commons Registration Act 1965, any period during which the servient tenement was requisitioned or grazing prevented for reasons of animal health must be deducted from a claim based on either period. The 1832 Act only applies to *profits appurtenant*.

12.12 Remedies for infringement of profits

These are the same as for easements, except that in the case of a profit the owner can sue a third party by proving possession without having to prove title.

12.13 Extinguishment of profits

Profits may be extinguished by the same method as easements.

In terms of extinguishment by statute it is important to note the effect of the Commons Registration Act 1965 on rights of common. The Act required common land, its owners and claims to rights of common over such land (except those held for a term of years or from year to year) to be registered with the appropriate local authority before 3 January 1970. Registration was provisional pending the hearing of any objections which had to be lodged prior to August 1972. Any such objections were considered by Commons Commissioners appointed under the 1965 Act. If land was not registered it ceased to be common land and the right of common was extinguished. The aim of the Act was to determine accurately the boundaries of land subject to rights of common as a forerunner to introducing more legislation in order to better utilise the same. New rights of common may arise (in respect of land over which no rights have previously been registered) and must be registered.

12.14 Worked example

Q Alf is the tenant of an isolated cottage, owned by Bert, adjoining Greenfield, which is also owned by Bert. Since 1985 Alf has used a path across Greenfield to get to the pub, and Bert has never commented on this. In 1997 Alf started to make pottery in his cottage, and Bert has allowed him by oral permission to set up a stall on the edge of Greenfield adjoining the main road to sell his wares to passing motorists.

Three months ago, Bert sold Greenfield to Chris who has told Alf to remove the stall and to stop walking across Greenfield.

Advise Alf.

Would the situation be different if in 2002 Bert sold the reversion of the cottage to Alf?

Comment
In this type of question the student is asked to determine whether someone has a right to do something over someone else's land, in other words, is there an easement or profit. Where it is an easement, which is more usual in examination questions, two questions must be asked:

1. Does the right claimed fulfil the four essentials of an easement?
2. If so, has the person claiming the easement acquired it?

If the answer to either is no, there is no easement, but there may be a licence, and the student should not forget to discuss that possibility.

A It is best to treat the two items separately.

Using the path

There is a dominant and a servient tenement and the use of this path would seem to benefit the dominant tenement. This is a right of way, long recognised as an easement, and the freehold owner was in possession of the servient tenement.

As Alf is a tenant he could not acquire an easement on his own behalf, but he could do so for his landlord. However, the landlord (Bert) is also the same person as the servient land owner. This will not present a problem as it is the diversity of occupation that counts: see *Borman* v *Griffith* (1930). Thus, all the essentials of an easement are present.

As Alf and Bert are strangers, Alf could only acquire the easement by express grant, or by prescription. There is no express grant in this case. In order to establish a prescription claim, the user must have been as of right. In this case there was no force used, the user was not secret and no permission was given, and so the user was as of right. In order to establish a claim under s2 Prescription Act 1832, Alf must show user for either at least 20 years or at least 40 years after any relevant deductions measured from the date at which legal proceedings are brought. There are no periods of deduction in this case, and so if Alf brought proceedings immediately he could show more than 20 years' user. It is important that he acts within the next *nine months* to start an action claiming a declaration that there is a right of way and an injunction restraining Chris from preventing its use, because if there is an interruption by the owner of the servient tenement which is acquiesced in by the person claiming an easement for more than 12 months after he has known of the obstruction and the person responsible for it, then the claim will be defeated. If the interruption ceases, time starts to run afresh.

If in 2002 Bert had sold the reversion of the cottage to Alf then there would have been a relationship of grantor and grantee and so easements could be acquired by implied grant. Prior to any such sale, Alf was Bert's tenant in respect of the cottage when he started using the path, and then in 1997 after he started to make pottery in his cottage Bert gave his oral permission to establish a stall on the edge of Greenfield to sell his wares to passing motorists. A sale in 2002 of the reversion of the cottage by Bert to Alf would rank as a conveyance for the purposes of s62 LPA 1925. Further, s62 has the effect of creating new easements out of all kinds of quasi-easements – not just those covered by the rule in *Wheeldon* v *Burrows* (1879) – provided the rights are those capable of being an easement. Given that there is no reservation of the right it would pass under s62 LPA 1925.

The stall

There is a dominant and a servient tenement and a capable grantor and grantee. While there does not appear to be a decided case concerning the right to erect a stall on another's land, except in the special case of markets, the right to store goods on another's land, provided that it does not amount to possession of the land, is a recognised easement (see *Copeland* v *Greenhalf* (1952), *Attorney-General of Southern Nigeria* v *John Holt & Co (Liverpool) Ltd* (1915) and *Grigsby* v *Melville* (1973)), which is similar to the right claimed here. It is doubtful, however, whether this particular right benefits the cottage, the dominant tenement, or merely the occupant Alf.

This case is somewhat similar to *Hill* v *Tupper* (1863) in that the right claimed is for the benefit of the occupant's business. If the premises had been let as a pottery the result would be different.

If this right is not an easement, then all Alf has is a licence. If there was no consideration, then the licence was terminable at will by Bert, and so a fortiori Chris can terminate it. Even if it was a contractual licence it is unlikely that a court will hold Chris, a stranger to the contract, to be bound by it: see *Ashburn Anstalt* v *Arnold* (1989), where the Court of Appeal held obiter that a contractual licence could not bind a third party.

Assuming that the right is capable of being an easement, then Alf could only have acquired it by express grant, which there was not, or prescription. However he does not have sufficient length of user to found a claim in prescription and, even if he did, a claim under the 20-year period would be defeated because Bert gave permission.

If in 2002 Bert had sold the reversion of the cottage to Alf, then again he would only have acquired a right to set up the stall if it is capable of being an easement. If it is not capable, then all he has is a licence. If it is capable of being an easement, then he could have acquired it by implied grant. It would not appear to come under the rule in *Wheeldon* v *Burrows* (1879) as the easement is not continuous, but it would pass under s62 LPA 1925 as being analogous with *Wright* v *Macadam* (1949).

13

Licences

13.1 Introduction

13.2 Bare licences

13.3 Licences coupled with an interest

13.4 Contractual licences

13.5 Licences protected by estoppel or in equity

13.1 Introduction

In English law there is no general right to enter on land in the possession of another. A person doing so without the permission of the occupier is a trespasser. Hence the familiar (although incorrect) warning sign: 'Trespassers will be prosecuted'. The sign should read 'Trespassers will be sued' as trespass is a tort, not a crime.

A licence is a permission given by the occupier of land (the licensor) which allows the licensee to do some act which would otherwise be a trespass, for example to lodge in his house, to enter his cinema to see a film, or to camp on his land.

The law relating to licences has, in the last 100 years and especially in the last 30 years, changed and expanded. It was previously well established that a licence was merely a contractual arrangement between two persons subject to the normal rules of privity. It did not confer any interest in the land on the licensee. There are two major consequences of this view of licences:

1. A licensee whose licence was revoked could not obtain specific performance of the licence, but was left to his contractual remedy of damages.
2. A licence bound only the original parties, not successors in title of either.

However, it is important to emphasise that the position is now different with regard both to revocability and to third parties. The courts have used licences *as a means of doing justice where the party had no recognised legal or equitable interest in the land, but it would be inequitable to deprive him of that land*. In doing so they have expanded the effect of licences so that they now have some of the characteristics of proprietary interests in the land. The law in this area is still developing and is not yet settled, particularly with regard to third parties. Cheshire at page 662 concludes:

'The law on this point is still in the process of development, but it seems that a new right in alieno solo has emerged in this century [ie the twentieth century] as did one in the previous century under the doctrine of *Tulk* v *Moxhay*.'

The land law aspects of licences must also be considered in two distinct areas: first, as a lease-substitute. This aspect was considered in Chapter 10, and attention is drawn in particular to section 10.5 above. Prior to the coming into force of the Housing Act 1988 on 15 January 1989 the licence was widely used as a method of overcoming the security of tenure provisions of the Rent Act 1977 and to a lesser extent of the Landlord and Tenant Act 1954 (to be able to enjoy such security of tenure an occupant has, inter alia, to have a *lease*).

Secondly, separate from the first point, the licence has developed into a distinct interest which merits the above conclusion by Cheshire that it is becoming 'a new right in alieno solo'. *It is this second aspect of the licence which will be considered in this chapter.*

With the coming into force on 15 January 1989 of the Housing Act 1988, which allowed landlords to create tenancies at full market rent, there has been less need for a landlord to try to avoid the Rent Acts by using a licence instead of a lease (see for example *AG Securities* v *Vaughan* and *Antoniades* v *Villiers* [1988] 3 WLR 1205). As a consequence the lease/licence debate may not be as prominent as hitherto.

Whether or not a licence is revocable or binds a third party will depend upon which type of licence has been created. There are four categories:

1. bare licences;
2. licences coupled with an interest;
3. contractual licences;
4 licences protected in equity or by estoppel.

In all discussions on licences it is as well to keep these four distinct categories in mind. They will be treated in this sequence in the subsequent sections.

13.2 Bare licences

These are licences granted otherwise than for valuable consideration – a mere permission and no more. Campers allowed to camp in a field free of charge would be bare licensees.

Revocability

A bare licence is revocable by the licensor at any time provided that he gives the licensee reasonable notice. Once the notice has expired, the licensee becomes a trespasser. In *Terunnanse* v *Terunnanse* [1968] AC 1086 it was held that a bare licence is automatically determined by the death of the licensor or the assignment of the land by the licensor.

Third parties

Bare licences are not binding on third parties, so if the licensor assigns the land the licensee cannot enforce the licence against the new owner and becomes a trespasser.

13.3 Licences coupled with an interest

The grant of a right to take something from the land of another, such as wood or game, creates an interest in land known as a profit à prendre (see Chapter 12, section 12.10). In order to exercise the right, the grantee must also be given a licence to enter onto the grantor's land. Such licences, because they are incidental to the enjoyment of an interest in land, are irrevocable and will bind third parties so long as that interest remains. The assignee of a profit à prendre will also acquire the licence.

The existence of the distinct rights should always be identified:

1. the licence to go on to the land;
2. the right to exploit the resources on the land, eg cutting timber.

13.4 Contractual licences

These are licences granted for valuable consideration. Provided the alleged consideration has some economic value the courts will not question its adequacy. The licence may form the whole subject matter of the contract, as with a platform ticket or the hire of a room for the night. Or the licence may be part of a larger contract, such as the licence granted to a builder so that he may enter onto land to carry out building works.

Revocability

At common law, licences were held to be inherently revocable, even where granted for consideration, because they did not confer any interest in the land. A licensor could revoke a licence in breach of the terms of the contract. The licensee would thereby become a trespasser and his only remedy would be an action for damages for breach of contract.

In *Wood* v *Leadbitter* (1845) 13 M & W 838 the plaintiff, who had bought a ticket to a race meeting, was forcibly ejected from the ground. He sued for assault. It was held that the defendant licensor was empowered to revoke the licence at any time, and once he did so the plaintiff became a trespasser who could be lawfully ejected with reasonable force. His only remedy was damages for breach of contract, which were nominal.

The position changed when the courts became willing to apply equitable remedies. Then the possibility arose that a licensee could prevent revocation of a contractual licence in breach of contract by injunction (from a licensee's perspective getting the equitable remedy of injunction was preferable to common law damages since the former would enable him to stay in possession of the land until the contract was completed).

In *Winter Garden Theatre (London) Ltd* v *Millennium Productions Ltd* [1948] AC 173 Lord Uthwatt said: 'The settled practice of the courts of equity is to do what they can by an injunction to preserve the sanctity of a bargain.' There the respondents were granted a licence for value to use the appellants' theatre. The agreement made no express provision for the revocation of the licence by the licensors. The House of Lords held that whether or not a contractual licence was revocable depended upon the terms of the agreement. In this case, a term must be implied that the licence was not intended to be perpetual, but that it could be revoked by the licensor, on reasonable notice to the licensee. Only if, on its true construction, the contract is irrevocable will breach be prevented by the grant of an injunction.

The contribution of equity in this area is not restricted to preventing breach by injunction. It can also enforce a right of entry by specific performance.

In *Verrall* v *Great Yarmouth Borough Council* [1981] QB 202, the council had entered into a contract with the National Front giving them a licence to use one of the council's halls for their annual conference. Before the conference, the Conservative council was replaced by a Labour one which purported to revoke the licence, admittedly in breach of contract. The National Front sought specific performance of the contract. The Court of Appeal granted an order for specific performance of the contract. Lord Denning MR stated:

> 'Since the *Winter Garden* case, it is clear that once a man has entered under his contract of licence, he cannot be turned out. An injunction can be obtained against the licensor to prevent his being turned out. On principle it is the same if it happens before he enters. If he has a contractual right to enter, and the licensor refuses to let him come in, then he can come to the court and in a proper case get an order for specific performance to allow him to come in.
>
> When arrangements are made for a licence of this kind of such importance and magnitude affecting many people, the licensors cannot be allowed to repudiate it and simply pay damages. It must be open to the court to grant specific performance in such cases.'

Analysis of contractual licence

In the course of his judgment in *London Borough of Hounslow* v *Twickenham Garden Developments Ltd* [1971] Ch 233 Megarry J made an analysis of the contractual licence, identifying four major points relating to such licences as:

1. A licence to enter land is a contractual licence if it is conferred by contract: it is immaterial whether the right to enter the land is the primary purpose of the contract or is merely secondary.

2. A contractual licence is not an entity distinct from the contract which brings it into being, but merely one of the provisions of that contract.
3. The willingness of the court to grant equitable remedies in order to enforce or support a contractual licence depends on whether or not the licence is specifically enforceable.
4. But even if a contractual licence is not specifically enforceable, the court will not grant equitable remedies in order to procure or aid a breach of the licence.

Domestic contractual licences

Where persons occupy land under an informal family arrangement which has broken down, the courts have to decide on their legal relationship even though originally there was no intention on the part of the persons involved that their arrangement was to have legal consequences. In most cases, the court cannot spell out a legal relationship from the actual intentions of the parties, as the situation which has arisen was not foreseen and no provision was made for it. In *Pettitt* v *Pettitt* [1970] AC 777 Lord Diplock put the matter thus:

> '... the court imputes to the parties a common intention which in fact they never formed and it does so by forming its own opinion as to what would have been the common intention of reasonable men as to the effect of the unforeseen event if it had been present to their minds.'

The original arrangement can usually be interpreted as giving rise to a variety of legal consequences, and the court must impose the legal relationship most appropriate in the present circumstances. A contractual licence will be imposed if that is the most fitting relationship (that is, if there has been or should be consideration and if the licence should be revocable), and the court will decide upon the terms of the contract according to what reason and justice require.

In *Tanner* v *Tanner* [1975] 1 WLR 1346, the Court of Appeal considered the case of an unmarried couple with children, where the father had bought the house for the mother and children to live in and the mother had given up a Rent Act protected flat to move into the house. The mother was found to have no proprietary interest in the house, but she did have a contractual licence (in leaving her Rent Act protected flat the mother had given up something of value, ie she had provided consideration) allowing her and the children to live there so long as they were of school age and the accommodation was reasonably required for her and the children (as the mother had in fact moved out of the house and did not ask to be put back she received £2,000 compensation for being wrongly turned out in lieu of the injunction that would otherwise have been granted). See also *Hardwick* v *Johnson* [1978] 1 WLR 683 and *Chandler* v *Kerley* [1978] 1 WLR 693.

It should be noted that there are no hard and fast legal rules in this area of the law. The courts tend to work backwards. Once it is decided what an acceptable outcome would be, the courts fit the acts of the parties into a legal framework which produces the desired result. Money paid by one party to another can be construed as supporting a contractual licence or an estoppel (see section 13.5) or a resulting trust, whichever result would be the most appropriate in the circumstances. Megarry and Wade conclude at page 1053:

> '... the contractual licence was employed as a flexible device for achieving an equitable result.'

Successors in title

Prior to 1952 it was clear law that a contractual licence could not bind a successor in title of the licensor, on the basis that a licence was a personal transaction which created no proprietary interest in land. In *Clore* v *Theatrical Properties Ltd* [1936] 3 All ER 483 a licence had been granted to sellers of refreshments allowing them the exclusive use of refreshment rooms at a theatre. A new owner of the theatre was able to prevent an assignee of the licensee from enforcing this right. The Court of Appeal held that the appropriate remedy was damages against the licensor (ie the contractual licence did not bind a third party). See also *King* v *David Allen & Sons Billposting Ltd* [1916] 2 AC 54.

The first signs of a new approach came with the Court of Appeal decision in *Errington* v *Errington & Woods* [1952] 1 KB 290. There the Court of Appeal held that a contractual licence for the occupation of a dwelling house would bind a person to whom the licensor left the house by will, and that a contractual licence gave rise to an equitable interest in land which would bind all-comers except a purchaser of the legal estate without notice of the interest.

Thereafter, there was uncertainty as to whether or not such a licence bound a successor in title of the licensor. Some decisions went one way, others the other. For example, in *Midland Bank Ltd* v *Farmpride Hatcheries Ltd* [1981] 260 EG 493 the Court of Appeal followed the 'new approach' and assumed that contractual licences were capable of binding successors in title as equitable interests. In contrast in *Binions* v *Evans* [1972] Ch 359 Stephenson LJ left open:

> '... the vexed question whether a contractual licence has been elevated to a status equivalent to an estate or interest in land.'

However, the matter was seemingly determined in *Ashburn Anstalt* v *Arnold* [1988] 2 All ER 147 where the Court of Appeal held obiter that a contractual licence did not create an interest in land capable of binding third parties (even a third party with notice) and disapproved of *Errington* v *Errington & Woods* on this point. The fact that *Ashburn Anstalt* v *Arnold* has been overruled by the House of Lords in *Prudential Assurance Co Ltd* v *London Residuary Body* [1992] 3 WLR 279 on an aspect of formalities of leases in no way affects the obiter on contractual licences. The fact that a contractual licence almost certainly does not now bind a third party means that it is a less attractive licence to establish from the perspective of a licensee.

13.5 Licences protected by estoppel or in equity

The equitable doctrines of estoppel and the constructive trust have been increasingly used by the courts to protect the position of licensees where it would be contrary to justice to allow strict legal principles to be applied. The courts are very flexible in their approach, and once the licensee has established that equity should intervene on his behalf the court will then consider how best to protect him. In effect the licence is made irrevocable or binding on third parties, but this result may be achieved by giving the licensee a recognised legal or equitable interest in the land. So a licensee may be held to be entitled to a full fee simple or a tenancy or an irrevocable licence under a constructive trust.

The equitable doctrines which empower the courts to interfere in this manner with established property rights are proprietary estoppel, constructive trusts, and mutual benefit and burden. These are all described below.

Proprietary estoppel

This is a type of estoppel which operates to prevent the revocation of a right affecting land which one party has been led by the other to believe to be permanent. When A, the owner of land, allows B to expend money on that land or otherwise act to his detriment under an expectation created or encouraged by A that he will be allowed to remain on the land or acquire an interest in the land, then A will not be allowed to defeat that expectation and deny B's right to remain on or to acquire an interest in the land. The principle was first expressed in this form in a dissenting judgment in *Ramsden* v *Dyson* (1866) LR 1 HL 129. In such problems a first requirement is to identify the necessary estoppel factor, which may be some active encouragement to proceed and/or the expenditure of money.

Proprietary estoppel differs from promissory estoppel (as propounded in *Central London Property Trust* v *High Trees House Ltd* [1947] KB 130) in that it acts as both a sword and a shield. In other words it can found a cause of action as well as a defence. As a sword, proprietary estoppel allows the promisee to enforce a promise to convey a legal estate, or convey an interest in land, or grant an irrevocable licence, where the promise would be unenforceable under normal land law principles. As a shield, proprietary estoppel protects the promisee from the exercise of the promisor's full legal rights, by raising an equity which the court must protect by the grant of an appropriate estate, interest or status in the land. See Cumming-Bruce LJ in *Pascoe* v *Turner* [1979] 1 WLR 431:

> 'One distinction between this class of case and the doctrine which has become known as promissory estoppel is that where estoppel by encouragement or acquiescence is found on the facts, those facts give rise to a cause of action. They can be relied upon as a sword not merely as a shield.'

The cases outlined below show how the doctrine has been applied. In many of the cases it will be seen that the estoppel factor is raised by the expenditure of money on the land of another person.

In *Dillwyn* v *Llewellyn* (1862) 4 De GF & J 517 a father gave possession of land to his son and attempted to convey the fee simple to him in writing. The son entered on the land and, with his father's assent, spent £14,000 on building a house for himself there. The father left the son only a life interest in the land by his will. After his father's death, the son claimed to be entitled to the full fee simple. The House of Lords held that the father's representations, together with the son's expenditure, gave the son the right to call for the imperfect transaction to be perfected, and the full fee simple should be vested in him. In this case the estoppel factor was the spending of the money by the son on building the house, together with the acquiescence of his father in his doing so.

In *Bannister* v *Bannister* [1948] 2 All ER 133 it was held that an irrevocable licence for life arose through proprietary estoppel, and that as the interest of the licensee fell within the definition set out in s20(1)(iv) SLA 1925, of 'a tenant for years determinable on life, not holding merely under a lease at a rent', she became a tenant for life under the SLA and was entitled to have the legal title vested in her (with the coming into force of the Trusts of Land and Appointment of Trustees Act 1996 on 1 January 1997 no new strict settlement can be created on or after that date).

This decision has been criticised, as the licensee acquired a far greater interest in the land than could have been intended, and it has not generally been followed, the minority judgment of Lord Denning in *Binions* v *Evans* [1972] Ch 359 being preferred. On the other hand the majority of the Court of Appeal in *Binions* v *Evans* did adopt this decision in spite of the consequences this could have had prior to 1 January 1997 under the SLA 1925.

In *Hopgood* v *Brown* [1955] 1 WLR 213, A and B owned adjoining plots of land. It was agreed between them that A could build a garage up to a certain boundary line. The garage in fact stood partly on B's land. B's successor in title claimed possession of that part of the land occupied by A's garage. The Court of Appeal refused possession. B was estopped by his conduct and A's expenditure from asserting his strict legal rights. A's bare licence was converted into either an irrevocable licence or an easement binding on B's successor in title because the latter had constructive notice of the encroachment from the title deeds.

The situation in *Inwards* v *Baker* [1965] 2 QB 29 began in 1931 when, at A's suggestion, B built a bungalow on A's land under the impression that he would be allowed to live there as long as he wished (the estoppel factor). A died in 1951. The trustees of his will were aware of B's occupation and allowed B to stay there until 1963 when they sought possession. Possession was refused by the Court of Appeal on the grounds that B had acquired, as against A, an irrevocable licence arising by proprietary estoppel. The licence gave B the right to remain in occupation for his lifetime. The trustees (A's successors in title) were bound by B's licence because they had acquiesced in B's continued occupation after they had notice of it. Lord Denning MR said:

> '... if the owner of land requests another, or indeed allows another, to expend money on the land under an expectation created or encouraged by the (owner of the land) that he will be able to remain there, that raises an equity in the licensee such as to entitle him to stay.'

In *Crabb* v *Arun District Council* [1976] Ch 179 the plaintiff owned two plots of land, only one of which (plot A) had an exit to the highway. In reliance upon the defendants' assurance that he would be allowed a right of way across their land onto the highway from plot B, the plaintiff sold plot A without reserving a right of way across it from plot B to the exit. There was no formal grant of an easement by the defendants. Shortly afterwards, the defendants fenced off the exit points from plot B, which they had themselves installed. The plaintiff sought an injunction. The Court of Appeal held that the defendants were estopped from going back on their assurance and that the interest that the plaintiff should be granted was a right of way across the defendants' land free of charge. Lord Denning MR took the opportunity to restate the fundamental principle as follows.

> '... the first principle upon which all courts of equity proceed, that is, to prevent a person from insisting on his strict legal rights ... when it would be inequitable for him to do so having regard to the dealings which have taken place between the parties'.

The case of *Pascoe* v *Turner* [1979] 1 WLR 431 dealt with the situation where, upon leaving his mistress (the defendant) for another woman, the plaintiff told her that the house they had shared (of which he held the fee simple) was hers, as was everything in it. He later repeated this assurance. In reliance upon this, the mistress spent money on furnishings and decoration, with the acquiescence of the plaintiff. Later the plaintiff sought possession, having purported to terminate the defendant's licence. The Court of Appeal held that the plaintiff's promise, together with the defendant's expenditure and the plaintiff's acquiescence in that expenditure, allowed the defendant to set up a proprietary estoppel. The defendant's equitable rights arising under that estoppel could only be satisfied by the grant to her of the fee simple of the house. Cumming-Bruce LJ concluded:

> '... the equity to which the facts in this case give rise can only be satisfied by compelling the plaintiff to give effect to his promise and her expectations. He has so acted that he must now perfect the gift. The plaintiff is ordered to execute a conveyance forthwith at his expense, transferring the estate to the defendant.'

In *Greasley* v *Cooke* [1980] 1 WLR 1306 Lord Denning MR further explored the detriment which must be suffered by the promisee to found proprietary estoppel. In 1938 the defendant, aged 16, came to live as a maidservant in a house occupied by a widower, his three sons, Kenneth, Hedley and Howard, and his mentally retarded daughter. After 1946 Kenneth and the defendant lived together as man and wife. From 1948 onwards the defendant received no wages, but continued to look after the house and nursed the daughter until she died in 1975. She had been given vague assurances by Kenneth and Hedley that she had taken to mean that she could live in the house as long as she wished, but after Kenneth's death in 1975, Hedley and Howard's daughters, in whom the house vested, sought possession. The Court of Appeal held:

1. The statements by Kenneth and Hedley were sufficient to amount to assurances for the purposes of proprietary estoppel.
2. That being so there was a rebuttable presumption that the defendant acted on the faith of those assurances, and it was for the plaintiffs to provide evidence that she did not.
3. There must be some detriment, but the expenditure of money was not a necessary element of such detriment. It was sufficient that the party to whom the assurance was given acted on the faith of it in circumstances in which it would be unjust and inequitable for the party making the assurance to go back on it.

The case is particularly noteworthy for the view of Lord Denning that while in most cases there will be expenditure of money that is not an indispensable element of estoppel. Here the remedy to give effect to the estoppel was that the defendant was entitled to remain in the house for so long as she wished.

Once an estoppel has been established can it be lost by virtue of the licensee's conduct? There is no conclusive authority on this point. However, the matter was considered in *Williams* v *Staite* [1978] 2 WLR 825. There the defendant had been held in previous proceedings to be entitled to an irrevocable licence for life, arising through proprietary estoppel and binding on the plaintiff's predecessor in title. The plaintiff purchased with notice of the licence. The issue was whether the defendant's behaviour (swearing at the plaintiff, blocking one entrance and committing other acts calculated to reduce the plaintiff's enjoyment of his property) entitled the plaintiff to revoke the licence. The Court of Appeal held:

1. The defendant's behaviour was not sufficiently improper to lead the court to deprive him of the equitable relief he sought, but there could be circumstances in which the court would refuse to restrain the revocation of an equitable licence. Thus certain conduct could make an irrevocable licence revocable, but that conduct did not arise in this case.
2. Where a party is seeking to establish a right to an *equitable licence* (rather than claiming protection for an existing licence) then the court must take that party's conduct into account in determining whether a sufficient answer to his equity has been made out by the other party. In other words the courts may refuse to recognise and enforce rights claimed under proprietary estoppel if there has been serious misconduct by the claimant.

In essence the Court took the view that an estoppel could be lost by conduct but only in exceptional circumstances.

In *Matharu* v *Matharu* (1994) 68 P & CR 93 the doctrine was used to give a widow a licence to occupy a house for life. In that case the plaintiff owned a house in which his son and daughter-in-law (the defendant) were living. The house was in the plaintiff's sole name. The son carried out extensive improvements to the house at his own expense with the plaintiff's approval. In 1991 the son died. Up until 1990 the defendant had assumed that the house was owned by her husband. Further, she claimed that she was encouraged in that belief by the plaintiff. During 1991 the defendant, at her own expense, installed a modern kitchen in the house. Subsequently the plaintiff claimed possession. The Court of Appeal held that the defendant was able to establish proprietary estoppel. However, on the facts the defendant had no beneficial interest in the property (there had been no common intention between the plaintiff, defendant and her husband that the property was to be shared beneficially). The defendant's equity could be satisfied by giving her a licence to remain in the house for life (or such shorter period as she might decide) provided that she was responsible for the outgoings on the house and kept the premises in good decorative repair. Accordingly, the plaintiff was unable to gain possession of the house.

The question whether an equitable interest arising under the doctrine of proprietary estoppel was exempt from overreaching fell to be considered in *Birmingham Midshires Mortgage Services Ltd* v *Sabherwal* (2000) P & CR 256. There the Court of Appeal concluded that an equitable interest arising under the doctrine was as much subject to overreaching as one arising from a trust. S relied upon two cases – *Shiloh Spinners Ltd* v *Harding* [1973] AC 691 and *E R Ives Investment Ltd* v *High* [1967] 2 QB 379 – in contending that an equitable right acquired by proprietary estoppel was exempt from overreaching. The former concerned an equitable right of entry, the latter an equitable easement. Although both these equitable rights were held to be outside the registration provisions and incapable of being overreached, the Court noted that neither could sensibly shift from the land affected by it to the proceeds of sale, whereas an equitable interest as a tenant in common (even if accompanied, as here, by the promise of a home for life) could, because the proceeds of sale could be used to acquire another home. To overreach an equitable right of entry and an equitable easement would have been to destroy them. Further, it would be a 'remarkable result' if the more precarious equitable right arising as a result of estoppel was not capable of being overreached, but any equitable right based on a direct financial contribution arising under a resulting trust could. Accordingly, the submissions made in reliance upon *Shiloh* and *E R Ives* were baseless.

Evidence of estoppel may be based on future prospective rights
The principle of proprietary estoppel is not limited to acts done in reliance on a belief relating to an existing right, but can be invoked to establish a right to property when the owner dies even though the property in question has been left by will to someone else. In *Re Basham (Deceased)* [1986] 1 WLR 1498 the court concluded

that on the facts the plaintiff had established that she had acted to her detriment in reliance on her belief, encouraged by the deceased, that she would ultimately benefit by receiving the deceased's property when he died. Accordingly, she was absolutely and beneficially entitled to the whole of the deceased's estate.

However, the doctrine of proprietary estoppel as explained in *Re Basham (Deceased)* seemed to suggest that it was enough for the promisee to act to his detriment on the promise even if the promisor (testator) did not realise he was doing so. Under this view of the matter it was necessary for the promisor to have encouraged the promisee's belief but not necessarily to have been aware of the promisee's action in reliance on that belief (ie an equity could arise over the promisor's estate without his knowledge). However, in *Gillett v Holt and Another* [1998] 3 All ER 917 Carnwath J questioned whether the judge in *Re Basham (Deceased)* had intended that to be the effect of his judgment. Rather in order to be bound Carnwath J concluded that the testator had to be aware that the promisee was acting to his detriment in reliance on his promise. There H made repeated promises and assurances to G over many years to the effect that he intended to transfer his farm by will to G. Following a new will in favour of the second defendant and excluding G completely, G sought equitable relief on the basis of proprietary estoppel (he claimed that H was bound by proprietary estoppel to bequeath substantially the whole of his estate to him). At first instance, G's action was dismissed. Carnwath J held that to establish proprietary estoppel it was necessary to show words and conduct going beyond a mere statement of intention and amounting to an irrevocable promise. G appealed. In allowing the appeal (*Gillett v Holt and Another* [2000] 2 All ER 289) the Court of Appeal emphasised that at the heart of proprietary estoppel was the fundamental principle that equity was concerned to prevent unconscionable conduct. It was necessary to look at a given claim 'in the round'. Here the assurances of H had been repeated over a long period of time and were unambiguous. They were intended to be relied upon and were relied upon by G to his detriment. Further, it was not necessary for them to be irrevocable. Equity could intervene to render an assurance irrevocable when the claimant had relied on the representations and suffered detriment in consequence. Here the assurances gave rise to an enforceable claim based on proprietary estoppel.

If the occupiers of a property carry out repairs and improvements which enhance the value of the property, they can only claim an interest in that property if they can prove they had acted in the belief that they would acquire an interest in the property and that belief had been encouraged by the landlord. In *Brinnand v Ewens* (1987) 19 HLR 415 no such belief could be proved. In his judgment Nourse LJ set out four ingredients which were necessary to establish proprietary estoppel:

1. The claimant must show that he had prejudiced himself or acted to his detriment.
2. Acting in that way must have taken place in the belief either that he had sufficient interest in the property or that he would obtain such an interest.

3. The belief must have been encouraged by the owner of the land or others acting on his behalf – this may be considered as the estoppel factor.
4. There must be no bar to the equity.

The courts continue to explore the limits of proprietary estoppel. In *J T Developments* v *Quinn* (1991) 62 P & CR 33 the Court of Appeal held that a proprietary estoppel could arise out of negotiations even where there was no binding agreement for a lease. Prior to the Land Registration Act 2002 such an estoppel appeared to be binding on third parties as an overriding interest under s70(1)(g) LRA 1925. The position under the 2002 Act is completely clear. It states in s116(a) LRA 2002 that an 'equity by estoppel' has effect 'from the time the equity arises as an interest capable of binding successors in title'. Accordingly, an equity of estoppel if supported with actual occupation by the claimant will override registered dispositions by virtue of Sch 3 of the Act. Finally, in the case of unregistered land it appears that such an estoppel is binding on third parties by virtue of the rules of notice.

Constructive trusts

The courts have also protected a licence by means of imposing a constructive trust on purchasers with notice of the licence. This was first developed by Lord Denning MR in his dissenting judgment in *Binions* v *Evans* [1972] Ch 359.

The defendant had been given a right to live in a cottage rent-free for the rest of her life on terms that only she was entitled to give notice. She was responsible for some repairs. The cottage was sold to the plaintiffs expressly subject to her right to live there, and the plaintiffs paid a lower price because of this. When the plaintiffs sought possession it was refused, the majority of the Court of Appeal following *Bannister* v *Bannister* [1948] 2 All ER 133 and holding that the true construction of the arrangement was that the defendant became a tenant for life under the Settled Land Act 1925 by virtue of s20(1)(iv), and that her interest had not been overreached on sale.

Lord Denning's minority reasoning was as follows:

1. The initial grant had been of no more than a contractual licence, revocable by the defendant.
2. The sale to the plaintiffs with express notice of and subject to the licence and at a lower price as a result meant that an equity arose, which took the form of a constructive trust imposed on the plaintiffs at the time of purchase to hold the cottage on trust for the defendant to occupy it for the rest of her life. Consequently the plaintiffs were not entitled to possession.

Constructive trusts have been used by the courts where the person seeking to revoke the licence is a successor in title of the licensor (as in *Binions* v *Evans*). The reason for this is that proprietary estoppel, strictly speaking, cannot be maintained against a third party who did not make the representations. But a constructive trust can be imposed upon a successor in title where it would be inequitable to allow him to disregard any rights the licensee might have.

Constructive trusts are exempted by s53(2) LPA 1925 from the requirement that the creation or disposition of equitable interests must be evidenced in writing. A constructive trust was used to bind a successor in title of the licensor in *Re Sharpe* (*A Bankrupt*) [1980] 1 WLR 219 where the original agreement had been oral. There the successor in title was the licensor's trustee in bankruptcy, who was bound by the bankrupt's equitable obligations, but not by merely contractual obligations.

In *Grant* v *Edwards* [1986] 3 WLR 114 the Court of Appeal held that where an unmarried couple lived in a house which was in *one name only* then the other party was entitled to a beneficial interest in the property if a constructive trust could be established by showing that it would be inequitable for the legal owner to claim sole beneficial ownership. It was possible to establish such a constructive trust by showing a common intention that both parties should have a beneficial interest together with the fact that the claimant had acted to his or her detriment on the basis of this common intention, believing that by so acting a beneficial interest would be obtained. On the facts there was the necessary common intention, and the plaintiff had acted to her detriment by making formal contributions to the household expenses, thus releasing money to make necessary mortgage repayments.

Some confusion as to the role of a constructive trust may have arisen from the decision of the House of Lords in *Lloyds Bank plc* v *Rosset* [1990] 2 WLR 867. Traditionally the courts have assumed that when a spouse or party not on the legal title to a property makes a *direct contribution* to its acquisition that will give rise to a *purchase money resulting trust*. However, in the latter case the House of Lords seemed to regard direct contributions as giving rise to a *constructive trust*. Lord Bridge put the matter thus:

> 'Direct contributions to ... [the] ... purchase price by ... [a] ... partner ... not the legal owner whether initially or by payment of mortgage instalments would readily justify ... the creation of a constructive trust ... [it is] ... extremely doubtful whether anything less would do.'

However, this is contrary to established principles (see Chapter 9, section 9.4 and in particular *Drake* v *Whipp* [1996] 1 FLR 826). Apart from this apparent confusion between resulting and constructive trusts, Lord Bridge in addition articulated a rather restrictive approach to the imposition of constructive trusts. He put the matter thus:

> 'The first and fundamental question which must always be resolved is whether, independently of an inference to be drawn from the conduct of the parties in the course of sharing the house as their home and managing their joint affairs, there has at any time prior to acquisition, or exceptionally at some later date, been any agreement, arrangement or understanding reached between them that the property is to be shared beneficially. The finding of an agreement or arrangement to share in this sense can only, I think, be based

on evidence of express discussions between the partners, however imperfectly remembered and however imprecise their terms may have been. Once a finding to this effect is made it will only be necessary for the partner asserting a claim to a beneficial interest against the partner entitled to the legal estate to show that he or she has acted to his or her detriment or significantly altered his or her position in reliance on the agreement in order to give rise to a constructive trust or proprietary estoppel.'

The courts are still exploring the limits of proprietary estoppel but take care not to extend the principle too far. This caution was seen in *Layton* v *Martin* [1986] 2 FLR 227.

So far there has been no decision dealing with the issue of whether a successor in title without notice is bound. As the licence by estoppel becomes established as a new right in alieno solo, a question to be considered is whether it should continue to rely upon the doctrine of notice for protection against third parties. A possible solution, which would have avoided the pre 1 January 1997 complications of the Settled Land Act 1925 and still give protection to the licensee against subsequent purchasers of the land, would be for the licence to become registrable under the Land Charges Act 1972. The advantage of such a procedure can be seen in cases with facts like those of *Inwards* v *Baker* [1965] 2 QB 29. A similar solution was adopted under what is now the Matrimonial Homes Act 1983 to protect the right of a deserted spouse to occupy the matrimonial home.

There is little doubt that this reliance upon the equitable doctrine of notice undermines the objects of the 1925 property legislation, which was designed to simplify conveyancing by collecting together as many third party rights as possible within the land charges register.

The lease-substitute aspect of the licence could also be seen to be undermining the legislation relating to security of tenure by creating 'sham' licences. This aspect received severe criticism from the House of Lords in *Street* v *Mountford* [1985] 2 WLR 877; that decision restores the role of the Rent Act in affording security of tenure to tenants. There are counter-views to this idea of making licences by estoppel registrable as land charges, and Cheshire at pages 660, 661 is strongly critical of the idea:

'... licences have been held not to be registrable under the Land Charges Act (1972). Indeed it would be a disaster for the licensee if they were ... if they were registrable and not registered they would be void against a purchaser who actually knew of the licence.'

No doubt a similar argument could be advanced in respect of the deserted spouse, but registration does bring certainty into an area where there is a singular lack of certainty at present.

In the case of land with registered title, as previously noted there is no doubt that a licence by estoppel will bind a successor in title of the licensor (s116(a) LRA 2002).

Mutual benefit and burden

Equity will also enforce a licence against successors in title with notice where the original licence also conferred a benefit on the licensor which the successor in title is enjoying. See *E R Ives Investments Ltd* v *High* [1967] 2 QB 379.

In these circumstances, the successor in title is not entitled to take the benefit acquired through the licence without submitting to the burden imposed by the licence. The rule was described by Lord Denning in *E R Ives* as follows:

'When adjoining owners of land make an agreement to secure continuing rights and benefits for each of them in or over the land of the other, neither of them can take the benefit of the agreement and throw over the burden of it.'

The application of a similar benefit and burden rule in relation to positive covenants was seen in *Halsall* v *Brizell* [1957] Ch 169 (see Chapter 11).

14

Mortgages

14.1 Introduction

14.2 Creation of a mortgage

14.3 Legal and equitable mortgages

14.4 The right to redeem and the equity of redemption

14.5 The rights of the mortgagor

14.6 Redemption

14.7 The rights of the mortgagee to enforce his security: remedies of the mortgagee

14.8 The remedies of the legal mortgagee

14.9 The remedies of the equitable mortgagee

14.10 Other rights of the mortgagee

14.11 The right to tack further advances

14.12 The right to consolidate

14.13 The rights common to both parties

14.14 Priority of mortgages

14.15 Priority of mortgages of an equitable interest

14.1 Introduction

A mortgage was defined by Lindley MR in *Santley* v *Wilde* [1899] 2 Ch 474 as:

> '... a conveyance of land or an assignment of chattels as security for the payment of a debt
> or the discharge of some other obligation for which it is given'.

The person who borrows the money and provides the security is called the *mortgagor*
and the person who lends the money the *mortgagee*. It is important to remember that
a mortgage is a security for money lent.

If the mortgagor has a legal interest in property and he gives the mortgagee a legal interest by way of security, then the mortgage is legal. If the mortgagor has merely an equitable interest, for example the beneficial interest of the tenant for life under the SLA 1925, then the mortgage must be equitable. A mortgagor with a legal interest can, however, create an equitable mortgage of that legal interest. The type of mortgage depends on what the mortgagee gets, not necessarily on what the mortgagor has.

In considering the law relating to mortgages the statutory rules set out in ss85–120 Law of Property Act 1925 should be considered as well as the extensive case law on the subject.

14.2 Creation of a mortgage

By s85 LPA 1925 a mortgage made after 1925 could be made *in one of two ways*:

1. By demise for a term of years absolute.
2. By charge of deed expressed to be by way of legal mortgage: s87 LPA 1925.

By demise for a term of years absolute

The mortgage is made in the form of a lease of the mortgagor's property with a proviso (known as the proviso for cesser on redemption) that the lease should be determined when the mortgage is redeemed, that is, when all the capital and interest are paid off. If the mortgage is of a freehold the term of the lease is usually 3,000 years, if of a leasehold then the mortgage is a sublease for about ten days less than the mortgagor's unexpired term.

Subsequent mortgages are created by granting a lease (or sublease in the case of mortgages of leaseholds) for at least one day longer than the previous mortgage.

A mortgage which purports to be by way of conveyance of the fee simple operates as a mortgage by demise for a term of 3,000 years (s85(2) LPA 1925). Under the Land Registration Act 2002 mortgages of registered land can no longer be created by demise or sub-demise (s23(1) LRA 2002). Rather the charge is now the only method of creating a mortgage over registered land.

By charge by deed expressed to be by way of legal mortgage: s87 LPA 1925

This method of creating a mortgage was first introduced by the LPA 1925, and is usually called a 'legal charge'. It is a simpler document than the mortgage by demise, but it imposes exactly the same rights on both mortgagor and mortgagee. Its main advantage is that freeholds and leaseholds can be mortgaged together in one document, which is not possible when the mortgage is by demise. The legal charge is a legal interest within s1(2)(c) LPA 1925 and will not be in breach of a covenant against subleasing which would be true of a mortgage by demise of leasehold property.

Even prior to the Land Registration Act 2002 the charge by deed was the method of creation more frequently used. Indeed, the lease method of creation was rarely encountered.

14.3 Legal and equitable mortgages

Legal mortgages

By virtue of the LRA 2002 a legal mortgage can now only be created by way of a legal charge and only in respect of a legal estate.

Equitable mortgages

An equitable mortgage which may be of either the legal estate or an equitable interest can be created in one of the following ways:

A mortgage of an equitable interest is always equitable. Such a mortgage can be made by conveyance of the whole equitable interest with a proviso for reconveyance on redemption. The mortgage need not be by deed, but it must be in writing signed by the mortgagor or his agent (s53 LPA 1925).

A mortgage of a legal estate not made by deed must be equitable. It acts as a contract to create a legal mortgage when made in writing and signed by or on behalf of both parties to the mortgage. See s2 Law of Property (Miscellaneous Provisions) Act 1989. Equity treats it as an actual mortgage, provided that the money has actually been advanced.

Formerly the deposit of title deeds was treated as an act of part performance, but the repeal of s40(2) LPA 1925 by s2 Law of Property (Miscellaneous Provisions) Act 1989 has seen the end of this form of equitable mortgage. This was confirmed in *United Bank of Kuwait plc* v *Sahib and Others* [1996] 3 All ER 215. There the Court of Appeal held that the deposit of title deeds (or land certificate in the case of registered land) took effect as a contract to mortgage and fell within s2 of the 1989 Act. Since there was no written document here the mere deposit of the land certificate by way of security could not create a mortgage or charge. To create a valid equitable charge by a deposit of title deeds or the land certificate there had to be a written mortgage agreement meeting the requirements of s2 of the 1989 Act. In practice the deposit of title deeds was usually accompanied by a written agreement in order to make the parties' intentions clear.

However, following the de-materialisation of deeds under the Land Registration Act 2002, the Land Registry no longer issue either land certificates or charges certificates. Consequently, the previous practice of creating an equitable mortgage by depositing a land certificate, effectively creating a lien on the deeds, is no longer possible.

Finally, to protect an equitable mortgage of registered land the mortgagee should register a notice under the LRA 2002 against the title in question.

Evaluation

The method of creating mortgages was simplified by the 1925 legislation. However, the whole process was still cumbersome. The process was further simplified by the LRA 2002 by virtue of which legal mortgages no longer involve a conveyance of the fee simple but instead, as noted above, are created by a legal charge (formerly they could also be created by a demise for a term of years). However, the fact that English law still recognises the creation of equitable mortgages means that the law of mortgages suffers from the same defects which were apparent in land law prior to the 1925 legislation, namely a plethora of interests both legal and equitable which can exist in the same piece of land.

Other consequences of recognising legal and equitable mortgages are: (i) two different schemes of protection; and (ii) complex rules for determining priorities of mortgages under the unregistered land regime. Legal mortgagees either protect themselves by taking title deeds, registering legal charges or puisne mortgagees (C(i) land charge), whereas equitable mortgagees have to register general equitable charges (C(iii)). Under the LRA 2002 a first legal mortgage triggers compulsory registration. The legal mortgage, in order to be protected, must be entered on the register as the legal charge. Where recognition is required for protection the normal rules apply making a mortgage void against a subsequent purchaser for want of registration. In consequence of the different types of mortgage, complex rules have evolved governing the determination of priorities between competing mortgages. Generally speaking, legal mortgages prevail over equitable, and the first in time has priority. Equitable mortgages are governed by the rule in *Dearle* v *Hall* (1828) 3 Russ 1 (as amended by ss138 and 139 LPA 1925) which provides that priority depends upon the order in which notice of the mortgages is received by the owner of the legal estate.

The aforementioned criticisms of the law of mortgages led the Law Commission in its Working Paper (*Land Mortgages*: Working Paper No 99) published in 1986 and in its 1991 Report (Law Com No 204) to recommend that all the existing methods of creating mortgages be abolished and replaced by a Formal Land Mortgage created by statute. Implementing the Commission's recommendation would have at least three main benefits. First, it would remedy the plethora of interests both legal and equitable which can exist at present in relation to the same piece of land. Second, the adoption of a single statutory mortgage which must be registered would eradicate a lot of the problems which currently arise as to priorities between competing mortgages. Third, the adoption of a single form of statutory mortgage would render the differing forms and methods of protection unnecessary.

14.4 The right to redeem and the equity of redemption

The right to redeem is the mortgagor's right to pay off all the capital and interest owing under the mortgage and take his land free from the mortgagee's rights. There are two distinct rights to redeem.

1. The *legal right to redeem* is the contractual right at law to redeem on the precise day fixed by the mortgage, neither before nor after. At common law, if the mortgage was not redeemed on the precise day fixed then the mortgagee took the land. Hence the intervention of equity to protect the mortgagor.
2. The *equitable right to redeem* is the right conferred by equity to redeem at any time after the legal date of redemption has passed on reasonable terms. Because of this right, it is possible for the legal date of redemption to be fixed for a day shortly after the mortgage is created (normally six months), although both parties intend that the mortgage should not in fact be redeemed for many years. An early legal date of redemption is normally specified in the mortgage deed because certain of the mortgagee's remedies do not arise until that date has passed.

The equitable right to redeem is not the same as the equity of redemption. The 'equity of redemption' is the total of the mortgagor's rights in the property given by equity, which arise as soon as the mortgage is made. The equity of redemption is an interest in land which can be dealt with just like any other interest in land. The two may be demonstrated in this way:

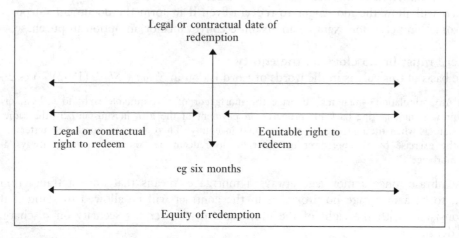

The language of the mortgage sometimes creates difficulties because of the date inserted in the mortgage deed when the money must be repaid. A literal interpretation of the mortgage would indicate that if the borrower failed to repay the mortgage on this date, he would forfeit the land. This is contrary to the concept that the land is no more than a security for the loan, and even though this contractual date for repayment has passed the borrower will be allowed to repay the loan and have the title to the land restored in his name free from the mortgage. It is this right that is known as the 'equitable right to redeem'. The sum of the contractual and equitable rights of the mortgagor are known as his 'equity of redemption'. In *Kreglinger* v *New Patagonia Meat and Cold Storage Co Ltd* [1914] AC 25 Lord Parker put the matter thus:

> 'The equity to redeem, which arises on failure to exercise the contractual right of redemption, must be carefully distinguished from the equitable estate which, from the first, remains in the mortgagor, and is sometimes referred to as an equity of redemption.'

14.5 The rights of the mortgagor

The right of redemption

Since a mortgage is only a security, any provision which prevents or unduly restricts the right of redemption is void as repugnant to the true nature of the transaction; the maxim is 'once a mortgage always a mortgage'. Equity will protect the mortgagor's rights of redemption from any attempt by the mortgagee to prevent the mortgagor from redeeming the mortgage. This takes the form of the following two rules:

The test of a mortgage is in substance not form

If the transaction is in substance a mortgage, it will be treated as such by equity, which will allow the mortgagor to redeem even if in form the document purports to be something else, for example an absolute conveyance or an option to purchase.

There must be no clogs on the equity

The basis of this rule is in the words of Lord Eldon in *Seton* v *Slade* (1802) 7 Ves 265:

> 'Any stipulation which may deprive the mortgagor of his equitable right to redeem or prevent him getting back his property on payment of the loan in substantially the same state as when the mortgage is made is void in equity. There must be no clog or fetter on the exercise by the borrower of the right to redeem, ie "once a mortgage always a mortgage".'

The phrase 'once a mortgage always a mortgage' means that once a transaction is seen to be a mortgage no provision in the contract will be allowed to stand if it is inconsistent with the right of the mortgagor to recover his security on discharging his debt.

This rule as to clogs on the equity of redemption may be dealt with under three headings:

1. The mortgage must not be irredeemable – 'once a mortgage always a mortgage'.
2. The mortgagor must be able to redeem free from conditions in the mortgage (the equity of redemption must not be clogged).
3. Rights of the mortgagor under the Consumer Credit Act 1974.

The mortgage must not be irredeemable – 'once a mortgage always a mortgage'.
Equity will not allow any term in a mortgage which expressly makes a mortgage irredeemable or redeemable only by a limited class of persons or for a limited period. Similarly, it will not allow a term which has the effect of preventing or limiting redemption. A term in a mortgage which gives the mortgagee an option to purchase the mortgaged property is void even if it is not oppressive. See *Samuel* v *Jarrah Timber and Wood Paving Corporation Ltd* [1904] AC 323 and *Lewis* v *Frank Love Ltd* [1961] 1 WLR 261. However, once the mortgage has been made, equity will not interfere if the mortgagor then gives the mortgagee such an option. The time between the two events must be at least one day. See *Reeve* v *Lisle* [1902] AC 461.

The right to redeem can be postponed. However, equity will not allow the right to be postponed for such a period of time that the right becomes illusory. The cases of *Fairclough* v *Swan Brewery Ltd* [1912] AC 565 and *Knightsbridge Estates Trusts Ltd* v *Byrne* [1939] Ch 441 illustrate clearly the approach of equity in this regard. The reason why a mortgagee may insert a term postponing the date of redemption is to ensure that the mortage will run for a minimum period of time. It is important to emphasise that a term postponing the right to redeem is usually only found in a commercial mortgage, not a domestic one. In *Fairclough* v *Swan Brewery Ltd*, F was the lessee for 17½ years (being the residue of a term of 20 years) of a hotel owned by the brewery company which he mortgaged to them to secure £500. The mortgage contained a clause postponing the contractual right of redemption for the whole of the residue of the term less six weeks. F also covenanted not to purchase beer from anyone other than the mortgagee brewery during the life of the mortgage. F offered to redeem and claimed to be free to purchase beer elsewhere, arguing that the covenant was void on the ground that it was a clog on his equity of redemption and he was entitled to redeem as a consequence. The Privy Council held that the provision rendered the equitable right to redeem illusory and was thus void. F was allowed to redeem after only three years.

In *Knightsbridge Estates Trusts Ltd* v *Byrne* the plaintiff company mortgaged to the defendants several freehold properties to secure a loan of £310,000. The mortgagors covenanted to repay the loan with interest by eight half-yearly instalments and not to redeem within the period of forty years, and the mortgagees covenanted that if instalments were so paid and if the mortgagors did not commit any breach of their obligations, the mortgagees would not require payment otherwise than by such instalments. The plaintiffs then claimed the right to redeem within the 40 years. The Court of Appeal held that a postponement of the contractual right to redeem for 40 years was not so unreasonable as to be void in equity. Sir Wilfred Greene MR concluded as follows:

'... equity may give relief against contractual terms in a mortgage transaction if they are oppressive or unconscionable and in deciding whether or not a particular transaction falls within this category, the length of time for which the contractual right to redeem is postponed may well be an important consideration. In the present case, no question of this kind was or could have been raised.

But, equity does not reform mortgage transactions because they are unreasonable. It is concerned to see two things – one that the essential requirements of a mortgage transaction are observed and the other that oppressive or unconscionable terms are not enforced. ...

The resulting agreement was a commercial agreement between two important corporations experienced in such matters and has none of the features of an oppressive bargain where the borrower is at the mercy of an unscrupulous lender. In transactions of this kind, it is notorious that there is competition among the large insurance companies and other bodies having large funds to invest and we are not prepared to view the agreement made as anything but a proper business transaction ...'

Here in contrast to the decision reached in *Fairclough* v *Swan Brewery* the Court concluded that the period of postponement – despite being 40 years – was not such as to render the right to redeem illusory. The former case concerned a mortgage of leasehold premises with the borrower being a private individual, whereas here the properties were freehold ones and the borrower was a company (with perpetual existence). The latter facts must have influenced the court in reaching the decision it did, together with the fact that this was a commercial agreement between two large corporations of equal bargaining strength (ie it was far removed from the situation of a vulnerable private individual borrower 'at the mercy of an unscrupulous lender'). The respective bargaining strength of the parties is invariably crucial in cases of this type because it is equity which protects the mortgagor's right of redemption from any attempt by the mortgagee to prevent the mortgagor from redeeming the mortgage.

The mortgagor must be able to redeem free from conditions in the mortgage (the equity of redemption must not be clogged). The basic purpose of a mortgage is to provide security for the repayment of the money lent by the mortgagee. However, in the case of commercial properties the lender may succeed in negotiating for some additional advantage (collateral advantages are not usually encountered in mortgages of domestic properties). For example, a brewery will often advance money on mortgage to the licensee of a public house, provided the borrower agrees to buy all his beer from the lending brewery. Comparable arrangements are often made between petrol companies and garage owners.

The original view of the courts was that all collateral advantages taken by a lender were void. This was because they were regarded as a disguised form of interest, contravening the old usury laws (see *Jennings* v *Ward* (1705) 2 Vern 520). In 1854 the last of the statutes dealing with usury was repealed and thereafter the attitude of the courts to collateral advantages began to change.

Equity divides collateral advantages into three classes. First, the collateral advantage may be held to be unconscionable and oppressive if it was imposed in a morally reprehensible way. In such a case the collateral advantage is void and therefore unenforceable even during the currency of the mortgage. In *Cityland &*

Property Holdings Ltd v *Dabrah* [1968] Ch 106 a term in the mortgage which imposed an extremely high premium, rather than requiring payment of interest, was held to be unenforceable as being oppressive and unreasonable because the whole balance of the premium and loan became immediately repayable on default. The mortgage was rewritten by the court.

Second, the collateral advantage may be regarded as fair and enforceable for the duration of the mortgage (many solus ties come within this second class). In *Biggs* v *Hoddinott* [1898] 2 Ch 307 a mortgage of a public house was granted by a brewer to a publican. The mortgage required the borrower to take all his beer from the mortgagee during the currency of the mortgage (ie a solus agreement).

The Court of Appeal upheld the collateral advantage as valid. Chitty LJ put the matter thus:

> 'The present appears to me to be a reasonable trade bargain between two businessmen who enter into it with their eyes open and it would be a fanciful doctrine of equity that would set it aside.' (p322)

So far as solus agreements are concerned, they come within the category of agreements in restraint of trade and must therefore be justified on the ground of reasonableness: see *Esso Petroleum Co Ltd* v *Harper's Garage (Stourport) Ltd* [1968] AC 269. Accordingly, in such cases, the test is unreasonableness not unconscionability. Equity will intervene if the solus agreement is unreasonable, ie an excessive restraint of trade.

Third, the collateral advantage may survive redemption of the mortgage. Normally a collateral advantage will not survive redemption of the mortgage (even if the mortgagor has agreed to a term that the collateral advantage shall continue beyond redemption), for otherwise the borrower would get back an estate encumbered in a way that the estate he mortgaged was not. Nevertheless, in the case of commercial mortgages entered into by parties bargaining on equal terms, the courts may be prepared to enforce a collateral advantage even after redemption by treating it as if it was a separate agreement, part of the consideration for entering the mortgage. The lead case in this regard is *Kreglinger* v *New Patagonia Meat Co Ltd* [1914] AC 25. There, a meat company mortgaged its property to a wool-broker. It was a term of the mortgage that the mortgagor would for five years offer its sheepskins to the mortgagee for purchase. Although the mortgage was redeemed after two years the House of Lords held that the option was valid even though it continued for three years after redemption. The option was regarded as being reasonable – it was for a short period of time and the mortgagee had to pay the best price for the sheepskins. The collateral advantage here was seen as forming part of a bigger commercial deal done between the two parties well capable of looking after their own interests (ie it was a separate agreement, not really part of the mortgage).

Equity endeavours to 'hold the ring' so far as collateral advantages are concerned. There is no rule of equity which prevents a mortgagee from stipulating for a collateral advantage. However, in certain circumstances, the courts will still be prepared to strike down a collateral advantage. The present position can be summarised as follows: a collateral advantage which exists until redemption can be valid, but will be struck down if it is oppressive or unconscionable; a collateral advantage which exists beyond redemption will be struck down unless it exists as an independent transaction.

There appears to be no objection to index-linked mortgages, even though the fluctuations in the respective values of the currency create a substantial rise in repayments. See *Multiservice Bookbinding Ltd* v *Marden* [1978] 2 All ER 489, where Browne-Wilkinson J held that there was nothing contrary to public policy in the index-linking arrangement. The parties were of equal bargaining power, and the terms were not unfair, oppressive or morally reprehensible. Index-linked arrangements by a building society were also held to be valid in *Nationwide Building Society* v *Registry of Friendly Societies* [1983] 3 All ER 296.

Rights of the mortgagor under the Consumer Credit Act 1974. The Consumer Credit Act 1974 establishes a code to regulate the supply of credit not exceeding £15,000 made to an individual or to partnerships. A personal credit agreement by which a creditor provides credit not exceeding £15,000 is a 'regulated consumer agreement'. A mortgage must come within the rules relating to regulated consumer agreements. Such agreements do *not* apply to loans over £15,000, building society mortgages or local authority mortgages. However, loans made by a *bank for house purchase* do come within the rules relating to regulated consumer agreements. Further, ss137–139 apply to extortionate credit bargains of any amount.

1. *Protection of the mortgagor: ss137–140*
   The court is given power to re-open a credit agreement if it is extortionate. This power extends to all credit bargains by an individual 'whenever made'. This provision (s137) covers regulated, exempt and credit bargains exceeding £15,000 unless the *mortgagor* is a corporate body.

   A court can only intervene, on the extortionate credit bargain basis, if the bargain has been grossly unfair to the borrower and this can be established if either the payments required to be made are grossly exorbitant or it has grossly contravened the principles of fair dealing.

   The wide discretion given to the court 'to do justice between the parties' is set out in s139. The court may re-open the agreement and, to relieve a debtor or surety from payment of any sum in excess of what is fairly due and reasonable, may direct accounts to be taken, or set aside the whole or part of the obligation, or alter the terms of the credit agreement.

   The law in this regard fell to be considered in *Paragon Finance plc* v *Nash and Another; Paragon Finance plc* v *Staunton and Another* [2002] 1 WLR 685. There the plaintiffs brought possession proceedings as mortgagee in two actions against the defendants on the grounds that they were in arrears with their mortgage interest repayments. Both mortgage agreements contained a variable interest clause. The defendants admitted the arrears of interest but contended by way of defence that the mortgage agreements had become extortionate credit bargains within s138 of the 1974 Act. They did not contend that the loan agreements were extortionate credit bargains at the outset. Rather that they had become such subsequently because of the rates of interest that they were required to pay (PF had not reduced its interest rates in line with the Bank of England or prevailing market rates). The defendants sought to plead an implied term that PF was bound to exercise its discretion to vary interest rates fairly and in good faith and not arbitrarily or unreasonably having regard to all relevant matters. The Recorder struck out the defendants' pleadings. The defendants appealed. The court held that the discretion to vary interest rates during the mortgage term given to a mortgagee in a mortgage agreement was not completely unfettered but was subject to an implied term that it was not to be exercised for an improper purpose, dishonestly, arbitrarily or in a way in which no reasonable lender would reasonably do. However, the fact that PF had set interest rates without reference to the prevailing or market rates did not show that PF was in breach of the implied term. A reason why PF charged interest rates above prevailing or market rates was because it was in serious financial difficulties because many of its borrowers had defaulted and this in turn resulted in the money markets charging PF higher rates because it was deemed to be at greater risk than other mortgage lenders and PF had passed those higher costs onto its borrowers. Accordingly, it could not be said that PF's discretion to set interest rates was being exercised arbitrarily, unreasonably or for an improper purpose.

The borrowers argument that the rates of interest were exorbitant so as to bring the agreements within s138 of the 1974 Act had 'no real prospect of success'. This was because only charges existing at the time of the bargain were to be taken into account in deciding whether a credit bargain was extortionate for the purposes of s138 – subsequent changes in interest rates had to be excluded from the calculation. Accordingly, the appeal would be dismissed.

2. *Postponement of the right to redeem and the 1974 Act*
Under s94 a debtor under a regulated agreement has the right, on giving notice to the creditor, to redeem prematurely at any time. Any provision in the agreement which limits his rights in this respect is void. A provision to postpone the contractual right to redeem in a regulated agreement would be void. Compare this with the decision in *Knightsbridge Estates Trusts Ltd* v *Byrne* [1939] Ch 441.

14.6 Redemption

Who can redeem?

The right to redeem may be exercised by any person who is interested in the equity of redemption, including assignees, subsequent mortgagees, and a lessee under a lease granted by the mortgagor but not binding on the mortgagee. The word 'redeem' means to pay off.

Method of redemption: s115 LPA 1925

After 1925 a mortgage is discharged by a receipt, endorsed on or annexed to the mortgage deed, which names the person paying the money and is signed by the mortgagee. The mortgagor who is exercising his right to redeem must pay the principal, all arrears of interest (for however long due) and all costs properly incurred by the mortgagee in exercising his powers under the mortgage.

If the payee is not the person entitled to the immediate equity of redemption the receipt operates as a transfer of the mortgage to him. On redemption the mortgagee will return any title deeds he is holding to the mortgagor, unless he is aware of a subsequent incumbrancer to whom he should transfer the deeds. A mortgagee who hands the deeds to the mortgagor will not thereby incur liability to a later incumbrancer if he has no notice of him; mere registration of a land charge is not sufficient, actual notice is required (s96(2) LPA 1925). This is another occasion where the equitable rules of notice still apply. As a result all subsequent mortgagees who do not obtain the title deeds should both register their mortgage, as appropriate, and give notice of their interest to all prior mortgagees.

Effect of redemption

Where the mortgage is redeemed by the mortgagor and there are no subsequent incumbrances, the effect is that the property is left free from incumbrances.

If the mortgage is redeemed by a subsequent mortgagee the effect is that the prior mortgage, with all its rights, is transferred to the subsequent mortgagee. If a prior mortgage is redeemed by the mortgagor he cannot take a transfer of this mortgage which might prejudice subsequent mortgagees; it must be discharged.

The following example involving R (mortgagor), E1 (first mortgagee) and E2 (second mortgagee) demonstrates who can redeem and the effect of redemption. R mortgages Blackacre to E1. Subsequently he mortgages it to E2. As a result of the second mortgage E2 has an interest in the equity of redemption of R. This is because if E1 enforces his security by selling Blackacre, E2 will want to ensure that there is enough left for him to be repaid after E1 has taken the sum owing to him. In such a situation E2 can redeem E1's mortgage because of his interest in R's equity of redemption (ie E1 could be paid off by either R or E2).

Extinguishment of the equity of redemption

The equity of redemption may be extinguished by:

1. Foreclosure.

2. Sale.
3. Limitation Act 1980 (see Chapter 15): this applies where the mortgagee has been in possession of the mortgaged land for 12 years without receiving any principal or interest money and without giving any written acknowledgement of the mortgagor's title.
4. The mortgagor surrendering the equity of redemption to the mortgagee, provided that there is no provision in the mortgage deed that this should be done. This would be void under the 'once a mortgage always a mortgage' rule.

The right to sue

As against third parties the mortgagor in possession has always been able to bring an action in his own name. The mortgagor can now bring an action in his own name against a tenant by s98 LPA, provided that the mortgagee has not given effective notice of his intention to enter into possession or enter into receipt of the rents and profits. Section 98 authorises the mortgagor to sue for possession, for the rent and profits and to protect the property, eg against a trespasser.

14.7 The rights of the mortgagee to enforce his security: remedies of the mortgagee

The mortgagee whose mortgagor defaults on payments under the mortgage is given several remedies. Some of these are primarily a method of recovering his capital, others are for enforcing payment of interest.

As a mortgage is merely a security for money lent, these remedies are given to the mortgagee solely to enable him to recover his money. The five major remedies may be presented as follows:

Remedies of the mortgagee

Common law	Statutory or express in deed	Equity
Possession	Sale	Foreclosure
Sue on the personal covenant	Appointing a receiver	

14.8 The remedies of the legal mortgagee

Sue on the personal covenant to repay

By taking this action the mortgagee is taking a normal action for debt, and is not seeking to enforce the security. The action will be barred after 12 years if the mortgage is by deed, six years in other cases (Limitation Act 1980). This remedy is available in addition to the others, so that if insufficient money to cover the mortgage debt is obtained when the security is realised the mortgagee could sue the mortgagor on the personal covenant for the remainder.

Foreclose

This is a very severe remedy which is a form of confiscation of the mortgagor's whole interest. Foreclosure is the process whereby a court declares that the mortgagor's equitable right to redeem is extinguished, leaving the mortgagee as the legal and equitable owner of the property. There are two conditions to the exercise of this remedy:

1. The legal date of redemption must have passed. This is because foreclosure is the extinguishing of the equitable right to redeem, which does not arise until the legal right to redeem has gone.
2. There must be a court order. The mortgagee must bring an action in the Chancery Division of the High Court, and all parties interested in the equity of redemption must be made parties, that is, all subsequent mortgagees to the mortgagee seeking to foreclose and the mortgagor. The writ requires the mortgagor to pay or be foreclosed, and if he does not pay a foreclosure order nisi is made requiring him to pay by a fixed date. If he does not do so the order is made absolute.

Foreclosure has the disadvantage for the mortgagee that even after the foreclosure order has been made absolute the foreclosure can be opened by the court, in other words, the equity of redemption can be revived, provided that it is equitable to do so. In general the court is reluctant to order foreclosure, especially if the value of the property is greater than the amount owing on the mortgage, and may instead order a sale at the request of any person interested (s91 LPA 1925). When the mortgaged property is or includes a dwelling house and the mortgage money is repayable by instalments (the common building society type of mortgage) the court has wide powers in the foreclosure action to adjourn the proceedings or suspend its order (s8(3) Administration of Justice Act 1973).

Sell

The mortgagee had no power of sale at common law and in equity, but this was remedied by statute, and the current provisions are contained in ss101–107 LPA 1925. The power of sale is the remedy most commonly used, as it enables a mortgagee to recover his capital speedily, and is usually combined with an action to obtain vacant possession to allow the best price to be obtained.

A distinction has to be made between when the power of sale *arises*, and when it becomes *exercisable*.

The power of sale (s101)
This *arises* when:

1. The mortgage has been made by deed.
2. The legal date of redemption has passed, see *Payne* v *Cardiff RDC* [1932] 1 KB 241 (in the case of repayment by instalments, the legal date for redemption arises when one instalment is overdue).
3. There is no contrary intention expressed in the mortgage deed.

If the mortgage money is not due this statutory power of sale is not available but, apparently, the court may be able to order a sale instead of foreclosure under s91 LPA 1925 – see *Twentieth Century Banking Corporation Ltd* v *Wilkinson* [1977] Ch 99.

Exercise of the power of sale (s103)
Once the power of sale has arisen it becomes *exercisable* when one or more of the following conditions is fulfilled:

1. Notice requiring repayment of the mortgage money has been served on the mortgagor and default has been made in payment of part or all of it for three months thereafter.
2. Some interest under the mortgage is two months or more in arrears.
3. There has been a breach of some provision contained in the LPA 1925 or the mortgage deed (other than the covenant for payment of the mortgage money or interest) which should have been observed or performed by the mortgagor or by someone who concurred in making the mortgage.

Until the power of sale has arisen the mortgagee has no power of sale, and any purported sale to a purchaser conveys only the mortgagee's mortgage, ie a transfer of the mortgage.

Once the power of sale has arisen the mortgagee can transfer good title even though the power has not in fact become exercisable, the mortgagor having a remedy in damages against the mortgagee if the power has been irregularly or improperly exercised (s104 LPA 1925). Thus a purchaser from a mortgagee must only satisfy himself that the power of sale has arisen, but he must act in good faith, and if he is aware that the power has not in fact become exercisable he will not get a good title.

A second or subsequent mortgagee can sell subject to any prior incumbrances or, if the prior mortgagee(s) concur(s), free from incumbrances.

Although the mortgagee only has a term of years, or its equivalent, he will convey the fee simple or other the whole interest of the mortgagor.

Mode of sale

The statutory power of sale is exercisable without a court order. The mortgagee is not a trustee of the power of sale, and may adopt any method of sale, but he must act in good faith and take reasonable care. In exercising the power of sale the non-building society mortgagee must obtain the true market value of the property. In *Cuckmere Brick Co Ltd* v *Mutual Finance Ltd* [1971] Ch 949 Salmon LJ put the matter thus:

> '... a mortgagee in exercising his power of sale does owe a duty to take reasonable precautions to obtain the true market value of the mortgaged property at the date on which he decides to sell.'

This duty is owed to both the mortgagor and any guarantor of the mortgagor's debt. See *Standard Chartered Bank* v *Walker* [1982] 3 All ER 938. In *Skipton Building Society* v *Bratley* (2000) The Times 12 January the Court of Appeal made clear that, in the event of a breach by a mortgagee of this duty, the amount of money for which a guarantor would be liable would be reduced pro tanto.

A similar obligation to achieve 'the best price that can reasonably be obtained' is imposed on building societies by s13(7) and Schedule 4 para 1(1)(a) of the Building Societies Act 1986. See *Tomlin* v *Luce* (1889) 43 Ch D 191 and *Cuckmere Brick Co* v *Mutual Finance Ltd* (above).

The duty of a mortgagee to obtain the best price reasonably obtainable on sale has fallen to be considered by the courts on a number of occasions recently and the following principles have been laid down. First, the mortgagee does not breach his duty to the mortgagor if he exercises his judgment on the relevant matters reasonably (see *Michael & Others* v *Miller* (2004) The Times 30 March). Second, in deciding whether a mortgagee has taken reasonable steps to obtain the 'best price' the matter has to be 'looked at in the round' and from a commercial perspective (see *Newport Farms Ltd* v *Damesh Holdings Ltd* (2003) 147 SJLB 1117). Third, when a mortgagee does sell the mortgaged property at an undervalue and thus in breach of its duty to take reasonable care to obtain the best price reasonably obtainable, the measure of damages to be paid to the mortgagor is the reduction in the value of the equity of redemption, ie the real loss (see *Adamson* v *Halifax plc* [2003] 1 WLR 60). Fourth, a 'bracket approach' to the valuation issue is not inappropriate, ie the mortgagee must sell within an acceptable bracket of valuations for the mortgaged property. This was laid down by the Court of Appeal in *Michael & Others* v *Miller* (2004) The Times 30 March. There, although the price obtained by the mortgagees was lower than the market value of the estate (£1.75 million), it was within an acceptable bracket for valuation (which ranged from £1.6 million to £1.9 million) and therefore the mortgagees had not been negligent. Fifth, it is for the mortgagee to decide whether a sale should be by public auction or private treaty (see *Warner* v *Jacob* (1882) 20 Ch D 220; confirmed in *Michael & Others* v *Miller* (2004) The Times 30 March).

The duty of a mortgagee to *third parties* upon exercising the power of sale was considered by the Court of Appeal in *Parker-Tweedale* v *Dunbar Bank plc (No 1)* [1990] 3 WLR 767. There the duty to the mortgagor to take reasonable care to obtain the true market value of the property at the time of sale was confirmed. This duty of care does not extend to the beneficiary under a trust of which the mortgagor was a trustee. In this case, as a result of three separation agreements, the wife became the sole legal owner and mortgagor of the property, but the plaintiff, the husband, was entitled to the net surplus proceeds from the sale of the property. Nourse LJ discussed the principle settled in *Cuckmere Brick Co Ltd* v *Mutual Finance Ltd* (above) that the mortgagee owes the mortgagor 'a duty to take reasonable care to obtain a proper price for the mortgaged property' at the sale. He then went on to say:

'But there is no support, either in the authorities or in principle, for the proposition that where the mortgagor was a trustee, even a bare trustee, of the mortgaged property, a like duty is owed to a beneficiary under the trust of whose interest the mortgagee had notice.'

He explained that the duty owed by the mortgagee to the mortgagor arose out of the particular relationship between them, and then concluded:

'Once it was recognised that the duty owed by the mortgagee to the mortgagor arose out of the particular relationship between them, it was readily apparent that there was no warrant for extending its scope so as to include a beneficiary under a trust of which the mortgagor was the trustee.'

The obligation on the mortgagee was to take reasonable care to obtain a proper price being the true market value. It is the mortgagee's decision when to sell once the power of sale has become exercisable. See *Countrywide Banking Corporation* v *Robinson* [1991] 1 NZLR 75.

However, it has been held that a mortgagee when exercising the power of sale owed a duty of care to the legal owner of land even if the owner was not the mortgagor. In *Freeguard* v *Royal Bank of Scotland plc* [2002] EWHC 2509, F (the claimant) acquired an option to purchase land but the option was never registered. Subsequently, the owners of the land charged it to RBS (the defendant) but the charge was never registered. F's option and RBS's charge were competing equities and proceedings to determine which had priority were resolved in favour of RBS. Notwithstanding this determination, F purchased the land subject to the charge even though she was not the mortgagor. Thereafter RBS sold the land in exercise of its power of sale as mortgagee. F issued proceedings contending that RBS had sold the land at an undervalue and that in so doing it had breached its duty of care towards her, the legal owner of the land (in essence she argued that there was such a duty even though she was not the borrower). The Deputy Master struck out F's claim on the basis that RBS did not owe her a duty of care. F appealed. The court held that a mortgagee owed a duty of care in equity not only to the mortgagor or any subsequent incumbrancer, but also to the legal owner of land even if the owner was not the mortgagor. This was because F, like a subsequent incumbrancer, had an interest which was subject only to a prior right (here the legal charge), and she would therefore suffer loss if RBS breached its duty of care. RBS owed F a duty of care and the Deputy Master had been wrong to strike out F's claim. Accordingly, the appeal would be allowed.

This decision constitutes a logical extension of the duty of care owed by a mortgagee when exercising its power of sale and is consistent with case developments in this field over the last decade.

In *Downsview Nominees Ltd* v *First City Corporation Ltd* [1993] AC 295 it was held that a mortgagee owed a duty of care not just to the mortgagor but also to any subsequent incumbrancer. In *Medforth* v *Blake* [2000] Ch 86 it was held that a receiver owed a duty of care not just to the mortgagor, but also to any other person who had an interest in the equity of redemption.

A sale by the mortgagee to himself, either directly or through a third party, may be set aside

In *Williams* v *Wellingborough Borough Council* [1975] 1 WLR 1327 a council house was sold to the tenant with the purchase money left on the mortgage. Following default, the purported sale by the council to itself was held to be void.

The problem of the mortgagee exercising his power of sale was considered by the Privy Council in *Tse Kwong Lam* v *Wong Chit Sen* [1983] 3 All ER 54, and it was held that there was no inflexible rule that a mortgagee exercising his power of sale under a mortgage could not sell to a company in which he had an interest. However, the mortgagee and the company had to show that the sale was made in good faith and that the mortgagee had taken reasonable precautions to obtain the best price reasonably obtainable at the time. This would be shown by taking expert advice as to the method of sale, the steps which ought reasonably to be taken to make the sale a success, and the amount of the reserve. Sale by auction did not necessarily prove the validity of the transaction, since the price obtainable at an auction which produced only one bid might be less than the true market value. On the facts, the mortgagee did not succeed in showing that all reasonable steps had been taken to achieve the best price reasonably obtainable.

Lord Templeman stated:

'In the result their Lordships consider that in the present case the company was not debarred from purchasing the mortgaged property but, in view of the close relationship between the company and the mortgagee and in view in particular of the conflict of duty and interest to which the mortgagee was subject, the sale to the company can only be supported if the mortgagee proves that he took reasonable precautions to obtain the best price reasonably obtainable at the time of sale.'

In *Newport Farms Ltd* v *Damesh Holdings Ltd & Others* (2003) 147 SJLB 1117 the Judicial Committee of the Privy Council again had to consider the situation of a mortgaged property being sold to a company in which the mortgagee was interested. There the Privy Council concluded that in deciding whether or not 'the mortgagee took reasonable precautions to obtain the best price reasonably obtainable at the time' (per Lord Templeman in *Tse Kwong Lam* v *Wong Chit Sen* [1983] 1 WLR 1349 at 1355) the mortgagee did not have to observe a set of inflexible rules. Rather, the matter turned on the circumstances of the case. There the mortgagor made much of the fact that the mortgagee had not followed the steps that Lord Templeman, in *Tse Kwong Lam*, said the mortgagee should have taken. Their Lordships dealt with this point by concluding that Lord Templeman's remarks had to be seen in the context of the facts of that case and that he did not intend to lay down inflexible rules to be observed in every subsequent case.

Proceeds of sale

The mortgagee is trustee of the proceeds of sale. The proceeds must be used in the following order:

1. discharge of any prior incumbrance, if the property was sold free from them;
2. discharge of the expenses of sale;
3. discharge of money due to the mortgagee under the mortgage;
4. pay the balance to the next subsequent mortgagee or, if none, to the mortgagor. The subsequent mortgagee will hold the balance on trust to discharge the money due to him and to pay the balance to the next person entitled.

Court order for sale

In addition to the power given to the mortgagee, the court is given a wide power to order a sale at the instance of any person interested by s91 LPA 1925: see *Twentieth Century Banking Corporation Ltd* v *Wilkinson* [1977] Ch 99. There the legal date for redemption was not until 1988, and so the statutory power of sale under s101 had not arisen. Templeman J held that the mortgagor was so seriously in arrears that he was in breach of a fundamental condition which barred the legal right of redemption. This allowed the mortgagee to foreclose, and a sale was ordered under s91 instead of foreclosure. The judge considered the basis of this right as follows:

> 'The defendants would in law be entitled to their property back if they complied with all their covenants ... In default of such compliance, the defendants have no legal right to recovery of their property, but equity accords them a right, namely an equitable right to redeem. That equitable right to redeem can, in a proper case, be terminated by an order for foreclosure. If the lenders are entitled to foreclose, the court in its discretion may order a sale instead.'

A court can order a sale of mortgaged property even against the wishes of the mortgagee. In *Palk* v *Mortgage Services Funding* [1993] 2 All ER 481 the plaintiffs decided to sell their home when the husband's company failed. The defendant mortgagee refused to agree to a sale negotiated by the plaintiffs because the sale price would not have been enough to pay off the mortgage debt. Furthermore, the mortgagees had secured a suspended possession order and were hoping to let the property in order to generate income pending an upturn in the housing market when they would sell it. Of central significance to the case was the fact that the sum due under the mortgage was increasing by about £43,000 per year whereas the anticipated income from letting was between £13,000 and £14,000 per year. The Court of Appeal stated that it had an unfettered discretion under s91(2) LPA 1925 to order a sale of mortgaged property even against the wishes of the mortgagee. In the exceptional circumstances of this case, they concluded that it was just and equitable to order a sale (even though a significant amount of the debt would remain outstanding and unsecured).

Take possession

The previous two remedies, foreclosure and sale, enable a mortgagee to recover his capital, while both this one and the next, appointing a receiver, leave the capital intact and enforce payments of interest.

The mortgagee has a right to possession as soon as the mortgage is executed: s95(4) LPA 1925. In *Four Maids Ltd* v *Dudley Marshall (Properties) Ltd* [1957] Ch 317 Harman J described the right as follows.

'The right of the mortgagee to possession in the absence of some contract has nothing to do with default on the part of the mortgagor. The mortgagee may go into possession before the ink is dry on the mortgage unless there is something in the contract, express or implied, whereby he has contracted himself out of that right. He has the right because he has a legal term of years in the property.'

The right arises even if the mortgagor is not in any default. This is because, if the mortgage was by demise, the mortgagee is a tenant and therefore entitled to possession as against the mortgagor, and a mortgagee whose mortgage is by legal charge has by statute the same rights as a mortgagee by demise.

There is nothing inconsistent about granting a mortgagee a possession order, suspended subject to conditions as to payment being met by the mortgagors, and a concurrent money judgment for the entire mortgage debt, suspended for as long as the possession order remains suspended. In *Cheltenham & Gloucester Building Society* v *Grattidge* (1993) The Times 9 April the building society started possession proceedings and claimed payment of the balance of the amount due because at the time there was widespread incidence of negative equity and it was concerned that the equity in the mortgaged property might not be enough to pay off the entire mortgage debt. The Court of Appeal held it could not make an immediately enforceable order for the payment of the entire mortgage debt. However there was no reason why it should not make a suspended order under s71(2) County Courts Act 1984 – suspended for as long as the possession order remained suspended.

The attitude of the court to an action for possession in the wrong circumstances is illustrated by *Quennel* v *Maltby* [1979] 1 WLR 318, in which the Court of Appeal held that so long as interest was paid and there was nothing outstanding, equity had the power to restrain any unjust use of the right to possession. In this case possession was being sought to defeat the protection afforded to a tenant by the Rent Act 1977, and the mortgagee was held not to be acting in good faith.

Relief of mortgagor

Even though the mortgagee has a right of possession he must obtain a court order before he can take possession. Before 1936 the action was brought in the King's Bench Division and the order was given automatically, but in that year possession actions were transferred to the Chancery Division, which thereafter refused an order if it was inequitable to grant it, and allowed an adjournment or stay of execution to give the mortgagor a chance to redeem the mortgage.

When the mortgaged property includes a dwelling house the court is given a discretion by s36 Administration of Justice Act 1970 (as amended) to adjourn the proceedings or to grant a stay of execution where it appears likely to the court that the mortgagor is likely within a reasonable time to pay any sums due to remedy any default.

When the mortgage is an instalment mortgage it is further provided by s8 AJA 1973 that the mortgagor may be required to pay off arrears only, not to pay the whole of the mortgage monies. This statutory discretion has been extended in favour of a mortgagor under an endowment mortgage: *Centrax Trustees Ltd* v *Ross* [1979] 2 All ER 952. In *Bank of Scotland* v *Grimes* [1985] 2 All ER 254 the Court of Appeal confirmed that s8 AJA 1973 was intended to cover both instalment mortgages and endowment mortgages. Griffiths LJ said:

> '… the words to defer payment were inserted in s8 to cover endowment mortgages where there was no obligation to repay the capital until the end of the duration of the loan.'

The question of what constitutes a 'reasonable period' for bringing payments up to date for the purposes of s36 AJA 1970 (as amended) fell to be considered in *Cheltenham & Gloucester Building Society* v *Norgan* [1996] 1 All ER 449. There N was sole owner of a period farmhouse which was subject to a mortgage. N's repayments faltered and the building society issued a summons to repossess the farmhouse. The county court judge estimated that N's arrears were £20,000 and that a period of two to four years was the maximum that would normally be allowed for clearing arrears (even though here the mortgage had 13 years still to run). He concluded that it would be impossible for N to meet that target and therefore the building society was entitled to have possession. N appealed and her appeal was allowed. A key consideration was what constituted a 'reasonable period' for bringing payments up to date for the purposes of s36 AJA 1970. The court unanimously agreed that 'the logic and spirit of the legislation' required that the court should take the full term of the mortgage as its starting point and pose at the outset the following question: 'Would it be possible for the borrower to maintain payment off of the arrears by instalments over that period?' The court identified a number of considerations which were likely to be relevant in establishing a reasonable period, including the following:

1. how much could the borrower reasonably afford to pay both now and in the future?;
2. if the borrower had a short term problem in meeting his mortgage commitments, how long was the difficulty likely to last?;
3. why had the arrears accumulated?;
4. how much remained of the original term?; and
5. were there any reasons affecting the security which should influence the length of the period for payment?

Accordingly, the case was remitted back to the county court to work out a new repayment scheme over the remaining 13 years of the loan.

This is unquestionably a landmark ruling. It formalises the process of capitalisation where the arrears are added to the original loan. In reality the court decided that the established practice of imposing a period of say two (or more) years as a 'reasonable period' for the payment of arrears within s36 AJA 1970 ought *not* to be followed as a matter of course. Clearly some home-owners who fall into arrears with their mortgages will now have a better chance of keeping their homes. In consequence of this decision it is likely that significant numbers of homeowners fighting repossession will now take their lenders to court in order to secure a comparable deal to that obtained by Mrs Norgan. However, the decision will clearly not help all home-owners facing repossession. Many people in that position are unable (because of redundancy, separation, etc) to meet their mortgage repayments, let alone try to pay off large arrears.

However, the 'dust' had barely settled after the *Norgan* ruling when it was qualified. In *Bristol & West Building Society* v *Ellis and Another* (1996) 73 P & CR 158 a subsequent Court of Appeal concluded that the *Norgan* starting point for determining a reasonable period for repayment of mortgage arrears for the purpose of the courts discretion under s36 AJA 1970 (ie the outstanding term of the mortgage) was *not* available to the mortgagor who could not discharge the mortgage arrears by periodic payments and whose only prospect of repaying the entire loan and accruing interest was by selling the property. In such cases, the reasonableness of the order was a matter for the court in the circumstances of the case. The most important factors in such a scenario were likely to be the extent to which the mortgage debt and arrears were secured by the value of the property and the effect of time on that security.

Further, the court can suspend a possession order under s36 AJA 1970 (as amended) when the proposed means of dealing with the arrears is a sale by the borrowers of the mortgaged property in order to discharge the entire debt, rather than (as is usually the case) a scheme whereby the mortgagor proposes only to repay the arrears while at the same time keeping the property. In *Target Home Loans* v *Clothier and Clothier* [1994] 1 All ER 439 the Court of Appeal postponed a possession order for three months to enable the defendant mortgagors to sell their home with a view to discharging the entire mortgage debt (the property in question was already on the market and an early sale was anticipated). In *National and Provincial Building Society* v *Lloyd* [1996] 1 All ER 630 the Court of Appeal confirmed that the court could invoke its discretion under s36 AJA 1970 to suspend a possession order pending a sale of the mortgaged property by the borrower provided the sale was likely to generate sufficient monies to pay the arrears due within a reasonable period. The Court stated that there was no rule of law to the effect that an order for possession of mortgaged property would only be suspended if the sale would take place within a short period of time. If there was clear evidence that the completion of a property sale, perhaps by piecemeal disposal, could take place within six months to a year there was no reason why a court could not conclude in exercising its discretion under s36 AJA 1970 that the borrower was 'likely to be able within a reasonable period to pay any sums due under the mortgage'. Further, the Court emphasised that the sale need not be in the immediate future provided the terms of s36 AJA 1970 were satisfied. The question of what was 'a reasonable period' to wait for the sale would be a question for the court in each individual case. Finally, the court emphasised that the prospect of a sale must not be fanciful (on the facts much of the evidence adduced by the borrower in this regard was a mere expression of hope).

Since a sale must be likely, a reasonable period to wait for it will not usually be the full term of the mortgage. Accordingly, are cases like *Target* and *Lloyd* at variance with *Cheltenham & Gloucester Building Society* v *Norgan*? They are not because there is a clear factual difference between the two types of case. The former two cases concern a situation where possession is being postponed to enable mortgage arrears to be paid by *sale monies* and thus a sale must be probable. In contrast in the *Norgan* situation possession is being postponed to enable arrears to be paid by *increased instalments*.

Finally, the protection provided to a borrower by s36 AJA 1970 only applies where the lender has brought an action for possession. This was established in *Ropaigelach* v *Barclays Bank plc* [2000] QB 263. There the lender had taken possession of mortgaged property by forceable entry (it was a residential property which was unoccupied by the mortgagor) and without first obtaining a court order. The mortgagee argued that by invoking this 'self help' remedy the mortgagor was not entitled to any of the protection afforded by s36 AJA 1970. In contrast the mortgagor (R) argued that Parliament could not have intended that the protection against ejectment which s36 AJA 1970 was plainly intended to give to borrowers in respect of their homes should be capable of being frustrated by a lender who resorted to self help (ie lender obtaining possession by entry without the assistance of the court). R argued that s36 AJA 1970 had to be construed in such a way as to make it unlawful to take possession of a dwelling-house except under an order of the court.

The Court of Appeal held that a mortgage lender was entitled to exercise its common law right to take possession of a mortgaged dwelling-house without first obtaining a court order. The protection provided to a borrower by s36 AJA 1970 *only* applied where the lender had brought an action for possession. In reaching the decision it did the Court rejected the purposive construction of s36 argued for by R. What was crucial here was that the house was unoccupied by the mortgagor.

Duties of a mortgagee in possession

A mortgagee who takes possession may use the income arising from the land in lieu of the interest payments due to him under the mortgage, and he may use any surplus to pay off the capital or may hand it over to the person next entitled. If he is a second or subsequent mortgagee he must make any payments due to prior mortgagees. A mortgagee in possession may not derive any personal advantages and must account strictly to the mortgagor. This means that he is liable for any loss caused by his own negligence. A brewery which let a free house as a tied house only selling its own beer was held liable for the difference in rent between a free house and a tied house in *White* v *City of London Brewery Co* (1889) 42 Ch D 237.

If the mortgagee occupies the premises himself he must pay a fair rent, and he must do reasonable repairs. In effect possession is only a satisfactory remedy where the mortgagee can collect fixed rents.

Possession and the question of undue influence

The question of fiduciary duty owed by a creditor who seeks possession and the possible effect of undue influence has become an increasing problem since safeguards were introduced to overcome the problems for mortgagees created by the decision in *Williams & Glyn's Bank* v *Boland* [1981] AC 487. In *National Westminster Bank plc* v *Morgan* [1985] 2 WLR 588 the House of Lords held that before a transaction could be set aside on the grounds of undue influence it had to be shown that it constituted a disadvantage to the person influenced and seeking to avoid it. Any question of presumption of undue influence will only become relevant if the transaction is shown to constitute such a disadvantage. On the facts of this case the proposals were designed to rescue the home from an earlier mortgagee's action for possession. Lord Scarman warned that:

> '... there was no precisely defined law setting limits to the equitable jurisdiction of a court to relieve against undue influence. A court in the exercise of such jurisdiction was a court of conscience ... and whether a transaction was or was not unconscionable ... depended on the particular facts of the case.'

The question of undue influence was also considered by the Court of Appeal in *Kingsnorth Trust Ltd* v *Bell* [1986] 1 WLR 119. There the Court of Appeal held that where, under the influence of her husband, a wife executed a mortgage of the matrimonial home without knowing his true purpose in wanting the advance, then her rights in the property retained their priority to the mortgagee's rights. Dillon LJ concluded:

> 'The moral was that where a creditor (or intending lender) desired the protection of a guarantee or charge on property from a third party other than the debtor and the

circumstances were such that the debtor would be expected to have influence over that third party, the creditor ought for his own protection to insist that the third party has independent advice.'

Barclays Bank *v* O'Brien

In recent years one of the most dynamic areas of mortgages has concerned the following situation – property jointly owned by husband and wife; wife provides security for her husband's business debts following undue influence etc by the husband; husband defaults on repayments; lender seeks to recover possession of the property and the wife alleges that her consent to the security was obtained by undue influence or misrepresentation on the part of her husband which is binding on the lender through actual or constructive notice. The leading case in this regard is that of the House of Lords in *Barclays Bank plc* v *O'Brien and Another* [1993] 3 WLR 786. There a matrimonial home was in the joint names of a husband and wife. The husband, but not the wife, had an interest in a company. In order to raise capital for this company the husband negotiated a loan from the bank, with the bank taking a legal charge over the matrimonial home as security. He misrepresented the transaction to his wife by telling her that she would be signing the mortgage for a fixed amount of £60,000 that would only last for three weeks and which would enable him to increase his shareholding in the relevant company (in fact they had guaranteed all the company's debts to the bank). The husband signed the relevant documents in the absence of his wife, and when the wife went to sign the legal charge the effect of the deal was not explained to her, nor was she advised to obtain independent legal advice despite the fact that the bank had asked its staff at the relevant branch to explain the deal to her and advise her to take such advice before signing. The company got into financial difficulties, the bank called in the guarantee, and when the husband failed to pay the sum owing the bank sought to realise its security by seeking a possession order in respect of the matrimonial home.

The House of Lords held that the wife was able to have the legal charge against the matrimonial home set aside because the bank was fixed with *constructive notice* of the husband's misrepresentation. This notice arose as follows: the bank was put on enquiry when the wife offered to stand surety for her husband's debts by a combination of two factors. First, the transaction on its face was not to the wife's financial advantage. Secondly, there was a substantial risk in such transactions that in getting a wife to act as surety the husband had committed a legal or equitable wrong that entitled the wife to set the transaction aside. To avoid such constructive notice it was necessary for the bank to have taken steps (in the absence of the husband) to bring home to the wife the risk that she was running as surety and advise her to take independent advice. This the bank had not done. Finally, their Lordships said that their ruling would also apply to unmarried couples, heterosexual or homosexual, in a relationship where there was a risk of one of them exploiting the other's emotional involvement and trust.

This decision of the House of Lords is undoubtedly a landmark ruling, since as a result of it wives (and others in an analogous position) who agree that their family homes can be used as security for their husbands' debts now have greater protection against the loss of their properties. However, it is important to emphasise the context of the decision – that of a wife signing a mortgage as surety for the debts of her husband. This reality was emphasised by the House of Lords in *CIBC Mortgages plc v Pitt and Another* [1993] 3 WLR 802. There a matrimonial home was in the joint names of husband and wife. The only encumbrance on it was a mortgage in favour of a building society. The husband told the wife that he wanted to borrow money on the security of their home in order to use the money so raised for buying shares on the stock market. The wife was unhappy with this idea but eventually agreed to it as a result of pressure from her husband. Both husband and wife signed the mortgage application form, which stated that the purpose of the loan was to pay off the existing mortgage and use the balance to buy a holiday home, and both signed the mortgage offer and legal charge. The wife did not read the documents before signing, nor was she advised to seek legal advice about the transaction. After the existing mortgage was discharged, the rest of the loan was paid into a joint account and the husband used the money to speculate on the stock market. Following the stock market crash of October 1987 the husband was unable to keep up the mortgage payments, and the plaintiffs applied for a possession order in respect of the matrimonial home. The wife contested the application on the basis that she had been induced to sign the relevant documents by undue influence on the part of her husband.

In dismissing the wife's appeal the House of Lords held that the rules laid down in *Barclays Bank plc v O'Brien and Another* (above) only applied to cases in which the wife was effectively a surety in that the money was given to her husband or her husband's company. Here Mrs Pitt was, with her husband, a joint borrower of the money. Although she had established undue influence by her husband, the plaintiffs would not be affected by it unless they had notice of it. Here they had no such notice because the loan had been advanced to the husband and wife jointly and there was nothing to suggest to the plaintiffs that it was anything other than a normal advance to a married couple for their joint benefit. The plaintiffs had no duty to advise the wife separately. The mere fact that there was a risk of undue influence because one of the borrowers was the wife of the other was not, in itself, enough to put the plaintiffs on inquiry.

In view of the clear factual differences between this case and *Barclays Bank v O'Brien*, the decision in the former is in no way inconsistent with that in the latter case.

Post O'Brien *developments*

There have been a number of important case law developments in this area since

Barclays Bank plc v *O'Brien and Another*, a number of which are featured in the ensuing paragraphs.

Range of circumstances in which the equitable right may arise

It is submitted that there are three situations in which the equitable right established in *O'Brien* may arise. First, where the mortgagee had *actual notice* of wrongdoing on the part of the husband mortgagor. Second, where the mortgagee had *constructive notice* of wrongdoing on the part of the husband mortgagor. Third, where the husband mortgagor acted as the lender's agent in procuring the wife mortgagor's signature to the document giving rise to the lender's legal rights.

Establishing the equitable right

In deciding whether or not an *O'Brien* equitable right can be established three questions need to be addressed.

First, did the husband, on getting his wife to enter into the loan transaction, commit an actionable wrong against his wife which entitles her, as against her husband, to have the transaction set aside?

Second, was the lender by virtue of the circumstances of the transaction put 'on inquiry' that an actionable wrong might have been committed? In *Barclays Bank plc* v *O'Brien and Another* the House of Lords, as previously noted, concluded that a lender was put on inquiry when the wife offered to stand surety for her husband's debts by a combination of two factors:

1. the transaction on its face was not to the wife's financial advantage;
2. there was a substantial risk in such transactions that in getting a wife to act as surety the husband had committed a legal or equitable wrong that entitled the wife to set the transaction aside (the 'two factor' test).

This view was challenged by the Court of Appeal in *Bank of Scotland* v *Bennett* [1999] 1 FLR 1115. There the Court advanced a different test for determining when a lender was put 'on inquiry', namely that it was necessary to look at all the circumstances of the transaction through the lender's eyes and only if there was a substantial risk that the wife's consent had been obtained by improper means on the husband's part would the lender be put 'on inquiry' (such a test was substantially at variance from that put forward in *O'Brien*). There a matrimonial home was in the sole name of the wife. The husband sought and obtained overdraft facilities from the plaintiff bank for a business which he controlled but in which his wife had a small shareholding (11.8 per cent). When the business foundered the bank sought to enforce its security. They obtained a judgment against H but W submitted that she had been subjected to undue influence by H in agreeing that her house could stand as security for the company's indebtedness. The bank knew that at the time when the security was given the prospects for the company seemed good; that the wife had been present at a number of meetings at which the future of the business had been considered; that she was being advised by a solicitor; and that the risks associated with the transaction were not such that a competent solicitor would advise against taking them. In essence the Court felt that it would be wrong to ignore such realities in deciding if the bank had been put 'on inquiry'. The Court of Appeal concluded that on the totality of the facts known to it, the bank was entitled to conclude that W's consent to the transaction had been freely given. Accordingly, they found for the bank using the aforementioned test for determining when a lender was put on inquiry.

In at least two factual respects this case is distinguishable from traditional *O'Brien* ones. First, the wife had an interest in the husband's business. Second, at the time the security was taken the prospects for the business appeared to be good. In the light of *Bennett*, in what circumstances will the *O'Brien* 'two factor' test apply? It is submitted that when a lender simply knows that a wife is providing security for her husband's business in which she has no interest then the two factor test will apply, especially if as is usually the case the business is in difficulty. Finally, in this regard it is important to make the precedent point that *O'Brien* was decided by the House of Lords while *Bennett* was a decision of the Court of Appeal. Accordingly, the *Bennett* test for determining whether a lender was put 'on inquiry' should be treated with some caution.

In the leading House of Lords case of *Royal Bank of Scotland plc v Etridge (No 2)* [2001] 4 All ER 449 the question of when a lender was put 'on inquiry' was again addressed. Their Lordships stated that a lender was placed on inquiry whenever a wife offered to stand surety for her husband's debts. The position was the same if the husband stood surety for his wife's debts; likewise in the case of an unmarried couple (whether heterosexual or homosexual), provided the lender was aware of the relationship. However, they emphasised that where money was advanced to a husband and wife jointly, the lender was not put on inquiry unless it knew the loan was being made for the husband's purposes rather than their joint purposes.

The question of where the burden of proof lies in respect of whether the lender has been put 'on inquiry' has also been determined. In *Barclays Bank plc v Boulter and Another* [1999] 1 WLR 1919 the Court of Appeal held that the burden was not on a wife to plead and prove that the bank had constructive notice of the alleged wrongdoing but rather on the bank to prove that it did *not* (ie the bank had to prove that it was not put on inquiry, as well as proving that it took reasonable steps to bring home to the wife the risk she was running in signing the legal charge, etc).

However, on appeal the House of Lords concluded that the Court of Appeal view of the matter could not be supported. Their Lordships held that in cases where a wife claimed that she had been induced to execute an instrument in favour of a bank by virtue of undue influence and misrepresentation by the husband, it was for the wife to demonstrate that the bank had constructive notice of the undue influence, etc. That burden was quite easily discharged. The wife only had to demonstrate that the bank knew that she was a wife living with her husband and that the transaction was not on its face for her financial advantage. The burden was then on the bank to establish that it took reasonable steps to satisfy itself that her consent was properly obtained.

Given that negative propositions are usually difficult to prove generally and that that difficulty would have been compounded in *O'Brien* cases where there was a significant time gap between the legal charge being signed and its validity being challenged in the courts, it is submitted that the conclusion reached by the House of Lords on the burden of proof issue is correct.

The third and final question is whether the lender (assuming it is 'on inquiry') has taken reasonable steps to ensure that a wife's consent has been properly obtained. In *Royal Bank of Scotland plc* v *Etridge (No 2)* [2001] 4 All ER 449 the House of Lords set out what steps the lender should take once it is put on inquiry. They made four main points. First, henceforward, a bank would be required to insist that a wife attended a private meeting with its representatives at which the nature of the risk would be explained to her and she would be urged to obtain independent advice. Second, it was neither desirable nor practicable that a bank should be required to discover for itself whether a wife's consent to the transaction was a consequence of her husband's undue influence. Third, the bank could not be expected to insist on confirmation from a solicitor that he was satisfied that the wife's consent had been so procured. Rather, the most that the bank could be expected to do was to take reasonable steps to satisfy itself that the practical consequences of the intended transaction had been explained to her in a meaningful way. Fourth, a bank would usually discharge this responsibility by relying on confirmation from the wife's solicitor that she had been appropriately advised.

However, in *National Westminster Bank plc* v *Amin* [2002] 1 FLR 735 a lender was not able to rely on such confirmation to discharge its responsibilities. There, in 1972, Mr and Mrs A emigrated from Uganda to the UK. They spoke Urdu. In 1988 their son, who had been educated in the UK, sought a loan from the National Westminster Bank offering as security for the same a charge over his parents' home. Although Mr and Mrs A had lived in the UK for a number of years, significantly neither of them spoke, read or wrote English. The bank wrote to a solicitor enclosing the mortgage document and asking him to ensure that Mr and Mrs A were aware of the terms and conditions contained therein, and to obtain and witness their signatures to the mortgage. For this purpose, the solicitor convened a meeting attended by Mr and Mrs A and their son which culminated in the parents signing the mortgage. The meeting was conducted in English and there was no request that Urdu should be spoken on that occasion. After the meeting, the solicitor confirmed to the National Westminster Bank that he had explained the terms and conditions of the mortgage to Mr and Mrs A. Subsequently the son found himself in financial difficulties and the National Westminster Bank (the claimant) brought possession proceedings against Mrs A (the defendant), her husband having died.

Mrs A raised the defence of undue influence, submitting that the mortgage should be avoided because of undue influence exerted upon her by her son (the debtor), for whose benefit the mortgage had been entered into.

The bank applied to have Mrs A's defence struck out, arguing that it could not be fixed with constructive notice of the son's alleged undue influence as it had acted in reliance on the solicitor's confirmation that he had explained the charge to Mrs A and her late husband. The House of Lords held that while the understanding of a mortgage transaction by a borrower could be inferred in ordinary cases, that was not the situation here where the solicitor explaining the mortgage document to the chargor spoke no Urdu, and the chargor neither spoke nor read English, and these communication difficulties were known to the mortgagee (the bank was aware that Mr and Mrs A could not speak English and therefore knew that they were especially vulnerable to exploitation).

In such circumstances there was a clear possibility that the bank knew, or ought to have known, that the advice given by the solicitor would be defective. Accordingly, it was appropriate that the case should be remitted to the county court for trial.

Role of solicitor

The decision of the House of Lords in *Royal Bank of Scotland plc* v *Etridge (No 2)* [2001] 4 All ER 449 is currently the leading authority on the role of solicitors in *O'Brien*-type cases.

The decision makes a number of points clear including the following:

1. The decision whether or not to proceed with the transaction rests with the wife not the solicitor.
2. If the solicitor considers the transaction not to be in the wife's best interests he should advise her accordingly.
3. The solicitor should only decline to act further in a case 'where it was glaringly obvious that the wife was being grievously wronged' (per Lord Nicholls).
4. The solicitor must explain to the wife the purpose for his involvement.
5. The solicitor must advise the wife as to the nature of the documentation, the extent of her liability under the guarantee and the fact that she has a choice.
6. There must be face-to-face discussions between the solicitor and the wife in the absence of the husband.
7. The solicitor may act for the husband provided he is satisfied that such an arrangement is in the wife's best interests.

As to conflict of interest the Court of Appeal in *Etridge (No 2)* [1998] 4 All 705 concluded that it was clearly unwise for the solicitor acting for the bank to advise the wife unless purely in a ministerial capacity at completion. However, a solicitor was not necessarily disqualified from acting for the wife simply because he was acting for the husband. Stuart-Smith LJ put the matter thus:

> 'If the marriage was secure and the indebtedness had been incurred by the business which provided the husband's livelihood and on which the family's prosperity depended there might be no real conflict between the interests of the husband and the wife.'

It was for the solicitor in the exercise of his professional judgment to decide whether he could advise the wife himself or advise her to go to another solicitor.

Finally, in *Barclays Bank plc* v *Coleman* [2000] 1 All ER 385 the Court of Appeal held that a bank was entitled to rely on a legal executive's certificate provided the advice given by the legal executive was independent of the bank and given with the authority of the legal executive's principal. This decision clearly accorded with the realities of contemporary solicitors' practice and was unsurprising given the progressive enhancement in the role of legal executives which has taken place in recent years. The Court made it clear that a solicitor who allows a legal executive to give advice from his practice address necessarily holds him out as having authority to do so.

Independent legal advice
A lender in *O'Brien*-type cases is required, as noted above, to insist that a wife attends a private meeting with its representative at which the nature of the risk would be explained to her and she would be urged to obtain independent legal advice in order to rebut a presumption of undue influence by the husband. The requirement of independent legal advice has fallen to be considered on a number of occasions. It has been accepted by the courts that a lender can delegate to a solicitor responsibility for advising a wife in an *O'Brien*-type case.

In *Credit Lyonnais Bank Nederland NV* v *Burch* [1997] 1 All ER 144 the Court of Appeal articulated a much stricter approach than hitherto as to what a lender had to do to avoid being fixed with notice of someone else's undue influence etc. There the court emphasised that what a lender had to do to avoid such notice depended upon the circumstances of the case including in particular the extent of the risk facing the person seeking to avoid the transaction. Here on the facts (see below) it was *not enough* for CLBN simply to advise B to seek independent legal advice (as it had done) before signing the deed of mortgage and guarantee. They had to do more because here the transaction was not just to the manifest disadvantage of B it was one which 'shocks the conscience of the court' (per Millett LJ). Further, it was not relevant that B had refused to follow CLBN's advice to get independent legal advice. Unfortunately the court was not particularly forthcoming as to the additional steps that CLBN could and should have taken to avoid being fixed with notice of the third party's undue influence here.

The charge
The court has also had to consider whether a charge which has been induced by misrepresentation should be set aside in full or should be upheld as valid to the extent to which the chargor thought the charge was valid. In *TSB Bank plc* v *Camfield* [1995] 1 All ER 951 a husband and wife entered into a transaction in order to secure loan facilities for the husband's company from the plaintiff bank. The security for the loan was the matrimonial home, over which the bank took a legal charge. The wife was induced to stand as surety by an innocent misrepresentation

by her husband that their maximum liability for the loan was limited to £15,000 when in fact it was unlimited. The husband's business failed and the bank brought proceedings against the husband and wife. The county court judge gave judgment for the bank against the wife for £15,000 and made an order for possession of the home, subject to the wife making payment in full within six months. The wife appealed, claiming that she was entitled to have the charge set aside in toto. The Court of Appeal allowed the appeal; the case came within the principles laid down in *Barclays Bank plc* v *O'Brien* (above). As to the bank's view that the court could set aside the charge on terms that the wife had acknowledged that it was a valid security for £15,000, the court agreed with the view expressed by Ferris J in the unreported first instance case of *Allied Irish Bank* v *Byrne* (1 February 1994) that the wife's right to set aside the transaction (because she could rely on misrepresentation by her husband to resist liability to the lender pursuant to a charge) was 'an all or nothing process'. Accordingly, the bank was not entitled to an order that the charge be partially enforceable against the wife.

However, in *Barclays Bank plc* v *Caplan* (1997) The Times 12 December the court concluded that neither of the aforementioned cases 'was authority for the proposition that setting aside was invariably an "all or nothing" process even in a case where the objectionable features of the document could readily be severed from the rest without rewriting it'. This retreat from the 'all or nothing' approach will clearly be welcomed by lending institutions. In essence the case decided that if part of a mortgage was rendered unenforceable because of undue influence/ misrepresentation, the tainted part might be severed leaving the untainted part enforceable against the debtor.

Employer/employee relationship

The Court of Appeal has followed the *O'Brien* principle in a case where the relationship between the debtor and the mortgagor was not that of husband and wife or of persons living together but one of employer and employee. In *Credit Lyonnais Bank Nederland NV* v *Burch* [1997] 1 All ER 144 B (the defendant) was an employee of P a holiday tour operator. She was ten years younger than P and had close links with him eg she did baby sitting at his home and visited his family at weekends. B had a lot of trust in P and she agreed at P's request to mortgage her flat as collateral security for the tour company's overdraft with the plaintiff bank (CLBN). As a junior employee she had no incentive to do this and at the relevant time she did not appreciate the extent of the tour company's indebtedness. CLBN's solicitor advised B to seek independent legal advice before signing the deed of mortgage and guarantee. However, she did not do so (although in a letter to the bank's solicitor she stated that she fully understood the nature and implications of the transaction). In due course, the tour company went into liquidation. After unsuccessfully seeking payment from P, CLBN proceeded against B and sought an order for possession of her flat. B in defence invoked the principle laid down in *Barclays Bank plc* v *O'Brien* [1993] 3 WLR 786 (ie she pleaded that there was a presumption of undue influence by her employer over her of which CLBN had constructive notice and therefore the mortgage and guarantee ought to be set aside). The court found that the relationship of trust and confidence between B and P was such that a presumption of undue influence had arisen. Further, B's liability under the guarantee was not just to the value of her flat but was an unlimited guarantee of her employer's business overdraft (ie the company's borrowing from CLBN past, present and future together with interest). The transaction was so manifestly disadvantageous to B (who had no direct interest in the company) that the steps taken by CLBN (advised B to take independent advice) were *not enough* to avoid them being fixed with constructive notice of P's undue influence over B when neither the extent of B's potential liability had been explained to her nor had she received independent advice. Accordingly, the transaction was set aside. Nourse LJ concluded that the case 'might broadly be said to fall under *Barclays Bank plc* v *O'Brien*' (although as the court itself recognised the terms of the mortgage were so harsh and unconscionable that it was hardly necessary for a court of equity to rely on that decision in order to avoid the transaction).

Mother/son relationship
In *Birmingham Midshires Mortgage Services Ltd* v *Sabherwal* (2000) 80 P & CR 256 the Court of Appeal concluded that the relationship between an adult son and a mother in her mid-fifties did not give rise to any general presumption of undue influence exerciseable by the former over the latter.

Replacement mortgage
The question whether a replacement mortgage taken out with the same lender as a condition of discharging an earlier voidable mortgage (because of undue influence) was voidable, even if there was no undue influence operating at the time of its execution, fell to be considered in *Yorkshire Bank plc* v *Tinsley* (2004) The Times 12 August. Prior to this case the point had not been determined. The Court of Appeal took the view that if an obligation incurred between two or more people was legally ineffective in any way any new obligation arising out of the release of the earlier obligation would also be legally ineffective. Longmore LJ quoted with approval the observation of Shakespeare's King Lear that 'nothing will come of nothing'. The case established that where a mortgage was voidable any replacement mortgage from the same lender would also be voidable provided the replacement mortgage was taken out as a condition of discharging the earlier voidable mortgage (ie the mortgages had to be inseparably connected). The fact that there was no undue influence operating when the replacement mortgage was taken out did not save it. However, if the replacement mortgage was made with a different lender, that lender could not be deemed to be aware of the matters of which the first lender was deemed to be aware.

Judicial forum

Finally, in *National Westminster Bank plc* v *Kosto Poulos* (2000) The Times 2 March, the Court of Appeal decided that the first instance court was usually best able to decide if a wife in an *O'Brien*-type case had raised an arguable defence of misrepresentation/undue influence and that the Court of Appeal should be slow to interfere with the same. In deciding in favour of the first instance court, the Court of Appeal recognised reality – the judge hears the parties/witnesses and has the best opportunity to assess their veracity.

Conclusion

The establishment of the *O'Brien* principle has a wider significance beyond that of conferring greater protection (against the loss of their properties) upon eg wives who agree that their family homes can be used as security for their husband's debts. One of the key aims of the 1925 property legislation was to facilitate conveyancing by moving away from unregistered conveyancing to registration of title. A hallmark of the registered land system is that the doctrine of notice is irrelevant. Lord Wilberforce put the matter thus in *Williams & Glyn's Bank* v *Boland* [1981] AC 487 at p503 '... the registered land system is designed to free the purchaser from the hazards of notice – real or constructive ... The only kind of notice recognised is by entry on the register'. It is submitted that the effect of the *O'Brien* principle is to reintroduce the doctrine of notice in respect of registered land since a registered interest (legal charge) may now be defeated where the mortgagee has constructive notice of the husband's (borrower's) wrongdoing (misrepresentation, undue influence etc) which induced the wife to stand surety for the husband's debts (see P O'Hagan 'A Specially Protected Class' [1994] NLJ 763).

Appoint a receiver

This achieves much the same result as taking possession without the responsibilities. It is a statutory power given by s101 LPA 1925, which *arises* and becomes *exercisable* under the same circumstances as the power of sale (see above). There is no requirement for a court order. The receiver is deemed to be the agent of the mortgagor (s109(2)). In registered land the mortgagee must be registered as proprietor before pursuing this remedy. In *Lever Finance Ltd* v *Needleman's Trustee and Kreutzer* [1956] Ch 375 a transferee of a mortgage of registered land sought to exercise his statutory power to appoint a receiver. It was held that he could not do so until he had obtained his own registration as proprietor of the charge. Until then the receiver was merely an ordinary agent of the mortgagee.

Income received by the receiver

This must be applied in the following order:

1. payment of rates, taxes and other outgoings;

2. payments which rank in priority to the mortgage;
3. his own commission and insurance premiums, and the cost of repairs if so desired in writing by the mortgagee;
4. interest due under the mortgage;
5. if the mortgagee so directs in writing, repayment of the principal sum, otherwise the surplus to be paid to the person next entitled.

14.9 The remedies of the equitable mortgagee

Sue the mortgagor for the debt

As with a legal mortgage (see section 14.8), the mortgagee can take a normal action to recover the debt.

Foreclose

This is the equitable mortgagee's main remedy. The court ordering the foreclosure will direct the mortgagor to convey the legal estate to the mortgagee. The court may order a judicial sale instead of foreclosure: s91 LPA 1925.

Sell

The statutory power of sale only applies when the mortgage is made by deed. A power of sale may be given expressly in mortgages not made by deed, but this has been held to give the mortgagee the power to sell only his equitable interest. This may be extended to a power to sell the legal estate by inserting a power of attorney or declaration of trust in the mortgage deed. Under the latter the mortgagor declares that he holds the legal estate on trust for the mortgagee and authorises the mortgagee to appoint himself or a third party as trustee instead of the mortgagor, to enable a conveyance of the legal estate to a third party to be effected.

Take possession

An equitable mortgagee has no right to take possession, but the court may award him possession.

Appoint a receiver

If the mortgage is by deed the equitable mortgagee has the statutory power to do this, otherwise he has the right to have a receiver appointed by the court (s37 Supreme Court Act 1981). A receiver appointed by the court is not strictly an agent and is personally liable for his actions as a receiver. He will be required by the court to provide a security.

14.10 Other rights of the mortgagee

The right to fixtures (quicquid plantatur solo, solo cedit)

The mortgagee is entitled to all fixtures on the land at any time during the mortgage unless the mortgage provides otherwise: see *Hulme* v *Brigham* [1943] KB 152 and *Gough* v *Wood & Co* [1894] 1 QB 713.

The right to title deeds

The first mortgagee is entitled to possession of the title deeds. The mortgagor is entitled to inspect the deeds and make copies of them on reasonable notice. In the case of registered land the mortgage must be registered as a registered charge. Prior to the Land Registration Act 2002, the land certificate was held by the Land Registry and the mortgagee received a charge certificate.

The right to insure against fire at the mortgagor's expense

This allows a mortgagee to protect the value of his security. In practice it is usually specified in the mortgage deed that the mortgagor will himself insure the mortgaged property. The statutory power in s101 LPA 1925 is not adequate because the amount insured must not exceed that on the mortgage deed or, if no amount is specified, two-thirds of the amount required to reinstate the property if totally destroyed.

Note the right under the Fires Prevention (Metropolis) Act 1774 of any person interested in the insured property (including the mortgagor) to require that the insurance money be applied to make good the damage.

14.11 The right to tack further advances

The right to tack is the right of a mortgagee under certain circumstances to add a subsequent loan to an existing loan on the same property mortgaged by the same mortgagor and so to gain priority for this subsequent loan over any intermediate loans by other mortgagees.

Before 1926 subsequent equitable mortgagees without notice of a prior equitable mortgage could buy out the legal mortgage and thus squeeze out any intermediate equitable mortgage. This method of buying priority was known as 'the plank in the shipwreck' – 'tabula in naufragio'. This form of tacking by a subsequent mortgagee was abolished by s94 LPA 1925. After 1925 the only form of tacking that may take place is by the prior mortgagee.

Tacking is best understood if demonstrated by a linear diagram in the following form:

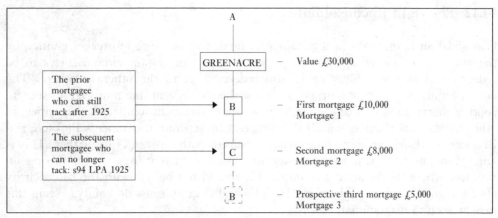

If A now wishes to borrow a further £5,000 on the security of Greenacre and B is prepared to lend the £5,000, he will wish to know whether he can 'tack' mortgage 3 to mortgage 1 in order to obtain priority for his combined loan of £15,000 before C.

Section 94 provides that the two loans may be tacked if one of three conditions is satisfied:

1. B has arranged with C to enable mortgage 1 and mortgage 3 to be added together.
2. There is an obligation in mortgage 1 to make further advances.
3. B has no notice of mortgage 2 created with C.

Thus the effect of s94 LPA 1925 is that the prior mortgagee (and only the prior mortgagee) has a right to make further advances which will rank in priority to subsequent mortgages created before the further advances provided that the following apply:

1. An arrangement to this effect has been made with subsequent mortgagees.
2. The prior mortgagee has no notice of the subsequent mortgage at the time of the further advance. A prior mortgagee may tack where he has no notice of intervening mortgages when he makes his further advance. Registration is notice for this purpose except where the prior mortgage was made expressly to secure a current account or other further advances, where only express notice will prevent tacking. A second mortgagee should give express notice of his mortgage to the first mortgagee as well as registering it. This exception to the rule that registration is equal to actual notice was designed to meet commercial needs. In the case of a bank a security to cover a customer's overdraft would not be as effective if further drawings were made dependent upon a search in the land charges register. It should be noted that this exception covers all mortgages where the contract contemplates further advances on the same security.
3. The prior mortgage imposes an obligation on the mortgagee to make the further advances, for example where an overdraft to a specified limit is secured by a mortgage.

14.12 The right to consolidate

Consolidation is the right of a person who holds two or more mortgages granted by the same mortgagor *on different properties* to refuse in certain circumstances to be redeemed as to one, unless he is also redeemed as to the other or others. The doctrine thus may force a mortgagor who wishes to redeem one mortgage to redeem another mortgage at the same time. The mortgagee can consolidate the securities, in other words treat them as one. If A mortgages by separate instruments Pinkacre and Blueacre to M, M can sometimes make A redeem both mortgages or neither. This is fair; M might have lent more money on Pinkacre than it was worth, relying on Blueacre where the security was ample. He should not be left with the bad security after the good has been redeemed. 'He who seeks equity must do equity.' Again this may be seen in diagrammatic form:

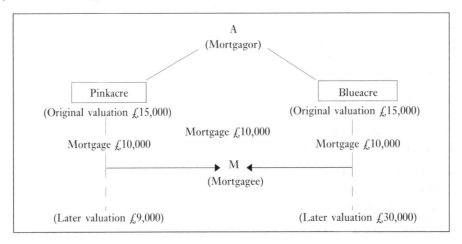

A enters into two separate mortgages of Pinkacre and Blueacre borrowing £10,000 on the security of each property. For some reason, perhaps a new road or a new industrial estate created nearby, the value of Pinkacre falls but the value of Blueacre reflects the current increase in land values. The total security is adequate at £39,000, but M is under-secured on Pinkacre. If A seeks to redeem Blueacre and leave M holding only Pinkacre, then M would be under-secured (£10,000 loan on property valued at £9,000). The doctrine of consolidation helps M by stating that if A seeks to redeem Blueacre he will only be allowed to do so on condition that he also redeems Pinkacre. M can insist on the simultaneous redemption of both mortgages. Waldock in *The Law of Mortgages* says:

> 'The principle upon which the court acts is that after the mortgagor is in default on his contract his right to redeem exists only in equity and, in seeking the assistance of equity, he must himself do equity.'

Before consolidation can take place, the following four conditions must be satisfied:

1. The right to consolidate must be reserved by at least one of the mortgage deeds, since s93 LPA 1925 forbids consolidation unless the right to consolidate is expressly reserved.
2. Both mortgages must have been created by the same mortgagor. If they have not been so created, there can never be consolidation, but according to *Sharpe* v *Rickards* [1909] 1 Ch 109 it is not necessary for them to have been created in favour of the same mortgagee.
3. The legal date of redemption must have passed on all the mortgages which it is desired to consolidate, as otherwise the mortgagor has a legal right to redeem which cannot be made subject to an equitable doctrine.
4. At one and the same time all the mortgages must have been vested in one person, and all the equities in another. If redemption is sought at that time, the mortgagee can consolidate. Even if this state of affairs has ceased when redemption is sought and the equities are then owned by different persons, a mortgagee who holds both mortgages can consolidate. The principle is that once a right to consolidate has arisen, a person who takes either of the equities takes subject to the right.

Note: There cannot be consolidation against a transferee of one of the equities by reason of anything which occurs after he acquires the property.

Examples

1.

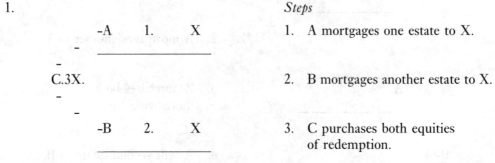

Steps

1. A mortgages one estate to X.

2. B mortgages another estate to X.

3. C purchases both equities of redemption.

Here there can be no consolidation since condition (2) above is not fulfilled. Both mortgages were not created by the same mortgagor.

2.

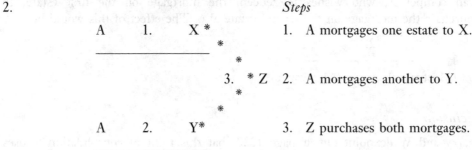

Steps

1. A mortgages one estate to X.

2. A mortgages another to Y.

3. Z purchases both mortgages.

Here Z can consolidate, provided that the right was reserved and the legal date for redemption has passed.

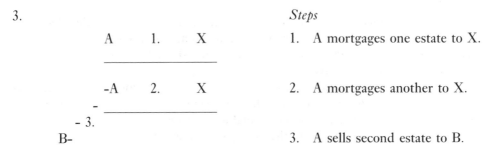

3.   *Steps*

A   1.   X   1. A mortgages one estate to X.

-A   2.   X   2. A mortgages another to X.

- 3.

B-   3. A sells second estate to B.

Here X acquired a right to consolidate after step 2. He can compel B, who purchased subject to that right, to take a transfer of the mortgage on the first estate if he wishes to redeem the mortgage on the second estate. This would leave the parties as:

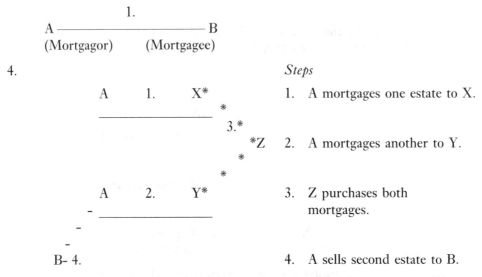

                    1.
A ————————————— B
(Mortgagor)   (Mortgagee)

4.   *Steps*

A   1.   X*   1. A mortgages one estate to X.

3.*

*Z   2. A mortgages another to Y.

A   2.   Y*   3. Z purchases both
                            mortgages.

B- 4.   4. A sells second estate to B.

Here Z acquired the right to consolidate after step 3 (see example (2) above). He can compel A, who wishes to redeem the mortgage on the first estate, to purchase the mortgage on the second estate also. The effect of this would be:

                    2.
B ————————————— A
(Mortgagor)   (Mortgagee)

Conclusion

Megarry and Wade point out at page 1222 that this right of consolidation 'causes less trouble than might be supposed'. On the other hand it can create problems for an innocent purchaser of a mortgage who may be presented with the requirement to redeem an unsuspected second mortgage, as in the case of B in example (3) above. Megarry and Wade conclude at page 1223:

> 'There may well be doubts as to the wisdom of equity in allowing a mortgagee who has made two distinct bargains, one good and one bad, to use the success of one to rescue him from the failure of the other. But the doctrine has existed almost as long as the equity of redemption itself and is too well settled to be questioned.'

14.13 The rights common to both parties

To grant a lease

1. A lease granted by the mortgagor before the mortgage is created is binding on the mortgagee provided that it is a legal lease or, if it is an equitable lease, it is registered as a land charge Class C(iv) if the land is unregistered, or the tenant is in actual occupation if the land is registered.
2. At common law, any lease granted by either party during the existence of the mortgage was not binding on the other without his consent.

By s99 LPA 1925 either party, provided that he is in possession or has appointed a receiver, can grant a lease binding on the other party, as long as:

1. No contrary intention is expressed in the mortgage deed.
2. If the lease is an agricultural or occupational lease, the term does not exceed 50 years, or 999 years for building leases.
3. The lease:

   a) reserves the best rent obtainable without a fine;
   b) takes effect in possession not more than 12 months after execution;
   c) contains a covenant by the tenant to pay the rent and a condition for re-entry on the rent being more than 30 days in arrear.

4. A counterpart executed by the lessee is delivered to the other party to the mortgage within one month.

The use of the statutory power of leasing by the mortgagor is often expressly excluded by the mortgage: *Rhodes* v *Dalby* [1971] 1 WLR 1325. If a mortgagor grants a lease when the statutory power is excluded it is void against the mortgagee although valid against the mortgagor: *Dudley and District Benefit Building Society* v *Emerson* [1949] Ch 707. If the mortgagee refuses to acknowledge such a lease and seeks to exercise one of his remedies against the mortgagor, the lessee may protect his interest by redeeming the mortgage.

In *Quennel* v *Maltby* [1979] 1 WLR 318 the Court of Appeal suggested that the mortgagee would only be able to exercise the remedies if they were used in good faith for the purpose of enforcing the security and not for any other ulterior motive, such as avoiding the effects of the Rent Act 1977.

To accept the surrender of a lease

By s100 LPA 1925 either party, if in possession or having appointed a receiver, can accept the surrender of a lease provided that within one month of the surrender he grants a new lease within his statutory powers for a term at least as long as that unexpired of the surrendered lease and at a rent at least equivalent to it. If these conditions are not complied with the surrender is void and the old lease continues.

14.14 Priority of mortgages

The position in respect of priority of mortgages has significantly changed following the coming into force of the Land Registration Act 2002. The new position can be summarised as follows:

1. As previously noted the creation of a legal mortgage in registered land under the LRA 2002 has to be by deed. The mortgage has to be registered. Priority of mortgages is by reference to the date of registration of the mortgages on the Charges Register, but mortgagees can agree a different priority by written agreement, which also needs to be registered.
2. Under the LRA 2002 as well as a mortgage of registered land being compulsorily registerable, a mortgage over an unregistered freehold interest, or an unregistered lease with a term unexpired of seven years will trigger registration.
3. As previously noted (see section 14.2) the situation in relation to the creation of equitable mortgages has changed since the coming into force of the LRA 2002. Following the de-materialisation of deeds under the 2002 Act, the Registry no longer issue either land certificates or charges certificates. Consequently, the pre LRA 2002 practice of creating an equitable mortgage by depositing a land certificate, effectively creating a lien on the deeds, is no longer possible.

    However, it would still be possible to create an equitable mortgage by, say, agreeing to grant a charge over registered land on a future date. This would not bind third parties unless a note of it is entered on the Register, either by a Unilateral Notice (broadly similar to cautions under the LRA 1925 regime) or an Agreed Notice (the rough equivalent of a Notice under the LRA 1925 regime).

14.15 Priority of mortgages of an equitable interest

This is governed by the rule in *Dearle* v *Hall* (1828) 3 Russ 1 as amended by ss137 and 138 LPA 1925.

The *Dearle* v *Hall* rule provides that priority depends upon the order in which the trustees received notice from the mortgagees. This rule originally applied to personalty, but s137(1) applies the rule to all dealings with equitable interests after 1925. It provides:

> 'The law applicable to dealings with equitable things in action which regulates the priority of competing interests therein, shall, as respects dealings with equitable interests in land, capital money, and securities representing capital money effected after the commencement of this Act, apply to and regulate the priority of competing interests therein.'

The object of the rule in *Dearle* v *Hall* was to enable a person to discover, by inquiries addressed to the trustees, whether the owner of an equitable interest had created any earlier incumbrances.

In the case of registered land the order of priority of equitable interests was formerly governed by s102(2) LRA 1925. This was repealed by s5 Land Registration Act 1986. The effect of this is to abolish the Minor Interests Index and provide that priority between dealings with equitable interests in registered land will also be determined by the rule in *Dearle* v *Hall*. The consequence of this is that in both registered and unregistered land the rule of priority for equitable mortgages will be the order in which notice is received by the trustees from the mortgagees.

15

Adverse Possession

15.1 General principles

15.2 Limitation periods

15.3 Running of time

15.4 Effect of lapse of time

15.5 Proof of squatter's title

15.1 General principles

Definition: 'adverse possession' means possession inconsistent with the title of the true owner.

Acquisition of title by adverse possession is one aspect of the law of limitation of actions: the prevention of stale claims and the prevention of endless litigation by the extinction of the right of action after a certain period of time are other aspects. Limitation of actions is purely statutory. Once an owner's right to take an action for possession against a squatter is barred by lapse of time his title to the land is extinguished, and the squatter acquires it by being in possession. The title he acquires, however, is only the title of the owner he dispossesses, so he may be evicted by a person having a better title.

15.2 Limitation periods

These are now laid down by the Limitation Act 1980. The main periods for land law purposes are:

1. Six years for simple contracts, arrears of rent, tort (s5).
2. Twelve years for actions on a deed (s15):

   'No action shall be brought to recover land after the expiration of 12 years from the date on which the right of action accrued.'

3. Twelve years for actions to recover money secured by a mortgage or charge (s20) and for a redemption action (s16).

When a mortgagee has been in possession of any mortgaged land for a period of 12 years no action to redeem such land can be brought by the mortgagor after the end of that period.

The limitation period in respect of land owned by the Crown or by a corporation sole is, however, 30 years (Schedule 1, Part II).

The interaction between s20 Limitation Act 1980 (which governs claims for a mortgage debt) and s5 of the 1980 Act (which governs claims under a simple contract) fell to be considered in *Bristol & West plc* v *Bartlett* [2003] 1 WLR 284. There B (mortgagor) had defaulted on his mortgage repayments. Thereafter BW (mortgagee) sold the property charged as security but for a price that left a significant shortfall in the amount due under the mortgage at the date of sale. The mortgagee brought proceedings to recover the shortfall after six years but before 12 years had elapsed. Under s20 Limitation Act 1980 the limitation period in respect of the principal claimed was 12 years from the time the cause of action accrued, but only six years in respect of claims for interest, whereas under s5 of the 1980 Act the limitation period was six years. B raised a defence of limitation to the action of BW for the shortfall, claiming that the effect of the sale was to discharge the liability arising under the covenant to pay in the mortgage deed. Accordingly, he contended that his only obligation to pay the outstanding mortgage debt arose as an implied term under a simple contract, that the matter was governed by s5 of the 1980 Act and that, on the facts, BW's action was time barred as being outside the relevant six-year period. The issue was whether a limitation period of six or 12 years applied to the claim of the mortgagee.

The Court of Appeal concluded that s20 Limitation Act 1980 and a 12-year limitation period applied to any action to recover *any principal sum* secured by way of mortgage in existence when the right to recover accrued and that it was not necessary for the principal sum to be still secured by the mortgage when the action was brought. The argument that the effect of a sale by a lender was to discharge the liability arising under the covenant to pay in the mortgage deed was rejected (ie no separate cause of action arose when the shortfall was ascertained). However, claims for interest were subject to a six-year limitation period.

15.3 Running of time

In order to determine when the action has become barred it is necessary to discover when time *began to run*, including any factors which could postpone this date, what will start time running afresh and what can suspend the running of time.

When time begins to run

When the owner is entitled to possession
Time begins to run as soon as:

1. The owner has been dispossessed or has discontinued his possession.
2. Adverse possession has been taken by some other person. As stated above, adverse possession is possession inconsistent with the title of the true owner, and whether the possession of the other person was adverse is a matter of fact depending on the circumstances of each case.

In *Wallis's Cayton Bay Holiday Camp Ltd* v *Shell-Mex and BP Ltd* [1975] QB 94 Lord Denning described the nature of the claim as follows:

'Possession by itself is not enough to give a title. It must be adverse possession. The true owner must have discontinued possession or have been dispossessed and another must have taken it adversely to him. There must be something in the nature of an ouster of the true owner by the wrongful possessor.'

The meaning of 'discontinued possession' or dispossession was further considered by Sir John Pennycuick in *Treloar* v *Nute* [1976] 1 WLR 1295:

'The person claiming by possession must show either (1) discontinuance by the paper owner followed by possession, or (2) dispossession ... (ouster) of the paper owner ... where the person claiming by possession establishes possession in the full sense of inclusive possession, that by itself connotes absence of possession on the part of the paper owner.'

There must be an intention to 'exclude the owner as well as other people'. This question of intention was explained by Slade J in *Powell* v *McFarlane* (1977) 38 P & CR 452 as follows:

'... the courts ... will require clear and affirmative evidence that the trespasser, claiming that he has acquired possession, not only had the requisite intention to possess, but made such intention clear to the world. If his acts are open to more than one interpretation and he has not made it perfectly plain to the world at large by his actions or words that he has intended to exclude the owner as best he can, the courts will treat him as not having had the requisite animus possidendi and consequently as not having dispossessed the owner.'

From the cases it is clear that adverse possession must be a question of fact in which circumstances such as the nature of the land and the way in which the land is enjoyed must be taken into account.

The intention to possess was the subject of further consideration by the Court of Appeal in *Buckinghamshire County Council* v *Moran* [1989] 2 All ER 225. A plot of land had been conveyed to the plaintiffs in 1955. To the south the plot was bounded by a laurel hedge; to the west there was a privet hedge; to the east there was a fence in poor condition along the road frontage and to the north was Dolphin Place with nothing to separate the plot from it. From about 1967 the previous owners of Dolphin Place had maintained the plot and treated it as part of their garden; they had mowed the grass and trimmed the hedges. In 1971 Dolphin Place was conveyed to the defendant

'together with ... all such estate right title and interest as the vendors may have in or over [the plot]'.

The vendors made a statutory declaration to the effect that since 1967 they had cultivated the plot and from time to time parked a horse-box there and that no one had challenged their right to occupy it. They further declared that their permission had been sought to lay an electric cable across the plot. The plaintiffs sought possession of the plot and the defendant claimed that they had been dispossessed by him more than 12 years before they instituted the proceedings. The judge found that the plaintiffs had never discontinued their possession of the plot, and that finding was not now challenged. Nevertheless, he declared that the defendant was the freehold owner of the plot, and the plaintiffs appealed.

The appeal was dismissed: the defendant had shown both factual possession and the requisite intention to possess.

Slade LJ concluded as follows:

'Under the Limitation Act 1980, as under the previous law, the person claiming a possessory title had to show either discontinuance by the paper owner followed by possession or dispossession (or, as it was sometimes called "ouster") of the paper owner ...

If the law was to attribute possession of land to a person who could establish no paper title to possession, he must be shown to have both factual possession and the requisite intention to possess (animus possidendi). A person claiming to have dispossessed another similarly had to fulfil both those requirements. However, a further requirement which the alleged dispossessor claiming the benefit of the [Limitation Act 1980 had to satisfy was] to show that his possession has been adverse within the meaning of ... paragraph 8 of Schedule 1 ...

The crucial question was whether Mr Moran was in adverse possession of the plot on 28 October 1973 ...

On the evidence it would appear clear that by 28 October 1973, Mr Moran had acquired complete and exclusive physical control of the plot. He had secured a complete enclosure of the plot and its annexation to Dolphin Place. Any intruder could have gained access to the plot only by way of Dolphin Place, unless he was prepared to climb the locked gate fronting the highway or to scramble through one or other of the hedges bordering the plot.

Mr Moran had put a new lock and chain on the gate and had fastened it.

He and his mother had been dealing with the plot as any occupying owners might have been expected to deal with it. They had incorporated it into the garden of Dolphin Place.

The more difficult question was whether Mr Moran had the necessary animus possidendi ... the animus possidendi involved the intention, in one's own name and on one's own behalf, to exclude the world at large, including the owner with the paper title, so far as was reasonably practicable and so far as the process of the law would allow.

As a number of authorities indicated, enclosure by itself prima facie indicated the requisite animus possidendi: *Seddon* v *Smith* (1877) 36 LT 168, 169.

However, the placing of the new lock and chain and gate did amount to a final unequivocal demonstration of Mr Moran's intention to possess the land.'

It must be shown that the claimant has accepted the assertion of the right by the paper owner, and the mere assertion alone by the true paper owner of a claim to possession in land contained in a letter sent to the squatter is not sufficient to prevent the squatter obtaining title by adverse possession.

The question of intention is a continuing problem for the courts.

The erection of a fence for some 24 hours was not a sufficient act of possession. This did not constitute a sufficient degree of exclusive physical control. In *Marsden* v *Miller* (1992) 64 P & CR 239, Scott LJ put the matter thus:

> 'To obtain possession of land, both a mental element and a factual element were requisite. The factual element had to involve an appropriate degree of exclusive physical control. The mental element, the Animus 2 precedent, had to consist of an intention to take possession to the exclusion of all others.'

The House of Lords has recently delivered an important decision on adverse possession in *J A Pye (Oxford) Ltd* v *Graham* [2002] 3 WLR 221. There P (the paper owner) purchased in 1977 a large estate. Subsequently, he sold the greater part of it, including Manor Farm, but retained 57 acres of farmland because of its development potential. In respect of this retained land he granted a grazing licence to the owners of Manor Farm. Thereafter, G became the registered proprietor of Manor Farm and when his written grazing licence expired in December 1983 he requested a renewal which was refused because of the possibility of P making a planning permission application in respect of the 'grazing land'. In 1985 a further request by G for a renewal was not answered. Despite this refusal, G remained in occupation of the relevant farm land and continued to use it as if he had a grazing licence. In January 1999, P commenced proceedings against G for possession of the 'grazing land', contending that the requisite 12 years had not elapsed. In support of this contention P argued that G's oral request to P for a further licence demonstrated an intention to submit to P's right of possession which was at variance with an intention to possess (in a written statement prepared for the trial G made clear that he would have accepted a new licence and paid for the same). At first instance the judge concluded that G had established a possessory title. However, on appeal the Court of Appeal held that G had not manifested an intention to possess the land. The defendants (G's widow and personal representatives) appealed. The issue was whether the squatter (G) had dispossessed the paper owner of the land (P) by ordinary possession of the land in question for the relevant time in the absence of consent from the owner.

Their lordships concluded that two requirements had to be satisfied in order to establish adverse possession. First, a squatter had to exercise a sufficient degree of physical custody and control (ie factual possession). In order to establish such possession, a squatter had to show absence of the paper owner's consent, a single and exclusive possession that he had been treating the land in the manner of an occupying owner and that no other individual had done so. Second, the squatter had to have an intention to possess the land. It was not necessary for him to demonstrate an intention to own or acquire ownership of the land. Rather, the requisite intention was to possess on his own behalf and to exclude the world at large, including the paper title owner, so far as was reasonably practicable. Accordingly, it was immaterial that the squatter would have been willing to pay the paper title owner to occupy the land if requested to do so. Given that G had been in factual possession of the land from January 1984 onwards (the licence expired in December 1983), and from September 1984 onwards had used it as his own, and since P had done nothing on the land and was effectively excluded from it throughout the relevant period, G had manifested an intention to possess the land. The judge had correctly concluded that G had established a possessory title. Accordingly, the appeal would be allowed.

This is an important decision on adverse possession for at least four reasons. First, the thrust of their Lordships' judgment was to move away from an emphasis upon 'adverse' possession. Lord Browne-Wilkinson put the matter thus: 'In my judgment much confusion and complication would be avoided if reference to adverse possession were to be avoided so far as possible and effect given to the clear words of the [Limitation] Acts. The question is simply whether the defendant squatter has dispossessed the paper owner by going into ordinary possession of the land for the requisite period without the consent of the owner' (at pp232–233). Secondly, establishing a sufficient degree of custody and control depends upon the circumstances of each case, and in particular the nature of the land and the manner of its usage. Thirdly, their Lordships emphasised a possessory justification for acquiring title by limitation – factual possession plus intention to possess. Finally, at first instance, Neuberger J concluded that the word 'action' in s15(1) Limitation Act 1980 only applied to proceedings brought in a court by an owner seeking to recover disputed land. It did not extend to an application to the Land Registry to warn off cautions, nor to an application by originating summons to remove cautions because neither application was an action to recover (the disputed) land.

Successive squatters

A squatter can give as good a title as he has. If the first squatter is dispossessed, the second squatter acquires any time which has already run, but if the first squatter abandons possession before the second takes possession, time starts running afresh.

The fact that where a squatter dispossesses another squatter, and the first squatter abandons his claim, then the second squatter can add the time enjoyed by the first squatter to achieve the necessary 12 years' adverse possession was confirmed by the Court of Appeal in *Mount Carmel Investments Ltd* v *Peter Thurlow Ltd* [1988] 3 All ER 129. There the first squatter had abandoned his claim and the defendants as second squatters were entitled to rely on the combined period of 14 years' possession to give them a title under s15(1) Limitation Act 1980.

Future interests

The remainderman or reversioner must sue for possession either within 12 years of the commencement of the adverse possession, or within six years of his interest vesting in possession, whichever is the longer. The second period is not available when the land is entailed and the reversioner or remainderman's interest could have been barred by the tenant in tail. (As noted previously no new entailed interests can be created after 31 December 1996: see Schedule 1 para 5 TOLATA 1996.)

Leaseholds

Time does not begin to run against the reversioner if the tenant is dispossessed until the lease expires, because until then he has no right to possession. A tenant cannot acquire title against his landlord during the currency of the lease because his possession is not adverse. See *Fairweather* v *St Marylebone Property Co Ltd* [1963] AC 510. Failure to pay the rent only bars the landlord's right to recover any unpaid instalment after six years. The landlord's title will, however, be barred if a third party is in adverse receipt of rent for 12 years ... in the case of a lease in writing under which a rent of 'not less than ten pounds a year' (Schedule 1 Part I para 6 of Limitation Act 1980) is reserved. In such a situation the landlord's right of action is deemed to accrue 'on the date when the rent was first received by the person wrongfully claiming to be so entitled and not on the date of the determination of the lease ...' (Schedule 1 Part I para 6 of Limitation Act 1980).

Tenants at will and at sufferance

Tenant at will. Formerly time ran from one year after the grant of the tenancy unless rent was paid or a written acknowledgement of the landlord's title was given, which caused time to start running afresh. This rule was abolished by the Limitation Act 1980, and now time runs in favour of a tenant at will from the time his tenancy comes to an end.

Tenant at sufferance. Time runs from the commencement of the tenancy because in one sense his possession is already adverse. A tenant who remains in occupation at the expiry of his lease whether periodic or for a term of years without paying rent and without the landlord's consent is a tenant at sufferance, and time begins to run from the expiry of the lease.

Rentcharges

A rentcharge is defined in s38(1) Limitation Act 1980 as a

'... periodical sum of money charged upon or payable out of land, except a rent service or interest on a mortgage of land'.

Time runs from the last payment of rent to the owner of the rentcharge.
Section 38(8) Limitation Act 1980 provides:

'References in this Act to the possession of land shall, in the case of ... rentcharges, be construed as references to the receipt of the ... rent, and references to the date of dispossession or discontinuance of possession of land shall, in the case of rentcharges, be construed as references to the date of the last receipt of rent.'

Mortgages

1. The mortgagor's right to redeem is barred after 12 years' possession by the mortgagee without receiving payment by or on behalf of the mortgagor. Receipt of rent and profits from the mortgaged land is not enough to stop time running.
   Note: this is an exception to the rule that the possession must be adverse.

2. Where a mortgagee in possession either receives any sum in respect of principal or interest or acknowledges the title of the mortgagor, an action to redeem the land may be brought at any time before the expiration of 12 years from the date of the last such payment or acknowledgement: s29(4) Limitation Act 1980.

3 As previously noted (see Chapter 14, section 14.8) a mortgagee in exercising its power of sale is under a duty to obtain a proper price. In *Raja* v *Lloyds TSB* (2001) 82 P & CR 19 R owned four residential properties which were repossessed and sold pursuant to a number of charges granted in favour of L (the defendant bank). R commenced an action against L (the mortgagee) claiming damages in respect of repossession and sale, contending that L had sold the properties at an under value in breach of the aforementioned duty. His claim was struck out as being statute-barred. Their Lordships held that such a claim by a mortgagor had to be bought within six years.

Trusts

By virtue of s21 of the Limitation Act 1980, an action by a beneficiary to recover trust property or in respect of any breach of trust cannot be brought after the expiration of six years from the date on which the right of action accrued. The date on which the right of action accrues is, in the case of a breach of trust, the date on which the breach occurred. However, no limitation period applies to an action by a beneficiary where the personal representative/trustee has either committed a fraudulent breach of duty or where he has converted the assets of the estate to his own use.

Schedule 1 para 9 of the 1980 Act provides that where 'settled land' or any land subject to a trust of land 'is in possession of a person entitled to a beneficial interest in the land or the proceeds of sale ... no right of action for its recovery shall be treated ... as accruing during that possession to any person entitled to a beneficial interest in the land or the proceeds of sale.'

In *Earnshaw and Others* v *Hartley* [2000] Ch 155 the Court of Appeal declined to give para 9 a literal interpretation. There a widow (MH) died intestate in 1983 leaving three adult children. Her estate included a farmhouse. However, no application for a grant of letters of administration was made at that stage. The son lived at the property throughout. In 1985 he married the defendant (JH) and by his will left his entire estate to her absolutely. After the son's death, his widow continued to reside at the property. In 1998 MH's daughters obtained a grant of letters of administration to their mother's estate and sought a sale of the farmhouse. JH contended that her husband and she by succession had been in adverse possession of the farmhouse for more than 12 years since MH's death in 1983 and therefore she had acquired a possessory title under the Limitation Act 1980. The question was whether the defendant's claim was defeated by para 9 of Schedule 1.

The plaintiffs contended that at all relevant times the farmhouse was 'in the possession of a person entitled to a beneficial interest in the land or in the proceeds of sale', namely the son, and that they were other persons 'entitled to a beneficial interest in the land or the proceeds of sale'. JH argued that since para 9 was expressed to apply to settled land or to land held on trust for sale it had no application here to the pre-grant period. This was not a case of settled land and since on the death of MH her estate was vested in the President of the Family Division until administration she argued that while the farm was so vested it was not held on a trust for sale (ie her argument was based on a literal interpretation of para 9).

In finding for the plaintiffs the Court of Appeal rejected this literal interpretaion of para 9 because it would have involved the court interpreting the provision in an unacceptable way. Further, while it was correct to state that the President of the Family Division was not a trustee of the farm while it was vested in him and that therefore it was not held on a trust for sale during that time he did hold it on a presumptive trust for sale. Nourse LJ concluded that it would be unrealistic 'for limitation purposes to distinguish between the state of affairs existing before and after the grant of administration'.

Finally, it is worth noting that it is no longer the case that when a person dies intestate his property vests in the President of the Family Division. Rather, from 1 July 1995, the property of such a person passes to the Public Trustee until the grant of administration (this is the effect of s14 of the Law of Property (Miscellaneous Provisions) Act 1994).

Adverse possession of trust property does not bar the trustee's title until all the beneficiaries are barred; for example, if land is held on a trust of land for X for life, then to Y for life and then to Z, 12 years' possession by S, a squatter, against X will bar only X; time will not start to run against Y until X's death, and similarly time will not run against Z until Y's death, and S will only bar the trustee's legal estate by 12 years' adverse possession after Y's death.

Section 18 Limitation Act 1980. A trustee can never acquire title by limitation against the beneficiaries. Time does not run in favour of a beneficiary against the trustees unless the beneficiary is solely and absolutely entitled. This would occur when a purchaser is let into possession before conveyance.

Postponement of the limitation period

The date from which time begins to run may be postponed by:

The owner being under a disability
If the owner was under a disability, for example was an infant or a patient under a Mental Health Act, when the adverse possession began he has an alternative period of six years from the end of his disability to take action, subject to a maximum period of 30 years from the beginning of adverse possession (s28(1) and (4) Limitation Act 1980). A supervening disability has no effect on the running of time; the disability must end at the time when the cause of action accrued.

Fraud, fraudulent concealment or mistake

Time does not begin to run until the claimant discovers the fact or could have discovered the fact with 'reasonable diligence' (s32(1) Limitation Act 1980).

Starting time running afresh

Time may be started running afresh by a payment or by a written and signed acknowledgement of the plaintiff's title (s29 Limitation Act 1980). Once the limitation period has elapsed the owner's title cannot be revived by any payment or acknowledgement.

Suspension of the period

Once time has started to run it will run continuously. Suspension of the running of time can only be done by statute; for example, during the Second World War, running of time was suspended against any person who was an enemy or detained in enemy territory by the Limitation (Enemies and War Prisoners) Act 1945.

Time no longer running in squatter's favour

The wording of s15(1) Limitation Act 1980 makes it clear that time stops running in a squatter's favour when a claimant brings his action for possession for the disputed land. In *J A Pye (Oxford) Ltd* v *Graham* [2000] 3 WLR 242 as previously noted, Neuberger J concluded that the word 'action' in s15(1) of the 1980 Act only applied to proceedings brought in a court by an owner seeking to recover disputed land. It did not extend to an application to the Land Registry to warn off cautions nor to an application by originating summons to remove cautions because neither application was an action to 'recover [the disputed] land'.

15.4 Effect of lapse of time

Once the limitation period has been achieved:

1. The owner's title is extinguished in that he can no longer take legal proceedings to recover the property. Section 17 Limitation Act 1980 provides:

    '... at the expiration of the period prescribed by this Act for any person to bring an action to recover land ... the title of that person shall be extinguished.'

2. The squatter acquires the title that the person he dispossessed had, subject to all third party rights. A squatter, not being a purchaser for value, takes subject even to unregistered registrable rights, but there is no actual transfer of title to him and his protection is negative in that he is protected from interference by the person who has been dispossessed. The nature of the squatter's title was

described by Lord Radcliffe in *Fairweather* v *St Marylebone Property Co Ltd* [1963] AC 510 as follows:

> 'He is not at any stage of his possession a successor to the title of the man he has dispossessed. He comes in and remains in always by right of possession, which in due course becomes incapable of disturbance as time exhausts the one or more periods allowed by statute for successful intervention. His title, therefore, is never derived through but arises always in spite of the dispossessed owner.'

3. Leases: unless the landlord has reserved a right of forfeiture for breach of covenant and a covenant is broken he cannot eject a squatter until the lease has expired. If, however, the dispossessed tenant surrenders his lease, the lease merges with the reversion and the landlord can sue immediately for possession.

   Fairweather v *St Marylebone Property Co Ltd* (above) was distinguished in respect of land with registered title by Browne-Wilkinson J in *Spectrum Investment Co* v *Holmes* [1981] 1 WLR 221. In the case of registered land, if the squatter registered his rights under the LRA 1925, once the limitation period has run, those rights could not be defeated by a subsequent surrender of the lease between the original lessee and the landlord. In *Fairweather* the House of Lords held that a surrender of the lease enabled the landlord to eject the squatter forthwith. The House of Lords did not have to consider the effect of registration of the squatter's title.

   A squatter is not entitled to relief from forfeiture under s146 LPA 1925.

Registered land

Pre Land Registration Act 2002
Section 75 LRA 1925 provided that the Limitation Act 1980 should apply to registered land in the same way as to unregistered land, with one important distinction: that when an interest would have been extinguished in the case of unregistered land then in the case of registered land it would not be extinguished. Instead it was deemed to be held in trust by the registered proprietor for the person who had acquired title against him.

The effect of s75 was that no legal title could vest in the adverse possessor until he had been registered as proprietor. Until then the registered proprietor's estate was held on trust for the adverse possessor.

In addition, s70(1)(f) LRA 1925 provided that 'rights acquired or in course of being acquired under the Limitation Acts' were overriding interests (see Chapter 7).

Land Registration Act 2002
The 'old' law on adverse possession which was considered to be unsatisfactory was replaced with an entirely new substantive system applicable only to registered land. See Chapter 7, section 7.8 at p85.

15.5 Proof of squatter's title

The fact of long possession alone is not enough to produce a good title between vendor and purchaser. In order to provide a good title by limitation a vendor must prove the following:

1. the title of the former owner to the particular land;
2. the extinction of that title in favour of the vendor.

This is a particularly heavy burden of proof because the vendor will normally have no documents of title in order to support his claim to be able to sell. Problems may well arise relating to restrictive covenants that remain in force. See *Re Nisbet and Pott's Contract* [1906] 1 Ch 386.

If a person has been in occupation of land for 14 years following a contract to purchase which was never completed by a conveyance, then possession is not adverse because there was always an answer to any action, namely that the possession was by virtue of the contract. See *Hyde* v *Pearce* [1982] 1 WLR 560.

16

Future Interests: The Rules against Perpetuities and Accumulations

16.1   Introduction

16.2   Vested and contingent interests

16.3   The rule against perpetuities

16.4   The common law rule against perpetuities

16.5   Modifications to the common law rule before 1964

16.6   Determinable and conditional interests

16.7   Perpetuities and Accumulations Act 1964

16.8   Powers

16.9   Exceptions to the perpetuity rule

16.10 The rule against accumulations

16.11 Revision summary

16.12 Proposals for reform

16.1 Introduction

The law dealing with perpetuities and accumulations should be considered purely as an exercise in logic. It has very little to do with the rest of land law, but once grasped the principles are very straightforward. The most important distinction is between vested and contingent interests (see section 16.2). The rule against perpetuities applies only to *contingent interests*.

It should also be noted that the rules apply only to *future interests*, that is, interests taking effect otherwise than in possession. An interest in possession gives an immediate right to the enjoyment of the land. A future interest gives a right of enjoyment at some time in the future. This is explained in Megarry and Wade at p291:

'A future interest in land is an interest which confers a right to the enjoyment of the land at a future time ...'

Future interests are divided into two categories:

1. Interest in reversion: this is that part of the grantor's interest not disposed of by the grant, which will revert back to him or his successors when the estates which have been created come to an end.
2. Interest in remainder: this is that part of the grantor's interest that is disposed of by the grant, provided that it is postponed to an interest in possession created at the same time. The future interest must be held by someone other than the original grantor, or his successors, and the name is derived from the fact that possession will remain away from the original grantor.

The grant by X, a fee simple owner, to A for life, remainder to B for life, remainder to C in tail creates:

a) one interest in possession: A's life interest;
b) two interests in remainder: B's life interest,
                                      C's fee tail;
c) one interest in reversion: X's fee simple.

The rule against perpetuities applies only to interests in remainder. This is because interests in reversion are always *vested*.

16.2 Vested and contingent interests

Interests in remainder can be either vested or contingent. An interest is vested when the grantee of the interest is certain that he will be entitled to the interest at some time in the future, as soon as the interests prior to his own have determined. An interest is contingent if the grantee cannot say with certainty whether or not he will be so entitled. The time at which it must be decided whether a grant is vested or contingent is the date at which the grant takes effect:

1. if by will, the date of the testator's death;
2. if inter vivos, the date of the grant.

Note: the word 'vested' does not mean that the grantee is entitled in possession. A future interest can be vested. The test to be adopted is to ascertain whether the owner is absolutely entitled at the present time to assume possession whenever it may fall vacant.

Vested interests

A future interest is vested provided that three conditions are satisfied:

1. the identity of the grantee or grantees must be known; and

2. all conditions attached to the grant must have been complied with; and
3. the respective shares of the beneficiaries must be known.

Contingent interests

An interest is contingent if any of the three aforementioned conditions is *not* satisfied. It will stay contingent until all the conditions are satisfied. Megarry and Wade explain this also at page 291:

> 'A contingent interest is one which will give no right at all unless or until some future event happens.'

It is vital to understand the distinction between vested and contingent interests, as the rule against perpetuities (see 'Importance of the distinction', and section 16.3 below) applies only to contingent interests.

Examples of vested and contingent interests

1. Gift by will 'to A for life, remainder to B'.
   At testator's death A and B are alive.
   B's interest in remainder is vested as all three conditions are satisfied.
2. Gift by will 'to A for life, remainder to B when he reaches 21'.
   At testator's death A is alive and B is 14.
   B's interest in remainder is contingent: condition 2 is not satisfied as B has not reached 21. The gift to B will vest when he reaches 21.
3. Gift by will 'to A for life, remainder to all the children of A'.
   At testator's death A is alive with two children.
   The children's interest in remainder is contingent. A may have more children. Thus condition 1 is not satisfied; the identity of all possible children of A is not known. Nor is condition 3 satisfied: the respective shares will depend on how many children A has. The gift will vest when A dies, as no more children can then be born to A.

Importance of the distinction

If someone holds a vested interest then he cannot lose it. If he holds a contingent interest, it is uncertain whether he will obtain the benefit from the property concerned. Thus at death a vested interest will always pass under the will or intestacy, but a contingent interest does not.

If an interest is contingent it is subject to the rule against perpetuities, but if it is vested it is not subject to the rule.

16.3 The rule against perpetuities

Unless and until an interest in land becomes vested, the interest cannot be sold. Before the Settled Land Act 1882, a landowner could ensure that land remained in the family by creating a long succession of future interests. These interests were not necessarily contingent, but often were, in order to provide for circumstances unknown to the settlor – whether, for instance, his grandson would have two or three sons.

In order to prevent land from being tied up in contingent (and hence inalienable) future interests for generations, the rule against perpetuities was developed. The common law rule was settled by the beginning of the nineteenth century, and its aim was to allow a landowner to tie up land in contingent future interests so as to benefit his children and grandchildren, but no further. To achieve this, gifts had to vest within the lifetime of persons alive at the date the gift took effect. A man's children were normally alive at his death, but his grandchildren need not be. As donors frequently made it a condition of receipt of the interest that the grandchildren should reach 21, 21 years was allowed in addition to the lifetime during which the gift had to vest.

The common law rule was very strictly interpreted by the courts, which applied pure logic rather than common sense. Hence many gifts failed because they might not vest within the period, even though it was highly likely that they would vest. The possibility of failure renders the gift void *ab initio*.

In response to these problems, the common law rules were supplemented by first the LPA 1925 and then the Perpetuities and Accumulations Act 1964, which applies to gifts taking effect after 15 July 1964 which would fail at common law.

In applying the rule against perpetuities the following steps should be followed:

1. Determine which interests are interests in remainder.
2. Determine whether any interests in remainder are vested or contingent (see section 16.2).
3. Apply the common law rules to the contingent future interests.
4. If the gift fails at common law and it took effect after 15 July 1964, apply the PAA 1964 rules.

16.4 The common law rule against perpetuities

The rule is as follows: the grant of a *contingent* interest is *void ab initio* at common law unless it is certain that the interest will *vest, if it vests at all*, within the perpetuity period. The perpetuity period consists of a *life or lives in being* when the grant takes effect, plus 21 years. The italicised words and phrases are explained below.

Contingent

This means the gift is not vested. That is, one or more of the three requirements for a vested interest have not been met:

1. The identity of the beneficiary or beneficiaries is not known.
2. A condition has not been fulfilled.
3. The respective shares of the beneficiaries are not known.

Void ab initio

The gift, if it fails at law, is void from the moment that it takes effect. The interest concerned will be held by trustees on trust for the residuary legatees.

Vest

A gift vests when all three conditions in 'Contingent' above become satisfied. It then ceases to be contingent.

If it vests at all

It is not necessary to show that the gift will actually vest. It must merely be shown that it is possible for it to vest within the period.

A life or lives in being

This means the lifetimes of persons alive at the date that the gift comes into effect.

Calculation of the perpetuity period

The period starts at the date the instrument takes effect, that is, the date of the testator's death if the gift is by will, or the date of the instrument if it is an inter vivos gift. The period stops after the lifetime(s) of the life/lives in being plus 21 years.

Lives in being at common law

A life in being is the lifetime of anyone alive when the gift takes effect. It is necessary to know the date of death of lives in being, and so it is obviously impractical to apply this wide definition. Lives in being are consequently limited to the following:

1. lives in being expressly nominated by the testator; or if there are no nominated lives,
2. lives in being relevant to whether or not the gift will vest (implied lives).

Nominated lives. It is common for a testator to nominate lives in being. There is no requirement that any of the nominated lives in being have any interest in the gift, hence a donor can ensure a relatively lengthy perpetuity period by nominating a number of lives in being.

It is necessary for the persons administering the gift to be able to ascertain when the nominated lives die, and so it is usual to select the descendants of a named monarch (the rationale being that such descendants are likely to enjoy the best living conditions, health care, etc and thus have the best chance of a long life). The monarch should be fairly recent as otherwise it will not be possible to trace all his descendants. In *Re Moore* [1901] 1 Ch 936, the testatrix nominated as lives in being all the persons alive at the date of her death. The gift was held void. In *Re Villar* [1929] 1 Ch 243, a testatrix who died in 1926 nominated all the descendants of Queen Victoria (died 1901, having had 11 children) alive at the time of her death. There were then approximately 120 descendants, scattered all over Europe. It was held that the difficulty in ascertaining their dates of death was not sufficient to render the gift void. The valid clause read:

'... ending at the expiration of 20 years from the day of the death of the last survivor of all the lineal descendants of her late Majesty Queen Victoria who shall be living at the time of my death'.

In *Re Leverhulme (No 2)* [1943] 2 All ER 274 a 'Queen Victoria' clause was held valid, but it was suggested that no further use be made of Queen Victoria's descendants. Today it is normal to use the descendants of George V, or George VI. The lives must be human lives and not trees: see *Re Kelly* [1932] IR 255.

Example of nominated lives in being.

'The lives in being are all those lineal descendants of George VI alive at my death.'

The testator died in September 1981. At that date there were ten lineal descendants of George VI alive, the youngest being a few weeks old. The perpetuity period runs from September 1981 until the death of the longest lived of those ten people plus 21 years.

Implied lives. If there are no expressly nominated lives, the lives in being are the lives of persons who are concerned in the gift. In practice, it is only necessary to consider the lifetimes of persons who are relevant to whether the gift will vest.

Example of implied lives in being.

1. Gift by will 'to my grandson, John'.
   The lives in being will be John and his parents, if they are alive when the gift takes effect.
2. Gift by will 'to all my grandchildren to attain 21'.
   At the date of the testator's death, two of his children and two of his grandchildren are alive. The lives in being are the two children and the two grandchildren. The perpetuity period will run from the death of the testator until 21 years after the death of the last of the lives in being to die. Note that any grandchildren born after the testator's death will *not* be lives in being.

The two children are lives in being because they are relevant to when the gift will vest. The gift must vest, if it vests at all, 21 years after the death of the last of the children, as it is only after those events that it is certain that no more grandchildren can be born, and that all the grandchildren will be 21.

Application of the common law rule

The following steps should be gone through:

1. Is the gift vested or contingent; have all three conditions been complied with?
2. If contingent, when will it vest; in other words, when will all three conditions be complied with?
3. Is it absolutely certain that the gift must vest, if it vests at all, within the lifetimes of persons alive at the time the gift takes effect plus 21 years?

Examples

1. Gift by will 'to A for life, remainder to A's first son to reach 21'.
   At the date of the testator's death, A is alive, a bachelor with no children.
   Apply aforementioned steps:

   a) A's gift is vested.
      The gift to A's son is contingent.
      His identity is unknown and he has not reached 21.
   b) The gift to A's son will vest when he reaches 21. (Note that A may never have a son. This does not matter. The test is whether any son that A might have would reach 21 within the period.)
   c) The life in being is A. Hence the perpetuity period is A's lifetime (which is extended to include the gestation period) plus 21 years. Any son born to A must be born within A's lifetime and must reach 21 within 21 years of A's death.

   Therefore, the gift will vest, if it vests at all, within the perpetuity period.

2. Gift by will 'to A for life, then to the first of A's sons to be called to the Bar'.
   On testator's death, A is alive with no children.
   Apply the above steps:

   a) A's interest is vested. His son's is not; his identity is not known and the condition (being called to the Bar) has not been fulfilled.
   b) The gift must vest when A's son is called to the Bar.
   c) The life in being is A. The perpetuity period is A's lifetime plus 21 years. The son must be born, at the latest, within nine months of A's death. But he may be called to the Bar more than 21 years after A's death.

   Hence, the gift to A's son is *void* at common law.

Future parenthood at common law

At common law any possibility, however remote, that a gift may not vest within the period renders the gift void. The law is not concerned with the probability that the gift will vest, but the possibility that it might not.

Consequently, the possibility that one of the lives in being may have another child (who would not be a life in being, and who might qualify under the terms of the gift after the perpetuity period) must be taken into account. The fact that it is extremely unlikely, or physically impossible, for such a child to be born is ignored. In *Jee* v *Audley* (1787) 1 Cox Eq Cas 324 a gift was held void because the court presumed that it was possible that a 70-year-old woman might have another child.

Megarry and Wade comment at page 306:

> 'Even when it can be proved that the birth of further children is a physical impossibility, the rule at common law maintains the same stubborn disregard for the facts of life.'

Example

Gift by will 'to all the grandchildren of A to reach 21'.

At the testator's death in 1958, A is a 64-year-old woman with two daughters and no grandchildren. The lives in being are hence A and her two daughters. At common law the gift fails. This is because the following sequence of events might occur:

1958 Testator dies.

1960 A has a daughter, B. B is not a life in being.

1967 A and her two elder daughters are all killed in a car crash. The perpetuity period now has 21 years left to run. B is seven years old.

1987 B has a child, A's grandchild. This grandchild will not be 21 until 2008. The perpetuity period ran out in 1988.

Legal impossibility is not ignored at common law. In *Re Gaite's Will Trusts, Banks* v *Gaite* [1949] 1 All ER 459 there was a gift by will to A for life and then to such of A's grandchildren living at the testator's death or born within five years thereof who should attain the age of 21 years. At the testator's death, A was a 67-year-old widow with children. The remainder to A's grandchildren was contingent.

It had to be assumed that A could have more children. These children would not be lives in being because they would not be alive at the testator's death; therefore those children could have children (A's grandchildren) who would reach 21 more than 21 years after the death of A and those of her children alive at the testator's death. Therefore, some of the beneficiaries under the will would fulfil the condition after the end of the perpetuity period.

However, the gift to the grandchildren was *valid*. This was because it was limited to grandchildren born within five years of the testator's death. Therefore to qualify, any grandchild of A would have to be born to A's hypothetical child before that child was five years old. This is a legal impossibility as the age of consent is 16.

The possibility that a trustee might not fulfil his duties under the trust is also ignored: see *Re Atkins' Will Trusts* [1974] 1 WLR 761.

The result of the decisions on future parenthood is that a contingent gift will fail at common law if the beneficiaries are the grandchildren of anyone alive at the testator's death.

Unborn spouses

The possibility that a life in being might marry a spouse who was not born at the date of the testator's death may cause a gift to fail at common law.

Example
Gift by will 'to my son A for life, remainder to his widow (if she survives him) for life, remainder to any of their children living at the death of the survivor'.

At the testator's death A is a bachelor. The life in being is thus A. A may marry a woman born after the death of the testator, and so his potential wife cannot be treated as a life in being. This makes the gift to A's children void, as A's widow might survive for more than 21 years after the death of A, so the gift to the children may not vest until after the perpetuity period.

Hence any gift to children to take effect on the death of the survivor of their parents will fail unless:

1. Both parents are alive at the testator's death.
2. The children to benefit are limited to the children of persons alive at the testator's death, which is done by naming both parents: 'the children of A and B'.

16.5 Modifications to the common law rule before 1964

There are three ways in which the harshness of the common law rule is modified in order to save gifts otherwise void:

1. Class closing under the rule in *Andrews* v *Partington*.
2. Age reduction under s163 LPA 1925.
3. Alternative contingencies.

These will be dealt with in turn.

Class closing under the rule in **Andrews** v **Partington**

The rules as to class closing apply only to class gifts. A class gift is a gift of property to all persons who come within some description, the property being divisible in shares varying according to the number of persons in the class. Thus gifts of property to 'all my children who attain 25', 'all the nephews and nieces of my late husband', or 'A, B, C, D, and E if living' are all class gifts.

The perpetuity rule applies to class gifts in two ways:

1. The gift cannot vest until the size of the respective shares is known. Hence if, at the date the gift comes into effect, it is possible that any class member could become entitled to a share after the end of the perpetuity period, the whole gift fails, and no member of the class can take any share.

    Example

    Gift by will 'to A for life, and remainder to all A's grandchildren'.

    If A is alive at the testator's death, the gift to the grandchildren will be void because A might have more children whose children might be born (and thus qualify for membership of the class of grandchildren) after the end of the perpetuity period.

2. If any member of the class might take a vested interest outside the perpetuity period, the whole gift fails, even though all the other members qualify inside the period.

    Example

    Gift by will 'to A for life, then to all the children of A to attain 25'.

    If A is alive at the testator's death, the gift to A's children is void, because a child might be born to A who might not reach 25 until after the end of the perpetuity period.

The rule in *Andrews* v *Partington* (1791) 3 Bro CC 401 is a *rule of convenience*, allowing members of a class to become entitled to their share as soon as they become qualified. It states that a numerically uncertain class closes as soon as the first member becomes entitled to claim his share. The class is thereupon limited to potential members who are already born. Potential members born later are not entitled to any share. As each member becomes entitled, he is given his share. If a potential member dies before qualifying, the shares of the remaining members of the class are adjusted.

The rule can save class gifts otherwise void for perpetuity only if one member of the class has qualified when the gift takes effect.

Examples
1. Gift by will 'to A for life, remainder to all the grandchildren of A'.

    If A is alive at the testator's death, the gift will be saved by the rule in *Andrews* v *Partington* if any grandchildren have been born by the testator's death. The class will then be limited to those grandchildren already born who are all lives in being and whose shares must vest within the perpetuity period.
2. Gift by will 'to A for life, remainder to all the children of A to attain 25'.

    If A is alive at the testator's death, the gift to the children will be valid only if one of the children is already 25. The class is then limited to those of A's children already born. If there are four, aged 26, 24, 22 and 21, they will be entitled to a quarter share each. If one of the younger ones dies before the age of 25, the shares are adjusted to a third each.

Note: the gift in the above example could also be saved by age reduction. See below.

Age reduction under s163 LPA 1925

Gifts conditional on the beneficiary reaching an age greater than 21 are often void at common law.

Example
Gift by will 'to all the children of A to reach 25'.
This gift could be valid only if:

1. A was dead at the time the gift took effect, so no more children could be born.
2. A was alive, but one of A's children was already 25 so the class could be limited to lives in being.

If A is alive, and no child has reached 25, the gift will fail at common law.

Section 163 LPA 1925 allows the age of 21 to be substituted for the excessive age provided that:

1. The gift came into effect after 1925 and before 15 July 1964.
2. The gift would otherwise be void.
3. The excess is in the age of a beneficiary or class of beneficiaries.

In the example above, the age of 21 can be substituted for 25 if the gift would otherwise fail. See also in this regard s4(1) of the Perpetuities and Accumulations Act 1964.

Alternative contingencies

Where the vesting of a gift is dependent upon the occurrence of either one or the other of two events, the strict common law rules are relaxed. If the gift is 'to A if X happens or if Y happens', and event X must occur within the perpetuity period, but event Y may occur outside the period, then by the strict common law rules, the gift is void. But in these circumstances the 'wait and see' principle of the PAA 1964 (see section 16.8 below) is applied at common law. It is not necessary to decide whether the gift is valid when it comes into effect. Instead the trustees can wait and see which of the two alternative events happens. If the validating event happens, the gift is valid; if it does not, the gift is void.

In *Re Curryer's Will Trusts* [1938] Ch 952 there was a gift by will to the testator's grandchildren to take effect on the death of the last surviving child of the testator or on the death of the last surviving widow or widower of the testator's children, whichever happened later. The gift to the grandchildren would be valid if it took effect on the death of the last surviving child of the testator. The alternative contingency was void because of the possibility of an unborn spouse (see section 16.4). It was held that the trustees could wait and see if all the widows and widowers did in fact die before the last surviving child.

In order for the 'wait and see' exception to apply, the alternative contingencies must be expressly stated in the instrument or will. In *Proctor* v *Bishop of Bath and Wells* (1794) 2 Hy Bl 358 property was left by will to the first son of A to become a clergyman or, if A had no sons, to B. Both A and B were alive at the date of the testator's death. B claimed the property on the death of A. It was held that the gift over to B in fact depended on two alternative contingencies. Either A had no sons, or none of his sons became a clergyman. As the alternatives were not expressed, the wait and see exception did not apply, and the gift over to B was void, as it was dependent upon a prior void gift.

16.6 Determinable and conditional interests

Determinable interests

Neither a determinable fee simple nor a possibility of reverter is subject to the rule against perpetuities at common law. But see section 16.7.

Conditional interests

Conditions precedent
These are subject to the perpetuity rule at common law. Hence a gift to 'A provided that he survives B' is subject to the rule and will be void if B could die outside the perpetuity period.

Conditions subsequent
The grant of a conditional interest involves both the grant of a conditional fee simple and the creation of a right of re-entry (see Chapter 6). The conditional fee simple is not affected by the rule, but the right of re-entry is void if it could take effect outside the perpetuity period. The conditional fee simple is converted into an absolute interest if the right of re-entry is void.

Example
Gift of 'fee simple in possession to testator's grandchildren provided that no grandchild marries outside the Jewish faith'.

The provision might not take effect until after the perpetuity period and is void; the grandchildren are absolutely entitled.

16.7 Perpetuities and Accumulations Act 1964

The PAA 1964 applies to gifts coming into effect after 15 July 1964 that are void at common law. The common law rules are applied first; the Act modifies the common law rules.

Section 1: the perpetuity period

A period of 80 years or less may be substituted for the normal perpetuity period in the instrument creating the gift. The statutory period has the advantage of certainty and for that reason it is frequently used by solicitors when drafting wills which will give rise to a trust.

Section 2: future parenthood

Where a gift would be void at common law because of the possibility of future parenthood, it may be valid under the PAA 1964. Section 2(1)(a) provides that for the purposes of the rule it shall be presumed that women are capable of having children only between the ages of 12 and 55, and that men's capacity is limited to the age of 14 or over.

Any presumption arising in the case of a living person under s2(1)(a) may be rebutted, and it would be possible to give evidence of actual capacity (s2(1)(b)). These presumptions only arise in any legal proceedings.

Section 3: wait and see

Under the common law the general rule was that it must be clear when the instrument took effect that the interest could not vest outside the perpetuity period. There was no 'wait and see' facility. Where a gift would be void apart from the provisions of s3, s4 (age reduction, class closing) and s5 (the unborn spouse), then s3 allows the trustees to wait and see if the gift does in fact vest within the perpetuity period. Under s3 the interest is to be treated as valid until it is clear that it cannot vest within the period.

Examples

1. Gift 'to A (a man), for life, remainder to those of A's grandchildren to reach 21'. If A is alive at the date of the gift, the gift to the grandchildren is void at common law. Under the Act, it is possible to wait and see whether the gift will in fact vest. This will be known when A dies. If he had no more children after the testator's death, the gift will vest, as the grandchildren's parents are lives in being (see below). If A did have more children, then any potential grandchildren as yet unborn at A's death can be excluded from the class: s4(4) (see below).

2. Gift 'to the first son of A to be called to the Bar'.
   If A is alive when the gift is made, it is void at common law. Under the Act, the trustees can wait and see whether any son of A does become a barrister within the perpetuity period.

Sections 3(4) and 3(5): lives in being

When the 'wait and see' provisions of this Act (see above) are to be applied, then the perpetuity period must be calculated with reference to statutory classes of lives in being, unless the donor has nominated a fixed period of 80 years or less. By s3(5) these classes are:

1. the person by whom the disposition was made – the donor;
2. a person to whom or in whose favour the disposition was made, that is to say:

   a) in the case of a disposition to a class of persons, any member or potential member of that class – the donee;
   b) in the case of an individual disposition to a person taking only on certain conditions being satisfied, any person as to whom some of the conditions are satisfied and the remainder may in time be satisfied – the donee;
   c) in the case of a special power of appointment exercisable in favour of members of a class, any member or potential member of the class – the donee;
   d) the first two provisions (above) equally apply to special powers of appointment – the donee;
   e) a person on whom any power, option or right is conferred – the donee;

3. a person having a child or grandchild who qualifies as a statutory life under (2) above or would if subsequently born so qualify – the donee's parents and grandparents;
4. any person on the failure or determination of whose prior interest the disposition is limited to take effect – the owner of a prior interest.

If any of these categories is too numerous for determination it may be disregarded.

The lives in being under the Act do not differ, in practical terms, from lives in being implied at law, although the Act is wider.

Section 3(5) does not apply unless the 'wait and see' provisions are applied. Where the gift was made before 1964, or is valid at common law, a royal lives clause can be used.

Section 4(1): age reduction

Where a gift would be void because it is limited to persons attaining an age of more than 21, then the age may be reduced to that which will allow the gift to be valid, so long as the reduced age is not less than 21. This provision differs from s163 LPA 1925 in that the reduction need not be to 21 years.

Example

Gift 'to all the grandchildren of A to attain 30.' A is alive, with no children.

The 'wait and see' provisions are applied until A's death. There are three grandchildren aged two, four and six. Section 4(1) can then be applied, reducing the qualifying age to 23, the age which will allow the gift to vest within the perpetuity period, that is, 21 years from A's death.

Section 163 LPA 1925 is repealed for gifts made after 15 July 1964.

Sections 4(3) and 4(4): class reduction

Class reduction under the Act operates in a fashion similar to, but more straightforward than the rule in *Andrews* v *Partington* (1791) 3 Bro CC 401 (see section 16.5).

Under s4(3), persons can be excluded from the class of potential beneficiaries where their inclusion would prevent the age reduction provisions from operating to save the gift.

Example

In the example above relating to s4(1), age reduction to 23 will not save the gift if any of A's children are still capable of having children. Section 4(3) can be used to exclude any potential unborn grandchildren from the class of beneficiaries.

Section 4(4) allows the exclusion of members from the class of beneficiaries where their inclusion would cause the gift to fail for remoteness, and age reduction is not appropriate.

Example

Gift 'to all the children of A who marry'.

If, at the end of the perpetuity period, any of A's children are not married, they can be excluded from the class, leaving only the married children as beneficiaries.

Section 5: unborn spouses

Section 5 prevents the possibility of an unborn spouse from causing a gift to fail. The 'wait and see' provisions are applied first, and if it becomes apparent that an unborn spouse will survive the perpetuity period, the gift can then be treated as though it were to take effect immediately before the end of the period.

Example

Gift 'to A for life, remainder to his widow (if she survives him), remainder to any of their children living at the death of the survivor.'

A is a bachelor, who marries a woman who was born after the death of the testator, and she survives A. The trustees should wait until the end of the perpetuity period, and if A's widow is still alive, the gift to the children can be saved by treating the gift to the children as taking effect immediately before the end of 21 years after the death of A, rather than upon the death of A's widow.

Section 9: options relating to land

The Act makes one important change to the common law rules on options, which make all options, except an option to renew a lease, subject to a 21-year perpetuity period. Under the Act, options are divided into two classes:

1. Options for a lessee, contained in a lease, to purchase the freehold or a superior tenancy: these options are not subject to the perpetuity rule, provided that the option ceases to be exercisable not later than one year after the end of the lease and is exercisable only by the lessee or by his successors in title.
2. All other options: these are subject to a perpetuity period of 21 years and no longer. The 'wait and see' principle applies, hence the owner of an option must use it within 21 years of its grant, after which time the option is void.

In all cases, the perpetuity rules apply only to options being enforced against successors in title. Prior to 1964 the perpetuity rule did not apply to the original parties to an option. Section 10 PAA 1964 changes the common law rule in respect of instruments taking effect after 15 July 1964, and as a result the perpetuity rule now applies to options to purchase between both the original parties and successors in title.

Section 12: determinable and conditional interests

The Act changes the common law rules for grants made after 15 July 1964 by making determinable interests subject to the perpetuity rule, so that the common law distinction between determinable and conditional interests no longer exists.

16.8 Powers

Powers, because they are concerned with the disposition of property, come within the perpetuity rule. The application of the rule depends on the type of power.

General powers

1. They must be *exercisable* within the perpetuity period.
2. They need not be *exercised* within the perpetuity period.
3. When they are exercised, the interest must vest within the perpetuity period reckoned from the date of their exercise (ie a second perpetuity period).

General testamentary powers

1. They must be *exercisable* within the perpetuity period.
2. They must be *exercised* within the perpetuity period.
3. When they are exercised, the interest must vest within the perpetuity period reckoned from the date of their exercise (ie a second perpetuity period).

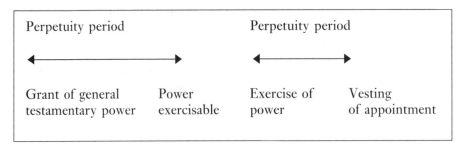

Special powers

1. They must be *exercisable* within the perpetuity period.
2. They must be *exercised* within the perpetuity period.
3. The interest appointed must vest within the original perpetuity period.

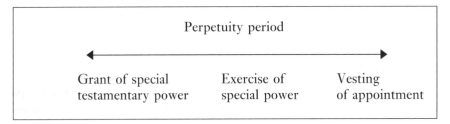

If a power cannot be exercised beyond the perpetuity period it is valid, even though an invalid appointment may be made under it.

For powers granted after 15 July 1964 the 'wait and see' provisions of the PAA 1964 apply. The Act also does not recognise any type of hybrid power except a general testamentary power, treating every power as special unless:

1. It is expressed by the instrument creating it to be exercisable by one person only.
2. The donee of the power, being of full age and capacity, can exercise it to transfer the whole appointable interest to himself unconditionally.

16.9 Exceptions to the perpetuity rule

1. Certain contracts, eg options to purchase (s9 PAA 1964): see section 16.7.

2. Limitations after entails: the 1964 Act has no effect. The Trusts of Land and Appointment of Trustees Act 1996 prevents the creation of any more entailed interests (Schedule 1, para 5 of the 1996 Act).
3. A gift to charity followed by a gift over to another charity: the gift over will not be void merely because the event may take place after the end of the perpetuity period.
4. Restrictive covenants.
5. Forfeiture clauses in leases by which the tenant agrees that if at any time the terms of the lease are broken the landlord may re-enter and bring the lease to an end.
6. Mortgages: it does not apply to the postponement of a mortgagor's right to redeem. See *Knightsbridge Estates Trusts Ltd* v *Byrne* [1939] Ch 441.
7. Resulting trusts: these were not subject to common law but are now subject to PAA 1964.
8. Right of survivorship in joint tenancy.
9. All powers and remedies for enforcing rentcharges are exempted by s11(1) PAA 1964.

Megarry and Wade state at page 356:

'The general effect of the exemptions is to enable rights which are merely ancillary to other valid interests to be exercised outside the perpetuity period.'

16.10 The rule against accumulations

An accumulation is a direction to add income from a fund to the capital rather than distributing it. Originally accumulations were subject only to the rule against perpetuities, but at the end of the eighteenth century a celebrated case, *Thellusson* v *Woodford* (1799) 11 Ves 112, caused a change in the law. The case showed that a long period of accumulation, which was valid under the rule against perpetuities, could theoretically result in a fund containing a significant part of the national wealth. Parliament hastily intervened by passing the Accumulations Act 1800, often said in the past to be one of the worst-drafted Acts on the statute book.

The present law is contained in the Law of Property Act 1925 ss164–166, as amended, for instruments taking effect after 15 July 1964, by the Perpetuities and Accumulations Act 1964 s13(1).

The statutory periods

Income can only be accumulated for one of the following periods:

1. the life of the settlor or settlors;
2. 21 years from the death of the settlor;
3. the minority or respective minorities of any persons living or en ventre sa mère at the death of the settlor;
4. the minority or respective minorities only of any person or persons who, under the limitations of the settlement would, if of full age, be entitled to the income directed to be accumulated;

} LPA 1925 s164

Plus

5. 21 years from the date of the settlement;
6. the duration of the minority or respective minorities of any person or persons in being at the date of the settlement.

} PAA 1964

Purchase of land

Where the accumulation is directed for the purpose of purchasing land, only period (4) may be selected: s160(1) LPA 1925. The choice of period is a matter of construction of the instrument directing accumulation.

Excessive accumulation

If the accumulation period may possibly exceed the perpetuity period, the direction to accumulate is totally void. The Perpetuities and Accumulations Act 1964 has not affected this rule.

If the accumulation period cannot exceed the perpetuity period but exceeds the relevant accumulation period, the direction to accumulate is good for the relevant accumulation period and only the excess is void.

If a direction to accumulate is wholly or partially void, the income for the void period passes to the person or persons who would have been entitled if no direction to accumulate had been made. There is no acceleration of subsequent interests.

The rule in *Saunders* v *Vautier* (1841) 4 Beav 115 enables a beneficiary of full age who has an absolute, vested and indefeasible interest in property to terminate any accumulation and require that the property be vested in him.

Exceptions to the rule against accumulations

Section 164(1) LPA 1925 gives three exceptions to the rule:

1. accumulation for the payment of the debts of any grantor, settlor, testator or other person;
2. accumulation to raise portions for children;
3. accumulation of the produce from timber or wood.

16.11 Revision summary

One of the problems with this area of land law is the collecting of the material into some cohesive whole for revision purposes. The following table is suggested as a method of revision, based on the normal style of question which invites the candidate to consider the law before and after the Perpetuities and Accumulations Act 1964 became effective.

Topic	*Before 16 July 1964 common law or LPA 1925*	*After 15 July 1964 Perpetuities and Accumulations Act 1964*
1 Perpetuity period	Lives in being – no restriction as to number selected	s1 – add a fixed period not exceeding 80 years
2 Possibility of vesting	Applied rigidly – any remote chance then void – 'fertile octogenarians': *Jee* v *Audley* (1787)	s2 – male under 14 and female under 12 or over 55 presumed incapable of having children
3 'Wait and see' rule	No general 'wait and see' rule – significant date was the moment of vesting	s3 – an interest is to be treated as valid until it is clear that it cannot vest within the period
4 Age contingencies	Fail if contingent on beneficiary attaining an age greater than 21: s163 LPA 1925 substituted 21 as the relevant age	s4(1) (repealed s163 LPA 1925) – substitutes the age nearest to that specified which will save it from being void for remoteness (no longer reduced to 21)
5 Class gifts	Composition of class and share of each member of the class must be known within perpetuity period – gift is wholly valid or wholly void. But – closing of classes – if uncertainty as to numbers, class will close as soon as first member becomes entitled: *Andrews* v *Partington* (1791)	ss4(3) and 4(4) – member whose interest can vest only outside the period and is not saved by reducing the age is excluded from the gift – and gift in favour of the rest of the class is valid
6 Accumulations	Rule applies to directions to accumulate income – the income could be accumulated for some period as property could be made inalienable, ie for the perpetuity period: *Thellusson* v *Woodford* (1799), then see Accumulations Act 1800, then ss164–166 LPA 1925	ss164–166 LPA 1925 and s13 of 1964 Act. Now a total of six possible accumulation periods, comprising life, or 21 years, or minority: see Megarry and Wade: 'In determining the appropriate period, the starting point is to ascertain which of the periods the testator or settlor seemingly had in mind.'

16.12 Proposals for reform

In 1998 a *Report on the Rules against Perpetuities and Excessive Accumulations* was published by the Law Commission (Law Com No 251). It concluded that there should be a major overhaul and simplification of the law concerning perpetuities. Some of the key recommendations of the Report are noted below.

1. The rule against perpetuities should only apply to interests and rights arising under wills and trusts. It should not apply to options nor to a restrictive covenant granted to take effect at a date in the future.
2. There should be one fixed perpetuity period of 125 years.
3. The 'wait and see' principle should apply.
4. Pension schemes should be excluded from the rule.
5. The reforms should usually be prospective – in effect not retrospective.

In relation to accumulations the Commission recommended that the rule against excessive accumulations should be abolished except in relation to charitable trusts.

The Commission's proposals, if implemented, would in essence create a third set of rules against perpetuities applicable to instruments made after the coming into force of the Act giving effect to its proposals. The two existing sets of rules are:

1. those applicable to instruments made before the coming into force of the Perpetuities and Accumulations Act 1964; and
2. those applicable to instruments made after the 1964 Act but before any new Act to implement the Commission's proposals became law.

However, it is difficult to see how three sets of rules against perpetuities would contribute to the simplification of the law sought for by the Law Commission

17

Statutory Restrictions on the Use of Land

17.1 Introduction

17.2 Planning control

17.3 Protection of tenants

17.4 Public health and housing provisions

17.5 Taxation

17.6 Environmental issues

17.7 Conclusion

17.1 Introduction

This very complex subject is dealt with in outline only. For more details see Cheshire, Chapters 30 and 31 (16th edn) and Megarry and Wade, Chapter 22 (6th edn). It is most unlikely to be the subject of a direct question (apart from the statutory rules relating to the protection of tenants), but a broad appreciation of the restrictions will help in an understanding of modern land law.

17.2 Planning control

This is well covered by Cheshire, Chapter 30, at page 1021. The system of planning control is governed by the Town and Country Planning Act 1990. Any person who wishes to 'develop' his land must first obtain planning permission from the local planning authority. 'Development' covers almost every type of building operation and material change of use, except alteration to a building which does not affect its external appearance or change to another use within the same category, for example from a theatre to a cinema. Once planning permission is granted, the benefit attaches to the land and for anyone who has an interest in the land. 'Development' is defined in s55(1) Town and Country Planning Act 1990 as:

'... the carrying out of building, engineering, mining or other operations in, on, over or under land or the making of any material change in the use of any buildings or other land'.

Section 55(2) contains a list of activities which do not amount to development under this definition. Any development that does not come within the exceptions set out in s55(2) must be the subject of an application for planning permission submitted to the local planning authority. In deciding whether to grant planning permission the local planning authority shall have regard to the provisions of the development plan and to any other material consideration (s70(1)). The development plan has priority.

The local planning authority may grant or refuse permission or grant permission subject to such conditions 'as they think fit'. Any conditions must:

'fairly and reasonably relate to the permitted development. The planning authority are not at liberty to use their powers for an ulterior object, however desirable that object may seem to them to be in the public interest.' (per Lord Denning MR in *Pyx Granite Co Ltd v Minister of Housing and Local Government* [1958] 1 QB 554)

If the applicant is not satisfied he can appeal to the Secretary of State within six months. This appeal may be made the subject of a public inquiry or be dealt with by correspondence only. The decision of the Secretary of State, or his inspector, can be challenged in the courts within three months on a point of law.

The use of land for caravan sites is more closely controlled, and there are special controls for historical buildings, conservation areas, national parks, advertisements and trees.

If there is a breach of planning control the local planning authority may serve an enforcement notice, specifying the steps to be taken to remedy the breach and giving a time in which this is to be done. Failure to comply is a criminal offence, and the local planning authority may itself enter the land and take steps to enforce the notice.

In certain cases the owner of the land which loses value because permission has been refused, or where the grant of permission reduces the value of the land or makes it virtually unsaleable ('planning blight'), may get compensation or may be able to make the local authority acquire the land by way of a purchase notice.

In furtherance of development plans for an area a local authority has powers to purchase property in the area compulsorily, the owner getting the open market value of the land in compensation. As compulsory purchase is an interference with private ownership, the acquiring authority must always have statutory authority to acquire land for the particular purpose. Once the compensation has been agreed the legal estate is vested in the acquiring authority by normal conveyancing procedures.

17.3 Protection of tenants

This has been dealt with in Chapter 10. The major statutes are:

Residential tenants: Rent Act 1977, Housing Acts 1980–1996.
Business tenants: Landlord and Tenant Act 1954.
Agricultural tenants: Agricultural Holdings Act 1986 and Agricultural Tenancies
                Act 1995.

17.4 Public health and housing provisions

There are a large number of provisions intended to prevent the serious deterioration of houses and to deal with those that have become uninhabitable. The obligations of landlords of certain types of tenanted property to repair under the Landlord and Tenant Act 1985 have already been discussed (see Chapter 10). Sections 8–10 provide for the declaration by the local authority of clearance areas when the majority of the buildings in the area have become unfit for human habitation or otherwise dangerous. The authority then has power to clear and redevelop the area. When an individual house becomes unsafe through lack of repair, the local authority can serve the owner with a dangerous structure notice, requiring the necessary repairs to be done. If individual rooms are not fit for human habitation, in particular basement rooms, the local authority can serve a closure order, which forbids the use of those rooms unless and until certain works are done to make them habitable.

17.5 Taxation

The pattern of land-holding has been greatly affected by the enormous increase in taxation that has taken place in the twentieth century, in particular the introduction of estate duty (now inheritance tax) which made the strict settlement of successive interests very expensive in terms of tax burdens (as previously noted following the coming into force of the Trusts of Land and Appointment of Trustees Act 1996 no new strict settlement can be created after 31 December 1996). If the land produces an income this is taxed as income tax.

Most settlements of land made today are designed to reduce the burden of taxation, and trusts are most usually varied (under the Variation of Trusts Act 1958) for that purpose.

17.6 Environmental issues

Protection of the environment is increasingly important and, influenced by the

European Community, a complex body of environmental law and policy has developed. The main statutes are the Environmental Protection Act 1990, the Water Resources Act 1991 and the Environment Act 1995.

Landowners must ensure that activities carried out on their land do not give rise to pollution – either pollution to the air, to water courses or to the land itself – by, for example, allowing certain types of waste to be deposited without contacting the relevant agency.

There are two control agencies, the local authority and the Environment Agency, the latter set up by the 1995 Act. Causing pollution can be a criminal offence and can result in a heavy fine and/or imprisonment.

17.7 Conclusion

The link between land law/conveyancing and social control must always be kept in mind. Megarry and Wade reminds the reader of this at page 1438:

> 'Formerly the conveyancer was concerned to see that his client obtained a good title to the land … But social control … has increased the burden. The client must not only obtain a good title to the land but also be assured that he will be able to use it as he wishes, without being frustrated by planning control or the rights of protected tenants.'

At first sight students find land law a rather daunting subject – not least because many of the concepts are unfamiliar to them. However, it is submitted that the more you get into the subject the clearer it becomes. It is hoped that this text has assisted in making land law a little easier to understand than it might otherwise be.

Index

Accumulation, rule against, *359–360*
  exceptions, *360*
  excessive accumulation, *360*
  purchase of land, *360*
  statutory periods, *359–360*
Adverse possession, *85–86, 330–341*
  general principles, *330*
  lapse of time, effect, *339–340*
    registered land, *340*
  limitation periods, *330–331*
    postponement, *338–339*
  proof of squatter's title, *341*
  running of time, *331–339*
    future interests, *335*
    leaseholds, *336*
    mortgages, *336–337*
    rentcharges, *336*
    successive squatters, *335*
    tenants at sufferance, *336*
    tenants at will, *336*
    trusts, *337–338*

Charges, *45*
Commonhold and Leasehold Reform Act 2002, *237–240*
Constructive trust, licence, and, *283–285*
Contingent interests, *344*
Conversion, doctrine of, *109*
  abolition, *114*
Conveyancing, simplification of, *42*
Co-ownership, *124–148*
  creation, *124–125*
  determination of type, *129*
  ending, *141–144*
  example, *146–148*
  house deposit, and, *140–141*
  joint tenancy *see* Joint tenancy
  legal and equitable interests, *127–129*
  legislation of 1925, under, *138–139*
  legislation of 1996, under, *139–140*
  other forms of, *145–146*
  resulting trusts, and, *132–137*
  rights between co-owners, *145*
  tenancy in common *see* Tenancy in common
  trust for sale, *139*
Coparcenary, *145*

Copyhold, *16*
Covenants, *211–244*
  creation, *213–214*
  effect of Contracts (Rights of Third Parties) Act 1999 *233*
  enforcement at common law between original parties, *214–215*
  enforcement at common law by assignees, *215–220*
    benefit, *216–217*
    burden, *217–220*
  enforcement between freeholders, *211–244*
  equity, enforcement in, *221–230*
    examples, *231–233, 240–244*
    original parties, *223–224*
    successors in title, *224–230*
    benefit, *224–229*
    burden, *230*
  example of running at common law, *220–221*
  meaning, *212–213*
  reform, *237–240*
  restrictive discharge, *233–237*

Easements, *44, 245–270. See also* Profits
  Access to Neighbouring Land Act 1992, *266*
  acquisition, *250–255*
    express grant or reservation, *251*
    implied grant or reservation, *251–255*
    statute, *251*
  equitable, *249–250*
  essentials, *248–249*
  examples, *245–248, 268–270*
  extent, *262–263*
  extinguishment, *265–266*
  legal, *68, 249–250*
  prescription, *255–261*
    Act of 1832, *258–261*
    common law, *256*
    deductions, *259*
    light, *260–261*
    lost modern grant, *256–258*
    statutory periods, *259*
    user as of right, *255–256*
    user in fee simple, *256*

Easements, prescription (*contd.*)
    user must be continuous, *256*
    user without interruption, *258–259*
  remedies for infringement, *263–264*
    abatement, *263–264*
    access order, *264*
    action, *264*
Electronic conveyancing, *82–83*
Environmental issues, *365–366*
Equity, *35–39*
  contributions to land law, *36*
  legal rights distinguished, *36*
  meaning, *35*
  notice, doctrine of, *36–38*
Escheat, *13*
Estates, *18–34*
  classification, *18–20*
  fee simple. *See* Fee simple
  freehold, *19*
  leasehold, *19–20*
  possession, *20*
  remainder, *20*
  reversion, *20*
  seisin, *20*
Estoppel, licence, and. *See* Licence

Fee simple, *21–27, 67*
  absolute, *21*
  creation of, *26–27*
  definition, *21*
  modified, *21–24*
  rights of owner, *24–27*
    right of alienation, *24*
    rights to everything in, on or over land, *24–26*
Fee simple absolute in possession, *43–44*
Fee tail, *27–28*
  creating, *27*
  definitions, *27*
  ending, *28*
Feudal system
  basis, *4–5*
  decline, *5–6*
  intervention of statute, *6–9*
  manor, *5*
  origins, *3*
  Statute Quia Emptores 1290, *6–7*
  Tenures Abolition Act 1660, *8–9*
  uses, *7–8*
Fixtures, *30–33*
  annexation, *30–31*
  chattels distinguished, *30–31*
  landlord and tenant, *32*

Fixtures (*contd.*)
  meaning, *30*
  moored houseboat, *31–32*
  mortgagor and mortgagee, *32*
  right to remove, *32–33*
  tenant for life and remainderman, *32*
  vendor and purchaser, *32–33*
Forfeiture, *13*
Future interests, *342–362*
  categories, *343*

Gavelkind, *14*
Grand serjeanty, *10*

Joint tenancy, *125–126, 140*
  creation, *129–130*
  severance, *126–127, 141–144*

Knight's service, *12*

Land charges register, *45–49*
Land law
  methods of study, *2*
  problem of, *1*
Leases, *149–210. See also* Tenancies
  assignment, *152–153*
  commencement date and duration of term, *157–159*
  covenant to insure, *173*
  covenant to pay rent, *172*
  covenants as to user, *173*
  covenants not to assign or underlet, *173–176*
  covenants to repair, *176–179*
    damages for breach, *178–179*
    estoppel, and, *178*
    scope, *177–178*
    standard of repair, *178*
  definitions, *151–156*
  enforceability of covenants, *189–201*
    Contracts (Rights of Third Parties) Act 1999, *198–201*
    general principles, *189–190*
    methods, *189–190*
    regimes, *190–198*
  equitable, *157*
  essentials, *154–159*
  exclusive possession, *159*
  express covenants in, *172–179*
  landlord's obligations, *168–171*
  legal, *67, 157*
  licence distinguished, *159–164*
  lives, for, *166–167*

Leases (*contd.*)
    perpetually renewable, *167–168*
    reversionary, *168*
    tenant's obligations, *171*
    terms implied into, *168–171*
Legislation of 1925, *1, 40–56*
    charges, *45*
    fee simple absolute in possession, *43–44*
    legal easements, *44*
    purpose, *41–42*
    reduction of legal estates and interests,
        42–45
    registration, *45–52. See also* Registration
    rentcharges, *44*
    rights of entry, *45*
    rules relating to real and personal property,
        41
    simplification of conveyancing, *42*
    term of years absolute, *44*
Licences, *271–286*
    bare, *272–273*
    constructive trust, and, *283–285*
    contractual, *273–276*
        analysis, *274–275*
        domestic, *275–276*
        revocability, *273–274*
        successors in title, *276*
    coupled with interest, *273*
    equity, mutual benefit and burden, *286*
    lease distinguished, *159–164*
    meaning, *271–272*
    proprietary estoppel, *277–283*
        evidence, *281–283*
Life estate, *28–29*
Limitation periods, *330–331*

Mortgages, *287–329*
    creation, *288–289*
        evaluation, *290*
    definition, *287–288*
    equitable, *289–290*
    equity of redemption, *291–292*
    legal, *68, 289*
    priority, *328*
        equitable interest, *329*
    protection of mortgagor, *296–297*
    redemption, *291–299*
        effect, *298*
        extinguishment of equity of redemption,
            298–299
        method, *298*
        right to sue, *299*
    remedies of equitable mortgagee, *321*

Mortgages, remedies of equitable mortgagee
    (*contd.*)
        appoint receiver, *321*
        foreclose, *321*
        sell, *321*
        sue, *321*
        take possession, *321*
    remedies of legal mortgagee, *300, 299–321*
        appoint receiver, *320–321*
        Barclays Bank v *O'Brien*, *311–312*
        foreclosure, *300*
        post *O'Brien* developments, *312–320*
        sell, *300–306*
        sue, *299–300*
        take possession, *306–311*
    rights common to both parties, *327–328*
    rights of mortgagee, *299, 322*
        fire insurance, *322*
        fixtures, *322*
        title deeds, *322*
    rights of mortgagor, *292–297*
        Consumer Credit Act 1974, *296–297*
    right to consolidate, *324–327*
    right to redeem, *291–292*
    right to tack further advances, *322–323*

Notice
    doctrine of, *36–38*
        registration of title, and, *60–62*

Overreaching, *49–50*
Overriding interests, *68–76, 84–85*
    effect, *68*
    meaning, *68*
    types, *68–76*

Perpetuities and accumulations, rules against,
    342–362
Perpetuities, rule against, *345*
    Act of 1964, *354–357*
        age reduction, *355–356*
        class reduction, *356*
        determinable and conditional interests,
            357
        future parenthood, *354*
        lives in being, *355*
        options relating to land, *357*
        perpetuity period, *354*
        unborn spouses, *356–357*
        wait and see, *354–355*
    age reduction under s163 LPA 1925, *352*
    alternative contingencies, *352–353*
    class closing rule, *350–352*
    common law rule, *345–350*

Perpetuities, rule against, common law rule
    (*contd.*)
        application,   *348*
        calculation of perpetuity period,
            346–348
        future parenthood,   *349–350*
        implied lives,   *347–348*
        modification before 1964,   *350–353*
        nominated lives,   *347*
        unborn spouses,   *350*
    conditional interests,   *353*
    determinable interests,   *353*
    exceptions,   *358–359*
    powers,   *357–358*
    reform,   *362*
    summary,   *361*
Petty serjeanty,   *13*
Planning control,   *363–364*
Powers,   *38–39*
    general,   *38*
    hybrid,   *38*
    special,   *38*
Prescription. *See* Easements
Primogeniture, rule of,   *13–14*
Priority notices,   *54*
Profits,   *245–270. See also* Easements
Profits à prendre,   *266–268*
    acquisition,   *267*
    extinguishment,   *268*
    remedies for infringement,   *267*
Property legislation 1925,   *1, 40–56*
Public health, housing provision, and,   *365*

Registration,   *45–56*
    effects of sale of unregistered land on legal
        and equitable rights,   *50*
    entries on land charges register,   *53*
    example,   *55–56*
    general effect of registration of land charges,
        50–51
    Local Land Charges Act 1975,   *52–53*
    overreaching,   *49–50*
    principles,   *46*
    priority notices,   *54*
    register of annuities,   *47*
    register of deeds of arrangement affecting
        land,   *47*
    register of land charges,   *47–48*
    register of pending actions,   *46–47*
    register of writs and orders affecting land,
        47
    registrable interests,   *46–47*
    searching in land charges register,   *54*

Registration (*contd.*)
    unregistrable interests,   *48–49*
    vacation of registration of land charge,   *55*
Registration of title,   *57–88*
    classes of rights,   *76–77*
    compensation,   *80–81*
    Crown land,   *87*
    doctrine of notice, and,   *60–62*
    first registration,   *83*
    independent adjudication,   *88*
    key principles,   *63–66*
        compulsory registration,   *63–64*
        contents of the title register,   *66*
        curtain,   *66*
        effect of non-compliance,   *64*
        mirror,   *66*
        insurance,   *66*
        time limit for registration,   *64*
        titles to freehold estates,   *64–65*
        titles to leasehold estates,   *65–66*
    Land Charges Act 1972,   *62–63*
    Land Registration Act 1988,   *59*
    Land Registration Act 1997,   *59–60*
    Land Registration Act 2002,   *60, 62, 81–88*
    minor interests,   *60–61, 77–78*
        protection of,   *77–78*
    minor interests index,   *58*
    notice, doctrine of,   *60–62*
    official search certificate,   *78–79*
    overriding interests,   *68–76, 84–85. See
        also* Overriding interests
    proof of title,   *58*
    protection of interests in land,   *58, 86–87*
    rectification of register,   *79–80, 87*
    registrable estates and interests,   *67–68*
    Registration of Title Order 1989,   *59*
Rentcharges,   *44, 336*
    legal,   *68*
Restrictive covenants, discharge,   *233–237*
Reverter of Sites Act 1987,   *33–34*

Settlements of land,   *89–123*
    ad hoc,   *110*
    capital money,   *104*
    creation,   *91–93*
    function of trustees,   *104*
    incompletely constituted,   *92–93*
    no tenant for life,   *94*
    powers of tenant for life,   *95–100*
        exercisable only with consent,   *99*
        exercisable on notice,   *97–98*
        exercisable without giving notice or
            obtaining consent,   *100*
        personal nature of,   *100*

Settlements of land, powers of tenant for life
  (*contd.*)
    powers remain with,   *101–102*
    protection of statutory powers,   *101*
    to compromise claims,   *99–100*
  registered land, and,   *110*
  Settled Land Act 1925, under,   *90–91*
  strict settlements,   *110*
  tenant for life,   *93–94*
    acquisition of settled land,   *102*
    death of,   *102*
    definition,   *93–94*
    dispositions, protection of purchasers and,
      102–104
    settlement coming to an end,   *103–104*
  trustees,   *94–95*
  trusts for sale,   *105–106*
    ad hoc,   *110*
    beneficiaries, position of,   *109*
    conversion,   *109*
    definition,   *105*
    position of trustees,   *106–108*
    strict settlement compared,   *111*
    types,   *105–106*
  Trusts of Land and Appointment of Trustees
    Act 1996,   *111–123*
Socage,   *13*
Statutory restrictions on use of land,   *363–366*

Tacking. *See* Mortgages
Taxation,   *365*
Tenancies,   *149–210. See also* Leases
  agricultural, statutory protection,   *208–209*
  at sufferance,   *166*
  at will,   *166*
  breach of covenant to repair,   *184–185*
  business, statutory protection,   *210*
  definitions,   *151–152*
  determination,   *179–181*
  disclaimer,   *181*
  enlargement,   *180–181*
  expiry,   *179*

Tenancies, (*contd.*)
  forfeiture,   *180, 181–189*
    breach of covenant to repair,   *184–185*
    evaluation,   *188–189*
    non-payment of rent,   *186–187*
    relief from,   *185–187*
    right to,   *181–182*
    s146 notice,   *183–184*
      exceptions to,   *185*
    waiver,   *182–183*
  frustration,   *180*
  merger,   *180*
  notice to quit,   *179*
  periodic,   *165–166*
  protection of tenants,   *365*
  residential, statutory protection,   *201–208*
  statutory protection,   *201*
  subtenancies,   *153–154*
  surrender,   *180*
  terms certain,   *165*
  types,   *165–168*
  yearly,   *165*
Tenancy by entireties,   *145*
Tenancy in common,   *126, 140*
  conversion to,   *142–144*
  creation,   *130–132*
  severance,   *141–142*
Tenures,   *10–17*
  free,   *10–14*
  in chivalry,   *10–13*
  in socage,   *13*
  inheritance of,   *13–14*
  spiritual,   *14*
  today,   *17*
  unfree,   *15*
Term of years absolute,   *44*
Title, registration of. *See* Registration of title

Vested interests,   *351–352*
Villeinage,   *15*

Waste,   *29–30*
  types,   *29–30*

Equity and Good Conscience

Second Edition

Margaret Halliwell, AIPM, LLB, ILTHE, TEP, Reader in Law at the Department of Law, City University, London

Since publication of the first edition, the principle of unconscionability in English law has developed considerably. It is now firmly recognised as the basis of proprietary estoppel, has been accepted as the basis of a change of position to personal restitutionary claims and is the current basis of liability for a third party who receives property in breach of trust. This timely opportunity has been taken to incorporate these developments in this second edition, as well as other developments in respect of illegality, undue influence and home ownership.

In *Equity and Good Conscience* Margaret Halliwell provides a critical analysis of the mass of English law concerning the remedying of unconscionable conduct. As well as considering new developments, the author undertakes comparisons with the relevant law in other Commonwealth countries. Detailed analysis covers the law of equity in the family and commercial context, which are seen as difficult and opaque. The author considers the various substantive areas of the law in the more general context of the jurisprudence of equity and, in particular, in assessing both the impact of the principle of unconscionability and the impact of the principle of unjust enrichment.

The first edition received very favourable reviews, and the author's aim has been to produce an even better second edition. *Equity and Good Conscience* will be of interest to all students of law and to practitioners, both in the area of equity and trusts and in other areas in which remedies for unconscionable conduct exist. An essential addition to any law library.

For further information on contents or to place an order, please contact:

Customer Services
Old Bailey Press
at Holborn College
Woolwich Road
Charlton
London
SE7 8LN

Telephone: 020 8317 6039
Fax: 020 8317 6004
Website: www.oldbaileypress.co.uk
E-Mail: customerservices@oldbaileypress.co.uk

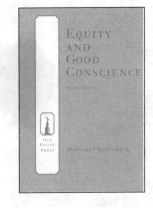

ISBN 1 85836 572 4
Soft cover 246 x 175 mm
176 pages
£19.95
Published December 2004

Internet Law

Dr Charles Wild, BSc (London), LLM, PhD (Sheffield), Pg Cert HE, CPE, LPC,
Head of the University of Hertfordshire School of Law,
Head of the Centre for International Law,
Mr Stuart Weinstein, BA (Williams), JD (Columbia), Attorney-at-Law
(California, District of Columbia and New York), Solicitor
and Mr Neil MacEwan, LLB, LLM, LPC

This new text offers, for the first time, a complete review of the area of Internet law. The discussion commences with an analysis of e-contracts, ranging from details of their formation, on-line terms and conditions through to a consideration of associated jurisdictional and choice of law issues. In addition, e-finance is considered, focusing on the use and regulation of credit cards on the Internet together with an evaluation of other methods of payment, including Smart Cards and electronic money. The text also covers intellectual property and data protection issues which specifically arise from the transfer and subsequent utilisation of data on the Internet, including responses in the form of cryptography, privacy enhanced technology and regional legislative responses. Finally, more specific topics such as domain names and spam will be included so as to provide the student with comprehensive coverage of this dynamic and challenging area of law. Whilst the legal content is UK based, the combination of UK, US and EU authors ensures that every aspect of this global subject is dealt with from a cross-jurisdictional perspective. An essential text for any student studying this subject or anyone interested in issues surrounding the Internet.

For further information on contents or to place an order, please contact:

Customer Services
Old Bailey Press
at Holborn College
Woolwich Road
Charlton
London
SE7 8LN

Telephone: 020 8317 6039
Fax: 020 8317 6004
Website: www.oldbaileypress.co.uk
E-Mail: customerservices@oldbaileypress.co.uk

ISBN 1 85836 573 2
Soft cover 246 x 175 mm
400 pages approx
£15.95
Due September 2005

Unannotated Cracknell's Statutes for Use in Examinations

New Editions of Cracknell's Statutes

Only £11.95   Due 2005

Cracknell's Statutes provide a comprehensive series of essential statutory provisions for each subject. Amendments are consolidated, avoiding the need to cross-refer to amending legislation. Unannotated, they are suitable for use in examinations, and provide the precise wording of vital Acts of Parliament for the diligent student.

Company Law
ISBN: 1 85836 563 5

Equity and Trusts
ISBN: 1 85836 589 9

Constitutional & Administrative Law
ISBN: 1 85836 584 8

European Union Legislation
ISBN: 1 85836 590 2

Contract, Tort and Remedies
ISBN: 1 85836 583 X

Family Law
ISBN: 1 85836 566 X

Criminal Law
ISBN: 1 85836 586 4

Land: The Law of Real Property
ISBN: 1 85836 585 6

Employment Law
ISBN: 1 85836 587 2

Law of International Trade
ISBN: 1 85836 582 1

English Legal System
ISBN: 1 85836 588 0

Medical Law
ISBN: 1 85836 567 8

Revenue Law
ISBN: 1 85836 569 4

For further information or to place an order, please contact:

Customer Services
Old Bailey Press at Holborn College
Woolwich Road, Charlton
London, SE7 8LN
Telephone: 020 8317 6039
Fax: 020 8317 6004
Website: www.oldbaileypress.co.uk
E-Mail: customerservices@oldbaileypress.co.uk

Old Bailey Press

The Old Bailey Press Integrated Student Law Library is tailor-made to help you at every stage of your studies, from the preliminaries of each subject through to the final examination. The series of Textbooks, Revision WorkBooks, 150 Leading Cases and Cracknell's Statutes are interrelated to provide you with a comprehensive set of study materials.

You can buy Old Bailey Press books from your University Bookshop, your local Bookshop, directly using this form, or you can order a free catalogue of our titles from the address shown overleaf.

The following subjects each have a Textbook, 150 Leading Cases, Revision WorkBook and Cracknell's Statutes unless otherwise stated.

Administrative Law
Commercial Law
Company Law
Conflict of Laws
Constitutional Law
Conveyancing (Textbook and 150 Leading Cases)
Criminal Law
Criminology (Textbook and Sourcebook)
Employment Law (Textbook and Cracknell's Statutes)
English and European Legal Systems
Equity and Trusts
Evidence
Family Law
Jurisprudence: The Philosophy of Law (Textbook, Sourcebook and
    Revision WorkBook)
Land: The Law of Real Property
Law of International Trade
Law of the European Union
Legal Skills and System
    (Textbook)
Obligations: Contract Law
Obligations: The Law of Tort
Public International Law
Revenue Law (Textbook,
    Revision WorkBook and
    Cracknell's Statutes)
Succession (Textbook, Revision
    WorkBook and Cracknell's
    Statutes)

Mail order prices:	
Textbook	£15.95
150 Leading Cases	£12.95
Revision WorkBook	£10.95
Cracknell's Statutes	£11.95
Suggested Solutions 1999–2000	£6.95
Suggested Solutions 2000–2001	£6.95
Suggested Solutions 2001–2002	£6.95
101 Questions and Answers	£7.95
Law Update 2004	£10.95
Law Update 2005	£10.95

Please note details and prices are subject to alteration.

To complete your order, please fill in the form below:

Module	Books required	Quantity	Price	Cost
		Postage		
		TOTAL		

For the UK and Europe, add £4.95 for the first book ordered, then add £1.00 for each subsequent book ordered for postage and packing.
For the rest of the world, add 50% for airmail.

ORDERING

By telephone to Customer Services at 020 8317 6039, with your credit card to hand.

By fax to 020 8317 6004 (giving your credit card details).

Website: www.oldbaileypress.co.uk
E-Mail: customerservices@oldbaileypress.co.uk

By post to: Customer Services, Old Bailey Press at Holborn College, Woolwich Road, Charlton, London, SE7 8LN.

When ordering by post, please enclose full payment by cheque or banker's draft, or complete the credit card details below. You may also order a free catalogue of our complete range of titles from this address.

We aim to despatch your books within 3 working days of receiving your order. All parts of the form must be completed.

Name

Address

Postcode

E-Mail
Telephone

Total value of order, including postage: £

I enclose a cheque/banker's draft for the above sum, or

charge my ☐ Access/Mastercard ☐ Visa ☐ American Express

Cardholder: ....

Card number

☐☐☐☐ ☐☐☐☐ ☐☐☐☐ ☐☐☐☐

Expiry date ☐☐☐☐

Signature: ....Date: ....